Edexcel
GCSE Modular Mathematics

higher

Mathematics

unit 3

Keith Pledger

Gareth Cole

Peter Jolly

Graham Newman

Joe Petran

www.heinemann.co.uk

✓ Free online support
✓ Useful weblinks
✓ 24 hour online ordering

01865 888058

Heinemann
Inspiring generations

Heinemann is an imprint of Pearson Educational Limited, a company incorporated in England and Wales, having its registered office at Edinburgh Gate, Harlow, Essex,CM20 2JE. Registered company number: 872828

www.heinemann.co.uk

Heinemann is the registered trademark of Pearson Education Limited

Text © Harcourt Education Limited, 2007

First published 2007

12 11 10 09 08
10 9 8 7 6 5 4 3 2 1

British Library Cataloguing in Publication Data is available from the British Library on request.

ISBN 978 0 435585 32 7

Typeset by Techset
Original illustrations © Harcourt Education Limited, 2007
Cover design by mccdesign
Cover photo/illustration © Digital Vision
Printed in Italy by Rotolito Lombarda S.p.A.

Acknowledgements
Harcourt would like to thank those schools who gave invaluable help in the development and trialling of this course.

The author and publisher would like to thank the following individuals and organisations for permission to reproduce photographs:

Morgue File **pp2, 203**; Getty Images / PhotoDisc pp**8, 12** top, **18** bottom, **30, 41, 43, 44** top, **49, 61, 141, 155, 260, 266**; Morgue File / Rupert Jefferies p**12** bottom; Harcourt Ltd / Malcolm Harris p**14**; Photos.com pp**15, 27, 29** bottom, **34** top, **34** middle, **71** bottom, **83, 89 179, 181**; iStockPhoto / April Turner p**18** top; Harcourt Ltd / Tudor Photography p**18** middle; Corbis pp**21** top, **32** bottom, **36** top, **37, 38** top, **51, 71** top, **90, 229, 275**; iStockPhoto p**21** bottom; Dreamstime / Mariana Raszkowska p**28** top; iStockPhoto / Amands Rohde p**28** middle; iStockPhoto / Melissa Carroll p**28** bottom; iStockPhoto / Vera Bogaerts p**29** top; Harcourt Ltd / Jill Birschbach p**32** top; Harcourt Ltd / Gareth Boden p**33**; iStockPhoto / Graeme Purdy p**34** bottom; iStockPhoto / Steven Miric p**35**; Brand X Pictures p**36** bottom; Digital Vision pp**38** bottom, **44** middle, **44** bottom; iStockPhoto / Tommy Ingberg p**42**; Harcourt Ltd / Jules Selmes p**59**; Alamy / ImageSource p**62**; iStockPhoto / Greg Nicholas p**146**; Harcourt Ltd / Chris Honeywell p**167**; Harcourt Ltd / Keith Gibson p**241**; iStockPhoto / Dan Mason p**261**

Every effort has been made to contact copyright holders of material reproduced in this book. Any omissions will be rectified in subsequent printings if notice is given to the publishers.

Quick reference to chapters

Contents

1 Calculations

2 Percentages

3 Ratio and proportion

4 Powers and surds

5 Simple linear equations and algebra

9 Quadratic graphs

10 Graphs and transformations of graphs

11 Transformations

12 Bearings, constructions and properties of shape

13 Pythagoras and trigonometry in 2-D and 3-D

14 Circle theorems

15 2-D and 3-D shapes

16 Vectors

About this book

This book has been carefully matched to the new two-tier modular specification for Edexcel GCSE Maths. It covers everything you need to know to achieve success in Unit 3. The author team is made up of the Chief Examiner, the Chair of Examiners, Principal Examiners and Senior Moderators, all experienced teachers with an excellent understanding of the Edexcel specification.

Key features

Chapters are divided into **sections**. In each section you will find:
- **key points**, highlighted throughout like this

> - Multiplying a number by its **reciprocal** gives 1.

- **examples** that show you how to tackle questions
- an **exercise** to help develop your understanding.

Each chapter ends with a **mixed exercise** and a **summary of key points**. Mixed exercises, which include past exam questions marked with an [E], are designed to test your understanding across the chapter.

Hint boxes are used to make explanations clearer. They may also remind you of previously learned facts or tell you where in the book to find more information.

> $\frac{1}{x^n}$ is the inverse operation of x^n because $\frac{1}{x^n} \times x^n = 1$.

An **examination practice** paper is included to help you prepare for the exam at the end of the unit.

Answers are provided at the back of the book to use as your teacher directs.

Quick reference and detailed Contents pages

Use the thumb spots on the **Quick reference page** to turn to the right chapter quickly.

Use the detailed **Contents** to help you find a section on a particular topic. The summary and reference codes on the right show your teacher the part(s) of the specification covered by each section of the book. (For example, NA3c refers to Number and algebra, section 5 Calculations, subsection c.)

Teaching and learning software

References to the Heinemann Edexcel GCSE Mathematics **Teaching and Learning Software** are included for you and your teacher. (The number refers to the relevant chapter from the linear course on which the software is based.)

> **8** Finding percentage multipliers

Use of a calculator

 These symbols show where you must, or must not, use a calculator.

1 Calculations

1.1 Written methods for multiplying and dividing decimals

- When you multiply decimals, the answer must have the same number of decimal places as the total number of decimal places in the numbers you multiply.

Multiplying and dividing decimals was covered in Chapter 2 of Higher Unit 3.

Example 1

Work out 4.56×2.4

$$
\begin{array}{r}
4\ 5\ 6 \\
\times\quad 2\ 4 \\
\hline
1\ 8_2 2_2 4 \\
9_1 1_1 2\ 0 \\
\hline
1\ 0\ 9\ 4\ 4 \\
\end{array}
$$

Multiply the numbers together, ignoring the decimals.

456×4

456×20

$456 \times 4 + 456 \times 20$

Answer = 10.944

The answer must have the same number of decimal places as the total number of decimal places in the numbers being multiplied.

- When you divide by a decimal, multiply the number you are dividing *by* by a power of 10 to change it into a whole number. Then multiply the number you are dividing *into* by the same power of 10.

Example 2

Work out $5.58 \div 0.15$

$0.15 \times 100 = 15 \qquad 5.58 \times 100 = 558$

$$
\begin{array}{r}
3\ 7\ .\ 2 \\
15\overline{)5\ 5\ 8\ .\ 0} \\
-\ 4\ 5\ \downarrow \\
\hline
1\ 0\ 8 \\
-\ 1\ 0\ 5\ \downarrow \\
\hline
3\ 0 \\
\end{array}
$$

Answer = 37.2

Multiply the number you are dividing by by a power of 10 to make a whole number.
Then do the same to the number to be divided.
$$\frac{5.58 \times 100}{0.15 \times 100} = \frac{558}{15}$$

Exercise 1A

Show all your working. In questions **1–10** work out the calculations.

1 3.56×3.7 **2** 7.52×0.19

3 2.25×5.4 **4** 35.2×4.3

5 $54.15 \div 0.15$ **6** $81.54 \div 0.18$

7 $303.62 \div 0.34$ **8** $12.88 \div 2.3$

9 $348.31 \div 6.1$ **10** 2.76×4.32

11 An electricity bill is made up of
- a service charge of 5.28p per day
- electricity at 7.30p per unit.

Work out the total electricity bill for 91 days and 1235 units of electricity.

1.2 Reciprocals

- Multiplying a number by its **reciprocal** gives 1.

> Zero has no reciprocal because you cannot divide by zero.

Example 3

Find the reciprocal of
(a) 4   (b) 0.8   (c) $\frac{3}{5}$

(a) 4 multiplied by its reciprocal = 1
$$4 \times x = 1$$
$$x = \frac{1}{4}$$

> Write x for the reciprocal of 4.

So the reciprocal of 4 is $\frac{1}{4}$

> The inverse of $\times 4$ is $\div 4$. $\div 4$ is the same as $\times \frac{1}{4}$. So $\frac{1}{4}$ is the multiplicative inverse of 4.

(b) $0.8 \times x = 1$
$$x = \frac{1}{0.8}$$
$$x = 1.25$$

The reciprocal of 0.8 is 1.25

> $\frac{1}{0.8} = 1 \div 0.8$
> $= 1.25$

(c) $\frac{3}{5} \times x = 1$
$$x = 1 \div \frac{3}{5}$$
$$= 1 \times \frac{5}{3}$$
$$= \frac{5}{3}$$

The reciprocal of $\frac{3}{5}$ is $\frac{5}{3} = 1\frac{2}{3}$

> The reciprocal of any number is 1 divided by that number.
> For example, the reciprocal of 5 is $\frac{1}{5}$.

Exercise 1B

1 Find the reciprocal of
   (a) 5   (b) 6   (c) 9
   (d) 3   (e) 10   (f) 18

2 Find the reciprocal of
   (a) 0.2   (b) 0.7   (c) 0.75
   (d) 0.6   (e) 0.05   (f) 0.125

3 Find the reciprocal, in its simplest form, of
   (a) $\frac{2}{5}$ (b) $\frac{4}{7}$ (c) $\frac{3}{4}$
   (d) $\frac{3}{8}$ (e) $\frac{4}{15}$ (f) $\frac{3}{10}$

4 Find the reciprocal of
   (a) n (b) m^3 (c) $\frac{1}{y}$ (d) $\frac{1}{x^2}$

1.3 **Multiplying and dividing negative numbers**

- This table shows the signs you get when you multiply or divide two numbers.

+	×/÷	+	=	+
+	×/÷	−	=	−
−	×/÷	+	=	−
−	×/÷	−	=	+

> Calculating with negative numbers was covered in Chapter 1 of Higher Unit 3.

Example 4

Work out
(a) 3×-4 (b) -2×-5
(c) $-18 \div -6$ (d) $24 \div -8$

(a) $3 \times -4 = -12$ (b) $-2 \times -5 = +10$
(c) $-18 \div -6 = +3$ (d) $24 \div -8 = -3$

 Exercise 1C

1 Work out
   (a) -2×4 (b) -5×-3 (c) -4×-5
   (d) 6×-3 (e) $12 \div -4$ (f) $-15 \div -3$
   (g) $-100 \div -100$ (h) -7×-8 (i) $-54 \div 6$

2 Copy and complete these tables.

(a)

÷	12	−16	48
−2			
+4			
−8			

2nd number

1st number

(b)

×	−3	5	−13
11			
−7			
−3			

2nd number

1st number

1.4 Using index laws

- $x^n \times x^m = x^{n+m}$
- $x^n \div x^m = x^{n-m}$ or $\dfrac{x^n}{x^m} = x^{n-m}$
- $(x^n)^m = x^{n \times m}$
- $x^0 = 1$ for all non-zero values of x.
- $x^{-n} = \dfrac{1}{x^n}$ (where $x \neq 0$).
- $x^{\frac{1}{n}} = \sqrt[n]{x}$
- $x^{\frac{m}{n}} = (\sqrt[n]{x})^m$ or $x^{\frac{m}{n}} = \sqrt[n]{x^m}$

> The index laws were covered in Chapters 1 and 3 in Higher Unit 3.

> $\dfrac{1}{x^n}$ is the inverse operation of x^n because $\dfrac{1}{x^n} \times x^n = 1$.

Example 5

Find the value of

(a) 5^0 (b) 2^{-2} (c) $9^{\frac{1}{2}}$ (d) $27^{-\frac{1}{3}}$ (e) $27^{\frac{2}{3}}$

(a) $5^0 = 1$

(b) $2^{-2} = \dfrac{1}{2^2} = \dfrac{1}{4}$

(c) $9^{\frac{1}{2}} = \sqrt[2]{9} = 3$

(d) $27^{-\frac{1}{3}} = \dfrac{1}{27^{\frac{1}{3}}} = \dfrac{1}{\sqrt[3]{27}} = \dfrac{1}{3}$

(e) $27^{\frac{2}{3}} = (\sqrt[3]{27})^2 = 3^2 = 9$

Example 6

Simplify and evaluate

(a) $4^{-\frac{1}{2}} \times 4^2$ (b) $\dfrac{3^2 \times 3^{-3}}{3^{-4}}$ (c) $(5^{\frac{1}{2}})^6$

(a) $4^{-\frac{1}{2}} \times 4^2 = 4^{-\frac{1}{2}+2} = 4^{\frac{3}{2}}$ $4^{\frac{3}{2}} = (\sqrt{4})^3 = 2^3 = 8$

(b) $\dfrac{3^2 \times 3^{-3}}{3^{-4}} = \dfrac{3^{2+(-3)}}{3^{-4}} = \dfrac{3^{-1}}{3^{-4}} = 3^{-1-(-4)} = 3^3$ $3^3 = 27$

> $-1 - (-4) = 3$

(c) $(5^{\frac{1}{2}})^6 = 5^{\frac{1}{2} \times 6} = 5^3$ $5^3 = 125$

Exercise 1D

1 Find the value of

(a) 9^{-2} (b) 3^{-2} (c) 5^{-3} (d) 3^{-4} (e) $49^{\frac{1}{2}}$

(f) 100^{-2} (g) $8^{\frac{1}{3}}$ (h) $1000^{\frac{2}{3}}$ (i) $64^{-\frac{1}{2}}$ (j) $36^{-\frac{1}{2}}$

(k) $125^{-\frac{1}{3}}$ (l) 12^0 (m) $125^{\frac{2}{3}}$ (n) $27^{\frac{5}{3}}$ (o) $49^{\frac{3}{2}}$

(p) $36^{-\frac{3}{2}}$ (q) $9^{-\frac{5}{2}}$

2 Simplify and evaluate

(a) $2^3 \times 2^{-4}$ (b) $3^{\frac{1}{2}} \times 3^{\frac{3}{2}}$ (c) $8^{-\frac{1}{3}} \times 8^1$

(d) $(2^4)^{\frac{1}{2}}$ (e) $\dfrac{6^1 \times 6^3}{6^6}$ (f) $\dfrac{4^{\frac{3}{2}} \times 4^{\frac{1}{2}}}{4^2}$

(g) $(8^{\frac{2}{3}})^3$ (h) $\dfrac{(4^{\frac{1}{2}})^5}{4^2}$ (i) $(4^2)^{-\frac{3}{2}}$

(j) $\dfrac{9^0 \times 9^{\frac{1}{2}}}{9^2}$ (k) $25^{0.5} \times 7^{-2}$ (l) $16^{\frac{1}{2}} \times 8^{\frac{2}{3}}$

(m) $27^{-\frac{2}{3}}$

1.5 Fraction calculations

- You need to be able to add, subtract, multiply and divide fractions.

See Chapter 2 of Higher Unit 3.

Example 7

(a) In January Mary is paid £1000. She spends £800. What fraction of the £1000 does she spend?

(b) In February she is paid £1000 and spends £750. What fraction of the £1000 does she spend?

(c) What fraction of the £2000 does she spend in total?

(d) Convert your answer to (c) to a decimal.

(a) $\dfrac{800}{1000} = \dfrac{8}{10} = \dfrac{4}{5}$

(b) $\dfrac{750}{1000} = \dfrac{75}{100} = \dfrac{3}{4}$

(c) $800 + 750 = 1550$

$\dfrac{1550}{2000} = \dfrac{31}{40}$

$\dfrac{\text{Total spent}}{2000}$

(d) $\dfrac{31}{40} = 0.775$

Use your calculator to work out $31 \div 40$

Example 8

Work out (a) $\frac{5}{6} - \frac{1}{4}$ (b) $3\frac{2}{3} + 1\frac{3}{5}$ (c) $3\frac{1}{4} - 1\frac{2}{5}$

(a) $\frac{5}{6} - \frac{1}{4} = \frac{10}{12} - \frac{3}{12}$

Change $\frac{5}{6}$ and $\frac{1}{4}$ to equivalent fractions with denominator 12.

$\qquad = \frac{7}{12}$

(b)

$3\frac{2}{3} + 1\frac{3}{5} = 4 + \frac{10}{15} + \frac{9}{15}$

Add the whole numbers.
Change $\frac{2}{3}$ and $\frac{3}{5}$ to equivalent fractions with denominator 15.

$\qquad = 4\frac{19}{15}$

$\qquad = 5\frac{4}{15}$

(c) $3\frac{1}{4} - 1\frac{2}{5}$

$= \frac{13}{4} - \frac{7}{5}$ Change to improper fractions.

$= \frac{65}{20} - \frac{28}{20}$ Change to equivalent fractions.

$= \frac{37}{20}$ Subtract.

$= 1\frac{17}{20}$ Change back to mixed fraction.

Example 9

Work out $1\frac{7}{9} \times 3\frac{3}{8}$

$1\frac{7}{9} \times 3\frac{3}{8} = \frac{\overset{2}{\cancel{16}}}{9} \times \frac{\overset{3}{\cancel{27}}}{\underset{1}{\cancel{8}}} = 6$

Change to improper fractions.
Cancel where possible.

Example 10

Work out $3\frac{5}{7} \div 5\frac{5}{21}$

$3\frac{5}{7} \div 5\frac{5}{21} = \frac{26}{7} \div \frac{110}{21}$

Change to improper fractions.

$= \frac{\overset{13}{\cancel{26}}}{\underset{1}{\cancel{7}}} \times \frac{\overset{3}{\cancel{21}}}{\underset{55}{\cancel{110}}} = \frac{39}{55}$

Invert the dividing fraction and multiply.
Cancel where possible.

Exercise 1E

1 Peter spends £40 out of his £240 wages.

  (a) What fraction is this?

  Peter then spends £60 of the remaining £200.

  (b) What fraction of the £200 is this?

  (c) What fraction of the £240 has he now spent?

2 Write 450 m as a fraction of 2 km.

3 Work out

(a) $\frac{2}{3} + \frac{7}{12}$

(b) $\frac{7}{8} - \frac{3}{4}$

(c) $1\frac{2}{3} + \frac{1}{6}$

(d) $2\frac{3}{4} - 1\frac{1}{5}$

(e) $2\frac{1}{2} - 1\frac{1}{8}$

(f) $3\frac{1}{4} + 2\frac{5}{8}$

(g) $4\frac{1}{5} - 2\frac{2}{3}$

(h) $2\frac{7}{12} + 1\frac{5}{8}$

4 Work out the following, simplifying your answers as much as possible.

(a) $3\frac{4}{5} \times 7$

(b) $4\frac{1}{2} \div 9$

(c) $3\frac{3}{4} \times 2\frac{1}{5}$

(d) $8\frac{1}{3} \times 4\frac{1}{5}$

(e) $5\frac{3}{5} \times 1\frac{3}{7}$

(f) $3\frac{1}{5} \times 1\frac{1}{8}$

(g) $1\frac{2}{7} \times 2\frac{2}{3}$

(h) $2\frac{5}{18} \times 4\frac{1}{2}$

(i) $4\frac{11}{16} \times 5\frac{3}{25}$

(j) $1\frac{1}{2} \times 1\frac{1}{4} \times 1\frac{3}{5}$

(k) $2\frac{2}{3} \times 1\frac{11}{16} \times 1\frac{5}{9}$

(l) $2\frac{2}{3}(3\frac{5}{8} - 2\frac{1}{5})$

(m) $1\frac{3}{5} \div \frac{4}{5}$

(n) $3\frac{6}{7} \div 2\frac{4}{7}$

(o) $4\frac{4}{5} \div 2\frac{2}{15}$

(p) $1\frac{9}{16} \div 2\frac{1}{2}$

(q) $9\frac{4}{5} \div \frac{7}{20}$

(r) $1\frac{6}{7} \div 4\frac{16}{35}$

(s) $4\frac{5}{7} \div 2\frac{1}{5}$

(t) $7\frac{1}{4} \div 8\frac{2}{7}$

1.6 Fractions and decimals

- To convert a fraction to a decimal, divide the numerator by the denominator. For a fraction in its simplest form, if the denominator's only prime factors are 2 and/or 5, the decimal **terminates**. Otherwise the decimal is **recurring**.

Example 11

Convert these fractions to decimals.

(a) $\frac{7}{160}$

(b) $\frac{5}{13}$

(a) $7 \div 160$

$= 0.043\,75$

(b) $5 \div 13$

$= 0.38\overset{\bullet}{4}61\overset{\bullet}{5}...$

$160 = 2^5 \times 5$
The decimal terminates.

The decimal recurs.

Exercise 1F

1 Use a calculator to convert each of the following fractions to a decimal.

   (a) $\frac{3}{8}$ (b) $\frac{7}{64}$ (c) $\frac{17}{25}$ (d) $\frac{97}{125}$

   (e) $\frac{217}{625}$ (f) $\frac{7}{24}$ (g) $\frac{8}{33}$ (h) $\frac{7}{13}$

   (i) $\frac{3}{22}$ (j) $\frac{77}{121}$ (k) $\frac{271}{999}$ (l) $\frac{14}{39}$

2 Which of these fractions can be written as terminating decimals?

   $\frac{3}{4}, \quad \frac{1}{6}, \quad \frac{7}{10}, \quad \frac{9}{50}, \quad \frac{4}{15}, \quad \frac{3}{15}$

Mixed exercise 1

1 Work out
   (a) 3.92×2.43 (b) $123.12 \div 0.27$

2 Find the reciprocal of
   (a) 9   (b) 8   (c) 0.5   (d) 0.625

   (e) $\frac{4}{5}$ (f) $\frac{5}{7}$ (g) m (h) $\frac{1}{y}$

3 Work out
   (a) $+24 \div -3$ (b) -5×-8 (c) 3×-7
   (d) $-2 \div -4$ (e) $-13 \times +11$ (f) $10 \div -5$

4 Work out
   (a) $\frac{2}{5} + \frac{1}{3}$ (b) $3\frac{1}{2} - 1\frac{1}{3}$ (c) $5\frac{3}{8} - 2\frac{1}{2}$
   (d) $3\frac{5}{6} + 1\frac{2}{3}$ (e) $2\frac{1}{7} \times 1\frac{2}{3}$ (f) $5\frac{2}{5} \div 1\frac{7}{11}$

5 Shireen earns £200 each month for her part-time job.
   She saves £45 each month.
   She pays £25 each month for her phone contract.
   (a) What fraction of her earnings does she save?
   (b) What fraction of her earnings does she have left to spend?

6 Use a calculator to convert these fractions to decimals.
   (a) $\frac{7}{8}$ (b) $\frac{77}{132}$ (c) $\frac{17}{19}$

7 Which of these fractions can be written as terminating decimals?
   $\frac{11}{18}, \quad \frac{14}{20}, \quad \frac{5}{22}, \quad \frac{19}{120}, \quad \frac{7}{8}, \quad \frac{9}{25}, \quad \frac{7}{12}$

Summary of key points

1 When you multiply decimals, the answer must have the same number of decimal places as the total number of decimal places in the numbers you multiply.

2 When you divide by a decimal, multiply the number you are dividing *by* by a power of 10 to change it into a whole number. Then multiply the number you are dividing *into* by the same power of 10.

3 Multiplying a number by its **reciprocal** gives 1.

4 This table shows the signs you get when you multiply or divide two numbers.

+	×/÷	+	=	+
+	×/÷	−	=	−
−	×/÷	+	=	−
−	×/÷	−	=	+

5 $x^n \times x^m = x^{n+m}$

6 $x^n \div x^m = x^{n-m}$ or $\dfrac{x^n}{x^m} = x^{n-m}$

7 $(x^n)^m = x^{n \times m}$

8 $x^0 = 1$ for all non-zero values of x.

9 $x^{-n} = \dfrac{1}{x^n}$ (where $x \neq 0$).

10 $x^{\frac{1}{n}} = \sqrt[n]{x}$

11 $x^{\frac{m}{n}} = (\sqrt[n]{x})^m$ or $x^{\frac{m}{n}} = \sqrt[n]{x^m}$

12 You need to be able to add, subtract, multiply and divide fractions.

13 To convert a fraction to a decimal, divide the numerator by the denominator. For a fraction in its simplest form, if the denominator's only prime factors are 2 and/or 5, the decimal **terminates**. Otherwise the decimal is **recurring**.

2 Percentages

2.1 Percentages, fractions and decimals

- per cent
  %   ⎫ mean 'out of 100'.
  pc   ⎭
- To change a percentage to a fraction, write it as a fraction with denominator 100.
- To change a percentage to a decimal, first change it to a fraction and then to a decimal.

Example 1

Write these percentages as (i) decimals (ii) fractions.

(a) 45%   (b) $62\frac{1}{2}\%$

(a)   (i) $45\% = \dfrac{45}{100} = 45 \div 100 = 0.45$

(ii) $45\% = \dfrac{45}{100} = \dfrac{9}{20}$

(b)   (i) $62\frac{1}{2}\% = \dfrac{62\frac{1}{2}}{100} = 62.5 \div 100 = 0.625$

(ii) $62\frac{1}{2}\% = \dfrac{62\frac{1}{2}}{100} = \dfrac{62\frac{1}{2} \times 2}{100 \times 2} = \dfrac{125}{200} = \dfrac{5}{8}$

- To change a decimal to a percentage, multiply the decimal by 100%.
- To change a fraction to a percentage, first change the fraction to a decimal and then multiply by 100%.
- To compare fractions with percentages, convert the fractions to percentages.

Example 2

Write as percentages.

(a) 0.55   (b) $\frac{8}{25}$ (c) 0.275   (d) $\frac{3}{8}$

(a) $0.55 \times 100\% = 55\%$

(b) $\frac{8}{25} = 8 \div 25 = 0.32$ $0.32 \times 100\% = 32\%$

(c) $0.275 \times 100\% = 27.5\%$

(d) $\frac{3}{8} = 3 \div 8 = 0.375$ $0.375 \times 100\% = 37.5\%$

Exercise 2A

1 Write these percentages as (i) decimals (ii) fractions.

(a) 75%   (b) 30%   (c) 65%

(d) 48%   (e) 64%   (f) $32\frac{1}{2}$%

(g) $87\frac{1}{2}$%   (h) $66\frac{2}{3}$%   (i) $33\frac{1}{3}$%

(j) $3\frac{1}{4}$%

2 Write as percentages.

(a) $\frac{3}{4}$ (b) 0.8   (c) 0.28

(d) $\frac{17}{20}$ (e) 0.95   (f) $\frac{7}{10}$

(g) 0.675   (h) $\frac{19}{40}$ (i) 0.225

(j) $\frac{5}{12}$

3 Copy and complete this table.

Fraction	Decimal	Percentage
		5%
$\frac{3}{10}$		
	0.64	
$\frac{15}{16}$		
		$83\frac{1}{3}$%

4 Natasha scores 60 out of 80 in a Science test.
In Art she scores 48 out of 60 and in French she scores 72%.
Which is the largest percentage score?

2.2 Finding a percentage of a quantity

- To find a percentage of a quantity, change the percentage to a fraction or a decimal and multiply it by the quantity.

Example 3

Work out

(a) 40% of 160   (b) $22\frac{1}{2}$% of £150   (c) 17.5% of £92

(a) 40% of 160 $= \dfrac{40}{100} \times 160 = \dfrac{4}{10} \times 160 = 64$

(b) $22\frac{1}{2}$% of £150 $= \dfrac{22\frac{1}{2}}{100} \times £150 = \dfrac{45}{200} \times £150 = £33.75$

(c) 17.5% of £92 $= 0.175 \times £92 = £16.10$

Simplify the calculations by cancelling.

Exercise 2B

1 Work out

(a) 30% of 190   (b) 70% of 600

(c) 55% of 220   (d) 25% of 336

(e) 18% of £107   (f) 36% of £255

(g) $17\frac{1}{2}$% of £500   (h) $52\frac{1}{2}$% of 1500 kg

(i) $33\frac{1}{3}$% of 300 g   (j) $66\frac{2}{3}$% of £81

2 A factory has 250 employees. 52% of these are female.
Find the number of

(a) female employees

(b) male employees.

3 A yogurt contains 3% fat.
How many grams of fat are there in 175 g of yogurt?

4 Lucy earns £20 500 a year. She pays 22% tax.
How much tax does Lucy pay on her earnings?

5 A book has 240 pages. 65% are text only.
The rest contain illustrations.
How many pages in the book contain illustrations?

6 A ticket for a concert costs £48.
The performer is paid $16\frac{2}{3}$% of the price of the ticket.
How much does the performer receive from each ticket sold?

7 An author is paid $12\frac{1}{2}$% royalties for each of her books sold.
Her book is sold for £18.
How much does the author receive in royalties per book?

2.3 Percentage increase and decrease

8 Finding percentage multipliers

- To increase a quantity by a percentage, use a multiplier *or* find the percentage of the quantity and add it to the original quantity.

Example 4

A shop increases all its prices by 5%.
Calculate the new cost of the following items.

(a) a coat costing £85

(b) jeans costing £30

(c) trainers costing £45

All the prices in the shop have been increased by 5%.
So the new prices are (100 + 5)% of the old prices.
105% as a decimal is 1.05

> 1.05 is the multiplier.
> All the new prices can be found by multiplying the old prices by 1.05

(a) Coat: old price = £85
    new price = £85 × 1.05 = £89.25

(b) Jeans: old price = £30
    new price = £30 × 1.05 = £31.50

(c) Trainers: old price = £45
    new price = £45 × 1.05 = £47.25

> Alternative method for (a)
> 5% of £85 = $\frac{5}{100}$ × £85 = £4.25
> New price = £85 + £4.25 = £89.25

- **Simple interest** is when the same interest is added each year. You find the interest for one year and multiply it by the number of years.

Example 5

Find the simple interest on £2000 invested for two years at 5% per annum.

> 'per annum' means every year

Year 1 interest = 5% of £2000 = $\frac{5}{100}$ × 2000 = £100

For two years, total interest = 2 × £100 = £200

- To decrease a quantity by a percentage, use a multiplier *or* find the percentage of the quantity and subtract it from the original quantity.

Example 6

During 2006 new car prices fell by 15%.
Calculate the prices of the following cars at the end of 2006.

Car	Price at start of 2006
Mini	£7 500
Clio	£12 600
Puma	£18 000

The prices of the cars at the end of 2006 are (100 − 15)% = 85% of the prices at the start of 2006. 85% as a decimal is 0.85

> The multiplier is 0.85

Car	Price at start of 2006	Price at end of 2006
Mini	£7 500	£7 500 × 0.85 = £6 375
Clio	£12 600	£12 600 × 0.85 = £10 710
Puma	£18 000	£18 000 × 0.85 = £15 300

Example 7

At the start of 2000 Sam's house was valued at £50 000. During 2000 house prices rose by 15%, but during 2001 they fell by 10%. Calculate the value of Sam's house at the end of 2001.

At the end of 2000 house prices were (100 + 15)% of the value at the start of 2000. 115% as a decimal is 1.15

At the end of 2001 house prices were (100 − 10)% of the value at the end of 2000. 90% as a decimal is 0.9

So the value of the house at the end of 2001 was

£50 000 × 1.15 × 0.9 = £51 750

> 1.15 is the multiplier for an increase of 15%.

> 0.9 is the multiplier for a decrease of 10%.

Exercise 2C

1 An electrical shop decreases all its prices in a sale by 12.5%. Calculate the sale prices of the following items.

   (a) LCD TV: normal price £400

   (b) games console: normal price £150

   (c) DVD recorder: normal price £225

2 A company gives all its employees a 4% pay rise. Calculate the new salary for the following employees.

   (a) office junior previously earning £13 500

   (b) team administrator previously earning £17 300

   (c) manager previously earning £24 700

3 Find the simple interest on £5000 invested at 5% for

   (a) 1 year   **(b)** 2 years   **(c)** 10 years.

4 VAT at the rate of $17\frac{1}{2}$% is added to all items sold in a builders' yard.
Calculate the cost of the following items including VAT.

Item	Price (excluding VAT)
Ladder	£82
Tin of paint	£6
Electric drill	£37.50

5 A frozen-food manufacturer has a '10% extra free' promotion. Calculate the promotional weights of these packets of food.

   (a) frozen peas: normal weight 400 g

   (b) oven chips: normal weight 1.5 kg

   (c) fish fingers: normal weight 225 g

6 A company tries to increase its profits by reducing the
   expenditure of the following departments by 7.5%.
   Calculate the target expenditure for each department.

   (a) Administration: original expenditure £734 000

   (b) Marketing: original expenditure £1 430 000

   (c) Production: original expenditure £2 300 000

   (d) Calculate the overall target saving by these three
        departments.

7 Jackie bought £3000 worth of shares in a company at the end of
   August. During September the value of the shares fell by 3%, then
   it rose again by 5% in October.
   Calculate the value of Jackie's shares at the end of October.

8 In August 2006 the annual rate of inflation for the previous
   12 months was calculated as 2.8%. A shopping basket of groceries
   cost £75.40 in August 2005. The cost of each item in the basket
   increased by the rate of inflation.
   What was the price of the same shopping basket of groceries in
   August 2006?

9 A house was bought in 1988 for £40 000. House prices fell by 30%
   in 1989. Between the end of 1989 and the end of 1994, house
   prices rose by 20%.
   Calculate the value of the house at the end of 1994.

2.4 Reverse percentages

- When an original amount is **increased** by R% to become a new
  amount,
  $$\text{Original amount} = \frac{\text{new amount}}{1 + \frac{R}{100}}$$

Example 8

A restaurant bill is £54.05 including VAT. VAT is charged at 17.5%.
Calculate the cost of the original bill (excluding VAT).

The bill including VAT is the cost of the original bill plus $17\frac{1}{2}$%.
So the bill including VAT is 117.5% of the original bill.
117.5% as a decimal is 1.175
So £54.05 = 1.175 × original bill

So original bill $= \dfrac{£54.05}{1.175} = £46$

$$1 + \frac{R}{100} = 1 + \frac{17.5}{100}$$
$$= 1.175$$

- When an original amount is **decreased** by R% to become a new amount,

$$\text{Original amount} = \frac{\text{new amount}}{1 - \frac{R}{100}}$$

Example 9

A shop reduces all its prices by 20% in a sale.
The sale price of a coat is £70.
Calculate the original price of the coat.

Sale price = $(100 - 20)$% of original price
So   £70 = 80% of original price
        £70 = $0.8 \times$ original price
So original price = $\frac{£70}{0.8}$ = £87.50

$$1 - \frac{R}{100} = 1 - \frac{20}{100}$$
$$= 0.8$$

Exercise 2D

Give your answers to a sensible degree of accuracy.

1 A shopkeeper includes a 25% profit margin on everything he sells.
   Calculate the cost to the shopkeeper of the following items.
   (a) a packet of biscuits: selling price 75p
   (b) a box of washing powder: selling price £4
   (c) 1 kg of apples: selling price £1.25

2 Mashoor is given a 7% pay rise. His new salary is £16 050.
   Calculate his original salary.

3 Sophie bought a house in 1996. She sold it in 2001 for £140 000.
   She made a 40% profit.
   Work out how much Sophie paid for her house in 1996.

4 The price of an MP3 player is reduced by 15% in a sale.
   The sale price of the MP3 player is £102.
   Calculate the price of the MP3 player before the sale.

5 A house is sold for £138 000. The sellers make a 15% profit.
   How much did the house cost originally?

6 Jack pays 22% tax on his salary. After paying tax, Jack gets £16 280.
   Calculate Jack's original salary.

7 The weight of a beefburger decreases by 12% during cooking. The cooked weight of the beefburger is 230 g. What was the uncooked weight of the beefburger?

8 A book sells for £15. This includes a 20% profit for the publisher. How much does the book cost before the profit is added?

9 The total cost of a CD is £11.75 including VAT at $17\frac{1}{2}$%. Calculate the cost of the CD before VAT is added.

10 Samira bought a car in 2002. She sold it in 2006 for £12 500. She calculates that the car depreciated by 35% over the 4-year period. Calculate the original cost of the car in 2002.

> 'Depreciation' means a loss in value.

11

Calculate the 'normal' weight of a Venus Choc Bar.

2.5 Finding one quantity as a percentage of another

- To write one quantity as a percentage of another:
  - ○ write one quantity as a fraction of the other
  - ○ change the fraction to a decimal
  - ○ multiply the decimal by 100%.

Example 10

In a box of 20 chocolates, 12 chocolates were soft-centred.
What percentage of the chocolates were soft-centred?

Write the quantities as a fraction: $\frac{12}{20}$

Change the fraction to a decimal: $\frac{12}{20} = 12 \div 20 = 0.6$

Multiply the decimal by 100%: $0.6 \times 100\% = 60\%$

60% of the chocolates were soft-centred.

- When a quantity changes (increases or decreases), find the percentage change using

  $$\text{Percentage change} = \frac{\text{actual change}}{\text{original quantity}} \times 100\%$$

Example 11

A shopkeeper buys apples at £1.30 per kilogram.
He sells them for £1.56 per kilogram.
Calculate his percentage profit.

$$\text{Percentage change (profit)} = \frac{\text{actual change (profit)}}{\text{original quantity}} \times 100\%$$

The original price is £1.30.

The actual profit is £0.26.

£1.56 − £1.30 = £0.26

$$\text{Percentage profit} = \frac{£0.26}{£1.30} \times 100\%$$

$$= 20\%$$

Exercise 2E

1   Faisal scored 36 out of 40 in a spelling test.
    Write this as a percentage.

2   A pet food manufacturer claims that 8 out of 10 cats prefer their
    cat food.
    What percentage of cats is this?

3   In a village of 2500 people, there are 650 children, 960 men and
    890 women.
    What percentage of the people in the village are

    (a) children   **(b)** men   **(c)** women?

4   Out of a flock of 150 sheep, 100 gave birth to twin lambs and the
    rest gave birth to single lambs.
    What percentage of the flock gave birth to

    (a) twin lambs   **(b)** single lambs?

5   The weight of a particular sort of chocolate bar is increased from
    60 g to 72 g.
    Calculate the percentage increase in weight of the chocolate bar.

6   The cost of a PC fell from £440 to £363.
    Calculate the percentage decrease in the cost of the PC.

7   The normal price of a pair of trainers is £50. In a sale they are
    sold for £37.50.
    Calculate the percentage reduction in the price of the trainers.

8   A carpenter makes kitchen tables. They cost him £240 to make.
    He sells them for £288.
    Calculate his percentage profit.

2.6 Compound interest

- **Compound interest** is interest paid on an amount *and* on the interest on that amount.

Example 12

Megan invests £300 in a savings account. The account pays 5% interest per annum. She leaves her money in the account for 10 years. How much money is in Megan's account after 10 years?

'per annum' means every year.

The account pays 5% per annum.
After 1 year the total in the account is (100 + 5)% of £300.
Amount after 1 year: $1.05 \times £300$

105% as a decimal is 1.05

This percentage increase is applied again in the next year.
Amount after 2 years: $1.05 \times 1.05 \times £300$ or $(1.05)^2 \times £300$
This happens every year for 10 years.
Amount after 10 years: $(1.05)^{10} \times £300 = £488.67$
                              to the nearest penny

- To calculate compound interest, find the multiplier.
    Amount after n years = original amount $\times$ multiplier^n

---

Example 13

£500 is invested for 6 years at $3\frac{1}{2}$% compound interest, which is paid annually.
Calculate the total amount of interest earned after 6 years.

After 6 years the total amount of money will be
        $£500 \times (100\% + 3.5\%)^6$
    $= £500 \times (1.035)^6$
    $= £614.627\,6\ldots$

The multiplier is 1.035

The interest earned is
        $£614.627\,6\ldots - £500$

The original investment

    $= £114.63$ to the nearest penny

Exercise 2F

1 Jessica invests £500 in a building society account on 1st January.
The building society pays interest on the account at a rate of 6.3% per annum.
Calculate the amount of money in the account at the end of

(a) 1 year   (b) 3 years   (c) 5 years.

2 Harry invests £1250 in a bank account for 5 years at a rate of interest of 7.5% per annum.
  Calculate the amount of interest earned over the 5-year period.

3 Hannah earns a salary of £12 000. At the end of each year she is given a 4% pay rise.
  Calculate her salary after 5 years.

4 Charlotte invests £500 in a savings account at the rate of 8% per annum.
  How long will it take her investment to reach £700?

5 Samina discovers that her grandfather invested £25 in a savings account 50 years ago at a rate of 8% per annum and forgot about it.
  How much will be in the account 50 years after the initial investment?

6 Calculate the total interest earned on £700 invested for 10 years at 4% per annum.

Mixed exercise 2

1 Write as percentages.
   (a) $\frac{3}{4}$ (b) $\frac{7}{8}$ (c) $\frac{4}{10}$
   (d) 0.45   (e) $\frac{11}{40}$ (f) $\frac{11}{12}$

2 Which is the better test score, $\frac{25}{40}$ or $\frac{75}{110}$ written as a percentage?

3 Work out the following.
   (a) 15% of £60   (b) 25% of 1.5 kg
   (c) 13% of £250   (d) 17.5% of 20 m

4 Hudson earns £18 000. He is given a pay rise of 5%.
  Work out how much his salary rises by.

5 In a sale a dress costing £25 is reduced by 15%.
  How much would a customer save by buying the dress in the sale?

6 VAT, at a rate of 17.5%, must be added to all the prices in a plumbers' merchants.
  Calculate the price of the following items including VAT.

Item	Cost excluding VAT
Bath	£80
Tap	£10.50
Tiles	£12 per dozen

7   A sports shop reduces all its prices by 15% in a sale.
    Work out the sale price of the following items.

    (a) trainers: original price £34.50

    (b) exercise bike: original price £145

    (c) football kit: original price £60

8   Rajinder bought a flat in 2000. He sold it in 2005 for £130 000.
    He made a profit of 65%.
    Calculate the original cost of the flat in 2000.

9   80 people take the practical driving test.
    85% of them pass the test.
    Write down the number of people who

    (a) pass the test

    (b) fail the test.

10 The cost of a television is £360 plus VAT. The rate of VAT is $17\frac{1}{2}$%.
    Calculate the total cost of the television.

11 A department store offers a 15% discount on all sports equipment
    on Bank Holiday Monday. A pair of trainers normally costs £44.
    Calculate the cost of the pair of trainers on Bank Holiday Monday.

12 Ellie scores 28 out of 35 on her driving theory test.
    What percentage is this?

13 Dougal buys a computer for £500. Two years later he sells it
    for £175.
    Calculate his percentage loss.

14 The weight of a cereal bar is increased from 80 g to 90 g.
    The manufacturers claim that this is a 15% increase.
    Is the manufacturers' claim correct? Give a reason for your
    answer.

15

SPECIAL OFFER
DIGITAL CAMCORDERS
only £435 + VAT

    VAT is $17\frac{1}{2}$%. Calculate the total cost of a digital camcorder.

16 A photocopier produces a copy of an original sheet of paper that
    is reduced by 42% of its original area. The area of the original
    sheet of paper is 600 cm². What is the area of the copy?

17 A shopkeeper buys a cooker for £180. He sells it for £207.
    Calculate his percentage profit.

18 Deepa bought a car for £8600. She sold the car for £6700 two years later. Calculate the percentage loss.

19 All items in a sale are reduced by 30%.
Alex bought a coat in the sale for £135.
Work out the pre-sale price of the coat.

20 On 1st January Eryl invests £700 in a building society savings account.
The account pays interest at a rate of 5.5% per annum.
Calculate the total amount of interest earned after 5 years.

21 £600 is invested at 4% per annum.
How long will it take for the investment to reach £700?

22 Hajra's weekly pay this year is £240.
This is 20% more than her weekly pay last year.
Bill says 'This means Hajra's weekly pay last year was £192'.
Bill is wrong.
   (a) Explain why.
   (b) Work out Hajra's weekly pay last year.   [E]

23 This item appeared in a newspaper.

Cows produce 3% more milk

A farmer found that when his cow listened to classical music the milk it produced increased by 3%.

This increase of 3% represented 0.72 litres of milk.

Calculate the amount of milk produced by the cow when it listened to classical music.   [E]

Summary of key points

1 per cent
    %   } mean 'out of 100'.
    pc

2 To change a percentage to a fraction, write it as a fraction with denominator 100.

3 To change a percentage to a decimal, first change it to a fraction and then to a decimal.

4 To change a decimal to a percentage, multiply the decimal by 100%.

5 To change a fraction to a percentage, first change the fraction to a decimal and then multiply by 100%.

6 To compare fractions with percentages, convert the fractions to percentages.

7 To find a percentage of a quantity, change the percentage to a fraction or a decimal and multiply it by the quantity.

8 To increase a quantity by a percentage, use a multiplier *or* find the percentage of the quantity and add it to the original quantity.

9 **Simple interest** is when the same interest is added each year. You find the interest for one year and multiply it by the number of years.

10 To decrease a quantity by a percentage, use a multiplier *or* find the percentage of the quantity and subtract it from the original quantity.

11 When an original amount is **increased** by R% to become a new amount,
$$\text{Original amount} = \frac{\text{new amount}}{1 + \dfrac{R}{100}}$$

12 When an original amount is **decreased** by R% to become a new amount,
$$\text{Original amount} = \frac{\text{new amount}}{1 - \dfrac{R}{100}}$$

13 To write one quantity as a percentage of another,
  ○ write one quantity as a fraction of the other
  ○ change the fraction to a decimal
  ○ multiply the decimal by 100%.

14 When a quantity changes (increases or decreases), find the percentage change using
$$\text{Percentage change} = \frac{\text{actual change}}{\text{original quantity}} \times 100\%$$

15 **Compound interest** is interest paid on an amount *and* on the interest on that amount.

16 To calculate compound interest, find the multiplier.
  Amount after n years = original amount $\times$ multiplier^n

3 Ratio and proportion

3.1 Simplifying ratios

- A **ratio** is a way of comparing two or more quantities.
- You can simplify a ratio by dividing the numbers by a common factor.
- A ratio has only whole numbers in its simplest form.

Example 1

A recipe for scones uses 8 oz flour and 2 oz butter.
Write the ratio of flour to butter in its simplest form.

The ratio of flour to butter is $8:2$

$$\div 2 \left(\begin{matrix} 8 & : & 2 \\ 4 & : & 1 \end{matrix} \right) \div 2$$

8 and 2 have common factor 2.

$8:2$ and $4:1$ are equivalent ratios.

Example 2

Write these ratios in their simplest form.
(a) $18:12$ (b) $2\frac{1}{2}:1\frac{1}{2}$
(c) $20:15:5$ (d) $1\,\text{m}:50\,\text{cm}$

(a) $\div 6 \left(\begin{matrix} 18 & : & 12 \\ 3 & : & 2 \end{matrix} \right) \div 6$

The HCF of 18 and 12 is 6.

(b) $\times 2 \left(\begin{matrix} 2\frac{1}{2} & : & 1\frac{1}{2} \\ 5 & : & 3 \end{matrix} \right) \times 2$

Multiply by 2 to remove the fractions.

(c) $20:15:5$
     $4:3:1$

Divide all 3 numbers by their HCF, 5.

(d) $1\,\text{m}:50\,\text{cm}$
     $= 100\,\text{cm}:50\,\text{cm}$
     $=   2:1$

Rewrite the ratio using the same units for both quantities. Then simplify.

- A ratio can be written in the form $1:n$ or $n:1$

Example 3

(a) Write the ratio $8:10$ in the form $1:n$
(b) Write the ratio 1 kg to 5 kg in the form $n:1$

(a) $\div 8 \left(\begin{array}{c} 8 \ : \ 10 \\ 1 \ : \ \frac{10}{8} \end{array} \right) \div 8$

Divide both sides by 8.

$= 1 : 1.25$

(b) $\div 5 \left(\begin{array}{c} 1\,\text{kg} \ : \ 5\,\text{kg} \\ \frac{1}{5} \ : \ 1 \end{array} \right) \div 5$

Divide both sides by 5.

$0.2 : 1$

Example 4

$\frac{1}{4}$ of a class are boys. What is the ratio of boys to girls?

$\frac{1}{4}$ of the class are boys, so the class has been divided into 4 parts.
1 part is boys, and the remaining 3 parts are girls.
So the ratio of boys to girls is

　　　1 part to 3 parts　or　1 : 3

Exercise 3A

In questions **1–3** write the ratios
(i)　in their simplest form　　　　(ii)　in the form $1 : n$
(iii) in the form $n : 1$

1 (a)　$10 : 5$　　　　(b)　$27 : 9$　　　　(c)　$36 : 9$
　　(d)　$4 : 8$　　　　(e)　$20 : 4$　　　　(f)　$36 : 24$

2 (a)　$4 : 1\frac{1}{2}$　　　(b)　$6 : 1\frac{1}{4}$　　　(c)　$1\frac{1}{2} : 3\frac{1}{2}$
　　(d)　$2\frac{1}{5} : 4\frac{4}{5}$　　(e)　$3.2 : 5$　　　(f)　$2.1 : 6$

3 (a)　$2\,\text{m} : 75\,\text{cm}$　　(b)　$2\,\text{kg} : 500\,\text{g}$　　(c)　$3\,\text{km} : 250\,\text{m}$
　　(d)　$2\,\text{min} : 30\,\text{s}$　　(e)　$3\,\text{h} : 1\,\text{h}\ 30\,\text{min}$　(f)　$2\,\text{km} : 1\,\text{km}\ 750\,\text{m}$

4 Write these ratios in their simplest form.
　　(a)　$3 : 6 : 9$　　　(b)　$24 : 12 : 6$　　(c)　$25 : 15 : 10$
　　(d)　$10 : 6 : 2$　　(e)　$12 : 8 : 2$　　(f)　$40 : 30 : 5$

5 The ratio of two gears is $5 : 2$. The smaller gear rotates 10 times.
　　How many times does the larger gear rotate?

6 $\frac{1}{5}$ of the pages in a book are printed in colour.
　　The rest are printed in black and white.
　　What is the ratio of colour pages to black and white pages?

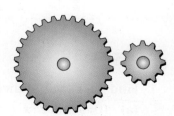

7 $\frac{3}{8}$ of a class of pupils catch a bus to school.
　　The rest of the class walk.
　　What is the ratio of pupils who catch the bus to those who walk?

3.2 Writing ratios as fractions

- Equivalent ratios can be written as equivalent fractions.
  If $a:b = x:y$ then $\dfrac{a}{b} = \dfrac{x}{y}$.

Example 5

(a) The ratios $8:4$ and $2:x$ are equivalent. Find x.

(b) In a box of chocolates the ratio of milk to plain chocolates is $2:3$. There are 18 milk chocolates in the box.
How many plain chocolates are there in the box?

(a) Writing the ratios as fractions gives
$$\frac{8}{4} = \frac{2}{x}$$

Write the fractions with the same numerator:
$$\frac{8}{4} = \frac{2 \times 4}{x \times 4} = \frac{8}{4x}$$

The denominators must be equal, so
$$4x = 4$$
$$x = 1$$

(b) The ratio of milk to plain chocolates is $2:3$. Use y to represent the number of plain chocolates. There are 18 milk chocolates, so the ratio of milk to plain chocolates is $18:y$.

$18:y$ is equivalent to $2:3$.

So $\dfrac{18}{y} = \dfrac{2}{3}$

$\dfrac{18}{y} = \dfrac{2 \times 9}{3 \times 9} = \dfrac{18}{27}$ | Write the fractions with the same numerator.

so $y = 27$

There are 27 plain chocolates.

Exercise 3B

1 Find x for each of these pairs of equivalent ratios.

(a) $10:5$ and $2:x$

(b) $12:3$ and $x:1$

(c) $15:10$ and $3:x$

(d) $8:x$ and $16:4$

(e) $x:5$ and $21:35$

(f) $x:42$ and $3:7$

(g) $2:5$ and $x:30$

(h) $4:5$ and $x:50$

2 The ratio of men to women in a company is 5 : 3. There are
15 men in the company. How many women are there?

3 The ratio of the sides of a rectangle is 7 : 4.
The length of the shorter sides of the rectangle is 16 cm.
Calculate the length of the longer sides of the rectangle.

4 The ratio of nuts to raisins in a packet of nuts and raisins is 4 : 5.
There are 24 nuts in the packet. How many raisins are there?

5 The ratio of the heights of two similar triangles is 5 : 2.
The height of the larger triangle is 24 cm.
Calculate the height of the smaller triangle.

6 Rachael and Mohammed are paid in the ratio 3 : 4.
Rachael earns £162.60 per week.
How much does Mohammed earn?

7 Jim makes a model of his school. He uses a scale of 1 : 50.
The area of the door on his model is 8 cm².
Work out the area of the door on the real school.   [E]

3.3 Dividing quantities in a given ratio

- Ratios can be used to share or divide quantities.

Example 6

(a) Divide £15 in the ratio 3 : 2.

(b) Jumana, Malik and Hala share £100 in the ratio 5 : 3 : 2.
How much does each person receive?

(a) 3 : 2 means 3 parts to 2 parts.
So £15 needs to be divided into 3 + 2 = 5 parts.
        1 part = £15 ÷ 5 = £3
so   3 parts = £3 × 3 = £9   2 parts = £3 × 2 = £6

(b) £100 is shared in the ratio 5 : 3 : 2.
                5 + 3 + 2 = 10 parts
        1 part = £100 ÷ 10 = £10

        Jumana receives 5 parts = 5 × £10 = £50
        Malik receives 3 parts = 3 × £10 = £30
        Hala receives 2 parts = 2 × £10 = £20

Example 7

Jill, Lesley and Marcia share £600 in the ratio of their ages.
Jill is 16, Lesley is 18 and Marcia is 26.

(a) Write the ratio of their ages in its simplest form.

(b) Calculate the amount of money each of them receives.

(a) $16:18:26$
is $8:9:13$ in its simplest form.

(b) $8:9:13$ means $8 + 9 + 13 = 30$ parts.
Jill has 8 parts, Lesley has 9 parts and Marcia has 13 parts.

So Jill has $\frac{8}{30} \times £600 = £160$

Lesley has $\frac{9}{30} \times £600 = £180$

Marcia has $\frac{13}{30} \times £600 = £260$

Exercise 3C

1 Divide the quantities in the ratios given.
   (a) 25 in the ratio $3:2$ (b) 100 in the ratio $7:3$
   (c) £30 in the ratio $4:1$ (d) £24.60 in the ratio $7:5$
   (e) 350 in the ratio $4:2:1$ (f) 150 cm in the ratio $3:1:1$
   (g) £240 in the ratio $4:3:1$ (h) £36.90 in the ratio $5:3:1$

2 Juan, Gabrielle and Kwame share £200 in the ratio of their ages,
   which is $12:8:5$. How much does each person receive?

3 The ratio of men, women and children in a village is $5:4:8$.
   The population of the village is 3400.
   How many women are there in the village?

4 The ratio of flour, fat and sugar in shortbread is $4:2:1$.
   What fraction of the shortbread is flour?

5 The sides of a triangle are in the ratio $3:4:5$. The perimeter of the
   triangle is 42 cm.
   Work out the length of the longest side of the triangle.

6 The ratio of nuts and fruit to other ingredients in a packet of
   muesli is $2:3$.
   (a) What fraction of the muesli is nuts and fruit?
   (b) Calculate the weight of nuts and fruit in a packet of muesli
       weighing 350 g.

7 George, Charlie and Ryan earn £60 for doing some gardening.
   They share the money in the ratio of the hours they work. George
   works for 5 hours, Charlie for 3 hours and Ryan for 2 hours.
   Work out the amount of money each boy should receive.

8 A DVD library has comedy, horror and action films in the
   ratio $1:3:5$. The shop has a total of 1800 DVDs.

   (a) What fraction of the DVDs are horror films?

   (b) What fraction of the DVDs are comedy films?

   (c) How many action DVDs does the shop have?

9 A box of 42 chocolates contains milk, plain and white chocolates
   in the ratio $3:2:1$.

   (a) What fraction of the chocolates are plain?

   (b) How many milk chocolates are there?

10 In a packet of sweet pea seeds the ratio of pink, purple and white
    flower seeds is $5:4:2$.

    (a) How many purple-flowered plants would you expect from a
         packet of 110 seeds?

    (b) What fraction of the plants would you expect to have
         white flowers?

3.4 More ratios

Example 8

Concrete is made from gravel, cement and sand in the ratio $3:2:1$.
A mixture of concrete is made using 12 kg of cement.
Calculate the amounts of the other items required for the mixture.

Cement is $\frac{2}{6}$ of the total mixture.

> So $\frac{2}{6}$ is 12 kg
>
> $\frac{1}{6}$ is 6 kg   1 part = 6 kg

The mixture needs $\frac{3}{6}$ gravel and $\frac{1}{6}$ sand.

> So the amounts required are
>   gravel: $3 \times 6\,\text{kg} = 18\,\text{kg}$ 3 parts
>   sand: $1 \times 6\,\text{kg} = 6\,\text{kg}$ 1 part

Exercise 3D

1 A recipe for fish pie uses cod, haddock and prawns in the
   ratio $4:2:1$. Sadie uses 300 g of cod.
   How much of each of the other ingredients should she use?

2 Bridget, Keith and David share a cash prize in the ratio $2:5:6$.
   David wins £60. Find

   (a) how much Bridget wins

   (b) the total amount of the prize money.

3 A chemical compound is made from three elements A, B and C in the ratio $2:5:7$.
2.6 mg of element A is used. Find

   (a) how much of element C is used

   (b) the total weight of the compound.

4 A box of sweets contains pink, blue and green sweets.
$\frac{1}{4}$ of the sweets are pink, and $\frac{3}{5}$ of the sweets are blue.

   (a) What fraction of the sweets are green?

   (b) Write the ratio for the coloured sweets in the box.

   (c) The box contains 15 pink sweets. How many sweets of each of the other colours are in the box?

5 £600 is shared between Paul, Douglas and Gillian in the ratio $2:x:4x$.
Paul receives £100.

   (a) Find the value of x.

   (b) Calculate how much Douglas and Gillian receive.

3.5 Direct and inverse proportion

• Two quantities are in **direct proportion** if their ratio stays the same as the quantities increase or decrease.

The distance travelled by a car is directly proportional to the amount of petrol used.
A car travels 59 km and uses 5 litres of petrol.
How far can the same car travel using 11 litres of petrol?

Method 1
The ratio of distance travelled to petrol used is

   $59:5$

The car travels x km on 11 litres of petrol.
The ratio of distance travelled to petrol used is

   $x:11$

$59:5$ and $x:11$ are equivalent ratios.
Write the ratios as fractions.

$$\frac{59}{5} = \frac{x}{11}$$

×2.2

So x must be $59 \times 2.2 = 129.8$ km.

Method 2 (unitary method)
On 5 litres of petrol the car travels 59 km
On 1 litre of petrol the car travels $59 \div 5 = 11.8$ km

So on 11 litres of petrol the car travels
$$11 \times 11.8 \text{ km} = 129.8 \text{ km}$$

> The unitary method involves finding the value of one unit of the quantity.

Example 10

18 pens cost £3.92.
How much will 30 pens cost?

Method 1
Ratio of pens to cost is $18 : 3.92$
30 pens cost x, so the ratio is $30 : x$

$$\times 1\frac{2}{3}$$
$$\frac{18}{3.92} = \frac{30}{x}$$

The cost of 30 pens is £3.92 $\times 1\frac{2}{3}$
$$= £6.53\frac{1}{3}$$
$$= £6.53 \text{ to the nearest penny}$$

> The answer £6.53$\frac{1}{3}$ isn't sensible, so round to the nearest penny.

Method 2 (unitary method)
18 pens cost £3.92
1 pen costs £3.92 $\div 18 = 0.21\dot{7}$
30 pens cost $30 \times 0.21\dot{7}$
$$= £6.5\dot{3}$$
$$= £6.53 \text{ to the nearest penny}$$

- Two quantities are in **inverse proportion** when one increases at the same rate as the other decreases.

Example 11

3 women take 15 days to landscape a garden.
How long would it take 5 women working at the same rate?

3 women take 15 days
1 woman takes $15 \times 3 = 45$ days
5 women take $45 \div 5 = 9$ days

> This is the unitary method.

Exercise 3E

1 A car travels at a steady speed of 50 km/h.
How far will the car travel in

(a) 2 hours   (b) 5 hours   (c) $\frac{1}{2}$ hour?

> A car travelling at a constant speed is an example of direct proportion. If the car travels for twice as long, it will go twice as far.

2 A train travels at a steady speed of 120 km/h.
How long will it take the train to travel

(a) 360 km   (b) 700 km   (c) 280 km?

3 8 books cost £12. How much will

(a) 1 book cost   (b) 13 books cost?

4 Climbing rope costs £18.70 for 5 metres. Work out the cost of

(a) 1 metre of rope   (b) 11 metres of rope.

5 A secretary can type 1000 words in $\frac{1}{4}$ hour.
How many words can he type in

(a) $1\frac{1}{2}$ hours   (b) 5 minutes   (c) 25 minutes?

6 The time taken for a microwave oven to heat up some soup is directly proportional to the amount of soup.
A microwave oven can heat up 400 ml of soup in 5 minutes.
How long will it take to heat up 750 ml of soup?

7 An 8 m tall statue casts a 6 m long shadow. The length of the shadow is directly proportional to the height of the statue.
Calculate the length of the shadow cast by a 5 m tall statue.

8 Jade is paid £56.80 for working 8 hours.
How much will she be paid for working 3 hours?

9 20 bales of hay will feed 5 horses for 20 days.
How long will 20 bales of hay feed

(a) 1 horse   (b) 4 horses?

10 3 dressmakers can make 6 bridesmaids' dresses in 5 days. How long will it take 5 dressmakers to make 6 bridesmaids' dresses?

11 The recipe for 24 shortcake biscuits requires the following ingredients:

     8 oz flour, 4 oz butter, 2 oz sugar.

What amount of each of the ingredients will be required to make 30 biscuits?

12 A student can write 400 words in 2 hours.
How long will the student take to write a 1000-word essay?

13 A bottle of shower gel lasts a family of four for 9 days.
How long will the same bottle of shower gel last a family of six?

14 A packet of hamster food lasts five hamsters for 15 days.
How long will the same packet of food last eight hamsters, to the
nearest day?

15 Five packets of sweets cost £1.90.
How much will eight packets of the same sweets cost?

16 Two workmen can complete a job in 7 hours.
How long will it take three workmen to complete the same job?

17 The voltage across a resistor is directly proportional to the current
flowing through it.
A voltage of 16.5 volts produces a current of 9.4 amperes.
(a) Calculate the voltage needed to produce a current of 5 amperes.
(b) Calculate the current produced by a voltage of 10 volts.

18 The distance travelled by a car is directly proportional to the
amount of petrol used.
A car travels a distance of 200 miles and uses 18.6 litres of petrol.
(a) How far will the car travel on 15 litres of petrol?
(b) How much petrol does the car use to travel 60 miles?

3.6 Repeated proportional change

Example 12

The number of colonies of bacteria in a Petri dish increases by
one quarter every hour.
There are 20 colonies at the start of the first hour.
How many colonies will there be after 5 hours?

After 1 hour the number of colonies will be

$20 \times 1\frac{1}{4}$ (or 1.25)

After 2 hours the number of colonies will be

$(20 \times 1.25) \times 1.25$

Number of colonies at the end of 1 hour.

1.25 is the multiplier.

This can be written as

$20 \times (1.25)^2$ ——— This is the number of hours.

So after 5 hours the number of colonies will be

$20 \times (1.25)^5 = 61.035\,156\ldots$
$\quad\quad\quad = 61$ colonies

This type of calculation
often gives answers with
lots of decimal places.
You need to decide what
degree of accuracy is
sensible for the question.

Example 13

The number of students in a school is predicted to fall by 5% every year for the next four years.
The school currently has 200 students.
How many students will there be in the school after four years if the prediction is correct?

After 1 year the number of students will be

$$200 \times (100\% - 5\%)$$
$$= 200 \times 95\% \text{ (or 0.95)}$$

After 4 years the number of students will be

$$200 \times (0.95)^4$$
$$= 162.901 \dots$$
$$= 163 \text{ students to the nearest whole number}$$

> 0.95 is the multiplier.

Exercise 3F

1 A puppy's weight increases by 10% every week during the first 6 weeks of its life.
   A puppy weighs 2 kg at birth.
   How heavy will the puppy be after 6 weeks?

2 During a particular year house prices increased by 2% every month.
   A house was valued at £60 000 at the start of the year.
   Calculate the value of the house at the end of the year.

3 In a science experiment on a bouncing ball some students found that the height of each bounce was $\frac{4}{5}$ of the height of the previous bounce.
   The height of the first bounce of the ball was 80 cm.
   Calculate the height of the fifth bounce.

4 The average attendance at a football club's matches fell by 7% every year for the 3 years from 2004 to 2006.
   The average attendance in 2003 was 21 500.
   Calculate the average attendance in 2006.

5 As part of his contract a rugby player is promised a 5% pay rise every year.
   The player's starting wage is £45 000.
   Calculate his wage after 4 years.

6 A population of rabbits increases by 10% every 2 weeks.
   At the beginning of March the population is 16.
   Assuming no rabbit dies, how many rabbits will there be after 20 weeks?

7 A population of hamsters increases by one third every month.
At the beginning of February there are 20 hamsters.
Assuming no hamster dies, how many hamsters will there be at the
end of June?

8 The population of a small country increases by 8% every year.
If it keeps increasing at this rate, how long will it take for the
country's population to double?

3.7 Finding proportionality rules from ratios

- You can use ratios to find the rule connecting quantities that are in
  direct or inverse proportion to one another.

Example 14

The distance travelled by a car is directly proportional to the
amount of petrol it uses.
A car travels 35.7 km and uses 7 litres of petrol.

(a) Find a rule connecting the distance travelled, d, and the
amount of petrol used, p.

(b) Find the distance that the car can travel on 11 litres of petrol.

(a) The distance-to-petrol ratio is
$$35.7 : 7$$
$$\frac{35.7}{7} = 5.1$$

The rule connecting distance travelled and petrol used
is $d = 5.1p$.

(b) Using the rule, when $p = 11$ litres then $d = 5.1 \times 11 = 56.1$ km

---

Example 15

The time taking to build a wall is inversely proportional to the
number of bricklayers building the wall.
Three bricklayers take 6 hours to build a wall. How long will it take
four bricklayers to build a similar wall, working at the same rate?

This information can be shown in a table:

$\times \frac{4}{3}$

Number of bricklayers	3	4
Number of hours	6	?

The number of bricklayers has been multiplied by $\frac{4}{3}$.

The number of hours taken is *inversely proportional* to the number of bricklayers. So to find the number of hours required we need to *divide* 6 by $\frac{4}{3}$.

$\times \frac{4}{3}$

Number of bricklayers	3	4
Number of hours	6	$4\frac{1}{2}$

$\div \frac{4}{3}$

So 4 bricklayers will take $6 \times \frac{3}{4} = 4\frac{1}{2}$ hours.

Exercise 3G

1 The mass of a book is directly proportional to the number of pages it contains. A book with mass 0.8 kg contains 320 pages. Calculate the mass of a similar book containing 220 pages.

2 The voltage V across a resistor is directly proportional to the current I flowing through it.
  A voltage of 10.9 volts produces a current of 6.2 amperes.
  (a) Find a rule connecting V and I.
  (b) Calculate the voltage needed to produce a current of 4.3 amperes.

3 The circumference of a circle is directly proportional to its radius. A circle has a radius of 6 cm and a circumference of approximately 37.7 cm.
  (a) Find a rule connecting the radius and circumference of a circle.
  (b) Use your rule to find the circumference of a circle with a radius of 8 cm.

4 A football team wins a trophy in a competition. The players in the team are each given a miniature replica of the trophy.
  The mass of a trophy is in direct proportion to its volume.
  The original trophy has a mass of 2.55 kg and a volume of 850 cm³.
  (a) Find a rule connecting the volume of the trophy and its mass.
  (b) A replica trophy has a volume of 425 cm³.
      Calculate the mass of a replica trophy.

5 A tree 6 metres tall casts a shadow 4 metres long. The length of the shadow is directly proportional to the height of the tree.
  (a) Find a rule connecting the length of the shadow and the height of the tree.
  (b) Calculate the length of the shadow cast by a tree 9.6 metres tall.
  (c) Calculate the height of a tree that casts a shadow of 12.6 metres.

6 Two variables, x and y, are inversely proportional to each other.
Copy and complete the table for these variables.

x	4	6	
y	15		6

7 The number of drinks that can be poured from a bottle of cola is inversely proportional to the size of glass used.
Six drinks can be poured from a bottle of cola using 250 m*l* glasses.
Drinks are poured from a similar bottle of cola using 300 m*l* glasses. Calculate the number of drinks that can be poured.

8 For rectangles of constant area, the length of the rectangle is inversely proportional to the width of the rectangle.
A rectangle has sides of 15 cm and 12 cm.
Calculate the length of a rectangle with the same area that is 10 cm wide.

Mixed exercise 3

1 Write these ratios in their simplest form.
  (a) 24 : 6
  (b) 8 : 4 : 2
  (c) $1\frac{1}{4}$: 3
  (d) 2.4 : 3
  (e) 3 kg : 500 g
  (f) 1 hour 15 minutes : 2 hours

2 Find x for these pairs of equivalent ratios.
  (a) 4 : 2 and x : 4
  (b) x : 7 and 20 : 35

3 The ratio of two sides of a rectangle is 7 : 2.
The length of the longer side is 17.5 cm.
Calculate the length of the shorter side.

4 Three children share £250 in the ratio of their ages. Their ages are

  Rebecca   15 years
  Dinesh   7 years
  Nilgun   3 years

How much does Dinesh receive?

5 $\frac{3}{5}$ of a bag of bulbs are tulips; the remainder are daffodils.
What is the ratio of tulip bulbs to daffodil bulbs in the bag?

6 9 pencils cost £1.17.
How much will 15 pencils cost?

7 A 12 m tall tree casts a shadow 9 m long. The length of the shadow is directly proportional to the height of the tree.
Calculate the length of the shadow cast by a 10 m tall tree.

8 The ingredients for 12 biscuits are as follows:

250 g flour, 100 g fat, 50 g sugar.

Work out the amount of each ingredient needed to make 30 biscuits.

9 A kitten increases its weight by 12% each week during the first 8 weeks of its life. A kitten weighs 400 g at birth. How heavy will the kitten be after 8 weeks?

10 A basketball is dropped from a height and bounces. Each bounce is $\frac{2}{3}$ of the height of the previous bounce. The height of the first bounce is 120 cm. Calculate the height of the fourth bounce.

11 Sue invests £400 for 5 years at 6% compound interest. Calculate the total value of her investment after 5 years.

12 Calculate the total interest earned on £300 invested for 3 years at a rate of 6% per annum.

13 £250 is invested at a rate of 3% per annum. How many years will it be before the total investment becomes more than £300?

14 A fish population is attacked by a disease. The disease kills 9% of the fish every week. If nothing is done, how long will it take the fish population to halve?

15 The population of the world is growing at the rate of 1.5% per annum. What single number can be used to calculate the world population growth over 50 years?

16 Paula, Sasha and Luisa share £4500 in the ratio 2 : 5 : 8.

(a) What fraction of the money does Sasha receive?

(b) How much money does Luisa receive?

17 Amy, Beth and Colin share 36 sweets in the ratio 2 : 3 : 4. Work out the number of sweets that each of them receives.   [E]

18 A fruit smoothie is made using 3 fruits in the ratio $x : 3 : 2x$. 450 ml is made. To make this amount, 150 ml of the second fruit is required.

(a) Find the ratio of the 3 fruits.

(b) How much of the third fruit is required?

19 A quantity of chicken feed will feed 12 chickens for eight days. How long would the same quantity of chicken feed last 15 chickens, to the nearest day?

20 8 kg of apples cost £4.80. How much will 5 kg of apples cost?

21 (a) The time, T seconds, it takes a water heater to boil some water is directly proportional to the mass of water, m kg, in the water heater.

When $m = 250$, $T = 600$.

Find T when $m = 400$.

(b) The time, T seconds, it takes a water heater to boil a constant mass of water is inversely proportional to the power, P watts, of the water heater.

When $P = 1400$, $T = 360$.

Find the value of T when $P = 900$. [E]

22 Two variables, a and b, are inversely proportional to each other. Copy and complete the table for these variables.

a	25	15	
b	36		100

23 The population of a village trebles every 4 years. The population was 682 in 1960.

What was the population of the village in

(a) 1972   (b) 1988?

Summary of key points

1 A **ratio** is a way of comparing two or more quantities.

2 You can simplify a ratio by dividing the numbers by a common factor.

3 A ratio has only whole numbers in its simplest form.

4 A ratio can be written in the form $1 : n$ or $n : 1$

5 Equivalent ratios can be written as equivalent fractions.

If $a : b = x : y$ then $\dfrac{a}{b} = \dfrac{x}{y}$.

6 Ratios can be used to share or divide quantities.

7 Two quantities are in **direct proportion** if their ratio stays the same as the quantities increase or decrease.

8 Two quantities are in **inverse proportion** when one increases at the same rate as the other decreases.

9 You can use ratios to find the rule connecting quantities that are in direct or inverse proportion to one another.

4 Powers and surds

4.1 Calculations using standard form

- A number in **standard form** is $A \times 10^n$ where $1 \leqslant A < 10$ and n is an integer.

Standard form was covered in Chapter 3 of Higher Unit 3.

Example 1

Work out   (a) $(3.4 \times 10^5) \times (2.6 \times 10^3)$ (b) $\dfrac{5.8 \times 10^4}{8.5 \times 10^6}$

Give your answers in standard form.

(a) $(3.4 \times 10^5) \times (2.6 \times 10^3)$

$= 3.4 \times 2.6 \times 10^5 \times 10^3$

$= 8.84 \times 10^{5+3}$

$= 8.84 \times 10^8$

Check that the answer is in standard form.

(b) $\dfrac{5.8 \times 10^4}{8.5 \times 10^6}$

$= \dfrac{5.8}{8.5} \times \dfrac{10^4}{10^6}$

$= 0.682\,352\ldots \times 10^{4-6}$

$= 0.682\,352\ldots \times 10^{-2}$

Answer is not in standard form.

$= 6.82 \times 10^{-3}$ (3 s.f.)

- Standard form can be used to make approximations and estimates.

Example 2

Work out an estimate for

(a) $537\,890 \times 0.003\,12$ (b) $0.0921 \div 0.000\,331$

(a) $537\,890 \times 0.003\,12$

$= 5.3789 \times 10^5 \times 3.12 \times 10^{-3}$

Rewrite in standard form.

$\approx 5 \times 10^5 \times 3 \times 10^{-3}$

$= 5 \times 3 \times 10^5 \times 10^{-3}$

Write the numbers correct to 1 s.f.

$= 15 \times 10^2$

$= 1500$

$\approx$ means 'is approximately equal to'.

(b) $0.0921 \div 0.000\,331 = \dfrac{9.21 \times 10^{-2}}{3.31 \times 10^{-4}}$

$\approx \dfrac{9 \times 10^{-2}}{3 \times 10^{-4}}$

$= \dfrac{9}{3} \times \dfrac{10^{-2}}{10^{-4}}$

$= 3 \times 10^{2}$

$= 300$

Exercise 4A

1 Evaluate these expressions, giving your answers in standard form.

(a) $(5 \times 10^{4}) \times (3 \times 10^{3})$ (b) $(2.1 \times 10^{-3}) \times (5 \times 10^{2})$

(c) $(1.8 \times 10^{7}) \times (2 \times 10^{-4})$ (d) $(4.8 \times 10^{-2}) \times (8 \times 10^{7})$

(e) $(2.7 \times 10^{-2}) \div (9 \times 10^{4})$ (f) $(6.4 \times 10^{6}) \div (1.6 \times 10^{3})$

(g) $\dfrac{5.5 \times 10^{3}}{1.1 \times 10^{2}}$ (h) $\dfrac{3.6 \times 10^{-6}}{4 \times 10^{3}}$

2 Evaluate these expressions, giving your answers as ordinary decimal numbers.

(a) $(3 \times 10^{4}) \times (7 \times 10^{3})$ (b) $(2.3 \times 10^{-2}) \times (1.6 \times 10^{4})$

(c) $(3.8 \times 10^{-4}) \times (8 \times 10^{-3})$ (d) $(6.2 \times 10^{3}) \div (4 \times 10^{2})$

(e) $\dfrac{4.8 \times 10^{-4}}{6 \times 10^{3}}$ (f) $\dfrac{3.55 \times 10^{-4}}{5 \times 10^{-2}}$

3 Estimate the value of

(a) $73\,261 \times 39.478$ (b) $896.25 \times 0.003\,21$

(c) 638.2×5.987 (d) $0.002\,58 \times 0.794$

(e) $82.63 \div 0.004\,23$ (f) $15.63 \div 0.0278$

(g) $9\,300\,000 \div 4187$ (h) $0.000\,28 \div 0.007\,38$

Hint: rewrite the numbers in standard form to 1 s.f.

4 The distance from the Earth to the Sun is 1.5×10^{8} km.
The distance from Neptune to the Sun is 4.5×10^{9} km.
How many times further from the Sun is Neptune than the Earth?

5 The United Kingdom has an area of 2.5×10^{5} km² and a
population of 5.9×10^{7} people.
Calculate the number of people per km² in the UK.

6 The mass of a neutron is 1.675×10^{-24} grams. Calculate the total
mass of 5×10^{6} neutrons. Give your answer in standard form.

4.2 Using a calculator for powers and roots

- A number can be raised to any power using the $\boxed{x^{y}}$ or $\boxed{y^{x}}$ key.
- The nth root of any number can be found using the $\boxed{\sqrt[x]{}}$ key.
- You may also need to use the brackets keys $\boxed{(}$ $\boxed{)}$.

Some calculators have different keys. Make sure you know how to work out powers and roots on your calculator.

Example 3

Use your calculator to work out the value of $\dfrac{\sqrt{15.7^3 - 800.1}}{12.8 \times 3.78}$

Give your answer correct to 2 decimal places.

Enter the calculation using brackets.

$(\sqrt{(15.7^3 - 800.1)}) \div (12.8 \times 3.78)$
$= 1.145\,124 \ldots$
$= 1.15$ (to 2 d.p.)

Example 4

Louise bought a car valued at £12 000.
The value of the car depreciates at a rate of 15% per year.
Work out the value of the car 6 years after Louise bought it.

'Depreciates by 15% per year' means that at the end of a year the
value of the car is 0.85 of its value at the start of the year.
So after 6 years the value of the car is
$(0.85)^6 \times 12\,000 = £4525.79$ (to the nearest penny).

Exercise 4B

1 Use your calculator to work out the value of $\dfrac{27.6 - 3.8^2}{5.2 - \sqrt{2.56}}$

Give your answer correct to 1 decimal place.

2 Use your calculator to work out the value of $\dfrac{\sqrt{12.3^2 + 7.9}}{1.8 \times 0.17}$

Give your answer correct to 1 decimal place.

3 The price of a new television is £423.
This price includes Value Added Tax (VAT) at $17\frac{1}{2}\%$.

(a) Work out the cost of the television **before** VAT was added.

By the end of each year, the value of a television has fallen by
12% of its value at the start of that year.
The value of a television was £423 at the start of the first year.

(b) Work out the value of the television at the end of the **third**
year. Give your answer to the nearest penny.

4 James and Donna bought a new flat for £130 000.
The value of the flat rose by 8% per year. Work out the value of
the flat 7 years after James and Donna bought it.

5 Use your calculator to work out the value of $\dfrac{(17.42^2 + 8.3)^{\frac{1}{3}}}{\sqrt{1.86 \times 3.54}}$

Give your answer correct to 1 decimal place.

6   Use your calculator to work out the value of $(17.38)^{\frac{1}{5}}$

7   Sumreen bought a new motorcycle for £8000 on 1 July 1998.
The value of the motorcycle depreciated by 12% per year.
Work out the value of the motorcycle on 1 July 2006.

4.3 Exponential growth and decay

- The function a^x, where a is a positive constant and x is a variable, is called an **exponential** function.
- If $a > 1$ then a^x is an example of **exponential growth** with multiplier a.
- If $a < 1$ then a^x is an example of **exponential decay** with multiplier a.

Example 5

If you place 1 grain of rice on the first square of a chessboard,
2 grains on the second square, 4 grains on the third square and so
on, doubling each time, how many grains of rice will be placed on
the 64th square?

The problem can be written as

Square 1: 1	or 1×2^0
Square 2: 1×2	or 1×2^1
Square 3: $(1 \times 2) \times 2$	or 1×2^2
Square 4: $(1 \times 2 \times 2) \times 2$	or 1×2^3
Square 5: $(1 \times 2 \times 2 \times 2) \times 2$	or 1×2^4

⋮

Square n: $1 \times 2^{n-1}$

So square 64: $1 \times 2^{63} = 9.22 \times 10^{18}$

Multiplier = 2

Use a calculator.

This is a famous mathematical problem. It is an example of exponential growth: the size of each new pile of rice is found by multiplying the number of grains in the previous pile by 2.

In reality it would be impossible to do this with real grains of rice. For example, by the 32nd square you would need 2 147 483 648 grains of rice. If you counted 100 grains per minute it would take around 40 years to count this number of grains.

Example 6

A population of bacteria is reduced by $\frac{2}{3}$ every hour.
If the population starts with 5 000 000 bacteria, how many will
remain after 6 hours?

After 1 hour the number of bacteria will be

$5\,000\,000 \times \frac{1}{3}$

Multiplier $= \frac{1}{3}$

So after 6 hours the number of bacteria will be

$5\,000\,000 \times \left(\frac{1}{3}\right)^6 = 6858.71\ldots = 7000$ (to 1 s.f.)

As the accuracy of the data is given to 1 significant figure, the answer has been given to 1 significant figure also. In some questions you will be asked to give your answer to a suitable degree of accuracy.

Exercise 4C

Give all answers to an appropriate degree of accuracy.

1 In Example 5, how many grains of rice would be placed on
   (a) the 8th square
   (b) the 16th square?

2 A cell divides into two every hour.
   Assuming that no cells die, how many cells will there be after
   (a) 24 hours
   (b) 1 week?

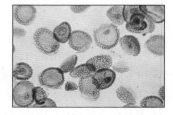

3 The population of a village doubles every 5 years.
   The population in 1980 was 1365.
   What was the population in 2005?

4 The size of a coral reef is halving every 3 years.
   The coral reef is currently $1\,250\,000\,\text{m}^3$.
   How big will it be in 30 years' time if it continues to shrink at
   this rate?

5 A population of insects trebles every 4 days.
   Initially the population is 240.
   Assuming that no insect dies, how many insects will there be after
   (a) 20 days
   (b) 32 days
   (c) 52 days?

6 The population of a particular type of fish is reduced by a disease.
   The population is reduced by one third every 3 months.
   The population of fish is 1.2×10^9.
   Assuming that the disease continues to destroy fish at the same
   rate and that no new fish join the population, how many fish
   will there be in the population after 2 years?

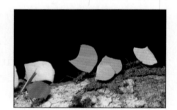

4.4 Using surds and π in calculations

- A number written exactly using square roots is called a **surd**.
  For example, $\sqrt{3}$ and $2 - \sqrt{5}$ are in surd form.
- Surds can be added, subtracted, multiplied and divided.
  $$\sqrt{a \times b} = \sqrt{a} \times \sqrt{b} \qquad \sqrt{\frac{a}{b}} = \frac{\sqrt{a}}{\sqrt{b}}$$
- Answers in surd form or in terms of π are **exact answers**.

Example 7

Simplify

(a) $\sqrt{20}$

(b) $\sqrt{\dfrac{18}{4}}$

(a) $\sqrt{20} = \sqrt{4 \times 5}$
$= \sqrt{4} \times \sqrt{5}$
$= 2\sqrt{5}$

(b) $\sqrt{\dfrac{18}{4}} = \dfrac{\sqrt{18}}{\sqrt{4}} = \dfrac{\sqrt{9 \times 2}}{2} = \dfrac{\sqrt{9} \times \sqrt{2}}{2} = \dfrac{3}{2}\sqrt{2}$

Example 8

A square has an area of 12 cm².
Find the exact length of the side of the square.

Call the length of the side of the square l.

$\quad$ Area of the square $= l^2$
$$l^2 = 12$$
$$l = \sqrt{12}$$
$$= \sqrt{4 \times 3}$$
$$= \sqrt{4} \times \sqrt{3}$$
$$l = 2\sqrt{3} \text{ cm}$$

Example 9

The shape below is made from a semicircle and a rectangle.
Calculate the exact area of the shape.

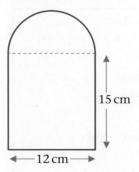

Area **A** $= 12 \times 15$
$\quad\quad\quad = 180 \text{ cm}^2$

Area **B** $= \dfrac{\pi \times 6^2}{2}$

$\quad\quad\quad = \dfrac{\pi \times 36}{2}$

$\quad\quad\quad = 18\pi \text{ cm}^2$

Total area $= (180 + 18\pi) \text{ cm}^2$

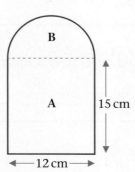

Area of circle $= \pi r^2$
Area of semicircle $= \frac{1}{2}\pi r^2$
For more on area of circles see Chapter 15.

Exercise 4D

1 Simplify

(a) $\sqrt{28}$ (b) $\sqrt{45}$ (c) $\sqrt{8}$ (d) $\sqrt{27}$

(e) $\sqrt{6} \times \sqrt{10}$ (f) $\sqrt{2} \times \sqrt{6}$ (g) $\sqrt{\dfrac{12}{9}}$ (h) $\sqrt{\dfrac{24}{16}}$

(i) $\sqrt{\dfrac{27}{25}}$

2 $ABCD$ is a rectangle.
$AB = 2\sqrt{3}$, $BC = \sqrt{6}$.
Calculate the area of the rectangle.

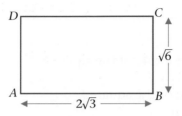

3 Work out the area and circumference of a circle with radius 6 cm.

> Circumference of a circle
> $= 2\pi r$

4 The area of a circle is 12π cm^2.

(a) Calculate the radius of the circle.

(b) Calculate the circumference of the circle.

4.5 More surds

- Accurate solutions to equations can be given in surd form.

Example 10

Solve the equation
$$x^2 - 2 = 25$$
Leave your answer in the most simplified surd form.

$$x^2 - 2 = 25$$
so $\quad x^2 = 25 + 2 = 27$
$$x = \pm\sqrt{27}$$
$$= \pm\sqrt{9 \times 3}$$
$$x = \pm 3\sqrt{3}$$

> For more on solving
> equations involving x^2
> see Chapter 8.

> Do not forget the $\pm$.

- A simplified (or 'rationalised') surd should never have a square root in its denominator.

Example 11

Simplify   (a) $\dfrac{1}{\sqrt{7}}$ (b) $\dfrac{50}{\sqrt{5}}$

(a) $\dfrac{1}{\sqrt{7}} \times \dfrac{\sqrt{7}}{\sqrt{7}} = \dfrac{\sqrt{7}}{7}$

(b) $\dfrac{50}{\sqrt{5}} = \dfrac{5 \times 10}{\sqrt{5}} = \sqrt{5} \times 10 = 10\sqrt{5}$ $\qquad \dfrac{5}{\sqrt{5}} = \sqrt{5}$

> Multiply by $\dfrac{\sqrt{7}}{\sqrt{7}}$ to get rid of the square root in the denominator.

Example 12

Simplify $(3 - \sqrt{5})^2$, giving your answer in the form $a + n\sqrt{b}$.

$$(3 - \sqrt{5})^2 = (3 - \sqrt{5})(3 - \sqrt{5})$$
$$= 3 \times 3 - 3 \times \sqrt{5} - 3 \times \sqrt{5} + \sqrt{5} \times \sqrt{5}$$
$$= 9 - 2 \times 3\sqrt{5} + 5$$
$$= 9 + 5 - 6\sqrt{5}$$
$$= 14 - 6\sqrt{5}$$

Example 13

Write $\dfrac{\sqrt{18} + 10}{\sqrt{2}}$ in the form $p + q\sqrt{2}$ where p and q are integers.

$$\dfrac{\sqrt{18} + 10}{\sqrt{2}} = \dfrac{\sqrt{2}(\sqrt{18} + 10)}{\sqrt{2} \times \sqrt{2}}$$
$$= \dfrac{\sqrt{36} + 10\sqrt{2}}{2}$$
$$= \dfrac{6 + 10\sqrt{2}}{2}$$
$$= 3 + 5\sqrt{2}$$

Exercise 4E

1 Find the exact value of x.
   (a) $x^2 = 20$ (b) $x^2 - 3 = 15$ (c) $2x^2 + 5 = x^2 + 7$

2 Rationalise
   (a) $\dfrac{1}{\sqrt{5}}$ (b) $\dfrac{2}{\sqrt{3}}$ (c) $\dfrac{14}{\sqrt{7}}$ (d) $\dfrac{20}{\sqrt{5}}$

3 Simplify
   (a) $(4 + \sqrt{3})^2$ (b) $(5 - \sqrt{2})(5 + \sqrt{2})$ (c) $(7 - \sqrt{5})^2$

4 (a) Find the value of
   (i) m when $\sqrt{128} = 2^m$
   (ii) n when $(\sqrt{8} - \sqrt{2})^2 = 2^n$
   (b) A rectangle has length 2^t cm and width $(\sqrt{8} - \sqrt{2})$ cm.
   The area of the rectangle is $\sqrt{128}$ cm^2. Find t.

5 Simplify $\dfrac{(7 - 3\sqrt{2})^2}{(3 - \sqrt{2})(3 + \sqrt{2})}$

6 Solve the equation $x^2 - 2 = 70$, leaving your answer in surd form.

7 Expand $(1 + \sqrt{3})^2$, giving your answer in the form $a + n\sqrt{b}$.

8 Write $\dfrac{\sqrt{12} + 5}{\sqrt{3}}$ in the form $p + q\sqrt{3}$ where p is an integer and q is a fraction.

4.6 Upper bounds and lower bounds

- If you make a measurement correct to a given unit, the true value lies in a range that extends half a unit below and half a unit above the measurement.

- The **lower bound** and **upper bound** are the minimum and maximum possible values of a measurement or calculation.

Example 14

A rectangle has length 8.5 cm and width 2.3 cm, measured to the nearest 0.1 cm.
Work out

(a) the lower bounds of the length and the width

(b) the upper bounds of the length and the width.

(a) The lower bound of the length is 8.45 cm.
The lower bound of the width is 2.25 cm.

(b) The upper bound of the length is 8.55 cm.
The upper bound of the width is 2.35 cm.

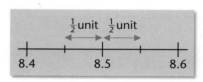

Exercise 4F

1 All these measurements are written to the nearest centimetre. Write down the smallest and largest possible values of the true length.

    (a) 12 cm   (b) 10.02 m   (c) 6 cm

    (d) 9.01 m   (e) 8.00 m

2 The distance between two towns is 23 km to the nearest kilometre. Write down the range of distances in which the true distance must lie.

3 Each number is written correct to the number of significant figures given in the brackets.
For each number write down the maximum and minimum value it could be.

(a) 180 (2 s.f.)   (b) 530 100 (4 s.f.)
(c) 0.002 (1 s.f.)   (d) 0.0032 (2 s.f.)

4 Linford ran 100 m. His time for the run was 12.3 seconds to the nearest tenth of a second.
Write down the upper bound and lower bound for his time.

5 A cuboid has dimensions of 2.4 cm, 4.5 cm and 6.8 cm, each to the nearest 0.1 centimetre. For each dimension write down

(a) the upper bound   (b) the lower bound.

4.7 Calculations involving upper and lower bounds

• When calculating using upper bounds (UB) and lower bounds (LB), use this table to help you.

Result	Calculation
UB	UB + UB
LB	LB + LB
UB	UB − LB
LB	LB − UB
UB	UB × UB
LB	LB × LB
UB	UB ÷ LB
LB	LB ÷ UB

Example 15

The sides of a rectangular lawn are 4.3 m and 2.5 m, to 1 d.p.
Calculate the upper bound and lower bound of the perimeter of the garden.

The largest value for the perimeter is found from the longest possible sides.

$2 \times (4.35 + 2.55) = 2 \times 6.9 = 13.8$ m

The upper bound for the perimeter is 13.8 m.

UB = UB + UB

The smallest value for the perimeter is found from the shortest possible sides.

$2 \times (4.25 + 2.45) = 2 \times 6.7 = 13.4$ m

The lower bound for the perimeter is 13.4 m.

LB = LB + LB

Example 16

Lauren travels from Bedford to Manchester by car. She measures the distance as 179 miles to the nearest mile and she uses 21.4 litres of petrol, to 1 d.p.
Calculate the upper bound and lower bound of the car's fuel economy in miles per litre.

> Fuel economy
> $= \dfrac{\text{number of miles}}{\text{number of litres of petrol}}$

For the upper bound for the fuel economy, use the largest possible distance and the smallest possible amount of petrol.

$\dfrac{179.5}{21.35} = 8.41$ miles per litre (to 3 s.f.)

> UB = UB ÷ LB

For the lower bound for the fuel economy, use the smallest possible distance and the largest possible amount of petrol.

$\dfrac{178.5}{21.45} = 8.32$ miles per litre (to 3 s.f.)

> LB = LB ÷ UB

Exercise 4G

Calculate the upper bound and lower bound for each of the quantities or calculations. The degree of accuracy for each measurement or number is given.

1   The area of a rectangle with sides 2.4 cm and 5.8 cm measured to the nearest millimetre.

2   The area of a circle with a radius of 5 cm measured to the nearest centimetre. Leave your answers in terms of π.

> $A = \pi r^2$

3   The length of the side of a rectangle with area 42.5 cm² correct to 1 d.p. and width 4.5 cm correct to the nearest millimetre.

4   The perimeter of a triangle with sides 12 cm, 11 cm and 17 cm measured to 2 s.f.

5   The average speed of a runner who runs a 200 m race in 23.2 seconds. The running track is measured to the nearest metre and the time to the nearest tenth of a second.

> Speed $= \dfrac{\text{distance}}{\text{time}}$

6   The temperature range on a day when the minimum and maximum temperatures are recorded as $-3\,°C$ and $11\,°C$ to the nearest degree.

7   The circumference of a circle with a radius of 0.23 m measured to 2 d.p. Leave your answers in terms of π.

> $C = 2\pi r$

8   The density of a block of wood of mass 240 g to the nearest gram and volume 80 cm³ correct to 1 s.f.

> Density $= \dfrac{\text{mass}}{\text{volume}}$

9 The value of $\dfrac{2.1 + 3.8}{4.5}$, with all figures correct to 1 d.p.

10 The value of $\dfrac{200(10 + 50)}{300}$, with all figures correct to 1 s.f.

Mixed exercise 4

1 Evaluate
   (a) $3^3 \times 3^{-5}$
   (b) $\dfrac{7^5 \times 7^{-2}}{7^4}$
   (c) $27^{-\frac{1}{3}} \times 27^2$

   (d) $(25^{\frac{1}{2}})^3$
   (e) $(10^2)^{-\frac{3}{2}}$
   (f) $\dfrac{2^0 \times 2^5}{2^{-4}}$

2 Work out
   (a) $(2.3 \times 10^{-2}) \times (5 \times 10^8)$
   (b) $(4 \times 10^{-3}) \times (3.1 \times 10^4)$

   (c) $(2.8 \times 10^4) \div (7 \times 10^{-3})$
   (d) $\dfrac{1.8 \times 10^5}{4 \times 10^3}$

   Give your answers in standard form.

3 Work out an estimate for
   (a) $878\,321 \times 0.004\,32$
   (b) $0.002\,56 \times 0.078$
   (c) $87.34 \div 0.002\,85$
   (d) $0.009\,21 \div 42\,100\,000$

4 A meteorite of mass 2.4×10^6 kg strikes the Moon. The mass of the meteorite is 3.06×10^{13} smaller than the mass of the Moon. Calculate the mass of the Moon.

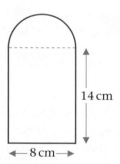

5 Simplify, without using a calculator
   (a) $\sqrt{20}$
   (b) $\sqrt{63}$
   (c) $\sqrt{6} \times \sqrt{8}$
   (d) $\sqrt{\dfrac{12}{16}}$

6 A square has area 27 cm².
   Calculate the exact length of one side of the square.

7 A window is made in the shape of a rectangle with a semicircular top, with dimensions as shown on the diagram.
   Calculate an exact value for the area of the glass.

Area of circle = πr^2

14 cm

8 cm

8 Simplify
   (a) $\dfrac{1}{\sqrt{13}}$
   (b) $\dfrac{42}{\sqrt{6}}$

9 Expand $(2 + \sqrt{5})^2$, giving your answer in the form $a + n\sqrt{b}$.

10 The lengths in question **7** were measured to the nearest 0.1 cm. Work out
   (a) the lower bounds of the length and width of the rectangle
   (b) the upper bounds of the length and width of the rectangle.

11 Stephanie ran 100 metres. The distance was correct to the nearest metre.

(a) Write down the shortest distance Stephanie could have run.

Stephanie's time for the run was 14.8 seconds. Her time was correct to the nearest tenth of a second.

(b) Write down
(i) her shortest possible time for the run
(ii) her longest possible time for the run.

(c) Calculate
(i) the lower bound
(ii) the upper bound for her average speed.
Write down all the figures on your calculator display.

(d) (i) Write down her average speed to an appropriate degree of accuracy.
(ii) Explain how you arrived at your answer. [E]

12 Brazil has an area of 8 500 000 km², correct to the nearest 100 000 km².

(a) Write down the limits between which the area of Brazil must lie.

The population density of a country is the average number of people per km² of the country.
Brazil has a population of 184 million correct to the nearest million.

(b) Calculate the maximum and minimum values of the population density of Brazil. [E]

13 An estimate of a calculation was made by rounding all numbers to 1 s.f.

The estimate was $\dfrac{300(40 \times 50)}{200}$.

Calculate the upper bound and lower bound of the estimate.

 14 Work out $\dfrac{\sqrt{4.83^3 - 1.62^4}}{12.8 \times 23.4}$

15 (a) Find the value of $16^{\frac{1}{2}}$

(b) Given that $\sqrt{40} = k\sqrt{10}$, find the value of k.

A large rectangular piece of card is $(\sqrt{5} + \sqrt{20})$ cm long and $\sqrt{8}$ cm wide.

A small rectangle $\sqrt{2}$ cm long and $\sqrt{5}$ cm wide is cut out of the piece of card.

(c) Express the area of the card that is left as a percentage of the area of the large rectangle. [E]

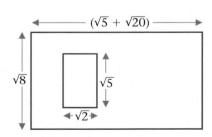

Diagram NOT drawn accurately

16 (a) Write down the value of $8^{\frac{1}{3}}$

$8\sqrt{8}$ can be written in the form 8^k

(b) Find the value of k.

$8\sqrt{8}$ can also be expressed in the form $m\sqrt{2}$ where m is a positive integer.

(c) Express $8\sqrt{8}$ in the form $m\sqrt{2}$

(d) Rationalise the denominator of $\dfrac{1}{8\sqrt{8}}$

Give your answer in the form $\dfrac{\sqrt{2}}{p}$ where p is a positive integer.   [E]

Summary of key points

1 A number in **standard form** is $A \times 10^n$ where $1 \leqslant A < 10$ and n is an integer.

2 Standard form can be used to make approximations and estimates.

3 A number can be raised to any power using the $\boxed{x^y}$ or $\boxed{y^x}$ key.

4 The nth root of any number can be found using the $\boxed{\sqrt[x]{y}}$ key.

5 You may also need to use the brackets keys $\boxed{(}\,\boxed{)}$.

6 The function a^x, where a is a positive constant and x is a variable, is called an **exponential** function.

7 If $a > 1$ then a^x is an example of **exponential growth** with multiplier a.

8 If $a < 1$ then a^x is an example of **exponential decay** with multiplier a.

9 A number written exactly using square roots is called a **surd**. For example, $\sqrt{3}$ and $2 - \sqrt{5}$ are in surd form.

10 Surds can be added, subtracted, multiplied and divided.
$$\sqrt{a \times b} = \sqrt{a} \times \sqrt{b} \qquad \sqrt{\dfrac{a}{b}} = \dfrac{\sqrt{a}}{\sqrt{b}}$$

11 Answers in surd form or in terms of π are **exact answers**.

12 Accurate solutions to equations can be given in surd form.

13 A simplified (or 'rationalised') surd should never have a square root in its denominator.

14 If you make a measurement correct to a given unit, the true value lies in a range that extends half a unit below and half a unit above the measurement.

15 The **lower bound** and **upper bound** are the minimum and maximum possible values of a measurement or calculation.

16 When calculating using upper bounds (UB) and lower bounds (LB), use this table to help you.

Result	Calculation
UB	UB + UB
LB	LB + LB
UB	UB − LB
LB	LB − UB
UB	UB × UB
LB	LB × LB
UB	UB ÷ LB
LB	LB ÷ UB

5 Simple linear equations and algebra

5.1 Solving simple equations

- In an **equation** a letter represents an unknown number.
- You can solve an equation to find the number that the letter represents. This number is called the **solution** of the equation.
- You can solve an equation by rearranging it so that the letter is on its own on one side of the equals sign.
- To rearrange an equation you can
  - add the same quantity to both sides
  - subtract the same quantity from both sides
  - multiply both sides by the same quantity
  - divide both sides by the same quantity.
- Whatever you do to one side of an equation, you must also do to the other side. This is called the **balance** method.

Example 1

Solve the equation $5x - 2 = 12$

$$5x - 2 = 12$$
$$5x - 2 + 2 = 12 + 2 \qquad \text{Add 2 to both sides}$$
$$5x = 12 + 2$$
$$5x = 14$$
$$x = 2\tfrac{4}{5} \qquad \text{Divide both sides by 5}$$

> $+2$ is the inverse operation of -2.

> On a flow diagram:
>
> $x \rightarrow \boxed{\times 5} \rightarrow \boxed{-2} \rightarrow 12$
>
> $2\tfrac{4}{5} \leftarrow \boxed{\div 5} \leftarrow \boxed{+2} \leftarrow 12$

Example 2

Solve the equation $3(x + 4) = 10$

Method 1
$$3(x + 4) = 10$$
$$3x + 12 = 10 \qquad \text{Expand the brackets}$$
$$3x = 10 - 12 \qquad \text{Subtract 12 from both sides}$$
$$3x = -2$$
$$x = -\tfrac{2}{3} \qquad \text{Divide both sides by 3}$$

Method 2
$$3(x + 4) = 10$$
$$x + 4 = \tfrac{10}{3} \qquad \text{Divide both sides by 3}$$
$$x = \tfrac{10}{3} - 4 \qquad \text{Subtract 4 from both sides}$$
$$= 3\tfrac{1}{3} - 4$$
$$x = -\tfrac{2}{3}$$

Exercise 5A

Solve these equations.

1 $4x + 5 = 17$

2 $3x - 5 = 16$

3 $5(x + 2) = 40$

4 $7(x - 4) = 21$

5 $\dfrac{x - 4}{6} = 2$

6 $\dfrac{x}{4} + 6 = 11$

7 $9x - 1 = 2$

8 $3(x + 5) = 6$

9 $2x + 3 = 10$

10 $5(x + 2) = 10$

11 $\dfrac{x}{3} + 6 = 2$

12 $3x + 7 = 2$

13 $4(x - 1) = 7$

14 $\dfrac{x + 10}{6} = 1$

15 $8x + 9 = 9$

16 $\dfrac{x}{3} - 1 = 5$

17 $2(3x - 1) = 3$

18 $\dfrac{4x - 3}{5} = 2$

19 $\dfrac{2x}{3} + 5 = 1$

20 $\dfrac{3(x + 4)}{2} = 5$

5.2 Equations with the unknown on both sides

- You can use the balance method to solve equations with the unknown on both sides.

Example 3

Solve the equation $8x - 1 = 3x + 2$

$$8x - 1 = 3x + 2$$
$$8x - 3x - 1 = 2 \qquad \text{Subtract } 3x \text{ from both sides}$$
$$5x - 1 = 2 \qquad \text{Collect like terms}$$
$$5x = 2 + 1 \qquad \text{Add 1 to both sides}$$
$$5x = 3$$
$$x = \tfrac{3}{5} \qquad \text{Divide both sides by 5}$$

You could subtract $8x$ from both sides:
$$1 = -5x - 2$$
but it is easier to work with a positive number in front of x.

Example 4

Solve the equation $7x + 9 = 4(x - 3)$

$$7x + 9 = 4(x - 3)$$
$$7x + 9 = 4x - 12 \qquad \text{Expand the brackets}$$
$$7x - 4x + 9 = -12 \qquad \text{Subtract } 4x \text{ from both sides}$$
$$3x + 9 = -12 \qquad \text{Collect like terms}$$
$$3x = -12 - 9 \qquad \text{Subtract 9 from both sides}$$
$$3x = -21$$
$$x = -7$$

Exercise 5B

Solve these equations.

1 $4x - 3 = 3x + 2$

2 $x - 1 = 7x - 4$

3 $7(x - 3) = 2x + 9$

4 $5(x + 2) = 3(x + 8)$

5 $3x - 8 = 5x - 2$

6 $8x + 5 = 5(x + 1)$

7 $5(x - 2) = 2x + 3$

8 $9(x + 3) = 5(x + 6)$

9 $3(x + 2) + 4(x - 5) = 5x + 3$

10 $8x + 7 - 5(x + 2) = x - 7$

11 $3x - 2 + (2x - 1) = 8x - 1$

12 $6(x + 3) - (2x - 7) = 7x + 1$

13 $3(4x + 9) + 4(2x - 1) = 6(4x + 7)$

14 $5(4x - 3) + 3(2 - 5x) = 8x$

15 $7(3x + 4) - 3(4x - 5) = 7 + 6(5x - 1)$

5.3 Equations with negative coefficients

- A **coefficient** is a number in front of an unknown.
- You can use the balance method to solve equations with negative coefficients.

> In $4 - 3x$ the coefficient of x is -3.

Example 5

Solve the equation $5 - 4x = 17$

Method 1

$5 - 4x = 17$

$\quad 5 = 4x + 17$ Add $4x$ to both sides

$\quad 4x = -12$ Subtract 17 from both sides

$\quad x = -3$ Divide both sides by 4

Method 2

$5 - 4x = 17$

$\quad -4x = 12$ Subtract 5 from both sides

$\quad x = -3$ Divide both sides by -4

Example 6

Solve the equation $5x + 2 = 7 - 4x$

$\quad 5x + 2 = 7 - 4x$

$\quad 9x + 2 = 7$ Add $4x$ to both sides

$\quad 9x = 5$ Subtract 2 from both sides

$\quad x = \frac{5}{9}$ Divide both sides by 9

> You could subtract $5x$ from both sides:
> $\quad 2 = 7 - 9x$
> but positive coefficients are easier to work with.

Example 7

Solve the equation $13 - 4x = 1 - 9x$

$$13 - 4x = 1 - 9x$$
$$5x + 13 = 1 \qquad \text{Add } 9x \text{ to both sides}$$
$$5x = -12 \qquad \text{Subtract } 13 \text{ from both sides}$$
$$x = -2\tfrac{2}{5} \qquad \text{Divide both sides by } 5$$

You could add $4x$ to both sides:
$$13 = 1 - 5x$$
but it is safer to get rid of negative coefficients.

Exercise 5C

Solve these equations.

1 $11 - 3x = 5$ **2** $7 - 5x = 22$ **3** $13 - 3x = x$

4 $8 - 7x = 3x$ **5** $4(5 - 3x) = 5$ **6** $3(1 - 2x) = 4x$

7 $4x + 9 = 13 - 2x$ **8** $9x + 10 = 3 - x$ **9** $3(x - 4) = 8 - 5x$

10 $6(x + 3) = 3 - 4x$ **11** $4x - 7 = 2(7 - 4x)$ **12** $2x + 5 = 3(1 - 2x)$

13 $4(3 - 2x) = x$ **14** $5(1 - 4x) = 2(x + 8)$ **15** $3(7x + 4) = 4(3 - 5x)$

16 $8 - 3x = 2(1 - x)$ **17** $5(3 - 2x) = 8 - 5x$ **18** $4(3 - 5x) = 3(6 - 7x)$

19 $3(4x + 1) - 5(3x - 2) = 9 - 7x$ **20** $4(2 - 3x) - 3(x - 1) = 5(3 - 2x)$

5.4 Expressions, equations and identities

- In algebra, an **expression** is a combination of letters, numbers, and $+$, $-$, $\div$, $\times$ signs.

  For example, $2a + 3b$ and $5n - 3$ are expressions.

- An equation is a mathematical statement that two expressions are equal. A letter can represent an unknown.

  For example, $4 + 5 = 9$, $y = 3x - 1$ and $2(x + 3) = 16$ are equations.

- An **identity** is an equation which is true for *all* values of the unknown.

  For example, $3x + 4x = 7x$ and $5(x - 3) = 5x - 15$ are identities.

Example 8

Cinema tickets cost £6 for adults and £4 for children. Write down an expression for the total cost, in pounds, of cinema tickets for a adults and c children.

There are many other possible expressions, such as
$$a + a + a + a + a + a + c + c + c + c,$$
but you should always write expressions as simply as possible.

$6a + 4c$

Example 9

Some of these equations are true for a particular value of x.
The rest are identities. They are true for all values of x.
For each equation, either solve the equation or explain why it is an identity.

(a) $3x + 4 + 2x - 1 = 5x + 3$ (b) $5x + 4 - 3x = x + 7$

(c) $5(x + 2) = 5x + 10$

(a) $3x + 4 + 2x - 1 = 5x + 3$
    $5x + 3 = 5x + 3$ Simplify the left-hand side by collecting like terms.
    This is an identity.

(b) $5x + 4 - 3x = x + 7$
    $2x + 4 = x + 7$ Simplify the left-hand side
    $x + 4 = 7$ Subtract x from both sides
    $x = 3$ Subtract 4 from both sides

(c) Expanding $5(x + 2)$ gives $5x + 10$.
    So $5(x + 2) = 5x + 10$ is an identity.

Exercise 5D

1 Write down an expression for the number of days in n weeks.

2 The length of each side of a regular pentagon is a centimetres.
Write down an expression for its perimeter.

3 There are 56 seats in a first-class railway carriage and 64 seats in a
standard-class carriage.
Write down an expression for the total number of seats on a train
with f first-class carriages and g standard-class carriages.

4 The sum of two numbers is 25. One of the numbers is n.
Write down an expression for the other number.

5 The product of two numbers is 36. One of the numbers is y.
Write down an expression for the other number.

6 For each equation, either solve the equation or explain why it is
an identity.

(a) $6x - 1 + 2x = 5x + 14$ (b) $7x + 2 - 3x - 5 = 4x - 3$

(c) $7(x - 3) = 7x - 21$ (d) $6(x + 2) = x - 3$

(e) $6(x - 5) = 3(2x - 10)$ (f) $6(x - 5) = 3x$

(g) $5(x - 1) - 3(x - 2) = 4x - 5$

(h) $5(x - 1) - 3(x - 2) = 2x + 1$

(i) $7x - 2x = 5x$

(j) $7x - 2x = 4x$

5.5 Using equations to solve problems

• You can write and solve equations to solve problems.

Example 10

I think of a number. I multiply it by 2 and subtract 19 from the result. The answer is the same as when I multiply my number by 3 and subtract the result from 71.
What is my number?

Let x stand for the number.

Then $2x - 19 = 71 - 3x$	
$5x - 19 = 71$	Add $3x$ to both sides
$5x = 90$	Add 19 to both sides
$x = 18$	Divide both sides by 5

The number is 18.

> Set up an equation involving the unknown number, x.
> Solve the equation to find x.

Example 11

The length of a rectangle is $x + 8$ centimetres and its width is $2x - 7$ centimetres. The perimeter of the rectangle is 56 cm.
Find the width of the rectangle.

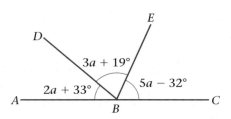

$$2(x + 8) + 2(2x - 7) = 56$$
$$2x + 16 + 4x - 14 = 56$$
$$6x + 2 = 56$$
$$6x = 54$$
$$x = 9$$

> Perimeter = 2 × length + 2 × width

Width of rectangle = $2x - 7 = 2 \times 9 - 7 = 11$ cm

Exercise 5E

1 In the diagram,
   ABC is a straight line.

   Find the size of angle DBE.

   In the diagram the angles at B are labelled $2a + 33°$, $3a + 19°$ and $5a - 32°$, with points D, E and C.

2 The sizes of the angles of a quadrilateral are $x + 38°$, $x + 46°$, $x - 31°$ and $x - 9°$.
   Find the size of the smallest angle.

3 In the diagram, triangle *PQR* is right-angled at *P*.
Find the size of angle *PQR*.

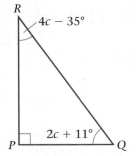

4 The lengths, in centimetres, of the sides of a triangle are $3d + 1$, $7d - 18$ and $41 - 2d$. Its perimeter is 64 cm.
Find the lengths of its sides.

5 I multiply a number by 3 and add 4 to the result.
The answer is the same as when I multiply the number by 5 and subtract 44 from the result.
Find the number.

6 The length of each side of a square is $3y - 2$ centimetres.
The perimeter of the square is 94 cm.
Find the value of *y*.

7 $5x + 8$, $29 - 4x$ and $3x - 4$ are three numbers. Their mean is 19.
Find the numbers.

8 Rashid is 34 years older than his daughter.
He is also 3 times as old as she is.
Find Rashid's age.

9 The width of a rectangle is 5 cm less than its length.
The perimeter of the rectangle is 58 cm.
Find its length.

10 I multiply a number by 3 and subtract the result from 49.
The answer is the same as when I multiply the number by 5 and subtract the result from 75.
Find the number.

11 The sum of two numbers is 46. Their difference is 12.
Find the numbers.

12 The sum of the present ages of Mrs Banerji and her daughter is 55 years.
Five years ago, Mrs Banerji was 4 times as old as her daughter.
Find Mrs Banerji's present age.

13 The sum of three consecutive **odd** numbers is 93.
Find the largest of these numbers.

14 The diagram shows a rectangle. Find the values of x and y.

$$5x - 7$$

$$4y - 13 \qquad\qquad 29 - 2y$$

$$2x + 17$$

15 Ffion has 26 coins in her purse. Some of them are 10p coins and the rest are 20p coins. Their total value is £4.
Find the number of 20p coins in her purse.

5.6 Equations with fractions

- To solve equations with algebraic fractions, first clear the denominators by multiplying both sides of the equation by the lowest common multiple of the denominators.

> Simplifying algebraic fractions was covered in Chapter 4 of Higher Unit 3.

Example 12

Solve the equation $\dfrac{4x + 3}{6} = \dfrac{x}{4} - 2$

The lowest common multiple of 6 and 4 is 12.
So multiply both sides of the equation by 12.

$$12\left(\frac{4x + 3}{6}\right)$$
$$= \frac{12}{6}(4x + 3)$$
$$= 2(4x + 3)$$
$$= 8x + 6$$

$$\frac{4x + 3}{6} = \frac{x}{4} - 2$$
$$12\left(\frac{4x + 3}{6}\right) = 12\left(\frac{x}{4} - 2\right)$$
$$8x + 6 = 3x - 24$$
$$5x = -30$$
$$x = -6$$

$$12\left(\frac{x}{4} - 2\right)$$
$$= 12 \times \frac{x}{4} - 12 \times 2$$
$$= 3x - 24$$

Exercise 5F

Solve these equations.

1 $\dfrac{x}{4} + 1 = \dfrac{x}{3}$

2 $\dfrac{x}{3} - 3 = \dfrac{x}{6} + 1$

3 $\dfrac{x + 2}{5} - 3 = 2$

4 $\dfrac{x}{4} + \dfrac{x}{5} = 9$

5 $\dfrac{2x - 7}{3} = 5$

6 $\dfrac{5x}{8} - \dfrac{x}{4} = 1$

7 $\dfrac{8 - 3x}{4} = 5$

8 $\dfrac{x}{8} + 5 = \dfrac{x + 4}{2} - 6$

9 $\dfrac{9 - 4x}{2} = 5x - 6$

10 $\dfrac{2x + 5}{3} = \dfrac{3x - 1}{4}$ **11** $\dfrac{7 - 2x}{4} = \dfrac{2x}{3}$ **12** $\dfrac{4x + 7}{3} =$

13 $\dfrac{x + 1}{2} = \dfrac{x - 4}{5} + 2$ **14** $\dfrac{3x + 1}{4} = \dfrac{4x - 1}{8} + 2$ **15** $\dfrac{4 - 7x}{4} =$

16 $2(x - 5) = \dfrac{x}{3} + 1$ **17** $\dfrac{7 - 4x}{3} = \dfrac{9 - 8x}{5}$ **18** $\dfrac{x + 2}{3} + \dfrac{x - 4}{5} = 2$

19 $\dfrac{2x}{5} + \dfrac{2x - 1}{4} = 2$ **20** $3(x + 4) = \dfrac{4x - 3}{2} + 9$ **21** $\dfrac{7x + 2}{5} + \dfrac{3x - 1}{10} = 2$

22 $2(4x + 1) = \dfrac{4x - 5}{3} + 7$ **23** $\dfrac{x}{3} - \dfrac{2x - 9}{5} = 1$ **24** $\dfrac{x - 1}{3} + 5 = \dfrac{x}{9} + 7$

25 $\dfrac{x + 3}{5} - \dfrac{x + 7}{6} = 1$ **26** $\dfrac{7 - 4x}{9} + \dfrac{4x - 1}{6} = 2$ **27** $\dfrac{x}{4} - \dfrac{2x - 1}{3} = 2$

28 $\dfrac{2x - 1}{3} - \dfrac{3x - 1}{4} = 1$ **29** $1 - \dfrac{4x - 3}{8} = \dfrac{5 - 6x}{4}$ **30** $\dfrac{x - 1}{3} - \dfrac{x + 6}{2} = \dfrac{x - 6}{4}$

5.7 Equations with the unknown in the denominator

- You can use the balance method to solve equations in which the unknown appears in the denominator.

For example
$\dfrac{20}{x} = 4$ and $\dfrac{5}{3x} = 2$

Example 13

Solve the equation $\dfrac{3}{x} = 5$

$\dfrac{3}{x} = 5$

$3 = 5x$ Multiply both sides by x

$x = \dfrac{3}{5}$ Divide both sides by 5

$x \times \dfrac{3}{x} = 3$
Cancel the xs.

Example 14

Solve the equation $\dfrac{15}{4x} = 2$

$\dfrac{15}{4x} = 2$

$\dfrac{15}{4} = 2x$ Multiply both sides by x

$\dfrac{15}{8} = x$ Divide both sides by 2

$x = 1\dfrac{7}{8}$

$\dfrac{15}{4} \div 2 = \dfrac{15}{4} \times \dfrac{1}{2}$

$= \dfrac{15}{4 \times 2}$

$= \dfrac{15}{8}$

ample 15

Solve the equation $\dfrac{2}{2x-1} = 3$

$$\dfrac{2}{2x-1} = 3$$

$2 = 3(2x - 1)$	Multiply both sides by $2x - 1$
$2 = 6x - 3$	Expand the brackets
$5 = 6x$	Add 3 to both sides
$x = \frac{5}{6}$	Divide both sides by 5

> $2x - 1$ 'moves' from the bottom on the left-hand side to the top on the right-hand side.
> This is sometimes called 'cross-multiplying'.

Exercise 5G

Solve these equations.

1 $\dfrac{36}{x} = 4$ **2** $\dfrac{5}{x} = 8$ **3** $\dfrac{8}{x} = 5$

4 $\dfrac{1}{x} = 6$ **5** $\dfrac{3}{2x} = 5$ **6** $\dfrac{13}{3x} = 2$

7 $\dfrac{12}{5x} = 1$ **8** $\dfrac{1}{8x} = 3$ **9** $\dfrac{2}{x-3} = 5$

10 $\dfrac{7}{x+5} = 2$ **11** $\dfrac{1}{3x-2} = 4$ **12** $\dfrac{3}{4x+5} = 2$

13 $\dfrac{4}{2x-5} = 3$ **14** $\dfrac{3}{2x+5} = 1$ **15** $\dfrac{6}{3x-8} = 1$

16 $\dfrac{7}{5x+7} = 1$ **17** $\dfrac{3}{4-x} = 2$ **18** $\dfrac{5}{1-x} = 3$

19 $\dfrac{2}{3-4x} = 1$ **20** $\dfrac{13}{3-2x} = \frac{1}{4}$ **21** $\dfrac{1}{2x+1} = \dfrac{13}{15x}$

5.8 Indices

- In the expression x^n, the number n is called the **index** or **power**.
- These are the laws of indices:
  - $x^m \times x^n = x^{m+n}$
  - $x^m \div x^n = x^{m-n}$
  - $(x^m)^n = x^{mn}$
  - $(ax^m)^n = a^n x^{mn}$

> The plural of index is **indices**.

Example 16

Simplify these expressions.

(a) $3x^2y^3 \times 5x^4y$ (b) $20x^6y^4 \div 4x^2y^3$ (c) $(2x^4)^3$

> An expression is a combination of letters and numbers.
> For more on expressions see Section 5.10.

(a) $3x^2y^3 \times 5x^4y = 3 \times x^2 \times y^3 \times 5 \times x^4 \times y^1$
$$= 3 \times 5 \times x^2 \times x^4 \times y^3 \times y^1$$
$$= 15 \times x^{(2+4)} \times y^{(3+1)}$$
$$= 15x^6y^4$$

(b) $20x^6y^4 \div 4x^2y^3 = \dfrac{20}{4}x^{(6-2)} \times y^{(4-3)}$
$$= 5x^4y^1$$
$$= 5x^4y$$

> Alternatively, you can write $20x^6y^4 \div 4x^2y^3$ as $\dfrac{20x^6y^4}{4x^2y^3}$ and then cancel.

(c) $(2x^4)^3 = 2^3 \times (x^4)^3$
$$= 8 \times x^{(3 \times 4)}$$
$$= 8x^{12}$$

> $(2x^4)^3$ means that each number and letter within the bracket is cubed. So $(2x^4)^3 = 2^3 \times (x^4)^3$

Exercise 5H

Simplify these expressions.

1 $x^2 \times x^7$ **2** $x^7 \div x^4$ **3** $(x^5)^2$

4 $2x^3 \times 7x^5$ **5** $5x \times 8x^5$ **6** $2x^5 \times 5x^6 \times 3x^2$

7 $18x^8 \div 3x^5$ **8** $20x^6 \div 4x^5$ **9** $24x^6 \div 6x$

10 $3(x^2)^4$ **11** $(4x)^3$ **12** $7x^4y^3 \times 3x^2y^4$

13 $5x^6 \times 4x^3y^5$ **14** $8xy^4 \times 7x^7y^2$ **15** $3x^4y^2 \times 2x^3y^5 \times 5x^2y$

16 $28x^7y^5 \div 4x^4y^2$ **17** $36x^6y^8 \div 12x^2y$ **18** $15x^9 \div 25x^4$

19 $20x^5y^3 \div 5x^2y^3$ **20** $5x^4 \times (4x^3)^2$ **21** $(4x^4y^5)^2$

22 $(2x^4y^2)^3 \times 5x$ **23** $\dfrac{6x^5 \times 4x^3}{8x^6}$ **24** $\dfrac{9x^5 \times 4x^6}{6x^3 \times 3x^4}$

25 $\dfrac{6x^3y^5 \times 8x^9y^4}{2xy \times 3x^5y^6}$

5.9 The zero index and negative indices

- $x^0 = 1$ for all non-zero values of x.
- $x^{-n} = \dfrac{1}{x^n}$ (where $x \neq 0$)

Example 17

(a) Evaluate   (i) $7a^0$ (ii) $\dfrac{15x^3}{5x^3}$

> Evaluate means 'work out the value of …'

(b) Copy and complete   (i) $\dfrac{1}{x^6} = x^?$ (ii) $x^{-4} = \dfrac{1}{x^?}$

(a) (i) $7a^0 = 7 \times 1 = 7$

    (ii) $\dfrac{15x^3}{5x^3} = \dfrac{15}{5}x^{3-3} = 3x^0 = 3$

> Alternatively, you can cancel by x^3.

(b) (i) $\dfrac{1}{x^6} = x^{-6}$

    (ii) $x^{-4} = \dfrac{1}{x^4}$

Example 18

Use the laws of indices to simplify these expressions.

(a) $\dfrac{6x^3}{2x^5}$

(b) $(x^{-2})^5$

(c) $(x^{-3})^{-4}$

(a) $\dfrac{6x^3}{2x^5} = \dfrac{6}{2}x^{3-5} = 3x^{-2}$

> You can write $3x^{-2}$ as $\dfrac{3}{x^2}$

(b) $(x^{-2})^5 = x^{-2 \times 5} = x^{-10}$

(c) $(x^{-3})^{-4} = x^{-3 \times -4} = x^{12}$

Exercise 5I

1 Evaluate

  (a) $9x^0$ (b) $\dfrac{18x^5}{12x^5}$ (c) $\dfrac{x^4}{2x^4}$ (d) $(4x)^0$ (e) $4 \times x^0$

2 Copy and complete.

  (a) $\dfrac{1}{x^3} = x^?$ (b) $x^{-8} = \dfrac{1}{x^?}$

3 Use the laws of indices to simplify these expressions.

  (a) $x^5 \times x^{-8}$ (b) $x^{-2} \times x^{-3}$ (c) $4x^{-5} \times 5x^7$

  (d) $x^5 \div x^8$ (e) $x^{-2} \div x^3$ (f) $x^2 \div x^{-4}$

  (g) $20x \div 5x^4$ (h) $\dfrac{24x^5}{3x^8}$ (i) $(x^{-2})^4$

  (j) $(x^{-3})^{-5}$ (k) $(3x^4)^{-2}$ (l) $\dfrac{x^5y^4}{x^2y^7}$

  (m) $4x^3 \div 2x^3$ (n) $\dfrac{(5x^2y)^3}{(5x^3y)^2}$

5.10 Substituting values into expressions

- **Substituting** means replacing a letter or letters in an expression with number values.

Example 19

Work out the value of $(3x)^2 + 2$ when $x = 5$

$\qquad (3 \times 5)^2 + 2 \qquad$ Replace x with 5
$\qquad = (15)^2 + 2 \qquad$ Brackets first
$\qquad = 225 + 2 \qquad$ Indices before addition
$\qquad = 227$

Remember the order of operations.

Example 20

Work out the value of $(3x - 2)^2 \times x^3$ when $x = 2$

$\qquad (3 \times 2 - 2)^2 \times 2^3 \qquad$ Replace x with 2
$\qquad = 4^2 \times 2^3$
$\qquad = 16 \times 8$
$\qquad = 128$

$3 \times 2 - 2 = 6 - 2$
$\qquad\qquad\quad = 4$

Exercise 5J

1 Work out the value of
    (a) $(2x)^2$ when $x = 5$ **(b)** $2x^2$ when $x = 5$
    (c) $3y^2 + 2$ when $y = 7$ **(d)** $2y - y^2$ when $y = 1$
    (e) $3y^2 - 2y$ when $y = -1$ **(f)** $(2x + 1)^2$ when $x = -2$
    (g) $(5z^2 - 2z)^2$ when $z = 1$ **(h)** $(2a^2 - 3)^3$ when $a = -2$

2 Work out the value of
    (a) a^2b when $a = 3$ and $b = 2$
    (b) ab^2 when $a = 2$ and $b = 5$
    (c) $3a^2bc$ when $a = 2$, $b = -3$ and $c = 1$
    (d) $2abc^2$ when $a = 2$, $b = 3$ and $c = 4$
    (e) a^2b^3 when $a = -2$ and $b = -1$
    (f) $(5ab - 3ac)^2$ when $a = 2$, $b = -1$ and $c = -3$

3 $w = 5$, $x = -\frac{1}{3}$, $y = 9$ and $z = 2\frac{2}{5}$
    Work out the value of
    (a) wxy **(b)** xyz **(c)** x^2y
    (d) $15x^3$ **(e)** $2w^2z$ **(f)** $3\frac{w}{z}y^2$

Mixed exercise 5

Solve the equations in questions **1–23**.

1 $3x + 7 = 15$

2 $5x - 2 = 1$

3 $4(x - 5) = 3$

4 $6(x + 3) = 11$

5 $\dfrac{2x + 7}{5} = 2$

6 $7x + 4 = 3x - 8$

7 $4(3x - 2) = 7(x + 1)$

8 $5x + 3 - (3x - 7) = x + 9$

9 $4(2x + 3) + 3(x - 5) = 6(x - 1)$ **10** $10 - 9x = 4$

11 $5 - 2x = 4x - 1$

12 $8 - 3x = 6 - 7x$

13 $8x - 7 = 3(x - 1)$

14 $5 + 3(3 - 2x) = 4x + 2(10 - 3x)$

15 $\dfrac{x}{3} + \dfrac{x}{4} - \dfrac{x}{6} = 2$

16 $\dfrac{9 - 4x}{3} = 4$

17 $\dfrac{2x - 7}{5} = 3 - 4x$

18 $\dfrac{3x + 7}{4} + \dfrac{2x - 5}{8} = 2x + 1$

19 $\dfrac{2(x - 1)}{3} - \dfrac{3(x - 2)}{4} = 1$

20 $\dfrac{5}{x} = 9$

21 $\dfrac{11}{2x} = 4$

22 $\dfrac{4}{3x + 5} = 1$

23 $\dfrac{11}{1 - 2x} = 2.5$

24 The size of each of the equal angles of an isosceles triangle is $x + 10°$. The size of the other angle is $98° - x$.
Find the size of each angle of the triangle.

25 I multiply a number by 3 and add 9 to the result.
The answer is the same as when I multiply the number by 2 and subtract the result from 94.
Find the number.

26 State which of these equations are identities and solve the remaining equations.
(a) $5x + 3x = 8x$
(b) $8(x + 4) = 8x + 32$
(c) $5x + 3x = 2(x + 12)$
(d) $3(2x - 5) + 4(3x - 1) = 19x - 18$
(e) $6(6x - 4) = 4(9x - 6)$
(f) $3(2x - 1) - 2(3x - 2) = 1$

27 Simplify these expressions.
(a) $x^5 \times x^3$
(b) $x^9 \div x^4$
(c) $(x^3)^5$
(d) $3x^4 \times 2x^6$
(e) $32x^7 \div 4x^2$
(f) $(2x^3)^5$
(g) $5x^4y^3 \times 4x^5y^2$
(h) $40x^6y^4 \div 5x^5y^4$
(i) $\dfrac{9x^3 \times 2x^8}{6x^7}$

28 Evaluate

(a) y^0 (b) $3y^0$ (c) $(3y)^0$

29 Use the laws of indices to simplify these expressions.

(a) $x^{-4} \times x^3$ (b) $3x^{-4} \times 5x^{-5}$

(c) $x^2 \div x^6$ (d) $18x^2 \div 6x^{-3}$

(e) $\dfrac{27x^4}{9x^9}$ (f) $(x^3)^{-2}$

(g) $(x^{-2})^{-6}$ (h) $(2x^5)^{-3}$

30 The two equal angles of an isosceles triangle are each $a°$. Write down an expression for the size, in degrees, of the other angle.

31 Work out the value of

(a) $3a^2(b - c)$ when $a = -2$, $b = 1$ and $c = \frac{1}{2}$

(b) $2(q^4 - p^3)$ when $p = -3$ and $q = 2$

(c) $xy^2 - x^2y$ when $x = -5$ and $y = -4.5$

32 In this question $a = -5$, $b = 6$ and $c = -2$.
Work out the value of

(a) $2ab + 3c$ (b) $2(a - 2c)$ (c) $abc + 2ac$

(d) $3a^2$ (e) $(3b + 5c)^2$ (f) $5b + 2c - a$

Summary of key points

1 In an **equation** a letter represents an unknown number.

2 You can solve an equation to find the number that the letter represents. This number is called the **solution** of the equation.

3 You can solve an equation by rearranging it so that the letter is on its own on one side of the equals sign.

4 To rearrange an equation you can
  - add the same quantity to both sides
  - subtract the same quantity from both sides
  - multiply both sides by the same quantity
  - divide both sides by the same quantity.

5 Whatever you do to one side of an equation, you must also do to the other side. This is called the **balance** method.

6 You can use the balance method to solve equations with the unknown on both sides.

7 A **coefficient** is a number in front of an unknown.

8 You can use the balance method to solve equations with negative coefficients.

9 In algebra, an **expression** is a combination of letters, numbers, and $+$, $-$, $\div$, $\times$ signs.

10 An equation is a mathematical statement that two expressions are equal. A letter can represent an unknown.

11 An **identity** is an equation which is true for *all* values of the unknown.

12 You can write and solve equations to solve problems.

13 To solve equations with algebraic fractions, first clear the denominators by multiplying both sides of the equation by the lowest common multiple of the denominators.

14 You can use the balance method to solve equations in which the unknown appears in the denominator.

15 In the expression x^n, the number n is called the **index** or **power**.

16 These are the laws of indices:
  ○ $x^m \times x^n = x^{m+n}$
  ○ $x^m \div x^n = x^{m-n}$
  ○ $(x^m)^n = x^{mn}$
  ○ $(ax^m)^n = a^n x^{mn}$
  ○ $x^0 = 1$ for all non-zero values of x.
  ○ $x^{-n} = \dfrac{1}{x^n}$ (where $x \neq 0$)

17 **Substituting** means replacing a letter or letters in an expression with number values.

6 Formulae

6.1 Writing a formula

- A **formula** uses algebraic expressions to describe a relationship or rule.
- A formula must contain an equals (=) sign.

The plural of 'formula' is **formulae**.

Example 1

(a) Write down a formula for the area, A, of a rectangle with length l and width w.

(b) Write down a formula for the perimeter, P, of this rectangle.

(a) Area = length × width
$$A = lw$$

(b) Perimeter = $l + w + l + w$
$$P = 2l + 2w$$
$$= 2(l + w)$$

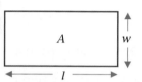

Exercise 6A

1 A motorist travels for t hours at an average speed of v miles per hour. Write down a formula for the distance travelled, d miles.

2 To cook a joint of pork, you allow 30 minutes per pound and an extra 30 minutes. Write down a formula for the time, T minutes, needed to cook a joint of pork weighing W pounds.

3 The cost, £C, of hiring a car is worked out by adding a fixed charge, £F, to a charge of £0.4 per mile. Write down a formula for the cost of a journey of m miles.

4 The length of each side of a regular hexagon is h centimetres. Write down a formula for the perimeter, P, of the hexagon.

5 A motorist travels d miles in t hours. Write down a formula for the average speed, v miles per hour.

6 Write down a formula for the area, A, of a triangle in terms of its base, b, and its vertical height, h.

7 Cartons of orange juice cost 47p each. Pat bought n cartons and paid for them with a £5 note. Write down a formula for the change, C pence, she should have received.

6.2 Evaluating formulae

- You can substitute numbers into a formula to find the value of a quantity.

Example 2

$s = ut - \frac{1}{2}gt^2$

Calculate the value of s when $u = 24$, $g = 10$ and $t = 3$.

$$s = 24 \times 3 - \frac{1}{2} \times 10 \times 3^2$$
$$= 72 - 45$$
$$= 27$$

Exercise 6B

1 $y = 3x + 7$ Calculate the value of y when $x = -4$.

2 $V = IR$ Calculate the value of V when $I = 12$ and $R = 20$.

3 $A = \pi rl$ Calculate the value of A, correct to 3 s.f., when $r = 7.3$ and $l = 9.1$.

4 $s = \dfrac{a + b + c}{2}$ Calculate the value of s when $a = 3.7$, $b = 4.2$ and $c = 5.3$.

5 $F = 1.8C + 32$ Calculate the value of F when $C = -40$.

6 $A = \frac{1}{2}(a + b)h$ Calculate the value of A when $a = 8$, $b = 7$ and $h = 5$.

7 $A = 4\pi r^2$ Calculate the value of A, correct to 3 s.f., when $r = 7.3$.

8 $v = u - gt$ Calculate the value of v when $u = 7$, $g = 10$ and $t = 2$.

9 $d = \dfrac{C}{\pi}$ Calculate the value of d, correct to 3 s.f., when $C = 16.8$.

10 $A = \dfrac{\pi d^2}{4}$ Calculate the value of A, correct to 3 s.f., when $d = 8.7$.

11 $y = 3x^2 - 5$ Calculate the value of y when $x = -2$.

12 $s = \dfrac{(u + v)t}{2}$ Calculate the value of s when $u = 19$, $v = 35$ and $t = 2\frac{1}{2}$.

13 $d = v + \dfrac{v^2}{20}$ Calculate the value of d when $v = 41$.

14 $D = \frac{1}{2}n(n-3)$ Calculate the value of D when $n = 12$.

15 $H = 17 - \dfrac{A}{2}$ Calculate the value of H when $A = 13$.

16 $E = \frac{1}{2}m(v^2 - u^2)$ Calculate the value of E when $m = 5$, $v = 7$ and $u = 10$.

17 $A = \pi(R + r)(R - r)$ Calculate the value of A, correct to 3 s.f., when $R = 8.9$ and $r = 5.7$.

18 $y = \dfrac{10}{x - 2}$ Calculate the value of y when $x = -\frac{1}{2}$.

19 $v = \dfrac{uf}{u - f}$ Calculate the value of v, correct to 3 s.f., when $u = 3.4$ and $f = 26.52$.

20 $F = \dfrac{mv^2}{r}$ Calculate the value of F when $m = 9$, $v = 13$ and $r = 5$.

21 $V = \frac{4}{3}\pi r^3$ Calculate the value of V, correct to 3 s.f., when $r = 14.3$.

22 $d = \dfrac{Wl^3}{3B}$ Calculate the value of d when $W = 18$, $l = 15$ and $B = 75$.

23 $P = 2l + \dfrac{100}{l}$ Calculate the value of P when $l = 8$.

24 $R = \dfrac{kl}{r^2}$ Calculate the value of R when $k = 0.000\,03$, $l = 280$ and $r = 2$.

25 $A = P\left(1 + \dfrac{R}{100}\right)^n$ Calculate the value of A, correct to 3 s.f., when $P = 2000$, $R = 6\frac{1}{4}$ and $n = 2$.

26 $v = \sqrt{2gh}$ Calculate the value of v, correct to 3 s.f., when $g = 9.81$ and $h = 23.8$.

27 $D = 5\sqrt{\dfrac{h}{2}}$ Calculate the value of D, correct to 2 s.f., when $h = 19.7$.

28 $T = 2\pi\sqrt{\dfrac{I}{MH}}$ Calculate the value of T, correct to 3 s.f., when $I = 125$, $M = 8$ and $H = 3$.

29 $v = \sqrt{u^2 + 2as}$ Calculate the value of v, correct to 3 s.f., when $u = 20$, $a = -3$ and $s = 35$.

30 $v = \omega\sqrt{a^2 - x^2}$ Calculate the value of v when $\omega = 8$, $a = 29$ and $x = 21$.

6.3 Manipulating formulae

- The letter that appears on its own on one side of the = sign and does not appear on the other side is called the **subject** of the formula.
- To find the value of a letter which is not the subject of a formula, substitute the given values into the formula and then solve the resulting equation.

Example 3

$s = ut - \frac{1}{2}gt^2$

Calculate the value of u when $s = 39$, $g = 10$ and $t = 3$.

$39 = u \times 3 - \frac{1}{2} \times 10 \times 3^2$	Substitute given values
$39 = 3u - 45$	Simplify
$84 = 3u$	Add 45 to both sides
$u = 28$	Divide both sides by 3

Exercise 6C

For π use a value of 3.14, or the π button on your calculator.

1 $y = 3x + 7$ Calculate the value of x when $y = 1$.

2 $V = IR$ Calculate the value of R when $V = 240$ and $I = 5$.

3 $A = \pi rl$ Calculate the value of r, correct to 3 s.f., when $A = 90$ and $l = 8.3$.

4 $s = \dfrac{a + b + c}{2}$ Calculate the value of a when $s = 12.6$, $b = 7.4$ and $c = 8.5$.

5 $F = 1.8C + 32$ Calculate the value of C when $F = 95$.

6 $A = \frac{1}{2}(a + b)h$ Calculate the value of b when $A = 112$, $a = 13$ and $h = 7$.

7 $A = 4\pi r^2$ Calculate the positive value of r, correct to 3 s.f., when $A = 150$.

8 $v = u - gt$ Calculate the value of t when $v = 4$, $u = 40$ and $g = 10$.

9 $d = \dfrac{C}{\pi}$ Calculate the value of C, correct to 3 s.f., when $d = 5.9$.

10 $A = \dfrac{\pi d^2}{4}$ Calculate the positive value of d, correct to 3 s.f., when $A = 85$.

11 $y = 3x^2 - 5$ Calculate the two possible values of x when $y = 43$.

12 $s = \dfrac{(u + v)t}{2}$ Calculate the value of u when $s = 136$, $v = 25$ and $t = 8$.

13 $H = 17 - \dfrac{A}{2}$ Calculate the value of A when $H = 12\frac{1}{2}$.

14 $E = \frac{1}{2}m(v^2 - u^2)$ Calculate the positive value of u when $E = 432$, $m = 12$ and $v = 11$.

15 $y = \dfrac{10}{x - 2}$ Calculate the value of x when $y = -2$.

16 $F = \dfrac{mv^2}{r}$ Calculate the positive value of v when $F = 20$, $m = 8$ and $r = 10$.

17 $V = \frac{4}{3}\pi r^3$ Calculate the value of r, correct to 3 s.f., when $V = 200$.

18 $v = \sqrt{2gh}$ Calculate the value of h when $v = 8$ and $g = 10$.

19 $D = 5\sqrt{\dfrac{h}{2}}$ Calculate the value of h when $D = 8.5$.

20 $v = \omega\sqrt{a^2 - x^2}$ Calculate the positive value of x when $v = 48$, $\omega = 6$ and $a = 17$.

6.4 Changing the subject of a formula

- You can rearrange a formula to make a different letter the subject.

Example 4

Make h the subject of the formula $A = bh$.

$A = bh$

$h = \dfrac{A}{b}$ Divide both sides by b

Example 5

Make t the subject of the formula $v = u + at$.

$v = u + at$

$v - u = at$ Subtract u from both sides

$t = \dfrac{v - u}{a}$ Divide both sides by a

Example 6

Make v the subject of the formula $E = \frac{1}{2}mv^2$

$E = \frac{1}{2}mv^2$

$2E = mv^2$ Multiply both sides by 2

$v^2 = \dfrac{2E}{m}$ Divide both sides by m

$v = \pm\sqrt{\dfrac{2E}{m}}$ Find the square roots

$v = \pm\sqrt{\dfrac{E}{\frac{1}{2}m}}$ is also correct but it is best not to have a fraction within another fraction.

Example 7

Make r the subject of the formula $A = \pi(R^2 - r^2)$

$A = \pi R^2 - \pi r^2$ Expand the brackets

$A + \pi r^2 = \pi R^2$ Add πr^2 to both sides

$\pi r^2 = \pi R^2 - A$ Subtract A from both sides

$r^2 = \dfrac{\pi R^2 - A}{\pi}$ Divide both sides by π

$r = \pm\sqrt{\dfrac{\pi R^2 - A}{\pi}}$ Find the square roots

Alternatively, you can start by dividing both sides by π

$\dfrac{A}{\pi} = R^2 - r^2$

which leads to the equivalent answer

$r = \pm\sqrt{R^2 - \dfrac{A}{\pi}}$

Example 8

Make m the subject of the formula $mv = (m + M)V$

$mv = mV + MV$ Expand the brackets

$mv - mV = MV$ Subtract mV from both sides

$m(v - V) = MV$ Factorise the left-hand side

$m = \dfrac{MV}{v - V}$ Divide both sides by $(v - V)$

The letter which you have to make the subject occurs twice. Get both terms involving m on the same side.

Exercise 6D

Make the letter in square brackets the subject of these formulae.

1 $P = IV$ $[I]$ **2** $A = \pi rl$ $[r]$

3 $y = 4x - 3$ $[x]$ **4** $t = 3n + 5$ $[n]$

5 $P = 2x + y$ [y] **6** $P = 2x + y$ [x]

7 $v = u - gt$ [u] **8** $v = u - gt$ [t]

9 $A = \frac{1}{2}bh$ [b] **10** $s = \dfrac{a + b + c}{2}$ [a]

11 $D = \dfrac{M}{V}$ [M] **12** $D = \dfrac{M}{V}$ [V]

13 $l = m(v - u)$ [v] **14** $l = m(v - u)$ [u]

15 $A = \frac{1}{2}(a + b)h$ [h] **16** $A = \frac{1}{2}(a + b)h$ [b]

17 $y = \frac{1}{3}x - 2$ [x] **18** $v = 2(x - 1)$ [x]

19 $x = 3(y + 2)$ [y] **20** $H = 17 - \dfrac{A}{2}$ [A]

21 $y = \dfrac{5 - x}{2}$ [x] **22** $3x - 2y = 6$ [x]

23 $3x - 2y = 6$ [y] **24** $mV + MV = mv$ [V]

25 $E = mc^2$ [c] **26** $c^2 = a^2 + b^2$ [a]

27 $d = \dfrac{v^2}{100}$ [v] **28** $A = \pi(R^2 - r^2)$ [R]

29 $d = L(1 + at)$ [t] **30** $T = k(L - a)$ [a]

31 $I = \frac{4}{3}Ma^2$ [a] **32** $E = \dfrac{Lx^2}{2a}$ [x]

33 $y = \dfrac{x}{a} + b$ [x] **34** $uf + vf = uv$ [f]

35 $uf + vf = uv$ [u] **36** $y = \frac{1}{2}x^2 - 5$ [x]

37 $mv^2 = 2E + mu^2$ [m] **38** $l = \frac{1}{3}M(a^2 + b^2)$ [a]

39 $A - P = \dfrac{PRT}{100}$ [R] **40** $A - P = \dfrac{PRT}{100}$ [P]

41 $\dfrac{x}{a} + \dfrac{y}{b} = 1$ [a] **42** $F = \dfrac{GMm}{r^2}$ [r]

43 $V = \frac{1}{6}\pi D^3$ [D] **44** $x = \dfrac{WL^3}{3EI}$ [L]

45 $I = M\left(\dfrac{r^2}{4} + \dfrac{a^2}{3}\right)$ [r] **46** $a = \sqrt{\dfrac{I}{m}}$ [I]

47 $v = \sqrt{2gh}$ [h] **48** $i = \sqrt{\dfrac{e - v}{R}}$ [v]

49 $d = 5\sqrt{\dfrac{h}{2}}$ [h] **50** $R = \sqrt{\dfrac{3M + m}{M}}$ [M]

51 $(a + y) = b(2y + c)$ [y] **52** $y = \dfrac{2x + 3}{x - 1}$ [x]

6.5 Substituting one formula into another

- You can sometimes **eliminate** one of the letters from a formula by substituting an expression from another formula.

Example 9

Two formulae used in the study of electricity are $P = IV$ and $V = IR$. Find a formula for P in terms of I and R.

$$P = IV$$
$$P = I \times IR \qquad \text{Replace } V \text{ by } IR$$
$$P = I^2R$$

Example 10

$y = 5x - 2$ and $x = 2t + 1$.
Express y in terms of t.

$$y = 5(2t + 1) - 2 \qquad \text{Substitute for } x$$
$$y = 10t + 5 - 2 \qquad \text{Expand the brackets}$$
$$y = 10t + 3 \qquad \text{Simplify}$$

Exercise 6E

1 $s = vt$ and $v = \frac{1}{2}gt$
Find a formula for s in terms of g and t.

2 $A = \pi r^2$ and $r = \frac{d}{2}$
Find a formula for A in terms of d.

3 $T = kx$ and $E = \frac{1}{2}Tx$
Find a formula for E in terms of k and x.

4 $V = \pi r^2h$ and $S = 2\pi rh$
Find a formula for V in terms of S and r.

5 The sum of the lengths of the edges of a cube is P centimetres.
Find, in terms of P, a formula for
(a) the total surface area, A cm^2, of the cube
(b) the volume, V cm^3, of the cube.

Mixed exercise 6

1 The cost of electricity is worked out by adding a fixed charge of £6.35 to a charge per unit of 8.25p.
Write down a formula for the total cost, C, when x units are used.

2 To find the sum, in degrees, of the interior angles of a polygon, you subtract 2 from the number of sides and multiply the result by 180. Write down a formula for the sum, $S°$, of the interior angles of an n-sided polygon.

3 The diagram shows a cuboid with a square base.
The length of each side of its base is x and its height is h.
T is the total length of the edges of the cuboid.

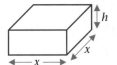

  (a) Find a formula for T in terms of x and h.

  (b) Show that $h = \dfrac{T - 8x}{4}$.

  (c) Find a formula in terms of x and T for the volume, V, of the cuboid.

4 The length of each side of a cube is d centimetres.
The total surface area of the cube is A cm^2.
Write down a formula for A in terms of d.

5 $e = V + IR$
  (a) Calculate the value of e when $V = 25$, $I = 7$ and $R = 4$.
  (b) Calculate the value of R when $e = 64$, $V = 19$ and $I = 5$.

6 $y = 5 - 3x$
  (a) Calculate the value of y when $x = -4$.
  (b) Calculate the value of x when $y = -16$.

7 $L = \pi(R + r) + 2c$
  (a) Calculate the value of L, correct to 3 s.f., when $R = 9.6$, $r = 5.3$ and $c = 8.7$.
  (b) Calculate the value of r, correct to 2 s.f., when $L = 53.8$, $R = 8.9$ and $c = 7.6$.

8 $I = \dfrac{kP}{d^2}$
  (a) Calculate the value of I when $k = 8$, $P = 15$ and $d = 4$.
  (b) Calculate the positive value of d when $I = 3$, $k = 80$ and $P = 15$.

9 $r = \sqrt{\dfrac{A}{4\pi}}$
  (a) Calculate the value of r, correct to 3 s.f., when $A = 70$.
  (b) Calculate the value of A, correct to 3 s.f., when $r = 4.8$.

10 $V = \pi h(R^2 - r^2)$
  (a) Calculate the value of V, correct to 3 s.f., when $h = 9.7$, $R = 8.2$ and $r = 4.5$.
  (b) Calculate the positive value of R, correct to 2 s.f., when $V = 1400$, $h = 8.9$ and $r = 1.7$.

11 $A = \sqrt{s(s-a)(s-b)(s-c)}$ and $s = \dfrac{a+b+c}{2}$.

Calculate the value of A when $a = 9$, $b = 12$ and $c = 15$.

12 For each formula, make the letter in square brackets the subject.

(a) $E = mgh$ $[h]$ (b) $V = \dfrac{D}{T}$ $[D]$ (c) $V = \dfrac{D}{T}$ $[T]$

(d) $V = e + IR$ $[I]$ (e) $S = \frac{1}{2}n(a + l)$ $[n]$ (f) $S = \frac{1}{2}n(a + l)$ $[l]$

13 Make y the subject of each formula.

(a) $a = \dfrac{y}{b} + c$ (b) $a(y + b) = c$ (c) $a = \dfrac{by^2}{c}$

(d) $a = by^2 + c$ (e) $ay = by + c$ (f) $ay = c - by$

(g) $a(y + b) = c(y + d)$ (h) $a = b(y^2 + c)$ (i) $ay^2 = by^2 + c$

(j) $ay^2 = b - cy^2$ (k) $a = \dfrac{by^3}{c}$ (l) $\dfrac{y + a}{y + b} = c$

14 $y = 5x - 2$ and $x = 2t + 1$

Find a formula for y in terms of t.

15 $a = \dfrac{v^2}{r}$ and $v = r\omega$

Find a formula for a in terms of r and ω.

16 $y = 4t + 3$ and $x = 2t - 1$

Find a formula for y in terms of x.

Summary of key points

1 A formula uses algebraic expressions to describe a relationship or rule.

2 A formula must contain an equals (=) sign.

3 You can substitute numbers into a formula to find the value of a quantity.

4 The letter that appears on its own on one side of the = sign and does not appear on the other side is called the **subject** of the formula.

5 To find the value of a letter which is not the subject of a formula, substitute the given values into the formula and then solve the resulting equation.

6 You can rearrange a formula to make a different letter the subject.

7 You can sometimes **eliminate** one of the letters from a formula by substituting an expression from another formula.

7 Linear and real-life graphs

7.1 Straight line graphs

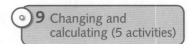 9 Changing and calculating (5 activities)

- A **straight line** has equation $y = mx + c$ where m is the gradient and the y-intercept is $(0, c)$.
- An **intercept** is a point at which a line cuts the y-axis or the x-axis.
- The **gradient** of a line is the increase in the y-value caused by an increase of 1 in the x-value.
- Lines with the same gradient (m) are parallel.
- To find the gradient of a straight line, draw a right-angled triangle below the line.

$$\text{Gradient} = \frac{\text{change in } y\text{-direction}}{\text{change in } x\text{-direction}} \text{ or } \frac{y_2 - y_1}{x_2 - x_1}$$

- The coordinates of any point on a straight line 'satisfy' its equation.

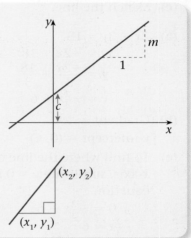

Example 1

(a) Work out the equation of the line **L**.

A second line **M** is parallel to **L** and passes through the point $(3, 5)$.

(b) Work out the equation of the second line **M**.

> Drawing linear graphs was covered in Chapter 5 of Higher Unit 3.

(a) The equation of the line **L** will be $y = mx + c$, where m is the gradient and $(0, c)$ is the y-intercept.
From the graph, $c = 2$.

$$\text{Gradient} = \frac{\text{change in } y\text{-direction}}{\text{change in } x\text{-direction}} = \frac{2}{1} = 2$$

The equation of line **L** is $y = 2x + 2$.

(b) Line **M** is parallel to line **L**, so they have the same gradient.
So the equation of **M** is $y = 2x + c$. Line **M** passes through the point $(3, 5)$, so $x = 3$ and $y = 5$ satisfy the equation.

$$5 = 2 \times 3 + c$$
$$5 = 6 + c$$
$$c = -1$$

The equation of line **M** is $y = 2x - 1$.

> Substitute $x = 3$ and $y = 5$ into $y = 2x + c$

Example 2

The equation of a straight line is
$$2x + 3y = 18$$
(a) Write the equation of the line in the form $y = mx + c$.
(b) State the values of the gradient and y-intercept.
(c) Sketch the line.

(a) $2x + 3y = 18$
$$3y = -2x + 18$$
$$y = \frac{-2x}{3} + \frac{18}{3}$$
$$y = -\frac{2}{3}x + 6$$

> Rearrange the equation to make y the subject.

(b) Gradient $= -\frac{2}{3}$
   y-intercept $= (0, 6)$

(c) To find where the line crosses the x-axis, substitute $y = 0$ into the equation.
$$0 = -\frac{2}{3}x + 6$$
$$\frac{2}{3}x = 6$$
$$x = 6 \times \frac{3}{2} = 9$$
The line crosses the x-axis at $(9, 0)$.

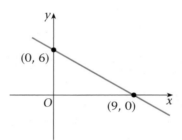

> Check: 3
> gradient $= \dfrac{y_2 - y_1}{x_2 - x_1}$
> $= \dfrac{6 - 0}{0 - 9}$
> $= -\dfrac{2}{3}$ ✓

Exercise 7A

1 Draw each of these graphs.
   (a) $y = 2x - 3$ (b) $y = \frac{1}{2}x + 5$ (c) $y = 12 - 3x$
   (d) $x + 3y = 6$ (e) $4x - 3y = 12$ (f) $6y + 4x = 30$
   For each graph find
   (i) the gradient   (ii) the y-intercept.

> Plot three points for each graph. Two is never sensible, in case you get one wrong.

2 The gradient of a line is 4. The point (6, 2) lies on the line. Find the equation of the line.

3 Line **L** has gradient $-\frac{2}{3}$ and passes through the point $(-2, 4)$. Find the equation of the line.

4 (a) Work out the equation of this line.

   A second line is parallel to the line shown and passes through the point $(-1, 1)$.
   (b) Work out the equation of the second line.

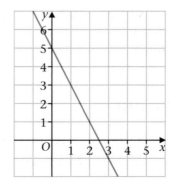

5 Work out the gradient and the y-intercept of the straight line
$4y - 9x = 24$

6 A straight line passes through the points (1, 1) and (4, 10).
Work out the equation of this straight line.

First work out the gradient.

7 Write down the pairs of equations which represent parallel lines.
(a) (i) $y = 3x - 2$ (ii) $y = 4 - 3x$
   (iii) $y = 2 + 3x$ (iv) $y = -2 - 3x$
(b) (i) $2y + 3x = 7$ (ii) $2y = 5 + 3x$
   (iii) $3y = 1 - 2x$ (iv) $3x - 2y = 17$
(c) (i) $y = \frac{1}{2}x + 1$ (ii) $2y = x + 3$
   (iii) $y + \frac{1}{2}x = 7$ (iv) $y - 2x = 0$

8 Work out the equation of the straight line which is parallel to
$y = 2x + 5$ and which passes through
(a) (0, 1)   (b) (1, 5)   (c) $(-2, -3)$

9 Work out the equation of the straight line which is parallel to
$2y + 3x - 2 = 0$ and which passes through
(a) (3, 3)   (b) $(-1, 5)$ (c) $(4, -3)$

10 The points A, B, C and D are the four vertices of a rectangle.
The coordinates of these four points are
    $A(1, 1)$ $B(1, 3)$ $C(5, 3)$ $D(5, 1)$
Work out the equations of the two diagonals AC and BD of the
rectangle.

11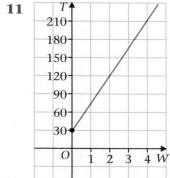

The graph above shows the time, T minutes, required to cook a
joint of meat weighing W kg.
T is given by the formula $T = mW + c$.
Work out the values of m and c.

7.2 Perpendicular lines

9 Perpendicular lines

- If a line has gradient m, a line perpendicular to it has gradient $-\dfrac{1}{m}$.
- If two lines are perpendicular, the product of their gradients is -1.

$m \times -\dfrac{1}{m} = -1$

Example 3

The equation of a straight line is

$$4y - 3x = 12$$

(a) Find
   (i) the gradient of this line
   (ii) the coordinates of its y-intercept.

A second line is parallel to $4y - 3x = 12$ and intercepts the y-axis at the point $(0, -5)$.

(b) Find the equation of this second line.

A third line is perpendicular to $4y - 3x = 12$ and passes through the point $(6, -1)$.

(c) Find the equation of this third line.

(a) $4y - 3x = 12$
$$4y = 3x + 12$$
$$y = \tfrac{3}{4}x + 3$$

> Rearrange the equation into the form $y = mx + c$

   (i) Gradient $= \tfrac{3}{4}$
   (ii) y-intercept $= (0, 3)$

(b) The second line is parallel to the first line, so it has gradient $\tfrac{3}{4}$. Its y-intercept is at $(0, -5)$.

So $y = \tfrac{3}{4}x - 5$

(c) The third straight line is perpendicular to the first one, so the third straight line has a gradient of

$$\frac{-1}{\tfrac{3}{4}} = -1 \div \tfrac{3}{4} = -1 \times \tfrac{4}{3} = -\tfrac{4}{3}$$

So the equation of the third line is $y = -\tfrac{4}{3}x + c$.

$(6, -1)$ lies on this line, so

$$-1 = -\frac{4 \times 6}{3} + c$$
$$-1 = -8 + c$$
$$c = 7$$

So the equation of the third line is

$$y = -\tfrac{4}{3}x + 7$$

> or $3y + 4x = 21$

Exercise 7B

1 Find the gradient of a line perpendicular to
   (a) $y = 2x + 3$
   (b) $3x + y = 5$

2 A line, **L**, is perpendicular to $2x - y = 1$ and passes through the point $(0, 5)$.
   Find the equation of the line **L**.

3 The equations of five lines are
   (a) $y = 3x + 2$ (b) $y - x = 1$ (c) $2y - x = 3$
   (d) $3x + 2y = 1$ (e) $5y - 2x = 7$
   For each line, write down the gradient of a line that is
   (i) parallel
   (ii) perpendicular to the line.

4 A straight line, L, passes through the points (2, 3) and (4, 9).
   (a) Work out the equation of the line L.

   A second straight line, M, is perpendicular to L and passes
   through the point with coordinates (0, −2).
   (b) Find the equation of this second straight line.

5 The equation of a straight line is $5y + 3x = 15$.
   (a) Find
        (i) the gradient of this line
        (ii) the coordinates of the point at which the line intercepts
             the y-axis.

   A second straight line is parallel to $5y + 3x = 15$ and passes
   through the point with coordinates (−10, 2).
   (b) Work out the equation of this second straight line.

   A third straight line is perpendicular to $5y + 3x = 15$ and passes
   through the point with coordinates (12, −1).
   (c) Find the equation of this third straight line.

6 A straight line passes through the points A and B.
   The coordinates of A and B are (2, 3) and (4, −7) respectively.
   A straight line, L, is perpendicular to AB and passes through the
   point (0, −3).
   Find the equation of the line L.

7 A: $y = 3x - 2$ B: $y = 2 - 3x$ C: $y = 5 - \frac{1}{3}x$
   D: $3y = x - 5$ E: $3y - x = 6$ F: $y = -2 - 3x$

   Write down the letters of any pairs of equations that represent
   (a) parallel lines
   (b) perpendicular lines.

7.3 Equations of real-life graphs

- You can draw a **line of best fit** for any data whose graph is almost a
  straight line.
- You can find the equation of a line of best fit by using the gradient
  and y-intercept.
- In real-life examples, m and c are rarely integers.

You may need to draw
a line of best fit for a
scatter graph.

Example 4

In an experiment the length of a spring is measured when different loads are hung from it.

The table shows the results.

Load (w) in kg	1	2	3	4	5
Length (L) in cm	25.8	27.8	29.0	31.2	32.9

(a) Plot the points.

(b) Draw the line of best fit.

(c) Find the equation of the line of best fit.

(a) (b)

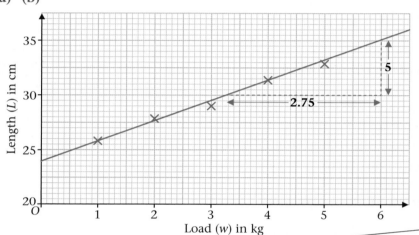

(c) The y-intercept is at (0, 24).

This is when there is no load.
It is the natural length of the spring.

$$\text{Gradient} = \frac{5}{2.75}$$

See the right-angled triangle drawn on the graph.

$$= 1.818...$$
$$= 1.8 \ (2 \text{ s.f.})$$

The equation is $L = 1.8w + 24$ where w is the load in kilograms.

Exercise 7C

For each question

(a) plot the points from the table

(b) draw the line of best fit

(c) find the equation of the line of best fit.

1

Age (years)	4	5	6	7	8
Depreciation (%)	62	70	75	80	83

2

Age (years)	11	12	13	14	15
Weight (kg)	40	45	53	62	70

3

Distance travelled (km)	120	150	200	270	350
Litres used	20	24	35	42	60

4

IQ	90	95	102	105	108
Total Key Stage score	8	9	13	14	15

5

Journey distance (miles)	55	83	120	134	165
Fare (£)	21	30	40	45	52

7.4 Interpreting real-life graphs

> **17** Distance–time graphs

- On a **distance–time graph**, the gradient gives the **speed**.
  A straight line represents **constant** speed.

Example 5

Here is the distance–time graph for Peter's cycle ride.

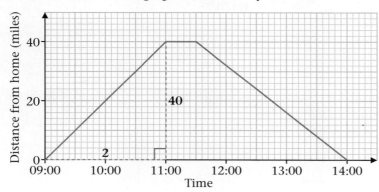

Work out Peter's average speed between

(a) 09:00 and 11:00

(b) 11:30 and 14:00.

$$\text{Average speed} = \text{gradient} = \frac{\text{change in } y\text{-direction}}{\text{change in } x\text{-direction}}$$

(a) Average speed $= \dfrac{40}{2} = 20\,\text{mph}$

(b) Average speed $= \dfrac{40}{2.5} = 16\,\text{mph}$

> Do *not* work out $\dfrac{40}{2.30}$

- On a **speed–time graph**, the gradient gives the **acceleration**.
- The area under a speed–time graph gives the **distance travelled**.

> Sometimes 'velocity' is used instead of 'speed'.

Example 6

The diagram shows the speed–time graph for one minute of a car journey.

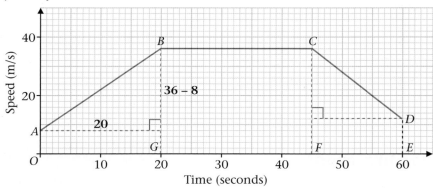

(a) Work out
  (i) the car's acceleration in the first 20 seconds
  (ii) the car's acceleration in the last 15 seconds.
(b) For how long did the car travel at constant speed?
(c) How far did the car travel during this one minute?

(a) (i) Acceleration = gradient = $\dfrac{36 - 8}{20} = \dfrac{28}{20} = 1.4\,\text{m/s}^2$

  (ii) Acceleration = gradient = $-\dfrac{24}{15} = -1.6\,\text{m/s}^2$

> From 20 to 45 seconds the car travelled at constant speed.

(b) $45 - 20 = 25$ seconds

(c) Distance = area under graph
    = area of trapezium $ABGO$ + area of rectangle $BCFG$
      + area of trapezium $CDEF$
    $= \frac{1}{2}(8 + 36) \times 20 + 25 \times 36 + \frac{1}{2}(36 + 12) \times 15$
    $= 440 + 900 + 360$
    $= 1700\,\text{m}$

> Area of trapezium = $\frac{1}{2}(a + b)h$

Example 7

The graph shows the electricity use in a small town one evening.
Describe the change in demand during the evening.

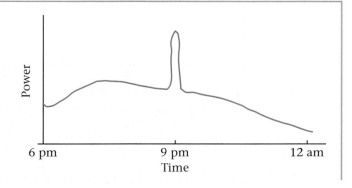

At the beginning of the evening there is a gradual increase in demand (possibly due to people coming home from work). It then tails off to a fairly constant rate with a sudden surge in demand at around 9:00 pm (typically caused at the end of a very popular TV programme). Demand declines as the evening passes (as people go to bed).

> Unless stated otherwise, the examiner is looking for the mathematical description rather than the speculation (which is in brackets).

Exercise 7D

1 Paul drove from Birmingham to Liverpool and back. Here is the distance–time graph for his journey.

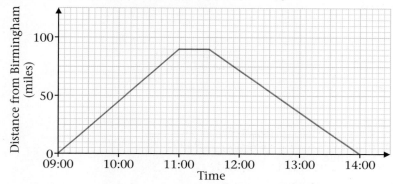

(a) Find his distance from Birmingham at 10:00.
(b) At what time did he reach Liverpool?
(c) For how long did he stay in Liverpool?
(d) Work out his average speed for
    (i) the journey from Birmingham to Liverpool
    (ii) the journey from Liverpool to Birmingham
    (iii) the whole journey, including his time in Liverpool.

2 Here is the speed–time graph for 25 seconds of a train's journey.

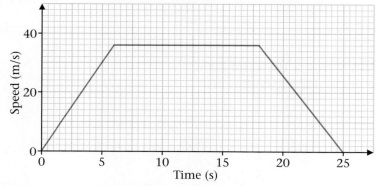

(a) Write down the train's speed after 4 seconds.
(b) For how long does the train travel at a constant speed?
(c) Work out the distance the train travels while its speed is constant.
(d) Write down the two times at which the train's speed is 18 m/s.

3 Aishya set off from home at 1 pm. She cycled 36 km in 2 hours and then rested for an hour. She cycled a further 12 km in half an hour and finally cycled the 48 km home, arriving at 7 pm.

Assume that she cycled at a constant speed during each stage of her journey.

   (a) Draw a distance–time graph for her journey.

   (b) Work out her average speed for the whole journey.

4 The graph shows the numbers of cars passing a traffic junction. Explain, with possible reasons, the pattern of traffic flow during the day.

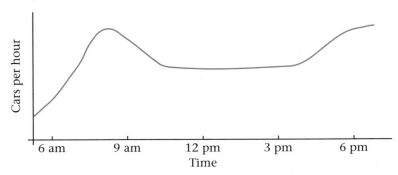

5 The graph shows the amount a hanging spring stretches as weight is added. Describe what happens.

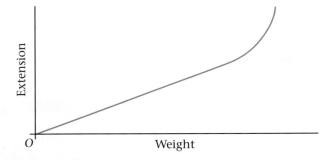

6 The graph shows house prices between 1980 and 2006. Describe what happened to prices during these years.

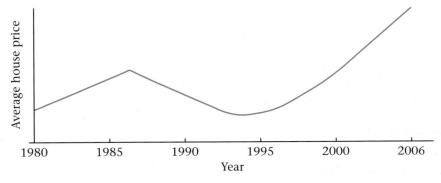

7 The distance–time graph shows the progress of a car.
Describe what happens during this part of the journey.

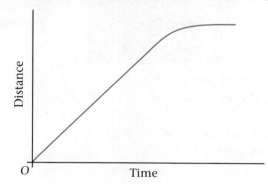

8 Sketch a graph to show the depth of fine sand in a
funnel that is full of sand as the sand flows out at a
constant rate.

Mixed exercise 7

1 Find the equation of the line parallel to $y = 2x + 3$ that goes
through the point
  (a) $(0, 5)$ **(b)** $(0, -2)$ **(c)** $(6, 6)$ **(d)** $(-2, 3)$

2 Write down the gradient and y-intercept for each of these lines.
  (a) $2x - 3y = 6$ **(b)** $x + 2y - 3 = 0$
  (c) $3y - 7 = 2x$ **(d)** $4x + 2y = 9$

3 **(a)** Work out the equation of the straight line which passes
    through $(2, 5)$ and $(4, 4)$.
  (b) Find the equation of the perpendicular to this line which
    passes through $(2, 5)$.

4 A line **L** passes through the points $(-2, 0)$ and $(0, 6)$.
A line **M** is perpendicular to **L** and passes through the
point $(2, 2)$.
Find the equation of the line **M**.

5 The table shows the estimated value of a piece of office
equipment at the end of each month, as a percentage of its
original value.

Time (months)	1	2	3	4	5	6	7	8	9	10	11	12
Value (%)	92	88	80	78	75	71	69	65	61	59	54	51

  (a) Plot the points from the table.
  (b) Draw a line of best fit.
  (c) Find the equation of the line of best fit.

6 Here is a distance–time graph for Mel's motorway journey.

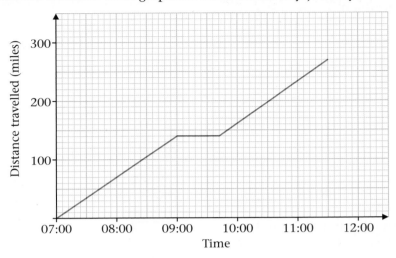

(a) Find the distance Mel had driven by 08:00.

(b) She was caught in a traffic jam from 09:00.
For how many minutes?

(c) Work out Mel's average speed for the first two hours of her journey.

(d) At what time had she covered 200 miles?

(e) Work out her average speed for the whole journey.

7 A train accelerates steadily for 3 seconds, increasing its speed from 14 m/s to 36 m/s. It travels at a constant speed of 36 m/s for 5 seconds and then decelerates steadily to rest in 4 seconds. Draw a speed–time graph for the 12-second period.

8 The five containers are all the same height and the same width.

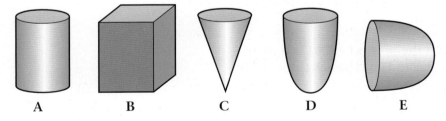

A   B   C   D   E

Each is full of water which is drained off from the base at a constant rate. The graphs show the depth of water, h, after time t. Match each container to its graph.

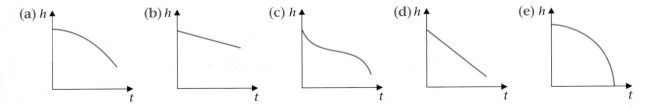

(a) h (b) h (c) h (d) h (e) h

9   Lester ran a 100 metres sprint in 10 seconds.
    The graph of his speed against time is shown below.
    Comment as fully as possible on his speed during the sprint.

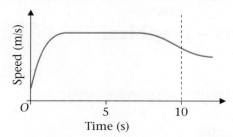

10 The diagram represents a goldfish bowl.
    Water is poured into the bowl at a
    steady rate.
    Draw a sketch of the height of the water
    against time.

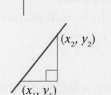

Summary of key points

1   A **straight line** has equation $y = mx + c$ where m is the gradient
    and the y-intercept is $(0, c)$.

2   An **intercept** is a point at which a line cuts the y-axis or the x-axis.

3   The **gradient** of a line is the increase in the y-value caused by an
    increase of 1 in the x-value.

4   Lines with the same gradient (m) are parallel.

5   To find the gradient of a straight line, draw a right-angled
    triangle below the line.

$$\text{Gradient} = \frac{\text{change in } y\text{-direction}}{\text{change in } x\text{-direction}} \quad \text{or} \quad \frac{y_2 - y_1}{x_2 - x_1}$$

6   The coordinates of any point on a straight line 'satisfy' its equation.

7   If a line has gradient m, a line perpendicular to it has gradient $-\frac{1}{m}$.

8   If two lines are perpendicular, the product of their gradients is -1.

$$m \times \frac{-1}{m} = -1$$

9   You can draw a **line of best fit** for any data whose graph is almost a straight line.

10 You can find the equation of a line of best fit by using the gradient and y-intercept.

11 In real-life examples, m and c are rarely integers.

12 On a **distance–time graph**, the gradient gives the **speed**.
    A straight line represents **constant** speed.

13 On a **speed–time graph**, the gradient gives the **acceleration**.

14 The area under a speed–time graph gives the **distance travelled**.

8 Solving equations and inequalities

8.1 Simultaneous equations – graphical solutions

9 Graphical solutions to simultaneous equations

- Two equations in two unknowns with a common solution are called **simultaneous equations**.
- You can solve simultaneous equations **graphically**.
  - Draw the two straight lines represented by the two simultaneous equations.
  - Their point of intersection represents the common solution.

Example 1

Does the point with coordinates (5, 2) lie on the line with equation $3x - 4y = 7$?

$$3 \times 5 - 4 \times 2 = 15 - 8$$
$$= 7$$

So $x = 5$ and $y = 2$ satisfy the equation $3x - 4y = 7$.
(5, 2) lies on the line $3x - 4y = 7$.

Substitute $x = 5$ and $y = 2$ into the expression $3x - 4y$.

Example 2

Solve the simultaneous equations
$$y = 2x - 1$$
$$y = 5 - x$$

Draw up a table of values and plot the graphs.

$y = 2x - 1$

x	0	1	3
y	-1	1	5

$y = 5 - x$

x	0	1	3
y	5	4	2

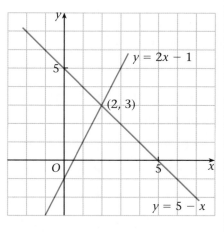

The coordinates of the point of intersection give the solution:
$$x = 2$$
$$y = 3$$

Check:
$2 \times 2 - 1 = 3$
$5 - 2 = 3 \checkmark$

Exercise 8A

1 Write down three pairs of integer values of x and y which satisfy
   each of these equations.
   (a) $x + y = 7$ (b) $x - y = 3$ (c) $y = 2x - 3$
   (d) $x + 2y = 8$ (e) $y = 3 - x$ (f) $y = 5 - 2x$

2 Which of the following points lie on the line with equation $3x - 4y = 12$?
   (a) $(4, 0)$ (b) $(-4, 0)$ (c) $(0, 3)$
   (d) $(0, -3)$ (e) $(8, 3)$ (f) $(-4, 6)$

3 Which of the following points lie on the line with equation $y = 4x + 5$?
   (a) $(5, 0)$ (b) $(0, 5)$ (c) $(1, 9)$
   (d) $(9, 1)$ (e) $(1, -1)$ (f) $(-1, 1)$

4 Which of the following equations are satisfied by $x = 2$ and $y = 3$?
   (a) $x + 2y = 8$ (b) $y = 4x - 5$ (c) $5x - 2y = 4$
   (d) $4x - 3y = 1$ (e) $y = 7 - 2x$ (f) $3x - 2y = 0$

5 Which of the following equations are satisfied by $x = 5$ and $y = -2$?
   (a) $2x + 3y = 4$ (b) $y = x - 3$ (c) $x - 2y = 9$
   (d) $y = 3 - x$ (e) $3x - 4y = 7$ (f) $y = 8 - 2x$

6 Use the diagram to solve
   the simultaneous equations
   $$2x + y = 1$$
   $$3x + 5y = 12$$

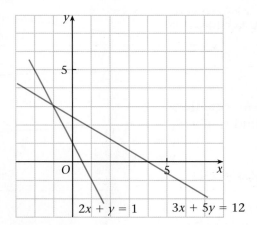

7 Use the diagram to solve
   the simultaneous equations
   $$2x + 3y = 12$$
   $$y = x - 1$$

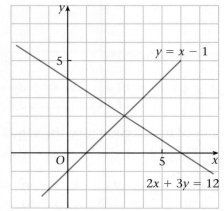

8 On separate diagrams, draw appropriate straight lines to solve these pairs of simultaneous equations.

(a) $x + y = 7$
$x - y = 3$

(b) $x + y = 8$
$y = x + 2$

(c) $2x + y = 8$
$x - y = 1$

(d) $y = x + 2$
$y = 2x - 1$

(e) $3x + 2y = 6$
$2x + y = 2$

(f) $2x - y = 5$
$3x - 4y = 10$

8.2 Simultaneous equations – algebraic solutions

- You can solve simultaneous equations **algebraically** by eliminating one of the unknowns.
  - If the coefficients of one of the unknowns are equal, subtract one equation from the other.
  - If the coefficients of one of the unknowns differ only in sign, add the two equations.
- Solve the resulting equation and substitute this value back into the original equation.

Example 3

Solve the simultaneous equations
$$6x + 5y = 7 \qquad (1)$$
$$3x + 5y = 1 \qquad (2)$$

$(1) - (2)$: $\qquad\qquad\qquad 3x = 6$
$\qquad\qquad\qquad\qquad$ so $x = 2$

Substitute in (2) to find y: $\ 6 + 5y = 1$
$\qquad\qquad\qquad\qquad 5y = -5$
$\qquad\qquad\qquad\qquad\ y = -1$

The solution is $x = 2$, $y = -1$.

Label the equations with a number or a letter.

The coefficients of y are equal (both 5), so subtract.

It does not matter which of the two original equations you substitute into, but you should check that your values fit the other one as well.

Exercise 8B

Solve these pairs of simultaneous equations.

1 $5x + y = 11$
$3x - y = 5$

2 $5x + 2y = 17$
$3x + 2y = 11$

3 $4x + 3y = 20$
$2x - 3y = 10$

4 $6x + 5y = 13$
$6x - y = 19$

5 $7x - 3y = 5$
$7x - 2y = 1$

6 $5x - 3y = 14$
$2x - 3y = 2$

7 $4x + 5y = 19$
$2x - 5y = 2$

8 $3x - 4y = -24$
$10x + 4y = -28$

9 $x + 4y = 3$
$x - 4y = -9$

10 $2x - 5y = 4$ $4x - 5y = 7$	**11** $3x + 5y = 3$ $6x - 5y = 21$	**12** $4x - 3y = 7$ $4x - 5y = 17$

8.3 Simultaneous equations with unequal coefficients

- If the coefficients are not equal, multiply the equation(s) by a number.

Example 4

Solve the simultaneous equations

$$3x + 4y = 6 \qquad (1)$$
$$5x - 6y = 29 \qquad (2)$$

$(1) \times 3:$ $\qquad\qquad 9x + 12y = 18 \qquad (3)$
$(2) \times 2:$ $\qquad\qquad 10x - 12y = 58 \qquad (4)$
$(3) + (4):$ $\qquad\qquad 19x = 76$
$\qquad\qquad\qquad\qquad x = 4$

Substitute in (1) to find y: $\quad 12 + 4y = 6$
$$4y = -6$$
$$y = -1\tfrac{1}{2}$$

The solution is $x = 4$, $y = -1\tfrac{1}{2}$.

> 12 is the lowest common multiple of 4 and 6. Multiply the equations so that the coefficients of y differ only in sign.

> Alternatively, you could multiply equation (1) by 5 and multiply equation (2) by 3, and then subtract.

Exercise 8C

Solve these pairs of simultaneous equations.

1 $3x + 2y = 14$ $5x + 6y = 26$	**2** $6x + y = 17$ $7x - 2y = 4$	**3** $3x - 4y = 4$ $9x - 7y = 22$
4 $8x + 3y = 18$ $12x - 5y = 8$	**5** $5x + 6y = 4$ $8x - 9y = 25$	**6** $7x - 10y = 16$ $4x - 15y = 37$
7 $4x + 3y = 24$ $3x - 2y = 1$	**8** $5x - 3y = 2$ $6x - 4y = 1$	**9** $5x + 4y = 12$ $2x - 5y = 18$
10 $6x + 5y = 4$ $4x - 3y = 9$	**11** $7x + 5y = 12$ $5x + 3y = 10$	**12** $9x - 7y = 6$ $11x - 9y = 8$
13 $2x + 5y = -17$ $x - 3y = 8$	**14** $3x - 2y = 18$ $2x + 5y = -7$	

8.4 Solving quadratic equations by factorising

- Equations where the highest power of x is x^2 are called **quadratic equations**, for example $x^2 - 9 = 0$, $x^2 + 2x - 3 = 6$.
- The quadratic equation $x^2 + bx + c = 0$ has two solutions (or roots), which may be equal.
- Some quadratic equations can be solved by **factorising**.
- If $xy = 0$, then either $x = 0$ or $y = 0$ or $x = y = 0$.

Factorising quadratic expressions was covered in Chapter 4 of Higher Unit 3.

Example 5

Solve the equation $(x + 5)(x - 6) = 0$.

Either
$$x + 5 = 0 \quad \text{or} \quad x - 6 = 0$$
The two solutions are $x = -5$, $x = 6$.

Example 6

Solve the equation $x^2 + 2x - 3 = 0$.

$$x^2 + 2x - 3 = 0$$
$$(x + 3)(x - 1) = 0 \qquad \text{Factorise}$$
Either
$$x + 3 = 0 \quad \text{or} \quad x - 1 = 0$$
The two solutions are $x = -3$, $x = 1$.

You must have zero on one side of a quadratic equation before you try to factorise the other side.

Example 7

Solve the equation $x^2 + 4x = 0$.

$$x^2 + 4x = 0$$
$$x(x + 4) = 0$$
Either
$$x = 0 \quad \text{or} \quad x + 4 = 0$$
The two solutions are $x = 0$, $x = -4$.

Don't divide both sides of the equation by x. If you do, you will lose the $x = 0$ solution.

Example 8

Solve the equation $x^2 - 9 = 0$.

Method 1
$$x^2 - 9 = 0$$
$$(x + 3)(x - 3) = 0$$
Either
$$x + 3 = 0 \quad \text{or} \quad x - 3 = 0$$
The two solutions are $x = -3$, $x = 3$.

Method 2
$$x^2 - 9 = 0$$
$$x^2 = 9$$
$$x = \pm\sqrt{9}$$
$$x = \pm 3$$

In general,
$x^2 - a^2 = (x + a)(x - a)$
This is called the 'difference of two squares'.
This was covered in Chapter 4 of Higher Unit 3.

Example 9

Solve the equation $16x^2 = 25$.

Method 1
$$16x^2 - 25 = 0$$
$$(4x + 5)(4x - 5) = 0$$
Either $4x + 5 = 0 \Rightarrow x = -\frac{5}{4}$
or $\quad 4x - 5 = 0 \Rightarrow x = \frac{5}{4}$
The two solutions are
$x = \frac{5}{4}$, $x = -\frac{5}{4}$
(or $x = 1.25$, $x = -1.25$)

Method 2
$$16x^2 - 25 = 0$$
$$16x^2 = 25$$
$$x^2 = \frac{25}{16}$$
$$x = \pm\sqrt{\frac{25}{16}}$$
$$= \pm\frac{\sqrt{25}}{\sqrt{16}}$$
$$x = \pm\frac{5}{4}$$

Exercise 8D

1 Solve these equations.

(a) $(x - 2)(x - 3) = 0$

(b) $(x + 8)(x - 5) = 0$

(c) $(x + 8)(x + 3) = 0$

(d) $x(x - 2) = 0$

(e) $(x - 7)(x + 4) = 0$

(f) $(x + 9)(x - 9) = 0$

(g) $(x - 6)(x + 6) = 0$

(h) $x(x + 8) = 0$

(i) $(x - 7)^2 = 0$

(j) $(x + 5)^2 = 0$

Parts **(i)** and **(j)** each have two equal solutions.

2 Solve these equations.

(a) $x^2 + x - 2 = 0$

(b) $x^2 - 3x + 2 = 0$

(c) $x^2 + 4x + 3 = 0$

(d) $x^2 - 4x - 5 = 0$

(e) $x^2 - x - 6 = 0$

(f) $x^2 + 8x + 7 = 0$

(g) $x^2 + 3x - 4 = 0$

(h) $x^2 + 2x - 8 = 0$

(i) $x^2 - 3x - 10 = 0$

(j) $x^2 + 7x + 12 = 0$

(k) $x^2 - 7x - 18 = 0$

(l) $x^2 + 5x - 14 = 0$

(m) $x^2 - 4x + 4 = 0$

(n) $x^2 + 8x + 16 = 0$

3 Solve these equations.

(a) $x^2 + 7x = 0$

(b) $x^2 - 5x = 0$

(c) $x^2 - x = 0$

4 Solve these equations.
   (a) $x^2 - 25 = 0$ (b) $x^2 - 1 = 0$ (c) $x^2 - 100 = 0$
   (d) $x^2 + 5 = 86$ (e) $4x^2 - 17 = 83$ (f) $36x^2 = 25$
   (g) $4x^2 = 49$

5 Solve these equations.
   (a) $x^2 - 6x - 16 = 0$ (b) $x^2 + 8x - 9 = 0$
   (c) $x^2 - 4 = 0$ (d) $x^2 - 2x + 15 = 0$
   (e) $x^2 - 4x = 0$ (f) $x^2 + 8x + 12 = 0$
   (g) $x^2 + 6x + 9 = 0$ (h) $x^2 + x = 0$
   (i) $x^2 - 5x - 24 = 0$ (j) $x^2 - 12x + 36 = 0$

8.5 More quadratic equations

- You may need to solve equations of the form $ax^2 + bx + c = 0$ where $a \neq 1$.
- You may need to rearrange the equation so that the right-hand side is 0.

Example 10

Solve the equation $10x^2 + 9x - 15 = 2x - 3$.

$$10x^2 + 9x - 15 = 2x - 3$$

Rearrange into the form $ax^2 + bx + c = 0$

$$10x^2 + 7x - 12 = 0$$
$$(2x + 3)(5x - 4) = 0 \qquad \text{Factorise}$$

Either $2x + 3 = 0$ or $5x - 4 = 0$

The two solutions are $x = -1\frac{1}{2}$, $x = \frac{4}{5}$.

Exercise 8E

1 Solve these equations.
   (a) $5x^2 - 15x + 10 = 0$ (b) $2x^2 - 4x - 48 = 0$
   (c) $7x^2 - 7 = 0$ (d) $4x^2 + 24x = 0$
   (e) $3x^2 + 21x + 36 = 0$ (f) $9x^2 - 36x + 36 = 0$
   (g) $6x^2 - 42x = 0$ (h) $4x^2 + 40x + 100 = 0$
   (i) $2x^2 - 50 = 0$ (j) $5x^2 - 35x - 90 = 0$

2 Solve these equations.
   (a) $5x^2 - 7x - 6 = 0$ (b) $2x^2 - x - 15 = 0$
   (c) $6x^2 - 13x + 5 = 0$ (d) $10x^2 - x - 21 = 0$
   (e) $4x^2 - 25 = 0$ (f) $9x^2 - 12x + 4 = 0$
   (g) $20x^2 - 23x + 6 = 0$ (h) $4x^2 + 28x + 49 = 0$
   (i) $9x^2 - 4 = 0$ (j) $8x^2 + 22x - 21 = 0$

3 Solve these equations.

(a) $2x^2 = x$ (b) $3x^2 = 48$

(c) $x^2 + x = 42$ (d) $x^2 + 4x - 5 = x + 13$

(e) $(x + 4)(x + 1) = x$ (f) $x^2 = 15 - 2x$

(g) $(x - 2)(x - 6) = 2x - 13$ (h) $12x^2 = 13x - 1$

(i) $(2x - 3)(3x - 5) = 5$ (j) $(5x - 2)^2 = 20(1 - x)$

8.6 Completing the square

19 Completing the square

- To make the expression $x^2 + 2ax$ a perfect square, you add a^2.

$(x + a)^2 = x^2 + 2ax + a^2$

- Completing the square: $x^2 + bx = \left(x + \dfrac{b}{2}\right)^2 - \left(\dfrac{b}{2}\right)^2$

p is $\frac{1}{2}$ the coefficient of x.

Example 11

Write each of the following in the form $(x + p)^2 + q$

(a) $x^2 + 10x$ (b) $x^2 - 8x + 21$

$(x + 5)^2 = x^2 + 10x + 25$
so you subtract 25.

(a) $x^2 + 10x = (x + 5)^2 - 25$

(b) $x^2 - 8x + 21 = (x - 4)^2 + 5$

$(x - 4)^2 = x^2 - 8x + 16$ so you add 5.

Example 12

Write $3x^2 + 24x + 55$ in the form $a(x + p)^2 + q$

$$3x^2 + 24x + 55 = 3(x^2 + 8x) + 55$$
$$= 3[(x + 4)^2 - 16] + 55$$
$$= 3(x + 4)^2 - 48 + 55$$
$$= 3(x + 4)^2 + 7$$

$(x + 4)^2 = x^2 + 8x + 16$

Exercise 8F

1 Write these expressions in the form $(x + p)^2 + q$

(a) $x^2 + 6x$ (b) $x^2 - 2x$ (c) $x^2 + 3x$

(d) $x^2 + 8x + 13$ (e) $x^2 - 4x + 7$ (f) $x^2 + 12x + 30$

(g) $x^2 - 10x + 35$ (h) $x^2 + 20x + 80$ (i) $x^2 - 5x + 4$

2 Write these expressions in the form $a(x + p)^2 + q$

(a) $2x^2 + 4x$ (b) $3x^2 - 30x$ (c) $5x^2 + 30x$

(d) $4x^2 - 16x + 21$ (e) $6x^2 + 36x + 47$ (f) $7x^2 - 14x + 10$

(g) $3x^2 - 3x + 1$ (h) $5x^2 + 15x + 9$ (i) $6x^2 - 30x + 37$

8.7 Solving quadratic equations by completing the square

> **Example 13**
>
> Solve the equation $x^2 - 6x + 4 = 0$.
> Give your answers **(a)** in surd form **(b)** correct to 2 d.p.
>
> **(a)** $x^2 - 6x = -4$ Subtract 4 from both sides
> $(x - 3)^2 - 9 = -4$ Complete the square for $x^2 - 6x$
> $(x - 3)^2 = 5$ Add 9 to both sides
> $x - 3 = \pm\sqrt{5}$ Square root both sides
> $x = 3 \pm \sqrt{5}$ Add 3 to both sides
>
>   In surd form, the solutions are $x = 3 + \sqrt{5}$, $x = 3 - \sqrt{5}$
>
> **(b)**   Correct to 2 d.p. the solutions are $x = 5.24$, $x = 0.76$

The square roots of all whole numbers except square numbers are surds e.g. $\sqrt{2}$, $\sqrt{3}$, $\sqrt{5}$.

Exercise 8G

1 Solve these equations by completing the square.
  Leave your answers in surd form.

  (a) $x^2 - 4x - 1 = 0$ **(b)** $x^2 + 8x + 5 = 0$

  (c) $x^2 - 10x + 8 = 0$ **(d)** $x^2 + 6x - 1 = 0$

  (e) $2x^2 + 12x + 5 = 0$ **(f)** $3x^2 - 12x - 7 = 0$

  (g) $x^2 - 5x + 3 = 0$ **(h)** $x^2 + 9x - 4 = 0$

2 Solve these equations by completing the square.
  Give your answers correct to 2 d.p.

  (a) $x^2 + 2x - 4 = 0$ **(b)** $x^2 - 8x + 9 = 0$

  (c) $x^2 - 6x + 3 = 0$ **(d)** $x^2 + 4x - 6 = 0$

  (e) $2x^2 + 4x - 1 = 0$ **(f)** $5x^2 - 20x + 2 = 0$

  (g) $x^2 - 3x + 1 = 0$ **(h)** $x^2 + 7x - 2 = 0$

8.8 Solving quadratic equations by using the formula

- The roots of the quadratic equation $ax^2 + bx + c = 0$, where $a \neq 0$, are given by the formula

$$x = \frac{-b \pm \sqrt{b^2 - 4ac}}{2a}$$

This formula will be on examination formulae sheets but you must know how to use it.

Example 14

Solve the equation $5x^2 - 9x + 2 = 0$.
Give your answers **(a)** in surd form **(b)** correct to 2 d.p.

In $5x^2 - 9x + 2 = 0$,
$a = 5$, $b = -9$ and $c = 2$

(a) $x = \dfrac{-b \pm \sqrt{b^2 - 4ac}}{2a}$

$x = \dfrac{9 \pm \sqrt{(-9)^2 - 4 \times 5 \times 2}}{2 \times 5}$

$= \dfrac{9 \pm \sqrt{81 - 40}}{10}$

$= \dfrac{9 \pm \sqrt{41}}{10}$

In surd form, the solutions are $x = \dfrac{9 + \sqrt{41}}{10}$, $x = \dfrac{9 - \sqrt{41}}{10}$

(b) Correct to 2 d.p. the solutions are $x = 1.54$, $x = 0.26$

Exercise 8H

1 Solve these equations by using the formula.
Leave your answers in surd form.

In parts **(a)**–**(d)**, $a = 1$.

(a) $x^2 - 3x + 1 = 0$ (b) $x^2 + 5x + 3 = 0$

(c) $x^2 - 6x - 2 = 0$ (d) $x^2 + 7x - 5 = 0$

(e) $2x^2 + 6x - 3 = 0$ (f) $3x^2 - 9x + 2 = 0$

(g) $4x^2 + 7x + 2 = 0$ (h) $5x^2 - 4x - 3 = 0$

(i) $3x^2 + 8x + 2 = 0$ (j) $4x^2 - 5x - 3 = 0$

2 Solve these equations by using the formula.
Give your answers correct to 2 d.p.

(a) $x^2 + 4x - 2 = 0$ (b) $x^2 - x - 9 = 0$

(c) $x^2 + 8x + 5 = 0$ (d) $x^2 - 7x + 4 = 0$

(e) $2x^2 - 5x - 1 = 0$ (f) $3x^2 + 7x + 3 = 0$

(g) $4x^2 - 10x + 5 = 0$ (h) $5x^2 + 3x - 4 = 0$

(i) $2x^2 + x - 7 = 0$ (j) $5x^2 - 9x + 2 = 0$

3 Solve these equations by using the formula.
Give your answers correct to 2 d.p.

(a) $x^2 + 7x - 2 = 2x + 1$ (b) $(x + 2)^2 = 7 - x$

(c) $(x + 3)(x - 3) = 3(x - 1)$ (d) $(x - 1)^2 + 5 = 6x$

(e) $2x(x + 3) = 5$ (f) $(2x + 1)(x + 4) = 3x + 1$

(g) $(2x - 1)^2 = 2(4x - 1)$ (h) $(3x - 2)(2x + 5) = 6x - 7$

(i) $3x^2 - 4x + 1 = x^2 + 2x - 1$

(j) $(2x - 3)^2 - (x - 2)^2 = 2$

8.9 **Showing inequalities on a number line**

⊙ 6 Showing inequalities on a number line

- An **inequality** is a statement which shows that one quantity is not equal to another quantity.
- You can show an inequality on a number line.
  ○ An open circle ○ means a number is not included.
  ○ A filled circle ● means a number is included.

> means 'is greater than'.
< means 'is less than'.
≥ means 'is greater than or equal to'.
≤ means 'is less than or equal to'.

Example 15

Show the inequality $x < 2$ on a number line.

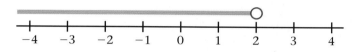

Example 16

Write down the inequality shown on this number line:

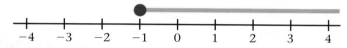

The inequality shown is $x \geq -1$.

Example 17

Show the inequality $-1 < x \leq 3$ on a number line.

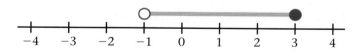

Exercise 8I

Write down the inequalities shown in questions **1–6**.

1
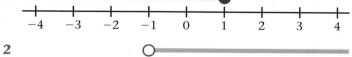

2
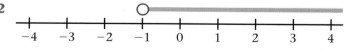

3
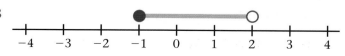

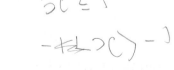

4
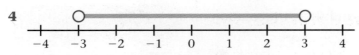

5

6
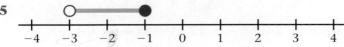

Draw number lines to show the inequalities in questions **7–15**.

7 $x < 1$

8 $x \geqslant 0$

9 $x \leqslant -1$

10 $x > -3$

11 $1 \leqslant x < 3$

12 $-2 \leqslant x \leqslant 1$

13 $-4 < x < -1$

14 $0 < x \leqslant 3$

15 $-1 \leqslant x < 2$

8.10 Solving inequalities

- To solve an inequality you can
  - ○ add the same quantity to both sides
  - ○ subtract the same quantity from both sides
  - ○ multiply both sides by the same **positive** quantity
  - ○ divide both sides by the same **positive** quantity.

  But you **must not**
  - ○ multiply both sides by the same **negative** quantity
  - ○ divide both sides by the same **negative** quantity.

> You solve inequalities in the same way as linear equations, except that you must not multiply or divide both sides by a *negative* number.

Example 18

Solve the inequality $3x - 10 < 7x - 1$ and show the solution on a number line.

$$3x - 10 < 7x - 1$$
$$-10 < 4x - 1 \qquad \text{Subtract } 3x \text{ from both sides}$$
$$-9 < 4x \qquad \text{Add 1 to both sides}$$
$$x > -2\tfrac{1}{4} \qquad \text{Divide both sides by 4}$$

> $-9 < 4x$ is equivalent to $4x > -9$

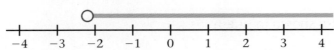

Exercise 8J

Solve the inequalities in questions **1–6**.

1 $5x + 3 < 18$

2 $9 - 4x \leqslant 7$

3 $-8x < 40$

4 $7x + 6 \leqslant 2x + 1$

5 $2x + 7 \leqslant 1 - x$

6 $3 - 4x > 5 - 6x$

In questions **7–15**, solve each inequality and show the solution on a number line.

7 $2x - 3 > 2$ **8** $4x - 1 < 6$ **9** $4 - 3x \leqslant 2$

10 $6x + 3 < 2x + 1$ **11** $2x + 5 < 5x - 2$ **12** $1 - 3x \geqslant 2x + 1$

13 $2x + 7 > 1 - 2x$ **14** $1 - x < 9 - 4x$ **15** $2 - 3x \leqslant 7 - x$

Solve the inequalities in questions **16–24**.

16 $2x - 7 < 6$ **17** $4x + 9 \geqslant 2$ **18** $9 - 7x < 4$

19 $2 + 9x > 3x - 10$ **20** $4x + 9 \geqslant 8x + 3$ **21** $13 - 4x \leqslant 2 - 7x$

22 $5 - 8x > 2 - 3x$ **23** $1 - 2x \geqslant 12 - 7x$ **24** $1 - 8x < 3 - 5x$

8.11 Integer solutions to inequalities

> **Example 19**
>
> List all the integers which satisfy the inequality $-9 \leqslant 4x < 8$.
>
> $$-2\tfrac{1}{4} \leqslant x < 2 \qquad \text{Divide each term in the inequality by 4}$$
>
> The integer solutions are $-2, -1, 0, 1$.

Integers are positive whole numbers, negative whole numbers and 0.

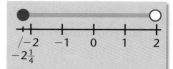

> **Example 20**
>
> Find the smallest integer which satisfies the inequality $2x \geqslant 4 - 3x$.
>
> $$2x \geqslant 4 - 3x$$
> $$5x \geqslant 4 \qquad \text{Add } 3x \text{ to both sides}$$
> $$x \geqslant \tfrac{4}{5} \qquad \text{Divide both sides by 5}$$
>
> The smallest integer which satisfies the inequality is 1.

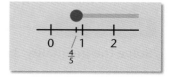

Exercise 8K

In questions **1–12**, list the integers which satisfy each of the inequalities.

1 $-2 \leqslant x < 3$ **2** $-9 < 3x \leqslant 3$ **3** $0 < 4x \leqslant 13$

4 $-17 \leqslant 5x < -3$ **5** $-3 \leqslant 2x \leqslant 1$ **6** $-5 < 6x \leqslant 18$

7 $13 < 2x < 20$ **8** $-20 \leqslant 3x < -13$ **9** $-3 < 4x \leqslant 8$

10 $-25 \leqslant 5x \leqslant -7$ **11** $-28 < 8x < 16$ **12** $-15 \leqslant 10x < 35$

13 Find the greatest integer which satisfies the inequality $5x + 2 \leqslant 4$.

14 Find the smallest integer which satisfies the inequality $6x - 1 \geqslant 2x - 7$.

15 Find the greatest integer which satisfies the inequality
$2x - 3 < 7 - 3x$.

16 If x is an integer, give all the possible solutions to
    (a) $3 < x + 3 \leqslant 5$ **(b)** $-2 \leqslant x - 2 \leqslant 3$
    (c) $-10 \leqslant 2x - 5 < 10$

> Consider the two inequalities separately in each part.

8.12 Regions

> **9** Graphical inequalities

- You can represent inequalities as **regions** on a graph.

Example 21

Draw a diagram to represent the inequality $y \leqslant 4$.

The **unshaded** region represents the inequality
$y \leqslant 4$.
Every point below the line $y = 4$ satisfies this
inequality.
Because the inequality is 'less than **or equal to**',
every point **on** the line $y = 4$ also satisfies the
inequality. It is drawn as a solid line to show
that it is included in the region.

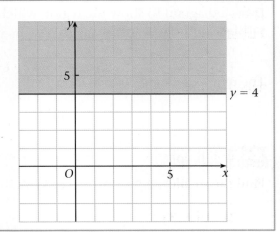

Example 22

Draw a diagram to represent the inequality
$2x + 5y < 10$

Points on the line $2x + 5y = 10$ do not satisfy
the inequality.
Draw the line with a dashed line.
To find which side of the line $2x + 5y = 10$ satisfies
the inequality, substitute the x- and y-coordinates of
a point into it.
Try $(0, 0)$: $x = 0$ and $y = 0 \rightarrow 2 \times 0 + 5 \times 0 < 10$.
So the point $(0, 0)$ lies inside the required region.
Shade the region that is not required.

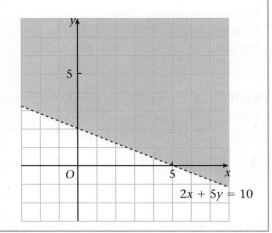

Example 23

Draw a diagram to represent the inequality $y \geqslant \frac{1}{2}x$.

The line $y = \frac{1}{2}x$ is solid, because points on the line satisfy the inequality.
The line passes through (0, 0), so test with a different point.
Test for (2, 0): $0 \geqslant \frac{1}{2} \times 2$ is **not** true.
(2, 0) does not lie in the required region.
Shade the region that is not required.

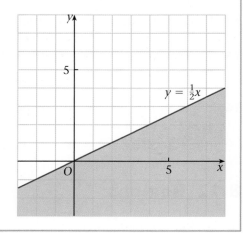

Example 24

Draw a diagram to show the region which satisfies all three of the inequalities
$$x \geqslant 1, \quad y > 2, \quad x + y \leqslant 7$$

The required region is **unshaded**.

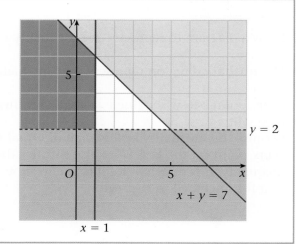

Example 25

Draw a diagram to show the region which satisfies all three of the inequalities
$$x + 2y > 8, \quad y < 6, \quad y \geqslant x - 1$$

Mark with a dot on your graph every point with integer coordinates which satisfy all three inequalities.

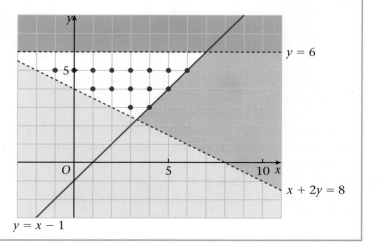

Exercise 8L

In questions **1–12**, draw diagrams to show the regions which satisfy
the inequalities. Shade the **unwanted** regions.

1 $x \leqslant 5$

2 $y > 4$

3 $x + y > 4$

4 $-2 \leqslant x < 3$

5 $y < 3x$

6 $2x + y > 8$

7 $y < x + 1$

8 $x - y \leqslant 3$

9 $y \geqslant 2x + 3$

10 $3x + 5y \leqslant 15$

11 $y < 6 - 2x$

12 $2x - 3y > 6$

In questions **13–16**, find the inequalities which describe the
unshaded regions.

13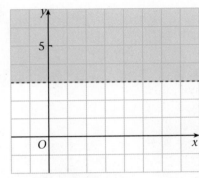

14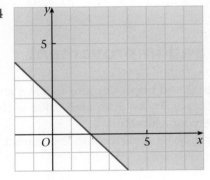

15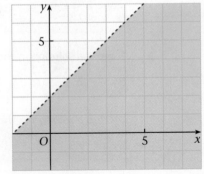

16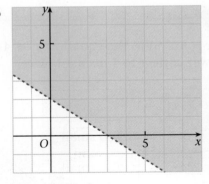

In questions **17–24**, draw diagrams to show the regions which satisfy
all the inequalities. Shade the **unwanted** regions.

17 $x > 2,\ \ y \geqslant 1,\ \ x + y < 6$

18 $x \geqslant 0,\ \ y < 4,\ \ y \geqslant x$

19 $y \leqslant x + 3,\ \ y \geqslant 0,\ \ x + 2y < 6$

20 $y < 2x,\ \ x + y \geqslant 2,\ \ x < 2$

21 $x \geqslant 0,\ \ y \geqslant 2x - 1,\ \ 2x + y < 6$

22 $x \geqslant 1,\ \ x - y < 2,\ \ y \leqslant \frac{1}{2}x + 1$

23 $x + y > 3,\ \ y < x + 3,\ \ 2x + 3y \leqslant 12$

24 $x + y \geqslant 2,\ \ y > x - 2,\ \ y < 8 - 2x,\ \ y \leqslant 3x + 2$

In questions **25–30**, draw a diagram to show the regions which satisfy all the inequalities. Mark with a dot on each graph every point with integer coordinates which satisfy all the inequalities.

25 $x \geqslant 3$, $y > 2$, $x + y \leqslant 7$

26 $x < 5$, $y \geqslant 2$, $y \leqslant x$

27 $x \leqslant 3$, $y < x + 2$, $2x + y \geqslant 4$

28 $y < 2x + 3$, $x + y \geqslant 3$, $2x + y < 6$

29 $y \geqslant 0$, $x - y \leqslant 4$, $y < \frac{1}{2}x$, $2x + y > 4$

30 $x \geqslant 0$, $x - y \leqslant 3$, $x + y > 5$, $3x + 4y < 24$

8.13 Trial and improvement

- You can use **trial and improvement** to solve an equation to any degree of accuracy. Try an estimated value in the equation. Then improve your estimate.
  Repeat, getting closer and closer to the correct value.

Example 26

Find a positive solution to the equation $x^3 + 4x^2 = 32$.
Give your answer correct to 1 decimal place.

x	$x^3 + 4x^2$	
1	5	Too small
2	24	Too small
3	63	Too large •
2.5	40.625	Too large •
2.2	30.008	Too small •
2.3	33.327	Too large •
2.25	31.640 625	Too small •

$x = 2.3$ (to 1 decimal place)

There is a solution in the range $2 < x < 3$
Try $x = 2.5$

There is a solution in the range $2 < x < 2.5$
Try $x = 2.2$

There is a solution in the range $2.2 < x < 2.5$
Try $x = 2.3$

There is a solution in the range $2.2 < x < 2.3$
Try $x = 2.25$

There is a solution in the range $2.25 < x < 2.3$
All variables in this range are 2.3 to 1 d.p.

You need to go to the next decimal place (2 d.p.) to confirm the solution.

Exercise 8M

In questions **1–8**, find the positive solution to each equation to the given level of accuracy.

1 $x^3 + 5x = 30$ (1 d.p.)   **2** $x^3 - 3x^2 = 10$ (1 d.p.)

3 $x^3 - 2x = 2$ (2 d.p.)   **4** $x^3 + 5x^2 = 100$ (2 d.p.)

5 $x^3 + 3x - 20 = 0$ (2 d.p.)   **6** $x^3 - 2x^2 - 25 = 0$ (2 d.p.)

7 $x^2 - \dfrac{3}{x} = 20$ (2 d.p.)   **8** $x - \dfrac{5}{x^2} = 4$ (2 d.p.)

9 The equation $x^2 + \dfrac{3}{x} = 19$ has *two* positive solutions.

     (a) One of the solutions lies between 0 and 1.
         Find this solution correct to 3 decimal places.

     (b) Find the other positive solution correct to 2 decimal places.

10 The diagram shows a prism which has a square as its cross-section. The length of each side of the square is x centimetres. The length of the prism is $x + 4$ centimetres. The volume of the prism is $200\,\text{cm}^3$. Find the value of x. Give your answer correct to 2 decimal places.

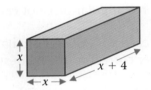

Mixed exercise 8

1 On separate diagrams, draw appropriate straight lines to solve these pairs of simultaneous equations.

     (a) $x + y = 6$ **(b)** $2x + y = 10$ **(c)** $3x + 2y = 18$
         $x - y = 2$ $y = x + 1$ $y = 2x + 2$

2 Solve these pairs of simultaneous equations algebraically.

     (a) $4x + 3y = 19$ **(b)** $7x + 2y = 17$ **(c)** $5x + 6y = 14$
         $5x - 3y = 17$ $7x - 5y = 31$ $7x + 6y = 16$

     (d) $3x + 5y = 3$ **(e)** $3x + 5y = 27$ **(f)** $8x - 3y = 13$
         $9x + 7y = 21$ $5x - 3y = 11$ $6x - 5y = 18$

3 Solve these equations.

     (a) $(x - 4)(x - 5) = 0$ **(b)** $(x + 3)(x - 8) = 0$

     (c) $(x + 8)(x + 1) = 0$ **(d)** $x(x - 6) = 0$

     (e) $(x - 7)(x + 2) = 0$ **(f)** $(x + 9)(x - 9) = 0$

     (g) $x(x + 2) = 0$ **(h)** $3(x + 6)(x - 4) = 0$

     (i) $(2x - 1)(3x - 2) = 0$ **(j)** $(2x - 5)(5x + 2) = 0$

4 Solve these equations.

(a) $x^2 - 5x + 6 = 0$ (b) $x^2 + 6x - 7 = 0$

(c) $x^2 + 10x + 16 = 0$ (d) $x^2 - 5x = 0$

(e) $x^2 - 4 = 0$ (f) $x^2 - 8x + 16 = 0$

(g) $x^2 + 9x = 0$ (h) $x^2 - x - 20 = 0$

(i) $x^2 - 100 = 0$ (j) $x^2 + 12x + 36 = 0$

5 Solve these quadratic equations.

(a) $x^2 + 2x - 35 = 0$ (b) $x^2 - 10x = 0$

(c) $x^2 - 81 = 0$ (d) $6x^2 + 17x - 45 = 0$

(e) $x^2 + 10x - 7 = 0$ (f) $x^2 - 7x + 4 = 0$

(g) $x^2 + 2x - 7 = 0$ (h) $2x^2 + 8x + 5 = 0$

(i) $3x^2 - x - 6 = 0$ (j) $4x^2 + 9x + 3 = 0$

6 Find the positive solution for these equations.
Give your answers correct to 2 decimal places.

(a) $x^3 - 4x = 60$ (b) $x^3 + 3x^2 = 80$ (c) $x^2 - \dfrac{2}{x} = 11$

7 The length of a rectangular piece of carpet is 5 m greater than its width.
The area of the carpet is 25 m². Calculate the width of the carpet.
Give your answer correct to the nearest centimetre.

8 A right-angled triangle is cut from the corner of a rectangular piece of paper that measures 12 cm by 5 cm.

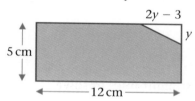

The base of the triangle is $2y - 3$ and its height is y.
The remaining piece of paper has area 54 cm².
Calculate the value of y, giving your answer to 2 significant figures.

9 Solve the equation
$$x^2 + 8x - 12x = 0$$
Give your answer in surd form.

10 The solution to a simple quadratic equation is $x = \pm 2\sqrt{5}$.
Write down the quadratic equation in its simplest form.

11 Draw number lines to show these inequalities.

(a) $x \leqslant 3$ (b) $x > -2$ (c) $-3 \leqslant x < 0$

12 Solve each inequality and show the solution on a number line.

(a) $2x + 7 \leqslant 4$ (b) $7x - 4 > 3x + 5$ (c) $5x + 9 \geqslant 9 - 3x$

13 Solve these inequalities.

    (a) $5x + 8 < 4$ (b) $7x - 3 \geqslant 3x + 11$

    (c) $4x + 1 > 5 - 2x$

14 List the integers which satisfy these inequalities and show them on a number line.

    (a) $-7 \leqslant 2x < 2$ (b) $0 \leqslant 3x \leqslant 8$ (c) $-5 < x - 2 < 10$

15 Draw diagrams to show the regions which satisfy these inequalities. Shade the **unwanted** regions.

    (a) $x > 3$ (b) $x + y > -1$ (c) $y \leqslant x + 4$

16 (a) Draw a diagram to show the regions which satisfy all these inequalities.

$$y < x + 3, \quad x + y \geqslant 3, \quad 2x + y \leqslant 6$$

    (b) Mark with a dot on the graph every point with integer coordinates which satisfy all the inequalities.

17 Only one of the solutions of the equation $x^3 + 4x = 100$ is a positive number. Use the method of trial and improvement to find this solution.

    Give your answer to 1 decimal place.

    You must show all your working.   [E]

18 The equation $x^3 - 2x = 67$ has a solution between 4 and 5.

    Use the method of trial and improvement to find this solution.

    Give your answer to 1 decimal place.

    You must show all your working.   [E]

Summary of key points

1 Two equations in two unknowns with a common solution are called **simultaneous equations**.

2 You can solve simultaneous equations **graphically**.
- Draw the two straight lines represented by the two simultaneous equations.
- Their point of intersection represents the common solution.

3 You can solve simultaneous equations **algebraically** by eliminating one of the unknowns.
- If the coefficients of one of the unknowns are equal, subtract one equation from the other.
- If the coefficients of one of the unknowns differ only in sign, add the two equations.
- If the coefficients are not equal, multiply the equation(s) by a number.
- Solve the resulting equation and substitute this value back into the original equation.

4 Equations where the highest power of x is x^2 are called **quadratic equations**, for example $x^2 - 9 = 0$, $x^2 + 2x - 3 = 6$.

5 The quadratic equation $x^2 + bx + c = 0$ has two solutions (or roots), which may be equal.

6 Some quadratic equations can be solved by **factorising**.

7 If $xy = 0$, then either $x = 0$ or $y = 0$ or $x = y = 0$.

8 You may need to solve equations of the form $ax^2 + bx + c = 0$ where $a \neq 1$.

9 You may need to rearrange the equation so that the right-hand side is 0.

10 To make the expression $x^2 + 2ax$ a perfect square, you add a^2.

> $(x + a)^2 = x^2 + 2ax + a^2$

11 Completing the square: $x^2 + bx = \left(x + \dfrac{b}{2}\right)^2 - \left(\dfrac{b}{2}\right)^2$

12 The roots of the quadratic equation $ax^2 + bx + c = 0$, where $a \neq 0$, are given by the formula

$$x = \frac{-b \pm \sqrt{b^2 - 4ac}}{2a}$$

13 An **inequality** is a statement which shows that one quantity is not equal to another quantity.

> $>$ means 'greater than'.
> $<$ means 'less than'.
> $\geqslant$ means 'greater than or equal to'.
> $\leqslant$ means 'less than or equal to'.

14 You can show an inequality on a number line.
   ○ An open circle ○ means a number is not included.
   ○ A filled circle ● means a number is included.

15 To solve an inequality you can
   ○ add the same quantity to both sides
   ○ subtract the same quantity from both sides
   ○ multiply both sides by the same **positive** quantity
   ○ divide both sides by the same **positive** quantity.
   But you **must not**
   ○ multiply both sides by the same **negative** quantity
   ○ divide both sides by the same **negative** quantity.

> You solve inequalities in the same way as linear equations, except that you must not multiply or divide both sides by a *negative* number.

16 You can represent inequalities as **regions** on a graph.

17 You can use **trial and improvement** to solve an equation to any degree of accuracy. Try an estimated value in the equation.
Then improve your estimate.
Repeat, getting closer and closer to the correct value.

9 Quadratic graphs

9.1 Drawing quadratic graphs

17 Plotting graphs

- Expressions of the type $ax^2 + bx + c$, where $a \neq 0$, are called **quadratic**.
- Graphs of functions of the form $y = x^2 + c$, where c can be positive or negative or 0, all have a ∪-shape.
  The bottom of the ∪-shape cuts the y-axis at $(0, c)$.
  The y-axis is a line of symmetry.
- Graphs of functions of the form $y = ax^2$, where a is positive, all have a ∪-shape.
  The greater the value of a, the narrower the ∪-shape.
  The y-axis is a line of symmetry.
- In general, graphs of functions of the form $y = ax^2 + bx + c$ have a ∪-shape if a is positive and a ∩-shape if a is negative.
  The ∪- or ∩-shape intercepts the y-axis at $(0, c)$.
- The ∪- or ∩-shape of the graph of a quadratic function is called a **parabola**.

Example 1

Draw the graph of the equation $y = x^2 + 3x - 18$.

One point is obvious. When $x = 0$, $y = -18$.
This is the intercept on the y-axis.
The intercepts on the x-axis are when
$$x^2 + 3x - 18 = 0$$
$$(x + 6)(x - 3) = 0$$

Therefore the x-intercepts are at $x = -6$ and $x = 3$.
The range of x-values needs to include -6 and 3 at least.
Make a table of values.

x	-7	-6	-5	-4	-3	-2	-1	0	1	2	3	4
x^2	49	36	25	16	9	4	1	0	1	4	9	16
$+3x$	-21	-18	-15	-12	-9	-6	-3	0	3	6	9	12
-18	-18	-18	-18	-18	-18	-18	-18	-18	-18	-18	-18	-18
y	10	0	-8	-14	-18	-20	-20	-18	-14	-8	0	10

So the graph is:

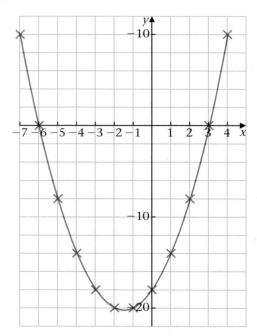

As a check, remember that quadratic graphs **always** have a line of symmetry.

Exercise 9A

Draw the graph of each of the following equations.
For questions **1–8** take values of x from -4 to 4.

1 $y = 2x^2$

2 $y = x^2 + 2$

3 $y = x^2 + 2x - 8$

4 $y = x^2 - 3x + 4$

5 $y = 2x^2 - 5x + 3$

6 $y = 3x^2 - 7x - 6$

7 $y = 4x^2 - 12x - 7$

8 $y = 5x^2 - 2x - 72$

9 $y = (x - 15)(x - 20)$

10 $y = (x + 6)(x + 10)$

11 $y = x^2 + 3x - 1$

12 (a) Draw the graph of $y = x^2 - 2x - 1$ for values of x from -2 to 4.

(b) Write down the minimum value of y and the value of x for which it occurs.

13 (a) Draw the graph of $y = x^2 - 4x + 4$ for values of x from -1 to 5.

(b) Draw the graph's line of symmetry and write down its equation.

14 (a) Copy and complete the table of values for $y = 2x^2 + 4x - 5$.

x	-4	-3	-2	-1	0	1	2
y		1			-5		

(b) Draw the graph of $y = 2x^2 + 4x - 5$.

(c) Draw the graph's line of symmetry and write down its equation.

(d) Write down the minimum value of y and the value of x for which it occurs.

15 (a) Draw the graph of $y = 3x^2 - 6x - 1$ for values of x from -2 to 4.

(b) Draw the graph's line of symmetry and write down its equation.

(c) Write down the minimum value of y and the value of x for which it occurs.

9.2 Solving quadratic equations graphically

- In a quadratic function the highest power of x is x^2.
- The general equation of a quadratic function is $y = ax^2 + bx + c$.
- The solutions of a quadratic equation are the values of x where the graph of the function cuts the x-axis.

Example 2

(a) For values of x from -3 to 2, draw the graph of $y = 3x^2 + 5x - 1$.

(b) Use your graph to find the approximate solutions to the equation
$$3x^2 + 5x - 1 = 0$$

(c) Use your graph to find the approximate solutions to the equation
$$3x^2 + 5x - 6 = 0$$

(a)

x	-3	-2	-1	0	1	2
$3x^2$	27	12	3	0	3	12
$+5x$	-15	-10	-5	0	5	10
-1	-1	-1	-1	-1	-1	-1
y	11	1	-3	-1	7	21

So the graph is:

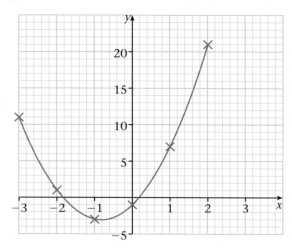

(b) The solutions of the equation $3x^2 + 5x - 1 = 0$ occur where the graph $y = 3x^2 + 5x - 1$ crosses the x-axis, i.e. where $y = 0$.

From the graph,

$$x = -1.8 \text{ and } x = 0.2$$

correct to 1 decimal place.

These are approximate solutions.

(c) To solve

$$3x^2 + 5x - 6 = 0$$

rearrange it to

$$3x^2 + 5x - 1 - 5 = 0$$

i.e. $3x^2 + 5x - 1 = 5$

The solutions are where the graph of $y = 3x^2 + 5x - 1$ crosses the line $y = 5$.

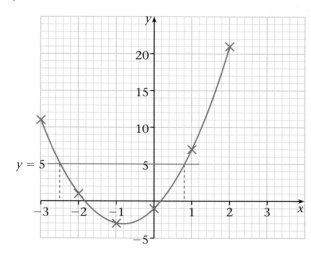

So the solutions are $x = 0.8$ and $x = -2.5$, correct to 1 decimal place.

Exercise 9B

1 (a) Copy and complete the table of values for $y = 2x^2 - 1$.

x	-3	-2	-1	0	1	2	3
y	17				1	7	

   (b) On a grid draw the graph of $y = 2x^2 - 1$.

   (c) Use your graph to
        (i)   solve the equation $2x^2 - 1 = 0$
        (ii) find the value of y when $x = 2.5$
        (iii) find the values of x when $y = 12.5$.

2 (a) For values of x from -4 to 4, draw the graph of
        $$y = 2x^2 - 3x - 8$$

   (b) Use your graph to find approximate solutions to the
        equation
        $$2x^2 - 3x - 8 = 0$$

3 (a) For values of x from -1 to 4, draw the graph of
        $$y = x^2 - 3x + 1$$

   (b) Use your graphs to find approximate solutions to the
        equation
        $$x^2 - 3x + 1 = 0$$

4 (a) For values of x from -4 to 4, draw the graph of
        $$y = 3 + x - x^2$$

   (b) Use your graph to find approximate solutions to the
        equation
        $$3 + x - x^2 = 0$$

9.3 The intersection of a line and a parabola

- You can find the coordinates of the points of intersection of a line and
  a parabola graphically.

- You can solve a linear equation and a quadratic equation
  simultaneously by drawing the graphs for the equations.
  Their points of intersection represent the common solutions.

Example 3

(a) Find graphically the coordinates of the points of intersection of the line with equation $y = x + 4$ and the parabola with equation $y = x^2 - 2$. Take values of x from -4 to 4.

(b) Use your answer to part (a) to solve the simultaneous equations $y = x + 4$ and $y = x^2 - 2$.

(a) Plot three points for $y = x + 4$, e.g. (0, 4), (1, 5) and (2, 6). Make a table of values for $y = x^2 - 2$.

x	-4	-3	-2	-1	0	1	2	3	4
y	14	7	2	-1	-2	-1	2	7	14

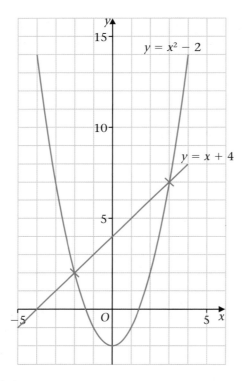

(b) From the diagram, the coordinates of the points of intersection are $(-2, 2)$ and $(3, 7)$.
The points of intersection represent the solutions of the simultaneous equations $y = x + 4$ and $y = x^2 - 2$.
So the solutions are $x = -2, y = 2$ and $x = 3, y = 7$.

> The x-coordinates of the points of intersection give the solutions of the quadratic equation $x^2 - 2 = x + 4$, which simplifies to $x^2 - x - 6 = 0$.

- You can solve a quadratic equation by finding the x-coordinates of the points of intersection of a parabola and a straight line.

Example 4

(a) Draw the graph of $y = x^2 + 2x - 1$.
Take values of x from -4 to 4.

(b) By drawing a suitable straight line, use your graph to solve the
quadratic equation $x^2 - x - 3 = 0$.
Give your answers correct to 1 decimal place.

(a) Make a table of values for $y = x^2 + 2x - 1$.

x	-4	-3	-2	-1	0	1	2	3	4
y	7	2	-1	-2	-1	2	7	14	23

The graph is drawn below.

(b) Write $x^2 - x - 3 = 0$ as $x^2 + 2x - 1 = 3x + 2$.
Then plot three points for the line with equation
$y = 3x + 2$, e.g. $(0, 2)$, $(1, 5)$ and $(2, 8)$, and draw
the line.

$$x^2 - x - 3 = x^2 + 2x - 3x - 1 - 2$$
$$= x^2 + 2x - 1 - 3x - 2$$
$$x^2 + 2x - 1 = 3x + 2$$

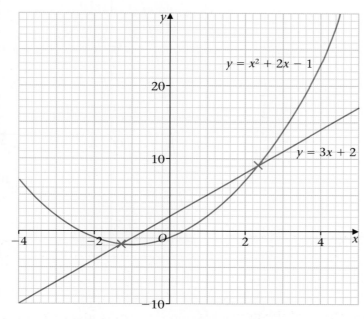

The x-coordinates of the
points of intersection
give the solutions to the
quadratic equation
$x^2 - x - 3 = 0$.

From the diagram, the solutions are $x = 2.3$ and $x = -1.3$.

Example 5

Solve graphically the simultaneous equations $x + y = 8$ and $y = 10 - x^2$.
Use values of x from -4 to 4.

Plot three points for $x + y = 8$, e.g. $(0, 8)$, $(2, 6)$ and $(4, 4)$.
Make a table of values for $y = 10 - x^2$.

x	-4	-3	-2	-1	0	1	2	3	4
y	-6	1	6	9	10	9	6	1	-6

From the graph, the solutions are
$\qquad x = -1, y = 9$ and $x = 2, y = 6$.

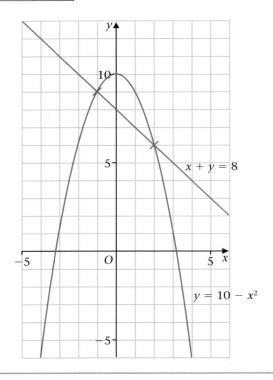

Exercise 9C

1 Find graphically the coordinates of the points of intersection of these parabolas and lines. Take values of x from -4 to 4.

(a) $y = x^2$ and $y = x + 2$
(b) $y = x^2$ and $y = 4x - 3$
(c) $y = x^2 + 4$ and $y = 1 - 4x$
(d) $y = 2 - x^2$ and $y = x$
(e) $y = x^2 + 2$ and $x + y = 8$
(f) $y = 9 - x^2$ and $2x + y = 6$
(g) $y = x^2 + 4x + 1$ and $y = x - 1$
(h) $y = x^2 - 2x + 1$ and $x + y = 3$

2 The graphs of $y = 2x^2$ and $y = 5 - 2x$ are drawn on the same axes.

Use the graphs to find approximate solutions to the equation

$$2x^2 + 2x - 5 = 0$$

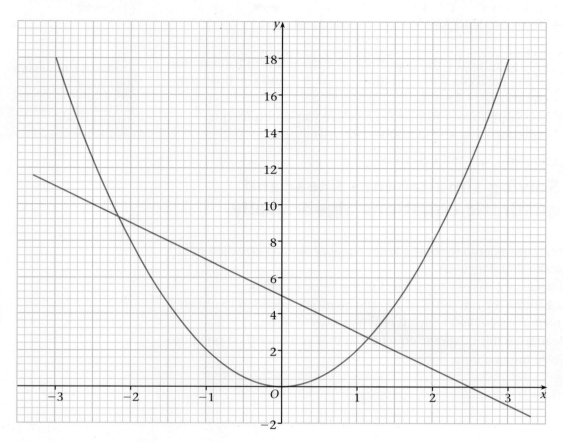

3 Solve these simultaneous equations graphically.
Take values of x from -4 to 4.

(a) $y = x^2$ and $y = x + 6$

(b) $y = x^2 + 1$ and $y = 3x - 1$

(c) $y = x^2 - 2$ and $y = 1 - 2x$

(d) $y = 4 - x^2$ and $y = 4x + 7$

(e) $y = 3 - x^2$ and $x + y = 1$

(f) $y = x^2 + 8$ and $3x + y = 6$

(g) $y = x^2 - 2x$ and $y = 2x - 3$

(h) $y = x^2 - 6x + 10$ and $x + y = 4$

4 (a) Draw the graph of $y = x^2 - x - 5$. Take values of x from -4 to 4.

(b) By drawing a suitable straight line, solve the quadratic equation $x^2 - 2x - 3 = 0$.

5 (a) Draw the graph of $y = x^2 + 3x + 1$. Take values of x from
        -4 to 4.
   (b) By drawing a suitable straight line, solve the quadratic
        equation $x^2 + x - 4 = 0$.
        Give your solutions correct to 1 decimal place.

6 (a) Find graphically the coordinates of the point of intersection
        of the parabola with equation $y = x^2 + 2$ and the line with
        equation $y = 2x + 1$.
   (b) Use your answer to part **(a)** to solve the simultaneous
        equations $y = x^2 + 2$ and $y = 2x + 1$.

> The line is a **tangent** to the parabola.
> The tangent to a curve just touches the curve at one point only.

9.4 Solving simultaneous linear and quadratic equations algebraically

- You can use algebra to solve a linear equation and an equation of a parabola simultaneously.
  - If necessary, make y the subject of the linear equation.
  - Substitute for y in terms of x in the quadratic equation to obtain a quadratic equation which is entirely in terms of x.
  - Rearrange this quadratic equation so that you have 0 on one side.
  - Solve the quadratic equation.

Example 6

Solve algebraically the simultaneous equations
$$y = x^2 - 2 \text{ and } y = 3x + 2$$

$$3x + 2 = x^2 - 2$$

> Substitute $3x + 2$ for y in the quadratic equation to obtain a quadratic equation which is entirely in terms of x.

$$x^2 - 3x - 4 = 0$$

> Rearrange this quadratic equation so that it has 0 on one side.

$$(x - 4)(x + 1) = 0$$

> Factorise the left-hand side.

$$x = 4 \text{ or } x = -1$$

> State the values of x.

Substitute each value of x into one of the original
equations to find the corresponding value of y:

   when $x = 4$, $y = 3 \times 4 + 2 = 14$
   when $x = -1$, $y = 3 \times -1 + 2 = -1$

The solutions are $x = 4$, $y = 14$ and $x = -1$, $y = -1$.

> Check that these solutions also satisfy $y = x^2 - 2$.

Example 7

Solve algebraically the simultaneous equations

$y = x^2 + 4$ and $y = 2x + 3$

$2x + 3 = x^2 + 4$ Substitute $2x + 3$ for y in the quadratic equation to obtain a quadratic equation which is entirely in terms of x.

$x^2 - 2x + 1 = 0$ Rearrange this quadratic equation so that it has 0 on one side.

$(x - 1)^2 = 0$ Factorise the left-hand side.

$x = 1$ State the value of x.

Substitute $x = 1$ into one of the original equations to find the corresponding value of y:

when $x = 1$, $y = 2 \times 1 + 3 = 5$ Check that this solution also satisfies $y = x^2 + 4$.

The solution is $x = 1$, $y = 5$.

Example 8

Solve algebraically the simultaneous equations

$y = 3x^2 + 8$ and $5x + y = 10$

$y = 10 - 5x$ Make y the subject of the linear equation.

$10 - 5x = 3x^2 + 8$ Substitute $10 - 5x$ for y in the quadratic equation to obtain a quadratic equation which is entirely in terms of x.

$3x^2 + 5x - 2 = 0$ Rearrange this quadratic equation so that it has 0 on one side.

$(x + 2)(3x - 1) = 0$ Factorise the left-hand side.

$x = -2$ or $x = \frac{1}{3}$ State the values of x.

Substitute each value of x into one of the original equations to find the corresponding value of y:

when $x = -2$, $y = 10 - 5 \times -2 = 20$

when $x = \frac{1}{3}$, $y = 10 - 5 \times \frac{1}{3} = 8\frac{1}{3}$ Check that these solutions also satisfy $y = 3x^2 + 8$.

The solutions are $x = -2$, $y = 20$ and $x = \frac{1}{3}$, $y = 8\frac{1}{3}$.

Exercise 9D

1 Solve these simultaneous equations algebraically.

(a) $y = x^2$ and $y = 5x - 4$ (b) $y = x^2$ and $y = 4x + 5$

(c) $y = x^2 + 1$ and $y = 9 - 2x$ (d) $y = x^2 - 8$ and $x + y = 12$

(e) $y = 9 - x^2$ and $y = 3x - 1$ (f) $y = x^2 - 3$ and $3x + y = 15$

(g) $y = x^2 + 9x + 4$ and $y = x - 3$ (h) $y = x^2 + 2x - 4$ and $y = 10 - 3x$

2 Solve these simultaneous equations algebraically.

(a) $y = 2x^2$ and $y = 7x - 3$

(b) $y = 3x^2$ and $x + y = 2$

(c) $y = 5x^2 + 2$ and $y = 2x + 5$

(d) $y = 2x^2 - 7$ and $y = x + 3$

(e) $y = 6 - 4x^2$ and $y = 4x + 3$

(f) $y = 12x^2 + 7$ and $5x + y = 10$

(g) $y = 6x^2 - 3x - 1$ and $y = 2x + 3$

(h) $y = 10x^2 + x - 13$ and $y = 5 - 2x$

3 Find the coordinates of the points of intersection of these lines and parabolas.

(a) $y = x^2 + 6$ and $y = 7x - 4$

(b) $y = 4 - x^2$ and $y = 8x - 5$

(c) $y = 2x^2$ and $y = 3x + 5$

(d) $y = 5x^2 + 2$ and $y = 18x - 7$

(e) $y = 3x^2 - 7x + 3$ and $y = 6x - 1$

(f) $y = 6x^2 + 6x + 5$ and $x + y = 3$

(g) $y = 12x^2 + x + 5$ and $10x + y = 20$

4 The line with equation $y = 6x - 1$ is a tangent to the parabola with equation $y = x^2 + 8$. Find the coordinates of the point at which the tangent touches the parabola.

5 Solve algebraically the simultaneous equations $4x + 2y = 19$ and $y = 9 - 2x^2$.

9.5 The points of intersection of a line and a circle

- $x^2 + y^2 = r^2$ is the equation of a **circle**, centre the origin and radius r. For example, $x^2 + y^2 = 16$ is the equation of a circle centre the origin and radius 4 units.

- You can find the coordinates of the points of intersection of a line and a circle graphically.

- You can solve a linear equation and an equation of a circle simultaneously by drawing the line and the circle.
  Their points of intersection represent the common solutions.

Example 9

(a) Find graphically the points of intersection of the line with equation $y = 2x - 5$ and the circle with equation $x^2 + y^2 = 25$.

(b) Use your answer to part (a) to solve the simultaneous equations $y = 2x - 5$ and $x^2 + y^2 = 25$.

> You need to use the same scale on both axes to get a circle.

(a) Plot three points for $y = 2x - 5$, e.g. (3, 1), (4, 3) and (5, 5).
$x^2 + y^2 = 25$ is the equation of a circle centre the origin with a radius of 5 units.
The coordinates of the points of intersection are (4, 3) and (0, −5).

(b) The points of intersection represent the solutions of the simultaneous equations $y = 2x - 5$ and $x^2 + y^2 = 25$.
So the solutions are $x = 4$, $y = 3$ and $x = 0$, $y = -5$.

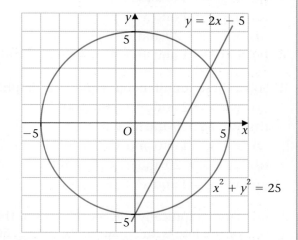

Example 10

Solve graphically the simultaneous equations $x + y = 2$ and $x^2 + y^2 = 100$.

Plot three points for $x + y = 2$, e.g. (0, 2), (1, 1) and (2, 0).

$x^2 + y^2 = 100$ is the equation of a circle centre the origin with a radius of 10 units.

The points of intersection represent the solutions of the simultaneous equations $x + y = 2$ and $x^2 + y^2 = 100$.

So the solutions are $x = 8$, $y = -6$ and $x = -6$, $y = 8$.

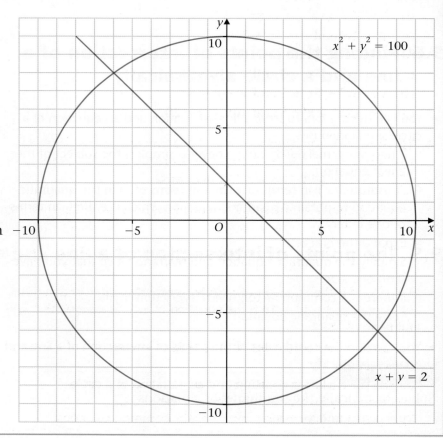

Exercise 9E

1 Find graphically the coordinates of the points of intersection of these circles and lines.
   (a) $y = x + 1$ and $x^2 + y^2 = 25$
   (b) $y = 3x - 10$ and $x^2 + y^2 = 100$
   (c) $x + y = 1$ and $x^2 + y^2 = 25$
   (d) $x + 2y = 20$ and $x^2 + y^2 = 100$
   (e) $y = 3 - x$ and $x^2 + y^2 = 9$

2 Solve these simultaneous equations graphically.
   (a) $y = x - 2$ and $x^2 + y^2 = 100$
   (b) $y = 3x + 5$ and $x^2 + y^2 = 25$
   (c) $x + y + 1 = 0$ and $x^2 + y^2 = 25$
   (d) $2y - x = 20$ and $x^2 + y^2 = 100$
   (e) $x + y = 4$ and $x^2 + y^2 = 16$

3 (a) Find graphically the coordinates of the point of intersection of the line with equation $3x - 4y = 50$ and the circle with equation $x^2 + y^2 = 100$.

    | The line is a tangent to the circle. |

   (b) Use your answer to part (a) to solve the simultaneous equations $3x - 4y = 50$ and $x^2 + y^2 = 100$.

9.6 Finding the points of intersection of a line and a circle algebraically

• You can use algebra to solve a linear equation and an equation of a circle simultaneously.
   ○ If necessary, make y or x (whichever is simpler) the subject of the linear equation.
   ○ Substitute for y in terms of x (or x in terms of y) in the quadratic equation to obtain a quadratic equation which is entirely in terms of one letter.
   ○ Expand the brackets.
   ○ Simplify the quadratic equation and rearrange it so that you have 0 on one side.
   ○ If there is a common factor, divide every term by it.
   ○ Solve the quadratic equation.

Example 11

Solve algebraically the simultaneous equations
   $y = x + 3$ and $x^2 + y^2 = 17$

$$x^2 + (x + 3)^2 = 17$$

Substitute $x + 3$ for y in the quadratic equation to obtain a quadratic equation which is entirely in terms of x.

$$x^2 + x^2 + 6x + 9 = 17$$

Expand the brackets.

$$2x^2 + 6x - 8 = 0$$

Simplify the quadratic equation and rearrange it so that it has 0 on one side.

$$x^2 + 3x - 4 = 0$$

2 is a common factor. So divide every term by 2.

$$(x - 1)(x + 4) = 0$$

Factorise the left-hand side.

$$x = 1 \text{ or } x = -4$$

State the values of x.

Substitute each value of x into one of the original equations to find the corresponding value of y:

when $x = 1$, $y = 1 + 3 = 4$
when $x = -4$, $y = -4 + 3 = -1$

The solutions are $x = 1$, $y = 4$ and $x = -4$, $y = -1$.

Check that these solutions also satisfy $x^2 + y^2 = 17$.

Example 12

Solve algebraically the simultaneous equations
$2x + y = 10$ and $x^2 + y^2 = 20$

$$y = 10 - 2x$$

Make y the subject of the linear equation.

$$x^2 + (10 - 2x)^2 = 20$$

Substitute $10 - 2x$ for y in the quadratic equation to obtain a quadratic equation which is entirely in terms of x.

$$x^2 + 100 - 40x + 4x^2 = 20$$

Expand the brackets.

$$5x^2 - 40x + 80 = 0$$

Simplify the quadratic equation and rearrange it so that it has 0 on one side.

$$x^2 - 8x + 16 = 0$$

5 is a common factor. So divide every term by 5.

$$(x - 4)^2 = 0$$

Factorise the left-hand side.

$$x = 4$$

State the value of x.

Substitute $x = 4$ into one of the original equations to find the corresponding value of y:

when $x = 4$, $2 \times 4 + y = 10$, so $y = 2$

The solution is $x = 4$, $y = 2$.

Check that this solution also satisfies $x^2 + y^2 = 20$.

Example 13

Solve algebraically the simultaneous equations
$$x - 2y = 3 \text{ and } x^2 + y^2 = 41$$

$$x = 2y + 3$$ | Make x the subject of the linear equation. | You could substitute $\frac{x-3}{2}$ for y but this would make the algebra more awkward.

$$(2y + 3)^2 + y^2 = 41$$ | Substitute $2y + 3$ for x in the quadratic equation to obtain a quadratic equation which is entirely in terms of y.

$$4y^2 + 12y + 9 + y^2 = 41$$ | Expand the brackets.

$$5y^2 + 12y - 32 = 0$$ | Simplify the quadratic equation and rearrange it so that it has 0 on one side.

$$(5y - 8)(y + 4) = 0$$ | Factorise the left-hand side.

$$y = 1\tfrac{3}{5} \text{ or } y = -4$$ | State the values of y.

Substitute each value of y into one of the original equations to find the corresponding value of x:

when $y = 1\tfrac{3}{5}$, $x = 2 \times 1\tfrac{3}{5} + 3 = 6\tfrac{1}{5}$

when $y = -4$, $x = 2 \times -4 + 3 = -5$

The solutions are $x = 6\tfrac{1}{5}$, $y = 1\tfrac{3}{5}$ and $x = -5$, $y = -4$.

Check that these solutions also satisfy $x^2 + y^2 = 41$.

Exercise 9F

1 Solve these simultaneous equations algebraically.
   (a) $y = x + 1$ and $x^2 + y^2 = 13$
   (b) $y = x - 2$ and $x^2 + y^2 = 34$
   (c) $x + y = 3$ and $x^2 + y^2 = 45$
   (d) $x - y = 7$ and $x^2 + y^2 = 49$
   (e) $y = 2x - 3$ and $x^2 + y^2 = 5$
   (f) $x - 2y = 1$ and $x^2 + y^2 = 2$

2 Solve these simultaneous equations algebraically.
   (a) $y = 2$ and $x^2 + y^2 = 40$
   (b) $y = x + 6$ and $x^2 + y^2 = 50$
   (c) $y = x - 5$ and $x^2 + y^2 = 17$
   (d) $y = x + 4$ and $x^2 + y^2 = 8$
   (e) $y = 3x + 1$ and $x^2 + y^2 = 29$
   (f) $x + y = 6$ and $x^2 + y^2 = 18$
   (g) $3x + y = 2$ and $x^2 + y^2 = 20$
   (h) $x - 2y = 1$ and $x^2 + y^2 = 65$

3 The line with equation $3y + 2x = 13$ is a tangent to the circle with equation $x^2 + y^2 = 13$. Find the coordinates of the point at which the line touches the circle.

Mixed exercise 9

1 (a) Draw the graph of $y = 2x^2 + 3x - 2$ for values of x from -3 to 3.
  (b) Use your graph to solve the equations
      (i) $2x^2 + 3x - 2 = 0$
      (ii) $2x^2 + 3x - 5 = 0$
  (c) On the same axes, draw the graph of
      $$y = x + 1$$
      Use your graphs to solve the equation
      $$2x^2 + 3x - 2 = x + 1$$
  (d) Explain why the solutions to the equation
      $$2x^2 + 3x - 2 = x + 1$$
      are also the solutions to the equation
      $$2x^2 + 2x - 3 = 0$$

2 (a) Draw the graph of $y = 3 + 4x - x^2$ for values of x from -1 to 5.
  (b) Draw the graph's line of symmetry and write down its equation.
  (c) Write down the maximum value of y and the value of x for which it occurs.

3 Solve these simultaneous equations graphically.
  Take values of x from -5 to 5.
  (a) $y = x^2 - 8$ and $y = x + 4$
  (b) $y = x^2 + 2$ and $y = 7 - 4x$
  (c) $y = 3 - x^2$ and $y = 2x - 5$
  (d) $y = x^2 + 3x + 5$ and $x + y = 2$
  (e) $y = x^2 + 2$ and $x + y = 8$
  (f) $y = 9 - x^2$ and $2x + y = 6$
  (g) $y = x^2 + 4x + 1$ and $y = x - 1$
  (h) $y = x^2 - 2x + 1$ and $x + y = 3$

4 The equation of a curve is
    $$y = x^2 - 8x + 14$$
  (a) Sketch the curve.
  (b) Find the minimum value of y.
  (c) Solve the equation $x^2 - 8x + 14 = 0$.
  (d) Solve the equation $x^2 - 8x + 6 = 0$.
  (e) By drawing a suitable straight line, solve the equation
      $x^2 - 10x + 10 = 0$.

5 Solve these simultaneous equations graphically.
  (a) $y = x - 1$ and $x^2 + y^2 = 25$
  (b) $y = x + 2$ and $x^2 + y^2 = 100$
  (c) $x + 3y = 15$ and $x^2 + y^2 = 25$
  (d) $x + y + 2 = 0$ and $x^2 + y^2 = 100$

6 Solve these simultaneous equations algebraically.
  (a) $y = x^2 - 6$ and $y = 3x + 4$
  (b) $y = x^2 + 3x - 5$ and $y = 1 - 2x$
  (c) $y = 2x^2 - 7$ and $y = 2x + 5$
  (d) $y = x^2 + 2$ and $y = 7 - 4x$
  (e) $y = 2x + 5$ and $x^2 + y^2 = 10$
  (f) $x + y = 4$ and $x^2 + y^2 = 58$
  (g) $3y - x = 2$ and $x^2 + y^2 = 20$
  (h) $x - y = 5$ and $x^2 + y^2 = 73$

7 Solve these simultaneous equations algebraically.
  (a) $y = 3x^2 - 1$ and $y = x + 1$
  (b) $y = 1 - x^2$ and $4x + y = 5$
  (c) $3x + y = 20$ and $x^2 + y^2 = 40$
  (d) $y = 2x - 7$ and $x^2 + y^2 = 17$

8 (a) Draw the graph of $y = x^2 - 4x + 1$.
      Take values of x from -3 to 7.
  (b) By drawing a suitable straight line, solve the quadratic
      equation $x^2 - 4x - 7 = 0$.
      Give your solutions correct to 1 decimal place.
  (c) By drawing a suitable straight line, solve the quadratic
      equation $x^2 - 6x + 6 = 0$.
      Give your solutions correct to 1 decimal place.

9 (a) The line with equation $x + y = 8$ is a tangent to the
      circle with equation $x^2 + y^2 = 32$. Find algebraically the
      coordinates of the point at which the line touches the circle.
  (b) The line with equation $x + y = c$ is a tangent to the circle
      with equation $x^2 + y^2 = r^2$. Show that $c^2 = 2r^2$.

10 AT is a tangent at T to a circle, centre O.
  $OT = x\,\text{cm}, \quad AT = (x + 5)\,\text{cm},$
  $OA = (x + 8)\,\text{cm}.$
  (a) Show that $x^2 - 6x - 39 = 0$.
  (b) Solve the equation $x^2 - 6x - 39 = 0$
      to find the radius of the circle.
      Give your answer correct to
      3 significant figures.

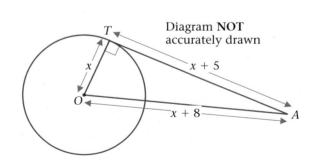
Diagram **NOT**
accurately drawn

11 (a) On a grid, with $-12 \leqslant x \leqslant 12$ and $-12 \leqslant y \leqslant 12$, draw the graphs of $x^2 + y^2 = 100$ and $2y = 3x - 4$.

(b) Use the graphs to estimate the solutions of the simultaneous equations

$$x^2 + y^2 = 100$$
and $\qquad 2y = 3x - 4$

(c) For all the values of x, $x^2 + 6x = (x + 3)^2 - q$.
Find the value of q.

(d) One pair of integer values which satisfy the equation $x^2 + y^2 = 100$ is $x = 6$ and $y = 8$.
Find one pair of integer values which satisfy

$$x^2 + 6x + y^2 - 4y - 87 = 0. \qquad \text{[E]}$$

Summary of key points

1 Expressions of the type $ax^2 + bx + c$, where $a \neq 0$, are called **quadratic**.

2 Graphs of functions of the form $y = x^2 + c$, where c can be positive or negative or 0, all have a ∪-shape.
The bottom of the ∪-shape cuts the y-axis at $(0, c)$.
The y-axis is a line of symmetry.

3 Graphs of functions of the form $y = ax^2$, where a is positive, all have a ∪-shape.
The greater the value of a, the narrower the ∪-shape.
The y-axis is a line of symmetry.

4 In general, graphs of functions of the form $y = ax^2 + bx + c$ have a ∪-shape if a is positive and a ∩-shape if a is negative.
The ∪- or ∩-shape intercepts the y-axis at $(0, c)$.

5 The ∪- or ∩-shape of the graph of a quadratic function is called a **parabola**.

6 In a quadratic function the highest power of x is x^2.

7 The general equation of a quadratic function is $y = ax^2 + bx + c$.

8 The solutions of a quadratic equation are the values of x where the graph of the function cuts the x-axis.

9 You can find the coordinates of the points of intersection of a line and a parabola graphically.

10 You can solve a linear equation and a quadratic equation simultaneously by drawing the graphs for the equations.
Their points of intersection represent the common solutions.

11 You can solve a quadratic equation by finding the x-coordinates of the points of intersection of a parabola and a straight line.

12 You can use algebra to solve a linear equation and an equation of a parabola simultaneously.
   - If necessary, make y the subject of the linear equation.
   - Substitute for y in terms of x in the quadratic equation to obtain a quadratic equation which is entirely in terms of x.
   - Rearrange this quadratic equation so that you have 0 on one side.
   - Solve the quadratic equation.

13 $x^2 + y^2 = r^2$ is the equation of a **circle**, centre the origin and radius r. For example, $x^2 + y^2 = 16$ is the equation of a circle centre the origin and radius 4 units.

14 You can find the coordinates of the points of intersection of a line and a circle graphically.

15 You can solve a linear equation and an equation of a circle simultaneously by drawing the line and the circle.
Their points of intersection represent the common solutions.

16 You can use algebra to solve a linear equation and an equation of a circle simultaneously.
   - If necessary, make y or x (whichever is simpler) the subject of the linear equation.
   - Substitute for y in terms of x (or x in terms of y) in the quadratic equation to obtain a quadratic equation which is entirely in terms of one letter.
   - Expand the brackets.
   - Simplify the quadratic equation and rearrange it so that you have 0 on one side.
   - If there is a common factor, divide every term by it.
   - Solve the quadratic equation.

10 Graphs and transformations of graphs

10.1 Graphs of cubic and reciprocal functions

17 Plotting graphs

- In a **cubic function** the highest power of x is x^3.
- The number in front of the x^3 is called the **coefficient** of x^3.
- The graph of a general cubic function is like this if the coefficient of x^3 is positive:

and like this if the coefficient of x^3 is negative:

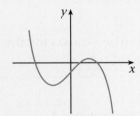

- Graphs of cubic functions have rotational symmetry.

Example 1

Plot the graph of $y = x^3 - 3x^2 + 2$.
Use your graph to solve $x^3 - 3x^2 + 2 = 0$.

x	-2	-1	0	1	2	3	4
x^3	-8	-1	0	1	8	27	64
$-3x^2$	-12	-3	0	-3	-12	-27	-48
$+2$	2	2	2	2	2	2	2
y	-18	-2	2	0	-2	2	18

So the graph is:

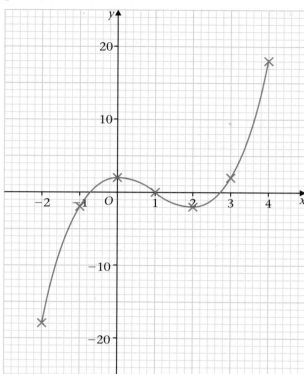

Join the points with a smooth curve.

The graph has rotational symmetry about the point (1, 0).

The solutions of $x^3 - 3x^2 + 2 = 0$ are where $y = 0$ (the x-axis) cuts the curve.
The solutions are $x = -0.7$, $x = 1$ and $x = 2.7$ (to 1 d.p.)

- To find the **reciprocal** of a number or expression, divide it into 1.
- The graph of $y = \frac{1}{x}$ is like this:

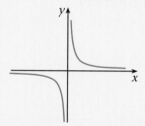

Example 2

Draw the graph of $y = \frac{1}{x} + x$ for $-5 \leqslant x \leqslant 5$.

x	-5	-4	-3	-2	-1	0	1	2	3	4	5
$\frac{1}{x}$	-0.2	-0.25	-0.33	-0.5	-1		1	0.5	0.33	0.25	0.2
$+x$	-5	-4	-3	-2	-1	0	1	2	3	4	5
y	-5.2	-4.25	-3.33	-2.5	-2		2	2.5	3.33	4.25	5.2

There is no value when $x = 0$ because you cannot divide by 0.
To find out what happens as x gets close to 0, try some more values:

x	-0.5	-0.4	-0.3	-0.2	0.2	0.3	0.4	0.5
y	-2.5	-2.9	-3.63	-5.2	5.2	3.63	2.9	2.5

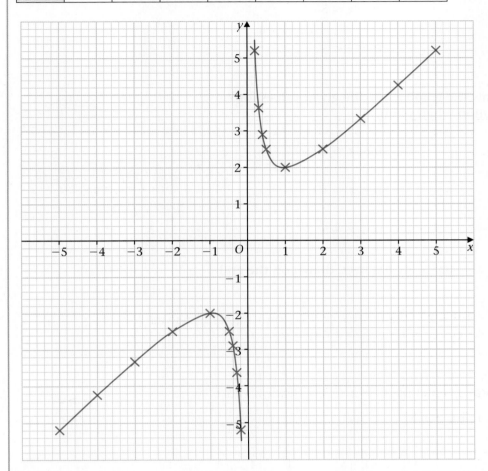

Exercise 10A

In questions **1–4** plot the graphs using the given values for x.
Use your graphs to find the value of x when $y = 0$.

1 $y = x^3 - 2x^2 + 3$ $\qquad\qquad -2 \leqslant x \leqslant 3$

2 $y = x^3 - 6x^2 + 9x$ $\qquad\qquad -1 \leqslant x \leqslant 5$

3 $y = 4x^3 - 15x^2 + 12x - 30$ $\qquad\quad 0 \leqslant x \leqslant 4$

4 $y = x^3 - 3x + 2$ $\qquad\qquad -3 \leqslant x \leqslant 3$

In questions **5–7** draw the graph using the given values for x.
Use it to find the solution when $y = 3$.

5 $y = \dfrac{1}{x}$ $\qquad\qquad\qquad\qquad 0 < x \leqslant 5$

6 $y = \dfrac{2}{x} + 3$ $\qquad\qquad\qquad\quad 0 < x \leqslant 5$

7 $y = 4 - \dfrac{1}{x}$ $\qquad\qquad\qquad\quad 0 < x \leqslant 5$

In questions **8–10** draw the graph using the given values for x.
Use it to find the solution when $y = 0$.

8 $y = \dfrac{1}{x} - x$ $\qquad\qquad\qquad\quad 0 < x \leqslant 10$

9 $y = \dfrac{5}{x} - 2x$ $\qquad\qquad\qquad\quad 0 < x \leqslant 10$

10 $y = x^2 - \dfrac{1}{x} + 1$ $\qquad\qquad\qquad 0 \leqslant x \leqslant 5$

11 The graph of $y = x^3 - 2x^2 - 4x$ has been drawn on the grid below.

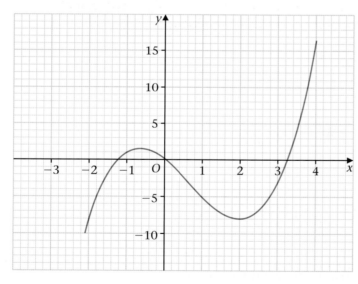

Use the graph to find estimates of the solutions to the equation
(a) $x^3 - 2x^2 - 4x = 0$
(b) $x^3 - 2x^2 - 4x = 1$ $\qquad\qquad\qquad\qquad\qquad$ [E]

10.2 Proportion

- The symbol $\propto$ means 'is proportional to'.
- $y \propto x$ means that y is directly proportional to x.
- When a graph connecting two quantities is a straight line through the origin, then one quantity is directly proportional to the other.
- When y is directly proportional to x, you can write a proportionality statement and a formula connecting y and x:
  - $y \propto x$ is the proportionality statement
  - $y = kx$ is the proportionality formula, where k is the constant of proportionality.
- When y is directly proportional to the square of x:
  - $y \propto x^2$ is the proportionality statement
  - $y = kx^2$ is the proportionality formula, where k is the constant of proportionality.
- When y is directly proportional to the cube of x:
  - $y \propto x^3$ is the proportionality statement
  - $y = kx^3$ is the proportionality formula, where k is the constant of proportionality.

Worked exam question

In a factory, chemical reactions are carried out in spherical containers.

The time, T minutes, that the chemical reaction takes is directly proportional to the square of the radius, R cm, of the spherical container.

When $R = 120$, $T = 32$.

Find the value of T when $R = 150$.

$T \propto R^2$

$T = kR^2$

$32 = k \times 120^2$ Substitute $T = 32$, $R = 120$

$k = \dfrac{32}{120^2}$

$k = 0.002\dot{2}$

So $T = 0.002\dot{2}R^2$

When $R = 150$, $T = 0.002\dot{2} \times 150^2 = 50$

- When y is inversely proportional to x:
  - $y \propto \dfrac{1}{x}$ is the proportionality statement
  - $y = k \times \dfrac{1}{x}$ or $y = \dfrac{k}{x}$ is the proportionality formula, where k is the constant of inverse proportionality.
- When y is inversely proportional to x^2:
  - $y \propto \dfrac{1}{x^2}$ is the proportionality statement
  - $y = \dfrac{k}{x^2}$ is the proportionality formula, where k is the constant of inverse proportionality.

Example 3

y is inversely proportional to x^2.
$y = 8$ when $x = 3$.
(a) Write y in terms of x.
(b) Calculate the value of y when $x = 2$.
(c) Calculate the exact values of x when $y = 7.2$.

(a) $y \propto \dfrac{1}{x^2}$ so $y = \dfrac{k}{x^2}$

When $x = 3$, $y = 8$, so $8 = \dfrac{k}{9}$

$k = 8 \times 9 = 72$

So $y = \dfrac{72}{x^2}$

(b) $y = \dfrac{72}{x^2} = \dfrac{72}{4}$ Substitute $x = 2$

So $y = 18$

(c) $7.2 = \dfrac{72}{x^2}$ Substitute $y = 7.2$

So $x^2 = \dfrac{72}{7.2} = 10$

$x = \pm\sqrt{10}$ Remember the $\pm$

Example 4

Match each statement to a sketch graph.
(a) y is directly proportional to x
(b) y is directly proportional to x^2
(c) y is inversely proportional to x

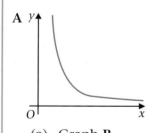 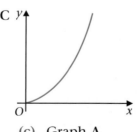

A   B   C

(a) Graph **B**   (b) Graph **C**   (c) Graph **A**

Exercise 10B

1 y is directly proportional to $\sqrt{x}$.
When $x = 9$, $y = 15$.
Write y in terms of x.

2 y is inversely proportional to x.
When $y = 3$, $x = 10$.
Find y in terms of x.

3 y is inversely proportional to x^2.
$y = 3$ when $x = 4$.

(a) Write y in terms of x.

(b) Calculate the value of y when $x = 5$.

(c) Calculate the value of x when $y = 12$.

4 y is directly proportional to x^2.
$y = 12$ when $x = 6$.

(a) Calculate y when $x = 5$.

(b) Calculate x when $y = 8$.

5 y is inversely proportional to x.
Sketch the graph of y against x.

6 y is directly proportional to x^3.
$y = 40$ when $x = 2$.

(a) Express y in terms of x.

(b) Calculate y when $x = 3$.

7 y is inversely proportional to x^2.
$y = 2$ when $x = \sqrt{3}$.
Work out the value of y when $x = 2$.

8 y is inversely proportional to x.
$y = 3$ when $x = 2$.
Prove that $xy = 6$.

9 y is directly proportional to $x^{\frac{1}{2}}$.
When $x = 16$, $y = 20$.
Work out the value of y when $x = 25$.

10 s is inversely proportional to t^2.
$s = 12$ when $t = 1$.

(a) Work out s when $t = 2$.

(b) Work out t when $s = 4$.

11 The cost of a square rug is directly proportional to the length of a side of the rug.
When the length of a side of the square rug is 4 m, the cost of the rug is £160.
Work out the cost of a similar square rug of side length 3 m.

12 The mass of a cube is directly proportional to the cube of the length of a side of the cube.

The mass of the cube is 32 grams when the length of a side is 2 centimetres.

(a) Calculate the mass of a similar cube when the length of a side is 5 cm.

(b) Calculate the length of a side of a similar cube when the mass is 4 kg.

10.3 Graphs of exponential and trigonometric functions

- The function a^x, where a is a positive constant and x is a variable, is called an **exponential function**.
- The graph of $y = a^x (a > 1)$ is like this:

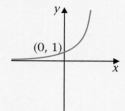

(0, 1)

Example 5

$y = 2^x$

(a) Complete the table of values for $y = 2^x$ for values of x from -3 to 3.

x	-3	-2	-1	0	1	2	3
y							

(b) Hence draw the graph of $y = 2^x$.

(a) $2^{-3} = \frac{1}{8} = 0.125$ $\qquad$ $2^{-2} = \frac{1}{4} = 0.25$ $\qquad$ $2^{-1} = \frac{1}{2} = 0.5$

$2^0 = 1$ $\qquad$ $2^1 = 2$ $\qquad$ $2^2 = 4$ $\qquad$ $2^3 = 8$

So the table is

x	-3	-2	-1	0	1	2	3
y	0.125	0.25	0.5	1	2	4	8

(b)

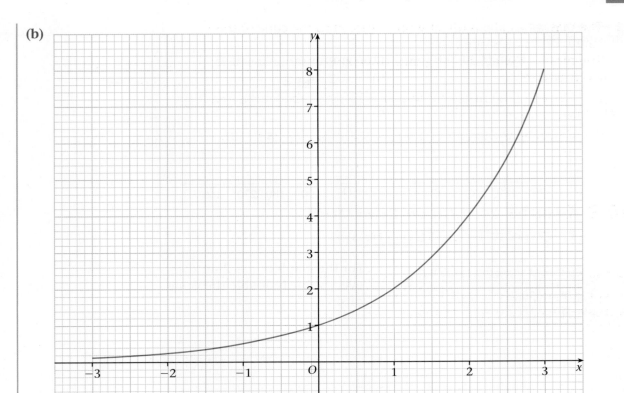

- The graph of $y = \sin x$ is like this:

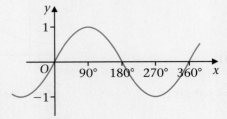

- The graph of $y = \cos x$ is like this:

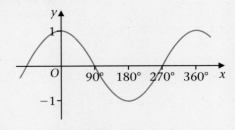

Example 6

For values of x from $0°$ to $360°$, sketch the graphs of
(a) $y = \sin x$
(b) $y = 2\sin x$

(a)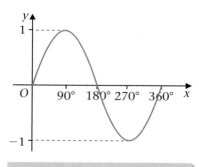

(b)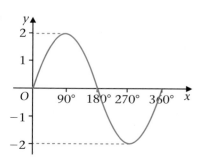

You should know this shape but can check it:
$\sin 0° = 0$, $\sin 45° \approx 0.7$,
$\sin 90° = 1$.

For the graph of $y = 2\sin x$, every value is double the value of $\sin x$.

Example 7

The diagram represents a sketch of part of the graph of
$$y = pq^x \qquad q > 0$$
The graph passes through the points $(1, 10)$ and $(3, 40)$.
(a) Work out the values of p and q.
(b) Work out the value of y when
   (i) $x = 4$ (ii) $x = -2$
(c) Work out the value of x when $y = 320$.

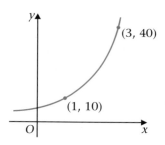

(a) Substituting $x = 1$ and $y = 10$ into $y = pq^x$ gives
$$10 = pq^1 \quad \text{or} \quad pq = 10 \qquad (1)$$
Substituting $x = 3$ and $y = 40$ into $y = pq^x$ gives
$$40 = pq^3 \quad \text{or} \quad pq^3 = 40 \qquad (2)$$
Dividing equations (1) and (2) gives
$$\frac{pq^3}{pq} = \frac{40}{10}$$
$$q^2 = 4$$
$$q = \sqrt{4} = \pm 2$$
Since $q > 0$, $q = 2$
Substituting $q = 2$ into $pq = 10$ gives
$$p \times 2 = 10$$
$$p = 5$$
So $p = 5$ and $q = 2$.

From the graph, when $x = 1$, $y = 10$.

When $x = 3$, $y = 40$.

(b) The equation is
$$y = 5 \times 2^x$$

(i) When $x = 4$
$$y = 5 \times 2^4$$
$$y = 5 \times 16 = 80$$

(ii) When $x = -2$
$$y = 5 \times 2^{-2}$$
$$y = 5 \times \tfrac{1}{4} = \tfrac{5}{4} \text{ (or 1.25)}$$

(c) The equation is
$$320 = 5 \times 2^x$$

So $2^x = \dfrac{320}{5} = 64$

But $2^6 = 2 \times 2 \times 2 \times 2 \times 2 \times 2 = 64$

So $x = 6$.

Example 8

Fiona and Rick bought a flat for £90 000 in July 2005.
They anticipate that the value of the flat will increase by 5% each year.
Draw the graph of the anticipated value of the flat from July 2005 to July 2015.

The value of the flat in July 2006 is 90 000 + 5% of 90 000

or 90 000 + 0.05 × 90 000 = 90 000 × 1.05

The value of the flat in July 2007 is

(value in 2006) × 1.05
i.e. 90 000 × 1.05 × 1.05
i.e. 90 000 × 1.05²

> Appreciation and compound interest are examples of exponential growth.
> Depreciation is an example of exponential decay.

n years after July 2005 the anticipated value of the flat will be
90 000 × $(1.05)^n$

This gives a table of values:

July	n	Anticipated value of the flat (£)
2005	0	90 000
2006	1	90 000 × 1.05 = 94 500
2007	2	90 000 × 1.05² = 99 225
2008	3	104 186.25
2009	4	109 385.56
2010	5	114 865.33
2011	6	120 608.59
2012	7	126 639.01
2013	8	132 970.96
2014	9	139 619.50
2015	10	146 600.47

Plotting the anticipated values against year gives this graph.

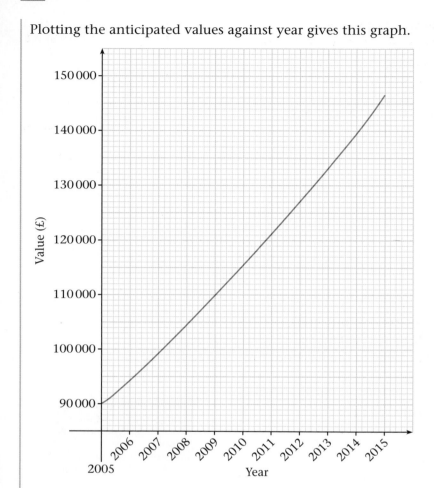

Exercise 10C

1 Sketch the graph of $y = \cos x$ for values of x from $0°$ to $360°$.

2 On the same axes, and for values of x from -3 to 3, draw the graphs of
   (a) $y = 3^x$ (b) $y = 2^{-x}$

3 On separate axes, sketch the graphs of
   (a) $y = \sin x$ for values of x from $0°$ to $360°$
   (b) $y = 3 \sin x$ for values of x from $-180°$ to $180°$
   (c) $y = \cos x$ for values of x from $0°$ to $360°$
   (d) $y = 3 \cos x$ for values of x from $0°$ to $360°$.

4 Afzal bought a new car for £12 000.
   The value of the car depreciates by 15% each year.
   Draw a graph of the value of the car from new until it is 6 years old.

5 The sketch shows part of the graph of $y = pq^x$.
The curve passes through the points (1, 12) and (3, 108).
  (a) Work out the values of p and q.
  (b) Work out the value of y when
      (i) $x = 4$ **(ii)** $x = -1$

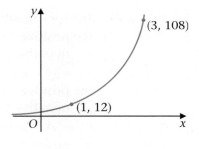

6 The diagram shows a sketch of part of the curve $y = \cos x$.

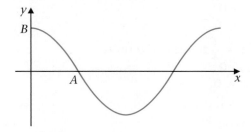

Write down the coordinates of the points A and B.

7 Here is a sketch of the graph of $y = \sin x$ for values of x between 0° and 360°.

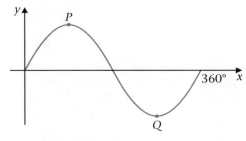

Write down the coordinates of the points P and Q.

8 The equation of a curve is
$$y = pq^x \qquad q > 0$$
The points (1, 10) and (3, 250) lie on the curve.
  (a) Work out the values of p and q.
  (b) Sketch the graph of the curve.
  (c) Work out the value of y when
      (i) $x = -2$ **(ii)** $x = 2$
  (d) Work out the value of x when $y = 1250$.

10.4 Applying transformations to graphs   25 Graph translations

- A **function** is a rule which shows how one set of numbers relates to another set.

$f(x)$, which denotes the output, is read as 'f of x'.

- The graph of $y = x + a$ is the graph of $y = x$ translated a units vertically in the **positive** y-direction if $a > 0$
  negative y-direction if $a < 0$.

- The graph of $y = x^2 + a$ is the graph of $y = x^2$ translated a units vertically in the **positive** y-direction if $a > 0$
  negative y-direction if $a < 0$.

- The graph of $y = x^3 + a$ is the graph of $y = x^3$ translated a units vertically in the **positive** y-direction if $a > 0$
  negative y-direction if $a < 0$.

- The graph of $y = \frac{1}{x} + a$ is the graph of $y = \frac{1}{x}$ translated a units vertically in the **positive** y-direction if $a > 0$
  negative y-direction if $a < 0$.

- For any function f, the graph of $y = f(x) + a$ is the graph of $y = f(x)$ translated a units vertically in the **positive** y-direction if $a > 0$
  negative y-direction if $a < 0$.

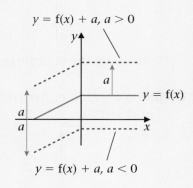

- The graph of $y = (x + a)^2$ is the graph of $y = x^2$ translated a units horizontally in the **negative** x-direction if $a > 0$
  positive x-direction if $a < 0$.

- The **vertex** of the parabola $y = (x + a)^2$ is at the point $(-a , 0)$.

- To sketch the graph of $y = x^2 + bx + c$, complete the square and apply a double translation to the parabola $y = x^2$.

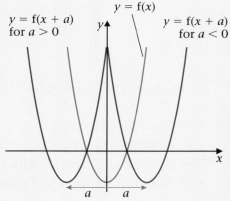

- The graph of $y = f(x + a) + b$ is the graph of $y = f(x)$ translated a units horizontally (in the **negative** x-direction if $a > 0$)
  (in the **positive** x-direction if $a < 0$)
  and then translated b units vertically (**upwards** if $b > 0$)
  (**downwards** if $b < 0$).

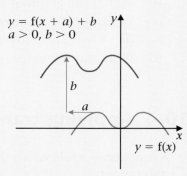

Example 9

The graph of f(x) = 2x + 6 is shown on the right.
Sketch the graph of f(x − 4).

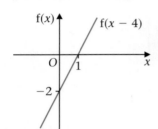

f(x) is translated 4 units in the positive x-direction.

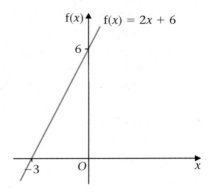

Example 10

The graph of y = f(x) is sketched below.

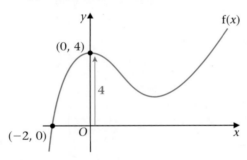

(a) Sketch the graph of y = f(x − 2).
(b) Sketch the graph of y = f(x) + 3.
y = f(x) is transformed to y = g(x):

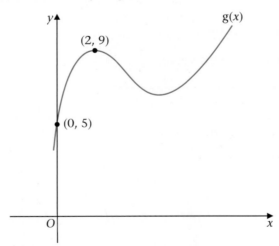

(c) State fully the single transformation which transforms f(x) to g(x).

(a) f(x − 2)

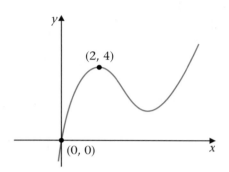

f(x) is translated
2 units in the positive
x direction.

(b) f(x) + 3

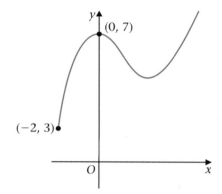

f(x) is translated 3 units
upwards.

(c)

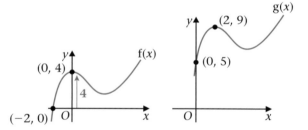

f(x) is translated 2 units across and 5 units up.

The single transformation is a translation with vector $\begin{pmatrix} 2 \\ 5 \end{pmatrix}$.

Example 11

The equation of a curve is

$$y = x^2 - 6x + 11$$

Sketch the graph of y against x.

By completing the square: $y = (x - 3)^2 - 9 + 11$

$$y = (x - 3)^2 + 2$$

So the sketch is:

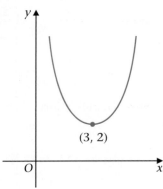

(3, 2)

$f(x) = x^2$ is translated 2 units upwards and 3 units in the positive x-direction.

i.e. $y = x^2$ translated along the vector $\begin{pmatrix} 3 \\ 2 \end{pmatrix}$.

Example 12

The graph of

$$y = \sin x$$

for values of x from $0°$ to $360°$ is sketched in the diagram.

(a) On the same diagram, sketch the graph of

$$y = 2\sin(x - 30°)$$

(b) Draw the curve $y = \sin x$, then on the same axes sketch the graph of

$$y = \sin 3x$$

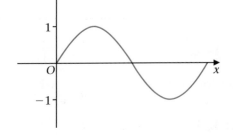

(a)

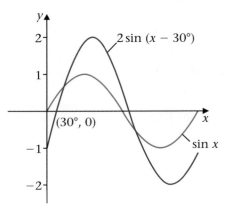

$2\sin(x - 30°)$

$(30°, 0)$

$\sin x$

(b)

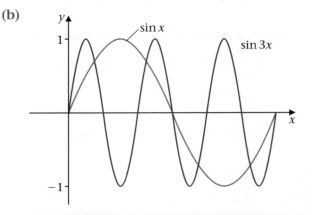

$\sin x$

$\sin 3x$

1 Translation $30°$ in positive x-direction
2 Sketch $\times 2$ parallel to y-axis.

Stretch $\times \frac{1}{3}$ parallel to the x-axis.

- For any function f, the graph of $y = -f(x)$ is obtained by reflecting $y = f(x)$ in the x-axis.

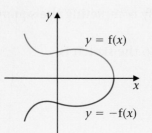

- For any function f, the graph of $y = f(-x)$ is obtained by reflecting $y = f(x)$ in the y-axis.

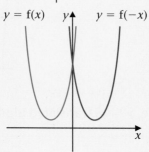

- Functions f which satisfy $f(-x) = f(x)$ are called **even functions**.
- Functions f which satisfy $f(-x) = -f(x)$ are called **odd functions**.

Exercise 10D

1 The equation of a curve is $y = f(x)$, where
$$f(x) = x^2 + 8x + 11$$
(a) Sketch the graph of $y = f(x)$.
(b) Obtain the minimum value of y and the value of x for which it occurs.

The graph of $y = g(x)$ is obtained by reflecting $y = f(x)$ in the x-axis.
(c) Express $g(x)$ as a quadratic function in x.

2 (a) Sketch the graph of $y = \cos x$ for values of x from $0°$ to $180°$.
(b) On the same axes, sketch the graph of $y = 3 \cos(x + 60°)$.
(c) On the same axes, sketch the graph of $y = \cos 2x$.

3 (a) Sketch the graph of
$$y = 13 - 6x - x^2$$
(b) Find the maximum value of $13 - 6x - x^2$.

The graph of $y = g(x)$ is obtained by reflecting $y = 13 - 6x - x^2$ in the line $x = 1$.
(c) Obtain $g(x)$ in terms of x.

4 Here is a sketch of the curve with equation $y = f(x)$:

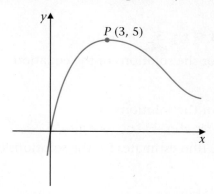

The curve has its only maximum point at the point P with coordinates $(3, 5)$.

Write down the coordinates of the maximum point for curves with each of these equations:

(a) $y = f(x + 1)$ (b) $y = f(x - 3)$ (c) $y = f(x) + 2$

(d) $y = f(-x)$ (e) $y = f(2x)$

5 This is a sketch of the graph of $y = \sin x°$ for values of x between 0 and 360.

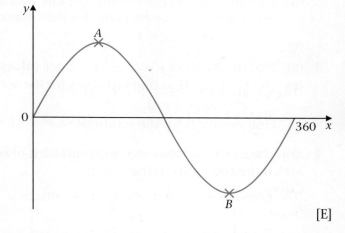

(a) Write down the coordinates of the points

   (i) A (ii) B.

(b) On the same axes sketch the graph of $y = \sin 2x°$ for values of x between 0 and 360.

[E]

6 The graph of $y = f(x)$ is sketched in the diagram.

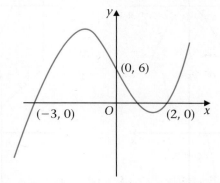

(a) Copy the diagram and sketch on it the graph of $y = f(x - 3)$.

(b) Make another copy of the diagram and sketch on it the graph of $y = f(x) - 4$.   [E]

Mixed exercise 10

1 (a) Plot the graph of $y = x + \dfrac{2}{x}$ for $0.1 \leqslant x \leqslant 5$.

   (b) Use your graph to find estimates for the solutions of the equation
$$x + \frac{2}{x} = 4$$

   (c) Use your graph to find estimates for the solutions of
$$x^2 + 2 = 3x$$

   (d) By drawing a suitable straight line, find estimates for the solutions of
$$3x + \frac{2}{x} = 5$$
   Give the equation for the line you used.

2 (a) Plot the graph of $y = x^3 - 3x^2 + 2$ for $-1 \leqslant x \leqslant 4$.

   (b) Use your graph to find estimates for the solutions of
$$x^3 - 3x^2 + 2 = 0$$

   (c) Use your graph to find estimates for the solutions of
$$x^3 - 3x^2 + 4 = 6$$

   (d) Find the equation of the straight line whose intercepts on this graph will give estimates for the solutions of
$$x^3 = 3x^2 + 2x - 1$$

3 (a) Plot the graph of $y = x^3 - 7x + 5$ for values of x between -3 and $+3$.

   (b) Use your graph to find estimates for the solutions of
$$x^3 - 7x + 5 = 0$$

   (c) Find estimates for the solutions of $x^3 - 5x = 3x + 5$.

4 Here are some sketches of graphs and a list of equations.
   Match the equations to the graphs.
   Curves

A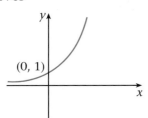

B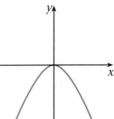

C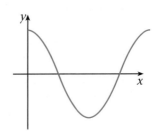

D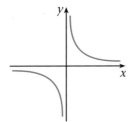

E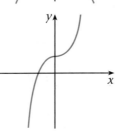

F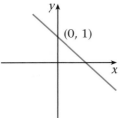

Equations

$y = \cos x$ $y = 5^x$ $y = x^3 + 2$ $y = \dfrac{5}{x}$ $y = -x^2$ $y = 1 - x$

5 On the same axes and for values of x from -3 to 3, plot the graphs of

$$y = x^3 + x \quad \text{and} \quad y = \frac{10}{x}$$

6 The points $(1, 4)$ and $(2, 256)$ satisfy the equation $y^k = 2x^m$.
Find the values of k and m.

7 The cost of hiring a holiday villa for a month is £2000.
The cost is fixed and does not depend on how many people hire the villa.
A group of people hire the villa for a month and share the cost equally.
Sketch the graph of the **cost per person** as the number of people in the group varies from 1 to 10.

8 d is directly proportional to the square of t.
$d = 80$ when $t = 4$.

(a) Express d in terms of t.

(b) Work out the value of d when $t = 7$.

(c) Work out the positive value of t when $d = 45$.   [E]

9 (a) The time, T seconds, it takes a water heater to boil some water is directly proportional to the mass of water, m kg, in the water heater.
When $m = 250$, $T = 600$.
Find T when $m = 400$.

(b) The time, T seconds, it takes a water heater to boil a constant mass of water is inversely proportional to the power, P watts, of the water heater.
When $P = 1440$, $T = 360$.
Find the value of T when $P = 900$.   [E]

10 Draw the graph of $y = \dfrac{1}{x + 1}$.

11 The diagram shows the accurate plot of the graph of a trigonometric function for values of x from $0°$ to $1440°$.
Work out the equation of this graph.

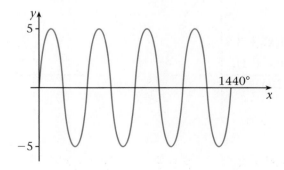

12 Sketch the graph of $y = (x - 1)^3$.

13 The graph of $y = a - b\sin(kt)$ is shown on the graph.
Use the graph to find values for a, b and k.

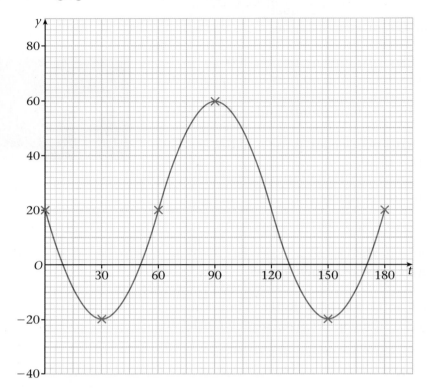

14 The diagram shows part of the graph of the function $y = f(x)$.
The function has a local maximum at $(1, 16)$.

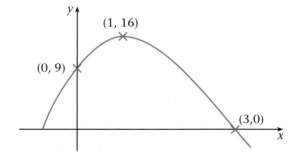

(a) Write down a maximum for $f(x) + 3$.

(b) Write down a maximum for $f(x + 1)$.

(c) Write down a maximum for $2f(x)$.

(d) Write down a solution for
    (i) $f(x - 3) = 0$
    (ii) $2f(-x) = 0$

Summary of key points

1 In a **cubic function** the highest power of x is x^3.

2 The number in front of the x^3 is called the **coefficient** of x^3.

3 The graph of a general cubic function is like this if the coefficient of x^3 is positive:

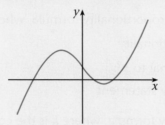

and like this if the coefficient of x^3 is negative:

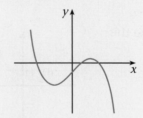

4 Graphs of cubic functions have rotational symmetry.

5 To find the **reciprocal** of a number or expression, divide it into 1.

6 The graph of $y = \frac{1}{x}$ is like this:

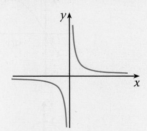

7 The symbol $\propto$ means 'is proportional to'.

8 $y \propto x$ means that y is directly proportional to x.

9 When a graph connecting two quantities is a straight line through the origin, then one quantity is directly proportional to the other.

10 When y is directly proportional to x, you can write a proportionality statement and a formula connecting y and x:
   ○ $y \propto x$ is the proportionality statement
   ○ $y = kx$ is the proportionality formula, where k is the constant of proportionality.

11 When y is directly proportional to the square of x:
   ○ $y \propto x^2$ is the proportionality statement
   ○ $y = kx^2$ is the proportionality formula, where k is the constant of proportionality.

12 When y is directly proportional to the cube of x:
- $y \propto x^3$ is the proportionality statement
- $y = kx^3$ is the proportionality formula, where k is the constant of proportionality.

13 When y is inversely proportional to x:
- $y \propto \dfrac{1}{x}$ is the proportionality statement
- $y = k \times \dfrac{1}{x}$ or $y = \dfrac{k}{x}$ is the proportionality formula, where k is the constant of inverse proportionality.

14 When y is inversely proportional to x^2:
- $y \propto \dfrac{1}{x^2}$ is the proportionality statement
- $y = \dfrac{k}{x^2}$ is the proportionality formula, where k is the constant of inverse proportionality.

15 The function a^x, where a is a positive constant and x is a variable, is called an **exponential function**.

16 The graph of $y = a^x (a > 1)$ is like this:

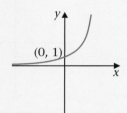

17 The graph of $y = \sin x$ is like this:

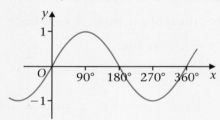

18 The graph of $y = \cos x$ is like this:

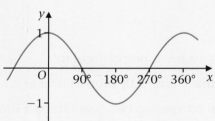

19 A **function** is a rule which shows how one set of numbers relates to another set.

> $f(x)$, which denotes the output, is read as 'f of x'.

20 The graph of $y = x + a$ is the graph of $y = x$ translated a units vertically in the **positive** y direction if $a > 0$
$\qquad\qquad\qquad\qquad$ **negative** y direction if $a < 0$.

21 The graph of $y = x^2 + a$ is the graph of $y = x^2$ translated a units vertically in the **positive** y direction if $a > 0$
$\qquad\qquad\qquad\qquad$ **negative** y direction if $a < 0$.

22 The graph of $y = x^3 + a$ is the graph of $y = x^3$ translated a units
vertically in the **positive** y direction if $a > 0$
negative y direction if $a < 0$.

23 The graph of $y = \frac{1}{x} + a$ is the graph of $y = \frac{1}{x}$ translated a units
vertically in the **positive** y direction if $a > 0$
negative y direction if $a < 0$.

24 For any function f, the graph of $y = f(x) + a$ is the
graph of $y = f(x)$ translated a units vertically in
the **positive** y direction if $a > 0$
negative y direction if $a < 0$.

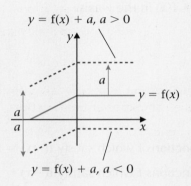

25 The graph of $y = (x + a)^2$ is the graph of $y = x^2$ translated
a units horizontally in the **negative** x direction if $a > 0$
positive x direction if $a < 0$.

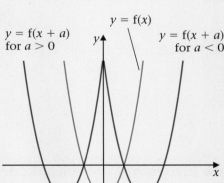

26 The **vertex** of the parabola $y = (x + a)^2$ is at the
point $(-a, 0)$.

27 To sketch the graph of $y = x^2 + bx + c$, complete
the square and apply a double translation to the
parabola $y = x^2$.

28 The graph of $y = f(x + a) + b$ is the graph of $y = f(x)$ translated
a units horizontally (in the **negative** x direction if $a > 0$)
(in the **positive** x direction if $a < 0$)
and then translated b units vertically (**upwards** if $b > 0$)
(**downwards** if $b < 0$).

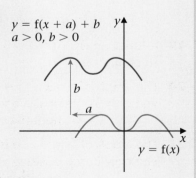

29 For any function f, the graph of $y = -f(x)$ is obtained by reflecting $y = f(x)$ in the x-axis.

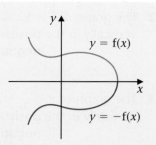

30 For any function f, the graph of $y = f(-x)$ is obtained by reflecting $y = f(x)$ in the y-axis.

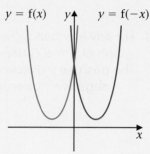

31 Functions f which satisfy $f(-x) = f(x)$ are called **even functions**.

32 Functions f which satisfy $f(-x) = -f(x)$ are called **odd functions**.

11 Transformations

11.1 Translation

- A **translation** moves every point on a shape the same distance and direction. A translation is described by a **vector** $\binom{x}{y}$.

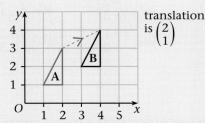

translation is $\binom{2}{1}$

- After a translation the object and image are exactly the same shape and size. They are **congruent**.

Example 1

Write down the vector describing the translation that maps **A** to **B**.

The translation is $\left(\begin{smallmatrix} 4 \\ -5 \end{smallmatrix}\right)$.

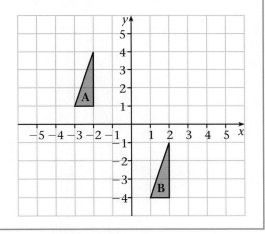

Exercise 11A

1 Write the vector describing the translation that maps **A** onto each of these other shapes.

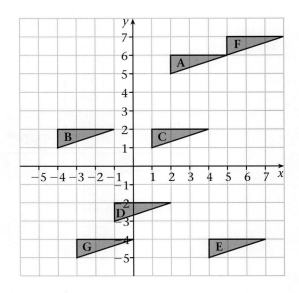

2 Use graph paper or squared paper.

Draw a set of axes and label each one from -7 to $+7$.

Draw a quadrilateral **Q** with vertices $A(-1, 2)$, $B(-3, 3)$, $C(1, 4)$ and $D(1, 2)$.

Translate **Q** using each of these vectors.

(a) $\begin{pmatrix} 2 \\ 1 \end{pmatrix}$ (b) $\begin{pmatrix} -1 \\ 1 \end{pmatrix}$ (c) $\begin{pmatrix} -2 \\ -3 \end{pmatrix}$ (d) $\begin{pmatrix} 4 \\ -1 \end{pmatrix}$

(e) $\begin{pmatrix} 1 \\ -1 \end{pmatrix}$ (f) $\begin{pmatrix} 3 \\ 0 \end{pmatrix}$ (g) $\begin{pmatrix} -1 \\ -2 \end{pmatrix}$ (h) $\begin{pmatrix} -2 \\ 3 \end{pmatrix}$

11.2 Reflection

- A **reflection** in a **line of symmetry** produces a mirror image.
- The image and object are equal distances from the mirror line.
- You describe a reflection by giving the equation of the mirror line.
- After a reflection the object and image are congruent.

Example 2

On the diagram draw a reflection of the shape in
(a) $y = x$ and (b) $y = -x$.
Label them **P** and **Q**.

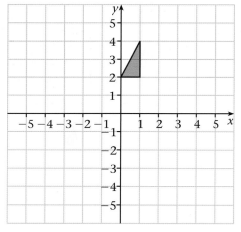

(a) (b)

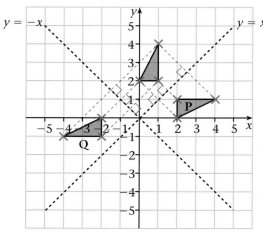

Draw in the lines $y = x$ and $y = -x$.

Take each vertex on the object and locate its image by drawing a line perpendicular to the line of symmetry. Join the points to produce the image.

- Regular polygons have the same number of lines of symmetry as they do sides.

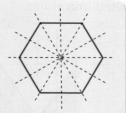

- A **plane of symmetry** divides a 3-D shape into two halves, and one is the mirror image of the other.

Example 3

Draw in all the planes of symmetry on this shape.

There are 3 possible planes.

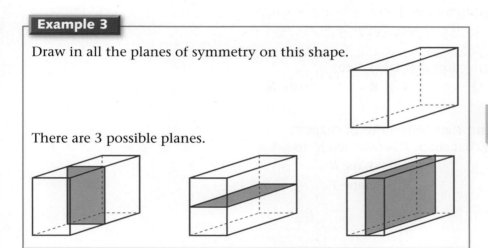

Shade the planes so that they show clearly.

Exercise 11B

1 Copy the diagram.

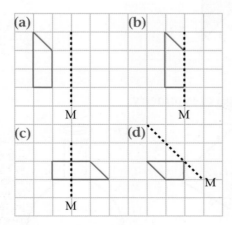

Reflect each shape in the mirror line M.

2 Shape **A** has been reflected four times.

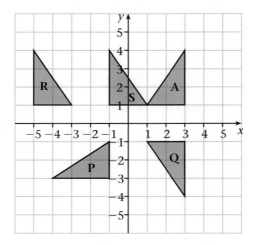

Describe fully the reflection that takes **A** to

(a) **P**   (b) **Q**   (c) **R**   (d) **S**

3 The shapes *Q*, *R*, *S* and *T* are reflections of shape *P*.
Write down the line that shape *P* is reflected in to get

(a) shape *Q*   (b) shape *R*
(c) shape *S*   (d) shape *T*

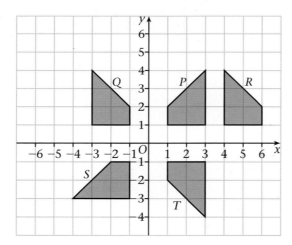

4 Copy each shape and draw in its planes of symmetry.

(a) 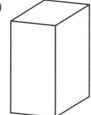   (b)    (c)

11.3 Rotation

- A **rotation** is described by giving
  - ○ a centre of rotation
  - ○ an amount of turn
  - ○ a direction of turn.

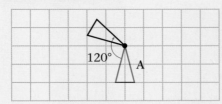

Triangle A is turned
120° clockwise about a
centre of rotation.

A clockwise direction may be indicated by a negative sign, and an
anticlockwise direction by a positive sign.

- After a rotation the object and image are **congruent**.

Example 4

Describe the transformation
which takes **A** to **B**.

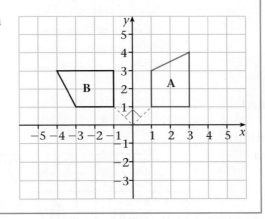

You can use tracing
paper to help you find
the angle and centre of
rotation.

Rotation through
90° anticlockwise with
centre (0, 0).

Example 5

Rotate shape **A** about the
origin through −90°.

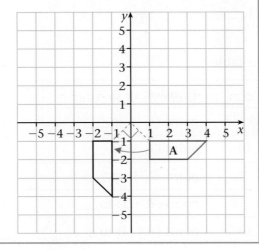

Rotate each vertex of **A**
through 90° clockwise.

- A 2-D shape with **rotational symmetry** looks the same as in its starting position two or more times during a full turn.
- The **order** of rotational symmetry is the number of times the original appearance is repeated in a full turn.
- The order of rotational symmetry of a regular polygon is the same as the number of sides.

Exercise 11C

1 Copy this diagram. Transform shape **R** by each of these rotations.

   (a) −270° with centre (0, 0)
   (b) +90° with centre (2, 1)
   (c) +180° with centre (−1, 2)
   (d) −90° with centre (0, 0)

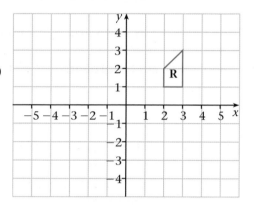

2 Shape **T** has been rotated four times. Describe fully the rotation that takes **T** to position

   (a) **A**   (b) **B**
   (c) **C**   (d) **D**

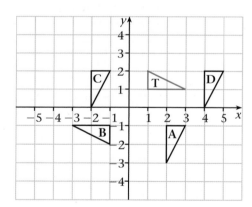

3 Copy and complete this table.

Rotation	Transforms
90° with centre (0, 0)	point (1, 2) to ___
−180° with centre (0, 0)	point (3, 5) to ___
−90° with centre (−1, 2)	point (2, 3) to ___
270° with centre (2, 4)	point (2, −1) to ___
−270° with centre (0, 0)	point (−1, 4) to ___

4 Write down the order of rotational symmetry of each shape.

(a)

(b)

(c)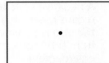

(d)

11.4 Enlargement

- An **enlargement** changes the size but not the shape of an object. The **scale factor** of the enlargement is the multiplier for the lengths.
- An enlargement is described by giving
  - the centre of enlargement
  - the scale factor.
- An enlargement with a scale factor smaller than 1 gives a reduced image.
- An enlargement with a negative scale factor means measuring in the opposite direction from the centre of enlargement.
- After an enlargement the object and image are **similar**.

Example 6

Enlarge trapezium $ABCD$ with scale factor $1\frac{1}{2}$ using the origin as the centre of enlargement.

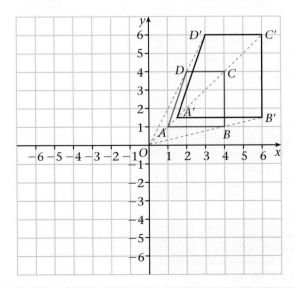

An enlargement with scale factor $1\frac{1}{2}$ multiplies the length of each side of the quadrilateral by $1\frac{1}{2}$ and each distance from the origin by $1\frac{1}{2}$.

$OA \times 1\frac{1}{2} = OA'$
$OB \times 1\frac{1}{2} = OB'$
$OC \times 1\frac{1}{2} = OC'$
$OD \times 1\frac{1}{2} = OD'$

$A(1, 1) \rightarrow A'(1\frac{1}{2}, 1\frac{1}{2})$
$B(4, 1) \rightarrow B'(6, 1\frac{1}{2})$
$C(4, 4) \rightarrow C'(6, 6)$
$D(2, 4) \rightarrow D'(3, 6)$

Example 7

Enlarge triangle *ABC* by scale factor −1 with centre (0, 0).

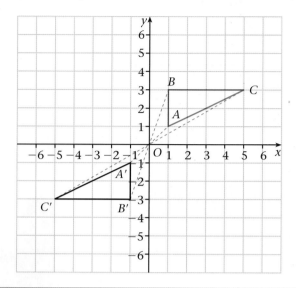

A negative scale factor means measuring in the opposite direction from the centre of enlargement.

$OA \times -1 = OA'$
$OB \times -1 = OB'$
$OC \times -1 = OC'$

Example 8

Work out the scale factor and centre of enlargement for these two similar triangles.

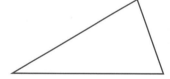

Similar triangles are the same shape but different sizes. One is an enlargement of the other.

Measure the lengths of two corresponding sides of the triangles. Divide one into the other. This gives the scale factor.

Small to large is ×2   Large to small is $\times\frac{1}{2}$

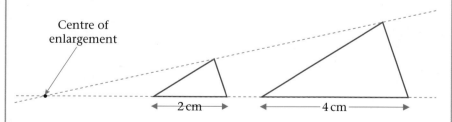

Centre of enlargement

←—2 cm—→   ←——4 cm——→

Join the corresponding vertices (corners) of the triangle with straight lines. Where the lines cross is the centre of enlargement.

Exercise 11D

1 Copy this diagram.
Draw the enlargement of the shape with

(a) centre (0, 0) and scale factor 2

(b) centre (1, 2) and scale factor 2

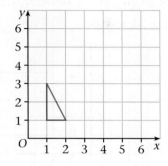

2 Copy this diagram.

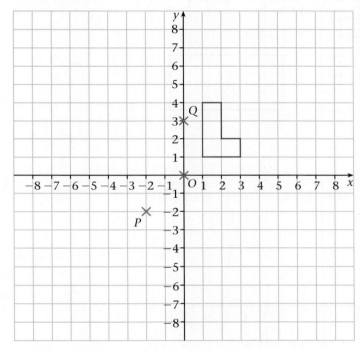

Enlarge the shape by

(a) scale factor 2 with centre O

(b) scale factor -1 with centre P

(c) scale factor $+0.5$ with centre O

(d) scale factor $1\frac{1}{2}$ with centre Q

(e) scale factor -1.5 with centre O

3 Look at the diagrams below.
Describe the enlargement that transforms

(a) **A to B**   (b) **A to C**   (c) **A to D**

(d) **A to E**   (e) **A to F**

> (b) and (e) are negative enlargements

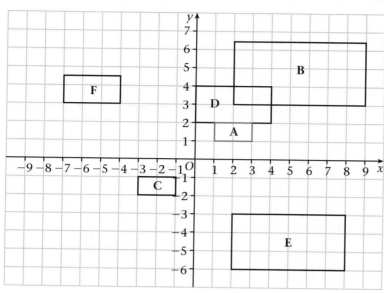

4 Copy this diagram.

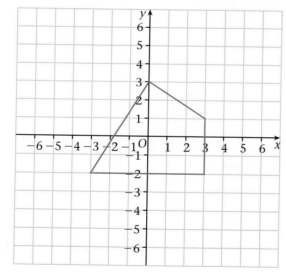

Enlarge the shape by scale factor -2 with centre $(0, 0)$.

5 Find the perimeter of the shape in question **2**.
Find the perimeters of your enlarged shapes.
What do you notice?

6 Find the area of the shape in question **2**.
Find the areas of your enlarged shapes.
What do you notice?

11.5 Combined transformations

○ 7 Transformations on a coordinate grid

- Transformations can be **combined** by performing one transformation and then another transformation on the image.

Example 9

(a) Reflect the shape in the *x*-axis.
(b) Reflect the image in the line $y = x$.
(c) Describe the single transformation equivalent to this combination of transformations.

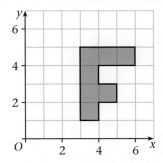

(a) (b)

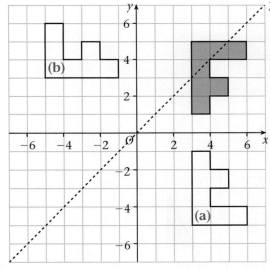

(c) The single transformation is a rotation through 90° anticlockwise about the origin.

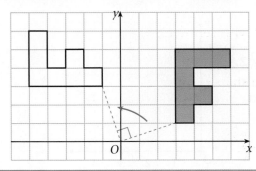

Example 10

(a) Reflect shape **A** in the
    y-axis. Label the image **B**.

(b) Reflect the image in the
    line $x = 4$; call it **C**.

(c) Describe the single
    transformation which
    maps **A** onto **C**.

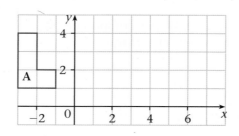

(a) (b)

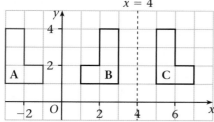

(c) The single transformation which maps **A** onto **C** is the
    translation $\begin{pmatrix} 8 \\ 0 \end{pmatrix}$.

- A reflection followed by a reflection is equivalent to
  - a rotation if the reflection lines are not parallel
  - a translation if the reflection lines are parallel.

Exercise 11E

1 Copy the diagram.
   (a) Reflect the triangle in the y-axis.
   (b) Reflect the image in the x-axis.
   (c) Describe the single transformation
       that is equivalent to (a) followed
       by (b).

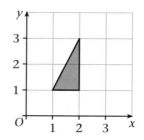

2 Copy the flag diagram.
   (a) Reflect the flag in the x-axis.
   (b) Reflect the image in the line $y = 2$.
   (c) Describe the single transformation
       that is equivalent to (a) followed
       by (b).

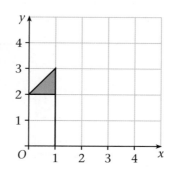

3 Copy and complete the coordinate grid so that x goes from -4 to 4 and y goes from -4 to 4.
Copy the triangle **A**.

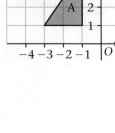

(a) Reflect **A** in the x-axis. Label the image **B**.

(b) Rotate **A** through $180°$ about the origin. Label the image **C**.

(c) Describe fully the transformation that maps **B** onto **C**.

4 Copy and complete the coordinate grid so that x and y both go from -10 to 10.
Copy the rectangle **D**.

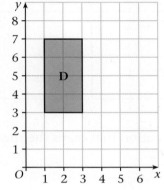

(a) Enlarge rectangle **D** with centre of enlargement $(0, 0)$ and scale factor -1.

(b) Describe this transformation in another way.

5 (a) Start with the same flag as in question **2**. Reflect the flag in the line $y = x$.

(b) Rotate the image through $90°$ anticlockwise about the origin.

(c) Describe the single transformation that is equivalent to (a) followed by (b).

6 (a) Start with the same triangle as in question **3**. Rotate the triangle through $-90°$ about the centre $(0, 0)$.

(b) Reflect the image in the line $y = x$.

(c) Describe the single transformation that is equivalent to (a) followed by (b).

> Remember: $-90°$ is the same as $90°$ clockwise.

Mixed exercise 11

1 How many planes of symmetry does a cube have?

2 Copy these diagrams and draw in all the planes of symmetry.

(a)

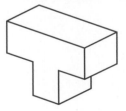

'T' made from 4 cubes

(b)

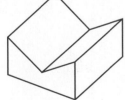

Prism with symmetrical cross-section

(c)

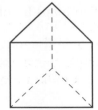

Equilateral triangular prism

3 Copy and complete this table to summarise the congruence and similarity of transformations.

	Reflection	Rotation	Translation	Enlargement
Sides stay the same length	Yes			
Angles stay the same size				
Orientation stays the same				
Image congruent				
Image similar		Yes		

4 (a) Describe the translation that maps the shaded shape onto each of **A**, **B** and **C**.

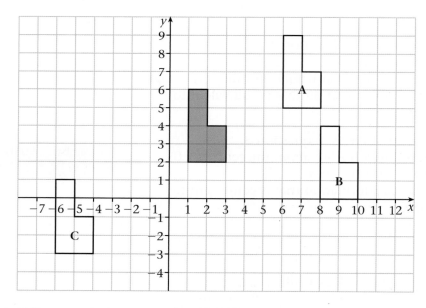

(b) What translation maps **C** onto **B**?

(c) What translation maps **B** onto **C**?

5 Copy the diagram.
   Draw each of these translations of the shape.

   (a) $\begin{pmatrix} 5 \\ 3 \end{pmatrix}$ (b) $\begin{pmatrix} 2 \\ -3 \end{pmatrix}$ (c) $\begin{pmatrix} -2 \\ 4 \end{pmatrix}$ (d) $\begin{pmatrix} -4 \\ -1 \end{pmatrix}$

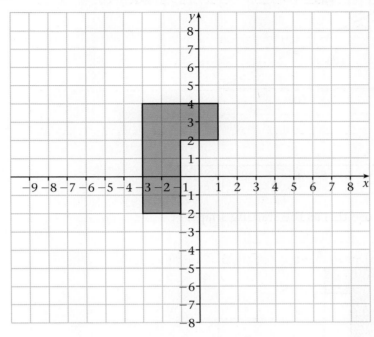

6 Copy the diagram and enlarge the shape by a scale factor of
   $2\frac{1}{2}$, using each of the three centres in turn.

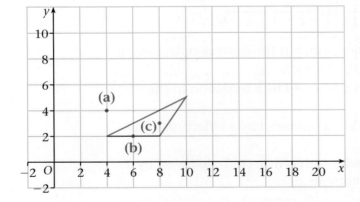

7 Copy the diagram and enlarge the shape by a scale factor of $\frac{1}{3}$, using each of the four centres in turn.

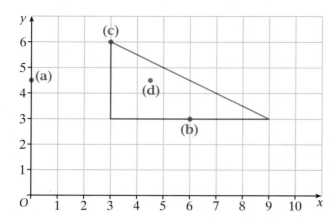

8 For each of parts **(a)**–**(f)** use this as the starting shape:

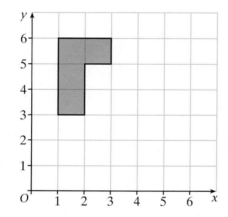

Find the single transformation which is the equivalent to each of these combinations of transformations.

(a) A reflection in the y-axis, followed by a reflection in the x-axis.

(b) A reflection in the line $y = x$, followed by a reflection in the x-axis.

(c) A rotation of 90° clockwise with centre (3, 3), followed by a rotation of 180° with centre (6, 3).

(d) A rotation of 90° clockwise with centre (1, 2), followed by a rotation of 270° clockwise with centre (4, 1).

(e) An enlargement with scale factor 3 and centre (0, 3), followed by an enlargement with scale factor $\frac{1}{2}$ and centre (3, 3).

(f) A translation of $\begin{pmatrix} 3 \\ -1 \end{pmatrix}$, followed by a half turn with centre (4, 2).

Summary of key points

1 A **translation** moves every point on a shape the same distance and direction.
  A translation is described by a **vector** $\begin{pmatrix} x \\ y \end{pmatrix}$.

2 After a translation the image and the object are exactly the same shape and size.
  They are **congruent**.

3 A **reflection** in a **line of symmetry** produces a mirror image.

4 The image and object are equal distances from the mirror line.

5 You describe a reflection by giving the equation of the mirror line.

6 After a reflection the object and image are **congruent**.

7 Regular polygons have the same number of lines of symmetry as they do sides.

8 A **plane of symmetry** divides a 3-D shape into two halves, and one is the mirror image of the other.

9 A **rotation** is described by giving
  ○ a centre of rotation
  ○ an amount of turn
  ○ a direction of turn.
  A clockwise direction may be indicated by a negative sign, and an anticlockwise direction by a positive sign.

10 After a rotation the object and image are **congruent**.

11 A 2-D shape with **rotational symmetry** looks the same as in its starting position two or more times during a full turn.

12 The **order** of rotational symmetry is the number of times the original appearance is repeated in a full turn.

13 The order of rotational symmetry of a regular polygon is the same as the number of sides.

14 An **enlargement** changes the size but not the shape of an object. The **scale factor** of the enlargement is the multiplier for the lengths.

15 An enlargement is described by giving
  ○ the centre of enlargement
  ○ the scale factor.

16 An enlargement with a scale factor smaller than 1 gives a reduced image.

17 An enlargement with a negative scale factor means measuring in the opposite direction from the centre of enlargement.

18 After an enlargement the object and image are **similar**.

19 Transformations can be **combined** by performing one transformation and then another transformation on the image.

20 A reflection followed by a reflection is equivalent to
  ○ a rotation if the reflection lines are not parallel
  ○ a translation if the reflection lines are parallel.

12 Bearings, constructions and properties of shape

12.1 Bearings

- A **bearing** is an angle measured clockwise from North.
  It is always a three-figure number.

> Bearings were also covered in Chapter 7 of Higher Unit 3.

Example 1

Find the bearing of A from B.

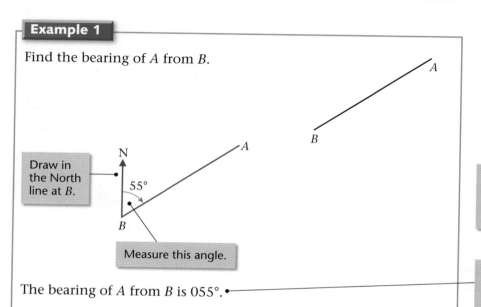

Draw in the North line at B.

Measure this angle.

'From B' means, stand at B and face North. What angle do you need to turn clockwise to face A?

The bearing of A from B is 055°.

For a bearing like this, add a zero to give it three figures.

Exercise 12A

1 Measure and write down the bearing of
   (a) A from B
   (b) B from A.

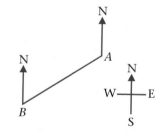

2 Measure and write down the bearing of
   (a) B from C
   (b) C from A
   (c) A from B
   (d) B from A.

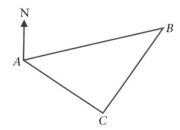

3 Using the map of East Anglia
   find the bearing of

   (a) Great Yarmouth from
      Norwich

   (b) Colchester from
      London

   (c) Cambridge from
      Luton

   (d) Cambridge from
      Kings Lynn

   (e) Spalding from
      Kings Lynn

   (f) Boston from Norwich

   (g) Ipswich from
      Bury St Edmunds

   (h) Southend from Boston.

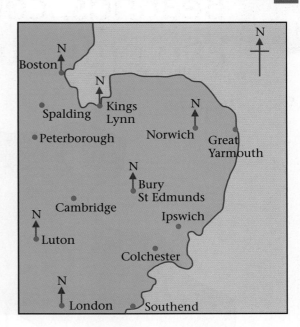

12.2 Maps and scale drawings

- A **scale** is a ratio which shows the relationship between a length on a drawing and the actual length in real life.
- A scale can be represented as a ratio (e.g. 1 : 25 000) or sometimes using an equals sign (e.g. 1 cm = 5 km).

Example 2

The scale of a map is 1 : 25 000.
(a) What is the actual distance between two points which are 5.6 cm apart on the map?
(b) Two places are 9 km apart.
    How far apart will they be on the map?

(a) Actual distance apart = 5.6 × 25 000 cm
                   = 5.6 × 250 m
                   = 1400 m
                   = 1.4 km

> 25 000 cm = 250 m

(b) 9 km = 9000 m = 900 000 cm
    Distance on the map = 900 000 ÷ 25 000
                       = 900 ÷ 25
                       = 36 cm

> First change to centimetres.

Exercise 12B

1 The scale of this map is 1 cm = 2 km.

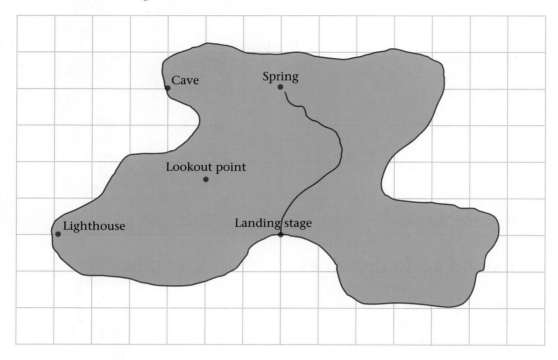

Find the actual distance between

(a) the landing stage and the lighthouse

(b) the landing stage and the spring

(c) the landing stage and the cave

(d) the landing stage and the lookout point

(e) the lighthouse and the lookout point.

2 (a) Construct an accurate drawing for this sketch.
Use a scale of 1 cm = 5 km.

> Use a ruler and
> protractor.

(b) How far is *A* from *C* in real life?

3 Copy and complete the distance chart.
Give the distances in km.

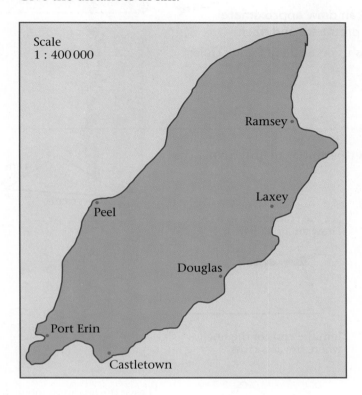

Scale
1 : 400 000

Ramsey

Laxey

Peel

Douglas

Port Erin

Castletown

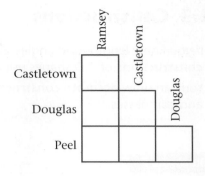

4 Make a sketch and construct an accurate drawing of the following
journey. Use a scale of 1 cm = 40 km.

170 km on a bearing of 120° followed by 220 km on a bearing
of 050°.

5 Make a sketch and construct an accurate drawing of the following
journey. Use a scale of 1 cm = 12 km.

66 km on a bearing of 250° followed by 78 km on a bearing
of 320°.

6 A surveyor's plan has a scale of 1 : 2500.
 (a) A plot of land measures 1 cm by 13 mm on the plan.
 Work out the actual size.
 (b) A road which is 10 m wide and 125 m long is to be marked
 on this plan. Work out the measurements on the plan.

7 The scale of an Ordnance Survey map is 1 : 50 000.
On the map Brownsea Island measures 4 cm by 2.5 cm.
Also, Bournemouth pier is 4.5 mm long.
Work out the real distances.

12.3 Constructions

⊙ 7 Constructing a triangle
7 Common constructions

- If you know lengths and angles, you can draw **approximate constructions** of 2-D shapes using a protractor and ruler.
- You can draw **accurate constructions** using a straight edge (ruler) and compasses.

Example 3

Construct a triangle with sides of length 4 cm, 5 cm and 6 cm.

Draw the longest side using a ruler.

Set the compasses to 5 cm. Draw an arc like this:

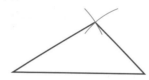

Set the compasses to 4 cm. Draw another arc like this:

Join the ends of the line to where the arcs cross.

Leave the arcs in to show the construction.

- **Perpendicular** lines meet at right angles.
- The **perpendicular bisector** of a line meets it at right angles and cuts it in half.

Example 4

Using a straight edge and compasses, construct accurately the perpendicular bisector of the line segment AB, which is 6 cm in length. Label the midpoint of the line segment AB with a letter M.

A ————————————— B
_____ 6 cm

A •————————————————— B

Draw a line segment 6 cm long and label its ends A and B.

Set the compasses to any radius greater than 3 cm (6 cm ÷ 2).With the point at A, draw arcs above and below the line segment, roughly where you expect the bisector to be.

A •————————————————— B

Keep the compasses at the same radius and repeat the process from B. Label the points where the arcs cross P and Q.

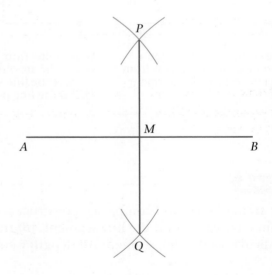

Draw a line segment joining P and Q. This is the perpendicular bisector of AB. Label with an M the point where the bisector crosses the line segment AB.
M is the midpoint of AB.

Example 5

Using a straight edge and compasses, construct accurately the line from P that is perpendicular to the line segment AB, which is 4 cm in length.

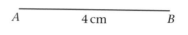

Set the compasses to any radius greater than the distance from P to AB. With the point at P, draw two arcs on the line AB.

Move the compass point to where one arc crosses AB, and draw a new arc roughly where you expect the perpendicular to be.

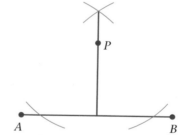

Keep the compasses at the same radius and repeat the process from the other arc on the line segment AB.

Draw a line from the point where the arcs cross through P to meet the line segment AB. This is the line perpendicular to AB.

Alternative method:
Set the compasses to the distance AP and draw an arc below the line, from A.

Then set the compasses to the distance BP and draw another arc below the line from B, crossing the other arc.

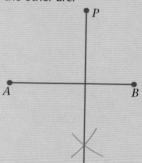

Draw a line from P to the point of intersection of the arcs.

This line is perpendicular to the line segment AB.

Example 6

Using a straight edge and compasses, construct accurately the line from P (any point on the line segment AB) that is perpendicular to the line segment AB (length 6 cm).

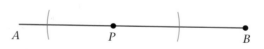

Draw a line segment AB that is 6 cm in length. Mark a point P on the line.

Set your compasses to any radius less than AP and PB. With the point at P, draw two arcs to cut the line segment AB.

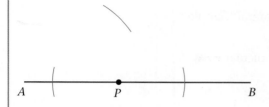

Make the radius on the compasses longer. Move the compass point to where one arc crosses *AB*, and draw a new arc roughly where you expect the perpendicular to be.

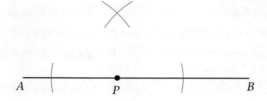

Keep the compasses at the same radius and repeat the process from the other arc on the line segment *AB*.

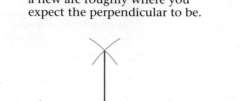

Draw a line from *P* to the point where the new arcs cross. This is the line from *P* that is perpendicular to the line segment *AB*.

• An **angle bisector** is a line that divides an angle into two halves.
• You can use a ruler and compasses to construct an angle bisector.

angle bisector

Example 7

Construct the angle bisector of angle *A*.

Put the compass point at *A*. Draw an arc that crosses both lines.

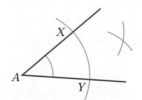

Put the compass point at *X*, then keeping the distance the same put it at *Y*, drawing two arcs that cross.

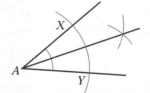

Draw a line to bisect the angle.

- You can construct a 60° angle by constructing an equilateral triangle.
- You can construct a 30° angle by bisecting a 60° angle.
- You can construct a 90° angle by constructing a perpendicular to a line.
- You can construct a 45° angle by bisecting a 90° angle.

Exercise 12C

1 Construct a triangle *ABC* with angle *A* = 40°, angle *B* = 50° and *AB* = 6 cm.

Use protractor and ruler.

For questions **2–7** use a straight edge and compasses.

2 Construct accurately an equilateral triangle *ABC* with side 4 cm.

3 Construct accurately the perpendicular bisectors of the following line segments.
  (a) *AB*, length 4 cm
  (b) *PQ*, length 7 cm
  (c) *RS*, length 11 cm

4 Draw a line segment *AB* that is 8 cm long. Label a point about 5 cm above the line segment with a letter *P*.
  Construct accurately the line from *P* that is perpendicular to the line segment *AB*.

5 Construct accurately on the line segment *AB*, which is 9 cm in length, the perpendiculars from the points *P*, *Q* and *R*, which are 3 cm, 4 cm and 6 cm respectively from point *A*.
  Draw a separate construction for each part.

6 Draw any two line segments *ABC* and *MBN*.

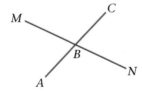

Use a straight edge and compasses to construct the angle bisector of angle *ABN*.

7 Construct these angles accurately.
  (a) 90°   **(b)** 60°   **(c)** 30°   **(d)** 45°   **(e)** 135°

12.4 Loci

○ 7 Loci demonstrator

• A **locus** is a set of points that obey a given rule. For example, in dressage, part of the test is to follow the path shown by the red line.
All points obey the rule:
  Each point is equidistant from *B* and *E*.
This path is called the **locus** of the points.

The plural of locus is **loci**.

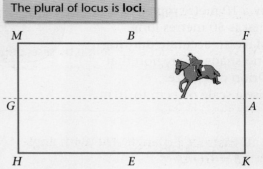

• The locus of the points equidistant from two points *A* and *B* is the perpendicular bisector of the line segment *AB*.

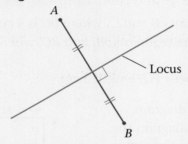

• The locus of the points a constant distance from a fixed point is a circle.

• The locus of the points a constant distance from a line segment *AB* is a pair of lines parallel to *AB* joined with semicircles whose centres are at *A* and *B*.

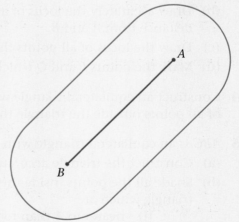

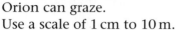

Example 8

Orion the horse is attached by a 10 metre rope to a bar that is 50 metres long. Make an accurate drawing and shade the region that Orion can graze. Use a scale of 1 cm to 10 m.

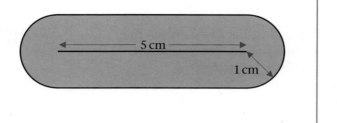

Exercise 12D

1 Construct the loci of the following points.

    (a) 4 cm from a point A

    (b) equidistant from the points B and C, where BC is 4 cm

    (c) equidistant from two line segments AB and BC, where angle ABC is 45°

    (d) 3 cm from the line segment PQ, length 5 cm

2 Make a full-size copy of this diagram.

    (a) Draw accurately on the diagram the locus of points which are the same distance from the line OA and the line OB.

    (b) Some points are the same distance from the line OA and the line OB and are also 4 cm from the point B. Mark these points with crosses.

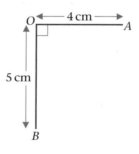

3 In triangle ABC, $AB = 5$ cm, angle $B = 38°$ and angle $A = 61°$.

    (a) Make an accurate drawing of triangle ABC.

    (b) Draw accurately the locus of all points that are the same distance from A and B.

    (c) Draw the locus of all points that are 5 cm from C.

    (d) Mark the points P and Q which are on both loci.

4 Construct an equilateral triangle with side 6 cm. Draw the locus of all points outside the triangle that are 2 cm from the sides.

5 ABC is an equilateral triangle with side 6 cm.

    (a) Construct the triangle accurately.

    (b) Shade all the points inside this triangle which are

            (i) nearer to A than to B

    and   **(ii)** less than 4 cm from C.

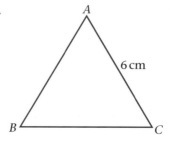

6 *PQR* is a right-angled triangle.

    (a) Construct the triangle accurately.

    (b) Shade all the points that are
            (i) nearer to *QR* than to *PR*
    and   **(ii)** nearer to *QR* than to *PQ*.

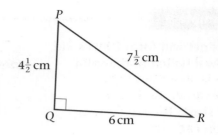

7 *ABCDE* are points on a circle, centre *O*, radius 6 cm.
ABCDE is a regular pentagon.

    (a) Construct this diagram accurately.

    (b) Shade all the points inside the pentagon
    that are
            (i) less than 4 cm from *O*
    and   **(ii)** more than 4 cm from *CD*.

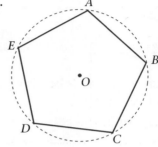

> For more on
> constructing
> regular
> polygons
> see Chapter
> 8 in Higher
> Unit 3.

8 *ABC* is an equilateral triangle with side 5 cm.

    (a) Construct the triangle accurately.

    (b) Shade all the points that are
            (i) more than 3 cm from *B*
    and   **(ii)** nearer to *BC* than to *BA*
    and   **(iii)** inside triangle *ABC*.

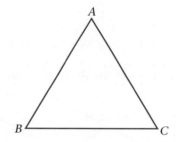

12.5 Nets

> **3** Introducing nets
> **3** Identifying nets

- A **net** is a 2-D shape that can be made into a 3-D shape.

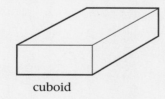

cuboid

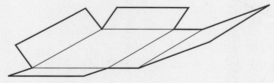

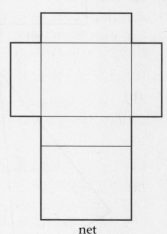

net

- You can construct accurate nets using a straight edge and compasses.

Example 9

This net will form a 3-D solid.
Draw a sketch of the solid.

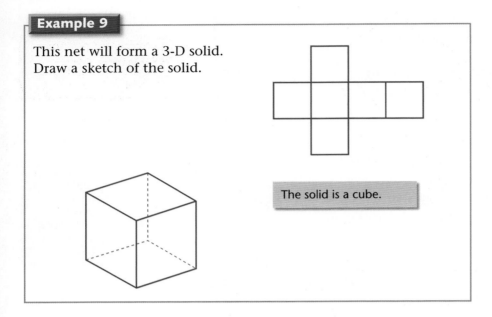

The solid is a cube.

Exercise 12E

You will need a ruler and a pair of compasses.

1 Construct accurate nets for these shapes.

(a)

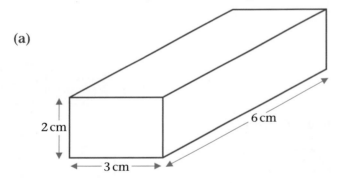

2 cm

6 cm

3 cm

(b)

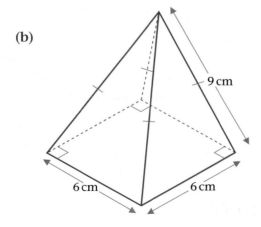

9 cm

6 cm   6 cm

(c)

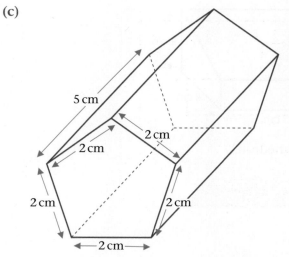

Construct the pentagon by division of a circle (see Chapter 8 in Higher Unit 3).

(d)

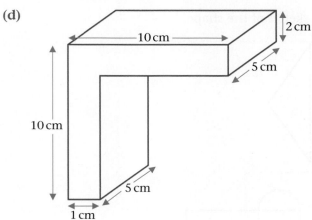

2 These nets will each form a 3-D solid.
Draw a sketch of each solid.

(a)

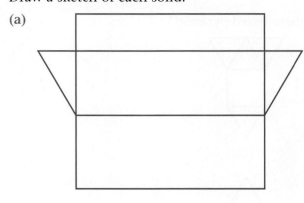

(b)

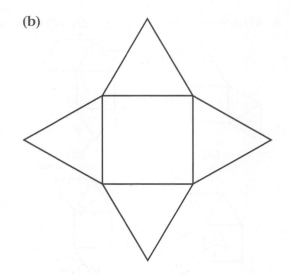

3 Find as many nets as possible which form the same cube.

4 Sketch a net for this prism.
Label all the lengths on
your sketch.

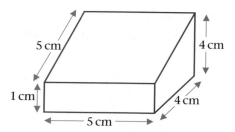

5 Construct an accurate net for a regular tetrahedron.

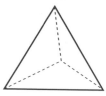

6 What shape will this net make? Draw a sketch of the shape.

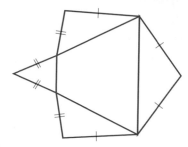

7 Could this be the net of a solid?
Give reasons for your answer.

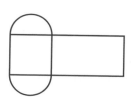

8 Which of these 2-D shapes are nets of a square-based pyramid?

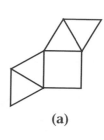

(a)

(b)

(c)

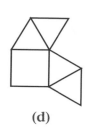

(d)

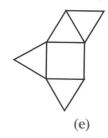

(e)

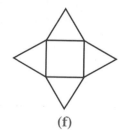

(f)

9 Draw accurate nets for the following 3-D shapes.

   (a) a square-based pyramid, slant height 5 cm and base side 3 cm

   (b) a cube of side 4 cm

   (c) a prism of height 6 cm whose cross-section is an equilateral triangle of side 4 cm

10 Copy and complete this 2-D shape to make it into a net of a cuboid.

12.6 Drawing on isometric grids

Example 10

Sketch a 1 cm cube on isometric paper.

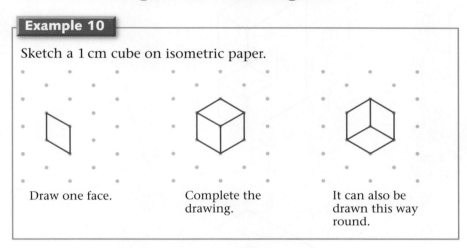

Draw one face.

Complete the drawing.

It can also be drawn this way round.

If you need to show hidden edges, use dotted lines.

Exercise 12F

The diagram shows three ways of drawing a shape on isometric paper.

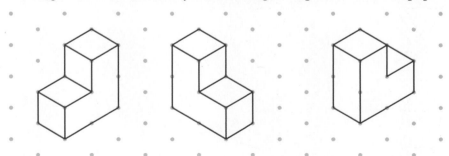

For each drawing on page 194, draw two other representations of the shape.

1

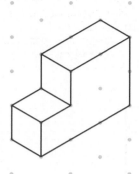

2

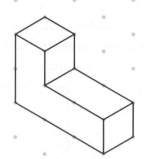

3

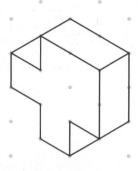

4

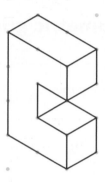

5

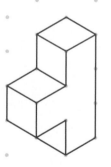

6

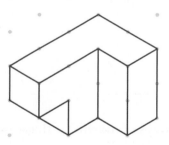

12.7 Plan and elevation

- The **plan** of a solid is the view when seen from above.
- The **front elevation** is the view when seen from the front.
- The **side elevation** is the view when seen from the side.

> 3 Introducing plans and elevations
> 3 Identifying plans and elevations

 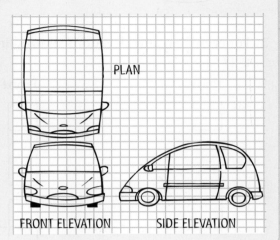

PLAN

FRONT ELEVATION   SIDE ELEVATION

Example 11

Draw the plan and elevations of this shape.

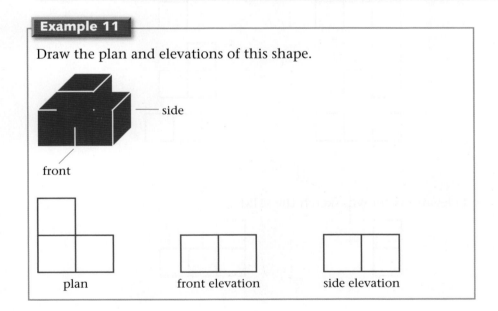

side

front

plan   front elevation   side elevation

Exercise 12G

1 Sketch the plan and elevations of these shapes.

(a)

(b)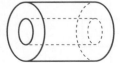

(c)

2 Construct accurately the plan and elevations of these shapes.

(a)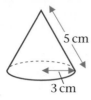

(b)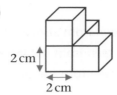

3 For each plan and elevations shown, draw the solid on isometric paper.

Plan	**Front elevation**	**Right side elevation**
(a) 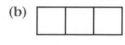		
(b) 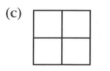		
(c) 		
(d)		

4 For each set of plan and elevations shown, sketch the solid.

(a)

(b)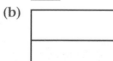

(c)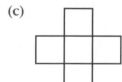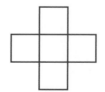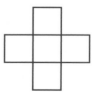

12.8 Polygons

- A **polygon** is a 2-D shape with any number of straight sides.

  This table shows the special names for polygons with a certain number of sides.

Number of sides	Name of polygon
3	triangle
4	quadrilateral
5	pentagon
6	hexagon
7	heptagon
8	octagon
9	nonagon
10	decagon

  The plural of vertex is **vertices**.

- The point where two sides meet is called a **vertex**.

- A polygon is a **regular polygon** if its sides are all the same length and its angles are all the same size.

Regular   Regular   Regular
pentagon   hexagon   octagon

- The sum of the exterior angles of any polygon is 360°.

- For a regular polygon,

  $$\text{Exterior angle} = \frac{360°}{\text{number of sides}}$$

- For a polygon,

  Interior angle + exterior angle = 180°

- The sum of the interior angles of a polygon with n sides is $(n - 2) \times 180°$.

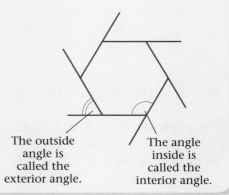

The outside angle is called the exterior angle.

The angle inside is called the interior angle.

Example 12

Work out (a) the exterior angle of a regular octagon
         (b) the interior angle of a regular octagon.

(a) Exterior angle = 360 ÷ 8
                = 45°

A regular octagon has 8 sides and 8 equal exterior angles.

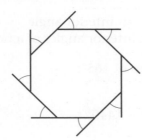

(b) Interior angle = 180° − 45°
$\qquad\qquad\qquad$ = 135°

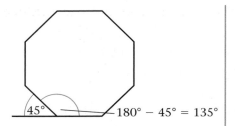

45° $\qquad$ 180° − 45° = 135°

Example 13

A regular polygon has interior angles of 156°.
How many sides does it have?

Each exterior angle = 180° − 156° = 24°
$\qquad$ 360 ÷ 24 = 15
The polygon has 15 sides.

> There are 15 exterior angles.

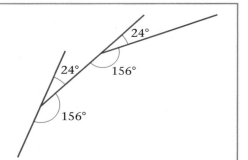

Example 14

Work out the missing angle for this polygon.

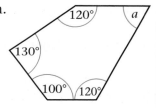

Sum of interior angles = $(n - 2) \times 180° = 3 \times 180°$
$\qquad\qquad\qquad\qquad\qquad$ = 540°
The angles given = 120° + 130° + 100° + 120°
$\qquad\qquad\qquad$ = 470°
So missing angle a = 540° − 470°
$\qquad\qquad\qquad$ = 70°

Exercise 12H

1 A regular nonagon has 9 sides.
$\quad$ Work out the size of
$\quad$ **(a)** an exterior angle $\qquad\qquad$ **(b)** an interior angle.
$\quad$ **(c)** Hence work out the sum of the interior angles of a nonagon.

2 A regular polygon has interior angles of 165°.
$\quad$ How many sides does it have?

3 The angle sum of a regular polygon is 1440°.
$\quad$ How many sides does it have?

4 Work out the size of the missing angles in these quadrilaterals.

(a)
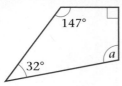

(b)
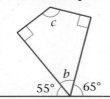

5 Work out the missing angle for each polygon.

(a)
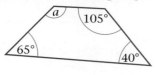

(b)
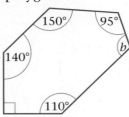

(c)
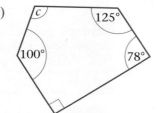

(d)
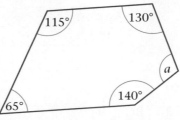

6 Explain why the angle sum of a quadrilateral is 360°.

Divide a quadrilateral into two triangles.

12.9 Similarity

- Two shapes are mathematically **similar** if one is an enlargement of the other.
  Corresponding angles are the same.
  Corresponding lengths are in the same ratio.

- Triangles are similar if one of these facts is true:

  - All corresponding angles are equal:
    $\hat{A} = \hat{X}$
    $\hat{B} = \hat{Y}$
    $\hat{C} = \hat{Z}$

  - All corresponding sides are in the same ratio:
    $\dfrac{PQ}{AB} = \dfrac{QR}{BC} = \dfrac{PR}{AC}$ = scale factor

  - Two pairs of corresponding sides are in the same ratio and the included angles are equal:
    $\dfrac{XY}{DE} = \dfrac{YZ}{EF}$ $\hat{Y} = \hat{E}$

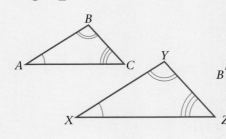

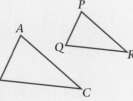

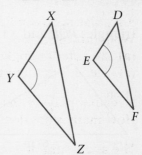

Example 15

ABC and XYZ are similar triangles.
Find the length of **(a)** AC **(b)** XY.

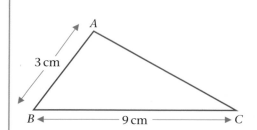

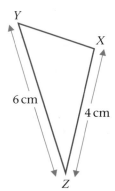

First identify corresponding angles.
Here angle A = angle X
angle B = angle Y
angle C = angle Z

Write the corresponding angles above each other.

A	B	C
X	Y	Z

Triangles $\dfrac{ABC}{XYZ}$ are similar, so

$$\frac{AB}{XY} = \frac{BC}{YZ} = \frac{AC}{XZ} = \frac{9}{6} = \frac{3}{2} \quad \left(\frac{BC}{YZ} = \frac{9}{6}\right)$$

The scale factor is $\frac{3}{2}$ or $1\frac{1}{2}$.

(a) $\dfrac{AC}{XZ} = \dfrac{AC}{4} = \dfrac{3}{2}$

$XZ = 4$ cm

$$AC = \frac{3}{2} \times 4 = 6 \text{ cm}$$

(b) $\dfrac{AB}{XY} = \dfrac{3}{XY} = \dfrac{3}{2}$

$AB = 3$ cm

$$XY = 3 \div \frac{3}{2}$$

$$= 3 \times \frac{2}{3}$$

$$= 2 \text{ cm}$$

Exercise 12I

1 Triangles PQR and XYZ are similar.

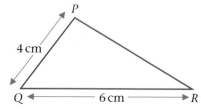

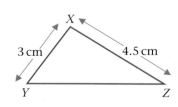

Find **(a)** YZ **(b)** PR.

2 Triangles *ABC* and *DEF* are similar.

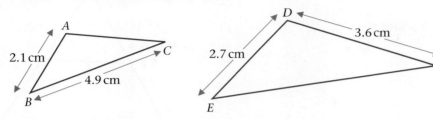

Find **(a)** *AC* **(b)** *EF*.

3 These rectangles are all similar.
Calculate the lengths marked by letters.

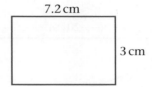

(a)

(b)   **(c)**

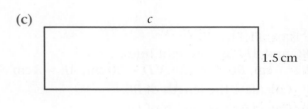

4 Identify the two similar triangles in each set of three.

(a) **(i)**   **(ii)**   **(iii)**

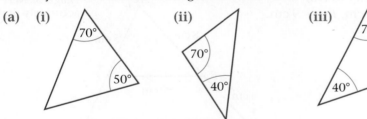

(b) **(i)**   **(ii)**   **(iii)**

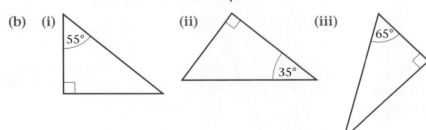

(c) **(i)**   **(ii)**   **(iii)**

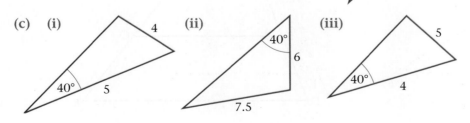

5 (a) Explain why the two triangles in this diagram are similar.

(b) Find the lengths of x and y.

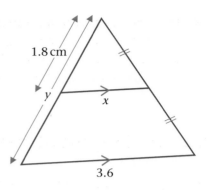

6

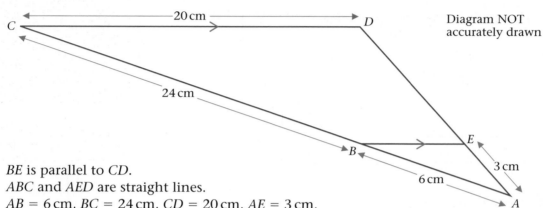

Diagram NOT accurately drawn

BE is parallel to *CD*.
ABC and *AED* are straight lines.
AB = 6 cm, *BC* = 24 cm, *CD* = 20 cm, *AE* = 3 cm.

(a) Calculate the length of *BE*.

(b) Calculate the length of *DE*. [E]

7 In the triangle *ADE*, *BC* is parallel to *DE*,
AB = 8 cm, *AC* = 5 cm, *BD* = 4 cm, *BC* = 9 cm.

(a) Work out the length of *DE*.

(b) Work out the length of *CE*.

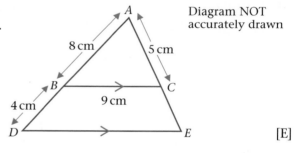

Diagram NOT accurately drawn

[E]

8 *BC* is parallel to *DE*.
AB is twice as long as *BD*.
AD = 36 cm and *AC* = 27 cm.

(a) Work out the length of *AB*.

(b) Work out the length of *AE*.

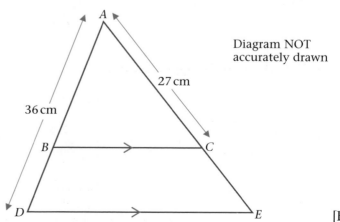

Diagram NOT accurately drawn

[E]

9 **(a)** Are any two squares mathematically similar?
Explain your reasoning.

(b) How about any two rectangles?

(c) How about any two circles?

12.10 Congruent triangles

3 Congruence
3 Identifying congruent shapes

- Shapes that are exactly the same size and shape are **congruent**.
- To prove that triangles are congruent you need to show that they satisfy one of these conditions.

Two sides and the enclosed angle the same.

○ **SAS (side, angle, side)**

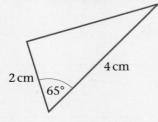 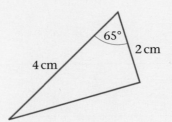

○ **ASA (angle, side, angle)**

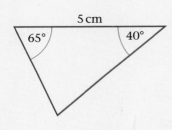 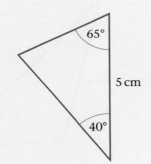

○ **SSS (side, side, side)**

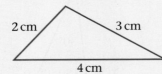 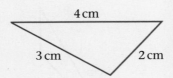

○ **RHS (right angle, hypotenuse, side)**

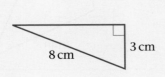 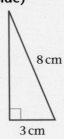

Example 16

(a) Write down the letters of the congruent triangles.

(b) Give a reason for your answer.

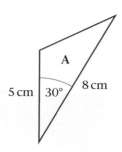

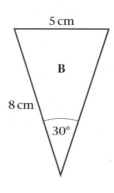

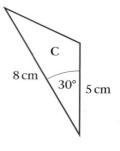

(a) Triangles **A** and **C** are congruent.

(b) Side, angle, side (SAS)

Example 17

Draw diagrams to show why two triangles, both with these measurements, are not necessarily congruent.

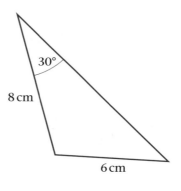

Because the angle given is not in between the two sides, two different triangles may share these measurements:

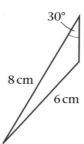

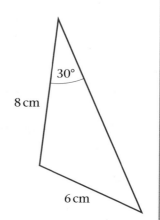

Exercise 12J

1 For each group of triangles write down the letters of the
   congruent triangles. Give a reason for your answer.

   (a)

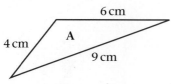 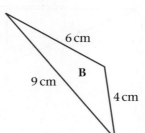 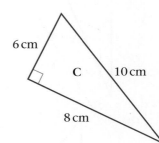

   (b)

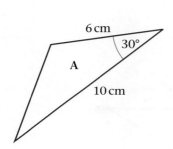 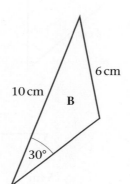 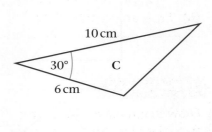

   (c)

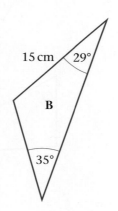 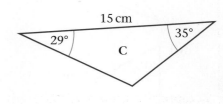

   (d)

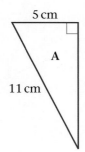 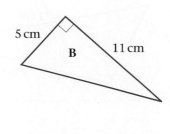 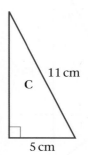

2 For each pair of triangles state whether they are congruent, and give a reason if they are.

(a)

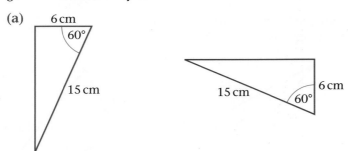

(b)

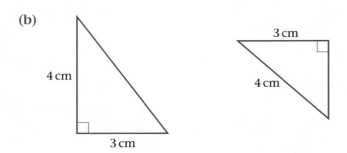

(c)

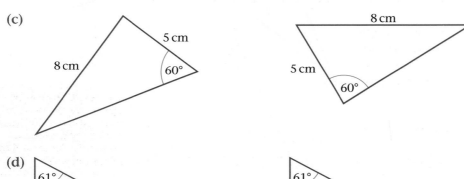

(d)

(e)

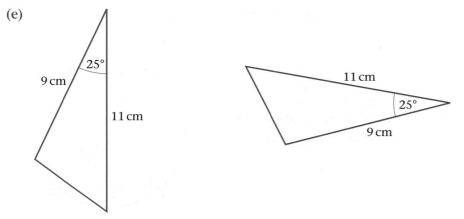

3 In parts **(a)** and **(b)**, draw diagrams to show why two triangles, both having the same measurements as shown, are not necessarily congruent.

(a)

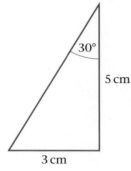

30°

5 cm

3 cm

(b)

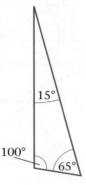

15°

100°

65°

12.11 Proof using congruence

Example 18

Prove that the base angles of an isosceles triangle are equal.

In the isosceles triangle, bisect angle A:

$AB = AC$ (the equal sides)
$AX = AX$ (the same side)
$BAX = CAX$ (angle A was bisected)

Therefore triangles AXB and AXC are congruent (SAS).
Therefore angle B = angle C.

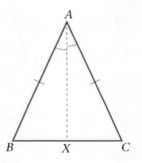

> This result can also be proved by joining A to the midpoint of BC (using SSS) or by drawing a perpendicular from A to BC (using RHS).

Example 19

Prove that the perpendicular to a chord from the centre of a circle bisects the chord.

In triangles OAX and OBX

$AO = BO$ (radii of the circle)
$OX = OX$ (same line)
$\angle OXA = \angle OXB = 90°$ (OX is perpendicular to AB)

Therefore triangles OAX and OBX are congruent (RHS).
Hence $AX = BX$

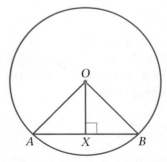

Exercise 12K

1   *ABCD* is a rectangle.
    Prove that triangles *ADC* and
    BCD are congruent.

2   *PQRS* is a parallelogram.
    Prove that triangles *SXR* and *QXP*
    are congruent.

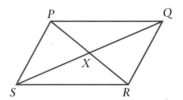

3   In the diagram, *D* and *E* are
    midpoints.
    CF is parallel to *BA*.
    Prove that triangles *DAE* and *FCE*
    are congruent.

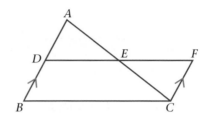

4   *ABCDE* is a regular pentagon.
    Prove that triangles *EAB* and *BCD*
    are congruent.

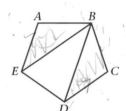

5   In the diagram, triangles *ABC* and
    AXY are isosceles.
    Prove that triangles *BXA* and *CYA*
    are congruent.

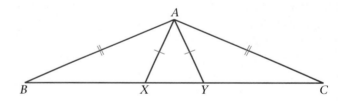

6   *WXYZ* is a kite.
    Prove that angle *X* and angle *Z*
    are equal.

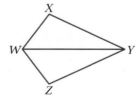

7   *ABCD* is a square.
    CXB and *BXY* are equilateral triangles.
    Show that triangles *ABY* and *ABX*
    are congruent.

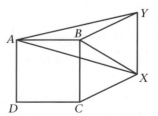

8   Prove that the line joining the midpoint of a chord to the centre
    of the circle is perpendicular to the chord.

Mixed exercise 12

1   Skillington lies on a bearing of 230° from Cliftonbury,
    at a distance of 10 km.
    Henlow lies on a bearing of 120°, 4 km from Cliftonbury.

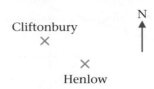

    (a) Draw a scale drawing to show these positions, using a scale of 1 cm to 1 km.

    (b) Meppershall water tower is equidistant from Cliftonbury and Skillington,
         and 7 km from Henlow. It is South of all 3 towns.
         Mark this position on your drawing.

2   This is a map of part of Northern England.

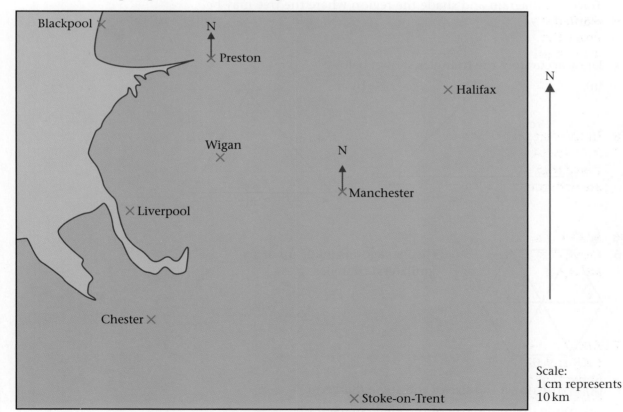

Scale:
1 cm represents
10 km

    A plane flies in a straight line from Preston to Stoke-on-Trent.

    (a) How far does it fly? Give your answer in kilometres.

    (b) Measure and write down the bearing of Preston from Manchester. [E]

3   Using a ruler and compasses, **construct** an angle of 15°.
    You must show **all** construction lines.

4   The diagram represents a triangular garden *ABC*.

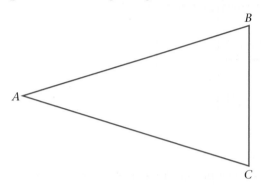

The scale of the diagram is 1 cm to represent 1 m.
A tree is to be planted in the garden so that it is
    nearer to *AB* than to *AC*
    within 5 m of point *A*.
Trace the diagram and shade the region where the tree may be
planted.   [E]

5   Draw accurately the triangles shown below.
    (a)   **(b)**

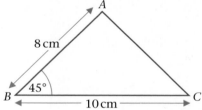
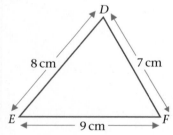

6

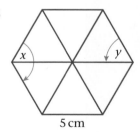

    This hexagon is made up of six
    equilateral triangles.

    (a)   Write down the size of the angle marked *x*.
    (b)   Write down the size of the angle marked *y*.
    (c)   Use a ruler and compasses to construct an equilateral triangle
          with sides of 5 cm.
    (d)   Use a ruler and compasses to construct a hexagon of side 5 cm.

7 The diagram shows a sketch of a net for a box.

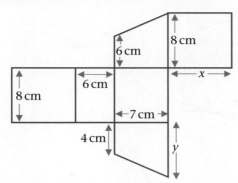

(a) Which measurement is wrong?

(b) Write down the values of *x* and *y*.

(c) Draw a sketch to show what the completed box looks like.

8 Construct an accurate net for each of these shapes.

(a)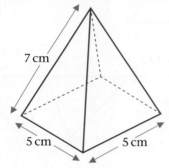

(b)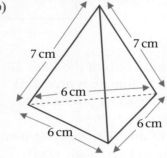

9 Here is a sketch of a
3-D shape.
Draw a sketch of the plan,
front and side elevations
of the shape.

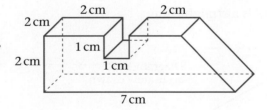

10 Here is a sketch of a 3-D shape.
Draw a sketch of the plan, front and side elevations.

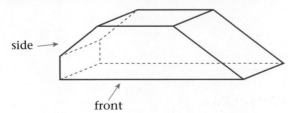

11 Work out

(a) the exterior angle of a regular 16-sided polygon

(b) the interior angle of a regular 16-sided polygon.

12 Work out the missing angle.

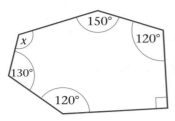

13 *BC* is parallel to *DE*.
BC = 10 cm, *DE* = 15 cm
BD = 5 cm, *AC* = 12 cm
  (a) Work out the length of *CE*.
  (b) Work out the length of *AD*.

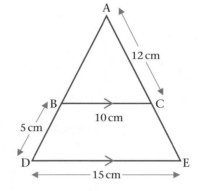

14 The points *D* and *E* are the midpoints of the sides *AB*
and *AC* of the triangle *ABC*. The line *BE* is produced
to *F* so that *BE* = *EF* and the line *CD* is produced to
G so that *CD* = *DG*.
  (a) Explain why triangles *AEF* and *BEC* are congruent.
  (b) Which triangle is congruent to triangle *ADG*?
  (c) Which angles are equal to ∠*FAE* and ∠*GAD*?
  (d) Explain why *GAF* is a straight line.

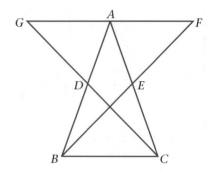

15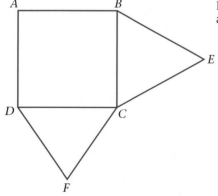
Diagram NOT
accurately drawn

ABCD is a square.
BEC and *DCF* are equilateral triangles.
  (a) Prove that triangle *ECD* is congruent to triangle *BCF*.
G is the point such that *BEGF* is a parallelogram.
  (b) Prove that *ED* = *EG*.   [E]

16 Here is a net of a 3-D shape.

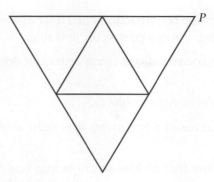

The net is folded to make the 3-D shape.
Two other vertices meet at *P*.
Sketch the net and mark each of these vertices with the letter *P*.

[E]

17

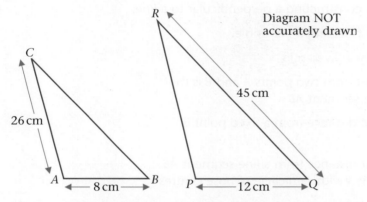

Diagram NOT
accurately drawn

The two triangles *ABC* and *PQR* are mathematically similar.

Angle *A* = angle *P*.
Angle *B* = angle *Q*.
AB = 8 cm.
AC = 26 cm.
PQ = 12 cm.
QR = 45 cm.

(a) Work out the length of *PR*.
(b) Work out the length of *BC*.

[E]

Summary of key points

1 A **bearing** is an angle measured clockwise from North. It is always a
   three-figure number.

2 A **scale** is a ratio which shows the relationship between a length on
   a drawing and the actual length in real life.

3 A scale can be represented as a ratio (e.g. 1 : 25 000) or sometimes
   using an equals sign (e.g. 1 cm = 5 km).

4 You can draw **approximate constructions** of 2-D shapes if you know lengths and angles, using a protractor and ruler.

5 You can draw **accurate constructions** using a straight edge (ruler) and compasses.

6 **Perpendicular** lines meet at right angles.

7 The **perpendicular bisector** of a line meets it at right angles and cuts it in half.

8 An **angle bisector** is a line that divides an angle into two halves.

9 You can use a ruler and compasses to construct an angle bisector.

10 You can construct a 60° angle by constructing an equilateral triangle.

11 You can construct a 30° angle by bisecting a 60° angle.

12 You can construct a 90° angle by constructing a perpendicular to a line.

13 You can construct a 45° angle by bisecting a 90° angle.

14 A **locus** is a set of points that obey a given rule.

15 The locus of the points equidistant from two points *A* and *B* is the perpendicular bisector of the line segment *AB*.

16 The locus of the points a constant distance from a fixed point is a circle.

17 The locus of the points a constant distance from a line segment *AB* is a pair of lines parallel to *AB* joined with semicircles whose centres are at *A* and *B*.

18 A **net** is a 2-D shape that can be made into a 3-D shape.

19 You can construct accurate nets using a straight edge and compasses.

20 The **plan** of a solid is the view when seen from above.

21 The **front elevation** is the view when seen from the front.

22 The **side elevation** is the view when seen from the side.

23 A **polygon** is a 2-D shape with any number of straight sides.

24 The point where two sides meet is called a **vertex**.

25 A polygon is a **regular polygon** if its sides are all the same length and its angles are all the same size.

26 The sum of the exterior angles of any polygon is 360°.

27 For a regular polygon,

$$\text{Exterior angle} = \frac{360°}{\text{number of sides}}$$

28 For a polygon,
Interior angle + exterior angle = 180°.

29 The sum of the interior angles of a polygon with n sides is $(n - 2) \times 180°$.

30 Two shapes are mathematically **similar** if one is an enlargement of the other.
Corresponding angles are the same.
Corresponding lengths are in the same ratio.

31 Triangles are similar if one of these facts is true:

○ All corresponding angles are equal:
$\hat{A} = \hat{X}$
$\hat{B} = \hat{Y}$
$\hat{C} = \hat{Z}$

○ All corresponding sides are in the same ratio:
$\dfrac{PQ}{AB} = \dfrac{QR}{BC} = \dfrac{PR}{AC} =$ scale factor

○ Two pairs of corresponding sides are in the same ratio and the included angles are equal:
$\dfrac{XY}{DE} = \dfrac{YZ}{EF} \qquad \hat{Y} = \hat{E}$

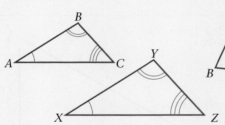

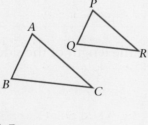

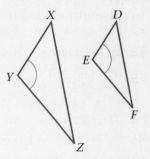

32 Shapes that are exactly the same size and shape are **congruent**.

33 To prove that triangles are congruent you need to show that they satisfy one of these conditions:

○ **SAS (side, angle, side)**

○ **ASA (angle, side, angle)**

○ **SSS (side, side, side)**

○ **RHS (right angle, hypotenuse, side)**

13 Pythagoras and trigonometry in 2-D and 3-D

13.1 Pythagoras' theorem

15 Introduction to Pythagoras' theorem
15 Pythagoras' theorem calculator
15 Pythagoras' theorem tool
15 Distance between two points

- Pythagoras' theorem states that in a right-angled triangle the square on the hypotenuse is equal to the sum of the squares on the other two sides.

  $a^2 + b^2 = c^2$

  or $c^2 = a^2 + b^2$

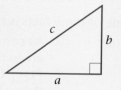

Example 1

In this right-angled triangle calculate the length of the side c.

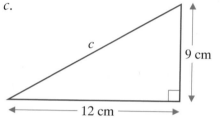

Using Pythagoras' theorem:

$$c^2 = a^2 + b^2$$
$$c^2 = 12^2 + 9^2$$
$$= 144 + 81$$
$$= 225$$

So $\quad c = \sqrt{225} = 15 \text{ cm}$

- Given the coordinates $A(x_1, y_1)$ and $B(x_2, y_2)$, the length

  $AB = \sqrt{(x_2 - x_1)^2 + (y_2 - y_1)^2}$

- To calculate one of the shorter sides in a right-angled triangle, use

  $a^2 = c^2 - b^2 \quad$ or $\quad b^2 = c^2 - a^2$

Example 2

Calculate the length AB between the points $A(2, 1)$ and $B(10, 7)$ on a coordinate grid.

Using Pythagoras:

$$AB^2 = 8^2 + 6^2$$
$$= 64 + 36$$
$$= 100$$
$$AB = \sqrt{100} = 10$$

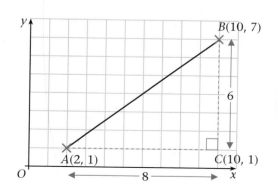

Plot the points A and B.
Construct a right-angled triangle ABC.
Length $AC = 10 - 2 = 8$
Length $CB = 7 - 1 = 6$

Example 3

Calculate the length of d correct to 3 significant figures.

$$d^2 = 23.4^2 - 12^2$$
$$= 547.56 - 144$$
$$= 403.56$$
$$\text{so} \quad d = \sqrt{403.56}$$
$$= 20.1 \text{ cm to 3 s.f.}$$

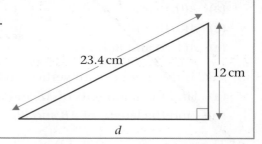

Example 4

Triangle PQR is isosceles.
Calculate the height of the triangle.

Using Pythagoras:
$$RM^2 = 12^2 - 4^2$$
$$= 144 - 16$$
$$= 128$$
$$\text{so } RM = \text{height} = \sqrt{128}$$
$$= 11.3 \text{ cm to 3 s.f.}$$

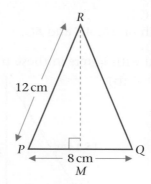

> Construct a perpendicular to PQ at its midpoint M. Remember that a perpendicular from the vertex to the unequal side of an isosceles triangle bisects the unequal side. PRM is a right-angled triangle with $PM = 4$ cm.

Exercise 13A

1 Calculate the lengths marked with letters in these triangles.

(a)

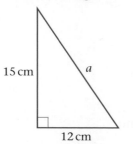

(b)

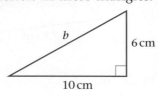

(c)

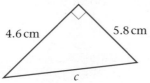

(d)

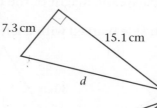

(e)

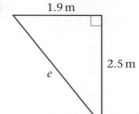

(f)

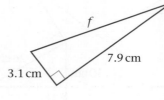

2 Calculate the length AB for the following pairs of points.

(a) $A(0, 0)$ and $B(3, 4)$ (b) $A(0, 0)$ and $B(9, 12)$

(c) $A(0, 0)$ and $B(4, 7)$ (d) $A(2, 3)$ and $B(5, 7)$

(e) $A(1, 9)$ and $B(4, 11)$ (f) $A(3, 12)$ and $B(7, 4)$

3 ABC is the triangle with vertices $A(1, 5)$, $B(3, 1)$ and $C(-5, -5)$.

(a) Find the midpoints of AB and BC.

(b) Find the length of AB and BC.

> Midpoint of the line segment joining (a, b) and (c, d) is
> $$\left(\frac{a + c}{2}, \frac{b + d}{2}\right)$$
> See Higher Unit 3.

4 The points $P(0, 2)$, $Q(8, 12)$ and $R(4, 6)$ form a triangle.
Find the midpoint and length of PQ and QR.

5 A is $(-3, 2)$, B is $(-5, 6)$ and C is $(7, -2)$.
Find the midpoint and length of AB, AC and BC.

6 Calculate the lengths marked with letters in these triangles.

(a)

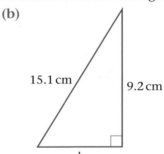

10 cm

a

6 cm

(b)

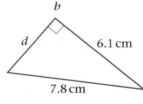

15.1 cm   9.2 cm

b

(c)

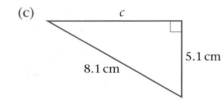

c

5.1 cm

8.1 cm

(d)

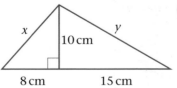

d 6.1 cm

7.8 cm

7 A rectangle measures 12 cm by 28 cm.
Calculate the length of a diagonal.

8 An isosceles triangle PQR has two equal sides 12 cm in length and a base 10 cm in length. Calculate the height of the triangle.

9 Calculate the length of each side marked with a letter.

(a)

x 10 cm y

8 cm   15 cm

(b)

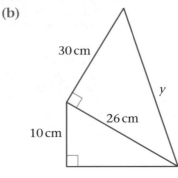

30 cm

y

26 cm

10 cm

(c)

(d)

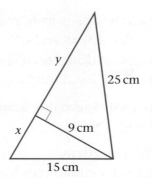

13.2 Pythagoras in 3-D

15 Using Pythagoras in 3-D shapes
15 Pythagoras' theorem in 3-D tool

- *AG* is one of the **longest diagonals** of this cuboid *ABCDEFGH*.
  The others are *BH*, *CE* and *DF*.

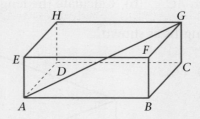

Remember
Pythagoras' theorem:

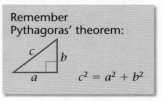

$c^2 = a^2 + b^2$

Example 5

A cuboid measures 3 cm by 5 cm by 10 cm.
Work out the length of the longest diagonal of this cuboid.

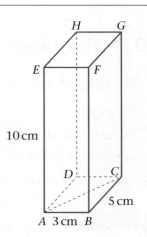

One longest diagonal is *AG*.

By Pythagoras: $AG^2 = AC^2 + CG^2$
where $CG = 10$ cm

To find *AC*, look at the base *ABCD*.

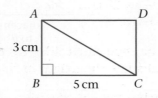

Using Pythagoras: $AC^2 = AB^2 + BC^2$
$$= 3^2 + 5^2$$
$$= 9 + 25$$
$$AC^2 = 34$$

No need to take the square root, as you need AC^2.

Then $AG^2 = AC^2 + CG^2$
$$= 34 + 10^2$$
$$= 34 + 100$$
$$AG^2 = 134$$

So $AG = \sqrt{134}$
$$AG = 11.58 \text{ cm to 2 d.p.}$$

You may be asked to leave the answer in surd form, i.e. $\sqrt{134}$ cm.

Exercise 13B

1 Calculate the length of the longest diagonal of a cuboid which has sides 4 cm, 7 cm and 15 cm.

2 Derive an expression for the longest diagonal of a cuboid which measures p cm by q cm by r cm.

3 A cuboid measures 5 cm by 10 cm by 20 cm.
   (a) Calculate the longest possible length across a face.
   (b) Calculate the longest diagonal through the cuboid.

4 A square-based pyramid has base $ABCD$ and vertex V directly above the centre of $ABCD$. $AB = 6$ cm and height $= 15$ cm.
   (a) Calculate the length AC.   (b) Calculate the length AV.

5 A prism $ABCDEF$ has lengths as shown.
   Calculate
   (a) EB (b) EC.

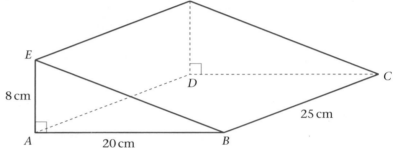

13.3 The tangent ratio

16 The tangent ratio

- The **tangent** ratio for any right-angled triangle is

$$\text{tangent of } \theta = \frac{\text{opposite side to } \theta}{\text{adjacent side to } \theta}$$

or for short, $\tan \theta = \dfrac{\text{opp}}{\text{adj}}$

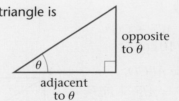

You need to remember this formula for the examination.

Example 6

Use your calculator to find   (a) $\tan 29.8°$
                               (b) θ when $\tan \theta = 1.5$

(a) $\tan 29.8° = 0.5727$ to 4 d.p.

(b) $\tan \theta = 1.5$
     You need to use the inverse tan function, $\tan^{-1}$ or arctan, to find θ.
        So $\theta = \tan^{-1} 1.5$
           $\theta = 56.31°$ to 2 d.p.

Make sure your calculator is in 'degree' mode. You normally need to work with four figures only.

Different calculators have different keys for the inverse tan function.

Example 7

Calculate the angle a in this triangle.

$$\tan a = \frac{\text{opp}}{\text{adj}}$$

So $\tan a = \dfrac{15}{8}$

$a = \tan^{-1}\dfrac{15}{8}$

$a = 61.9°$ to 3 s.f.

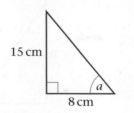

opposite = 15
adjacent = 8

Example 8

Calculate the length p in this triangle.

$$\tan \theta = \frac{\text{opp}}{\text{adj}}$$

So $\tan 32° = \dfrac{4.8}{p}$

$p \times \tan 32° = 4.8$ Multiply both sides by p

$p = \dfrac{4.8}{\tan 32°}$ Divide both sides by $\tan 32°$

$p = 7.68\,\text{cm}$ to 3 s.f.

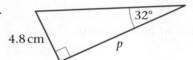

Exercise 13C

1 Use your calculator to find these tangents correct to 3 s.f.

  (a) $\tan 79°$

  (b) $\tan 8°$

  (c) $\tan 51.3°$

  (d) $\tan 29.1°$

2 Use your calculator to work out the values of θ correct to 3 d.p.

  (a) $\tan \theta = 1.8$

  (b) $\tan \theta = 0.57$

  (c) $\tan \theta = 4.49$

  (d) $\tan \theta = 2.6$

  (e) $\tan \theta = 6.19$

  (f) $\tan \theta = 0.75$

3 Calculate the lettered angles in these triangles.

(a)

8 cm

a

12 cm

(b)

16 cm

b

5 cm

(c)

13 cm

18 cm

c

(d)

9.8 cm

8.2 cm

d

(e)

4.2 cm

e

10.1 cm

(f)

15.7 cm

f

9.3 cm

4 Bedford is 16 miles North of Hitchin and 3 miles to the West.

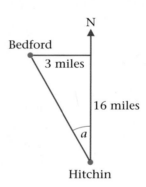

N

Bedford

3 miles

16 miles

a

Hitchin

    (a) Calculate the angle marked *a*.

    (b) Hence write down the bearing of Hitchin from Bedford.

5 Calculate the lettered lengths in these triangles.

(a)

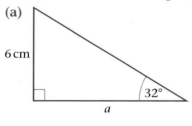

6 cm

32°

a

(b)

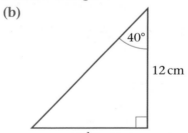

40°

12 cm

b

(c)

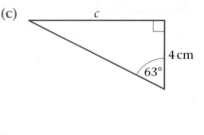

c

4 cm

63°

(d)

24°

9.6 cm

d

(e)

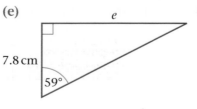

e

7.8 cm

59°

(f)

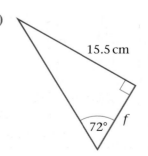

15.5 cm

72°

f

6 A ladder rests against a wall and makes
an angle of 71° with the ground.
The bottom of the ladder is 1.8 m
from the wall.
Calculate the height the ladder
reaches up the wall.

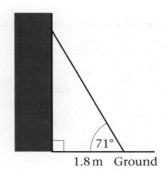

71°
1.8 m   Ground

7 Calculate the length of this rectangle.

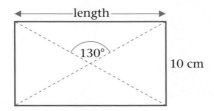

length

130°

10 cm

13.4 The sine ratio

16 The sine ratio

- The **sine** ratio for a right-angled triangle is

$$\text{sine of } \theta = \frac{\text{opposite to } \theta}{\text{hypotenuse}}$$

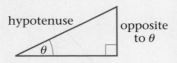

hypotenuse   opposite
to θ

θ

or for short, $\sin \theta = \dfrac{\text{opp}}{\text{hyp}}$

You need to remember
this formula for the
examination.

Example 9

Calculate the angle marked a in the diagram, correct to 3 s.f.

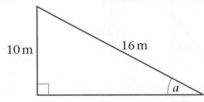

10 m   16 m

a

$$\sin \theta = \frac{\text{opp}}{\text{hyp}}$$

so $\sin a = \dfrac{10}{16}$

opposite = 10
hypotenuse = 16

$\sin a = 0.625$
$a = \sin^{-1} 0.625$
$a = 38.7°$ to 3 s.f.

Use the inverse sine
function on a calculator.

Example 10

Calculate the length of the side marked b in the diagram, correct to 3 s.f.

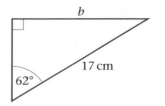

$$\sin \theta = \frac{\text{opp}}{\text{hyp}}$$

So $\sin 62° = \dfrac{b}{17}$

$\theta = 62°$
hypotenuse $= 17$ cm
opposite $= b$

$17 \times \sin 62° = b$ Multiply both sides by 17

So $b = 15.0$ cm to 3 s.f.

Exercise 13D

In this exercise give your answers correct to 3 s.f.

1 Calculate the lettered angles in these triangles.

(a)
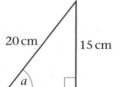

(b)
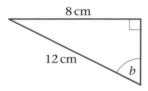

(c)
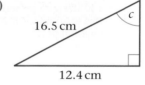

(d)
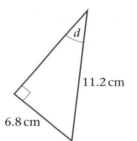

2 In these triangles calculate the lengths marked with letters.

(a)
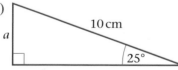

(b)
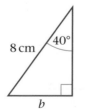

(c)
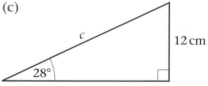

(d)
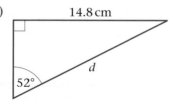

(e)
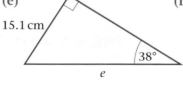

(f)
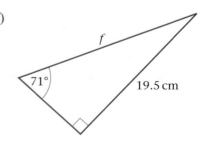

3 Calculate the missing sides in these isosceles triangles.

(a)

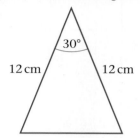

(b)

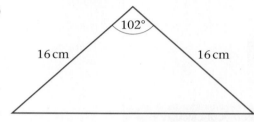

13.5 The cosine ratio

● 16 The cosine ratio

● The cosine ratio for a right-angled triangle is

cosine of $\theta = \dfrac{\text{adjacent side to } \theta}{\text{hypotenuse}}$

or for short, $\cos \theta = \dfrac{\text{adj}}{\text{hyp}}$

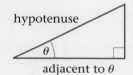

You need to remember this formula for the examination.

Example 11

Calculate the length a in the diagram.

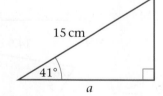

$$\cos \theta = \frac{\text{adj}}{\text{hyp}}$$

$\theta = 41°$
hypotenuse $= 15$ cm
adjacent $= a$

So $\cos 41° = \dfrac{a}{15}$

$15 \times \cos 41° = a$ \qquad Multiply both sides by 15

So $a = 11.3$ cm to 3 s.f.

Example 12

Calculate angle x in the diagram.

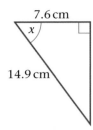

7.6 cm

x

14.9 cm

$$\cos \theta = \frac{\text{adj}}{\text{hyp}}$$

$\theta = x$
adjacent $= 7.6$ cm
hypotenuse $= 14.9$ cm

$$\cos x = \frac{7.6}{14.9}$$

$\cos x = 0.5100\ldots$ ────── Keep this value on your calculator.

$x = \cos^{-1} 0.5100\ldots$

$x = 59.3°$ to 3 s.f.

Exercise 13E

In this exercise give your answers correct to 3 significant figures.

1 Calculate the lengths marked with letters in these triangles.

(a)

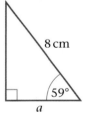

8 cm

59°

a

(b)

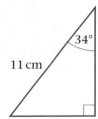

34°

11 cm

b

(c)

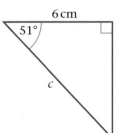

6 cm

51°

c

(d)

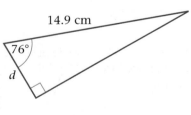

14.9 cm

76°

d

(e)

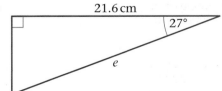

21.6 cm

27°

e

2 Calculate the lettered angles in these triangles.

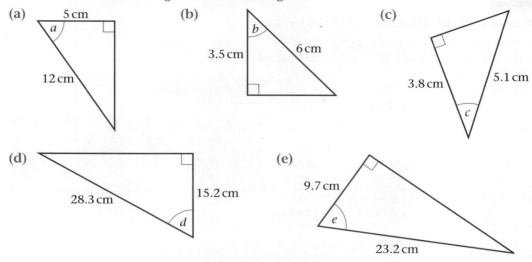

(a) 5 cm, a, 12 cm

(b) b, 3.5 cm, 6 cm

(c) 3.8 cm, 5.1 cm, c

(d) 28.3 cm, 15.2 cm, d

(e) 9.7 cm, e, 23.2 cm

3 Martin walks 16 m from the centre of a church, and measures the angle to the top of the tower as 39°.
How long would a rope need to be to go from the ground where he is standing to the top of the tower?

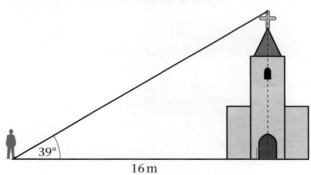

39°
16 m

13.6 Using trigonometry

- If you look up from the ground to the top of a tower, the **angle of elevation** is measured from the horizontal upwards.

- If you look down from the top of a cliff to a marker buoy in the sea, the **angle of depression** is measured from the horizontal downwards.

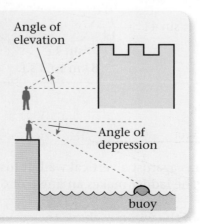

Angle of elevation

Angle of depression

buoy

Example 13

Morgan stands at the top of a vertical cliff 83 m high.
The angle of depression of a yacht in the sea is 32°.
Calculate the distance of the yacht from the base of the cliff.

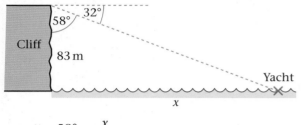

First draw a diagram.

Here $\theta = 58°$, **adj** = 83,
opp = x = distance of yacht from cliff
so use
$$\tan \theta = \frac{\text{opp}}{\text{adj}}$$

$$\tan 58° = \frac{x}{83}$$
$$x = 83 \times \tan 58°$$
$$x = 133 \text{ m correct to 3 s.f.}$$

Example 14

Radek walks from point A to point B on a bearing of 049°,
a distance of 14 km. How far East and how far North is he from A?

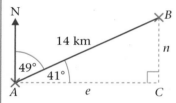

First draw a diagram.

angle $BAC = 90 - 49 = 41°$

To find distance East, e: $\quad \cos \theta = \dfrac{\text{adj}}{\text{hyp}}$

$$\cos 41° = \frac{e}{14}$$
$$e = 14 \times \cos 41°$$
$$e = 10.6 \text{ km to 3 s.f.}$$

To find distance North, n: $\quad \sin \theta = \dfrac{\text{opp}}{\text{hyp}}$

$$\sin 41° = \frac{n}{14}$$
$$n = 14 \times \sin 41°$$
$$n = 9.18 \text{ km to 3 s.f.}$$

Exercise 13F

1 A 9 m long ladder leans against a vertical wall. It just reaches
an upstairs window. The ladder makes an angle of 69° with the
horizontal ground.
Calculate the height of the window above the ground.

2 Bhavana stands at the top of a tower. Proshotam, her father, is
   on the ground 60 m from the bottom of the tower. The angle of
   depression of Proshotam from Bhavana is 38°.
   Calculate the height of the tower.

3 Maxwell runs from point *X* to point *Y* on a bearing of 062°,
   a distance of 25 km. How far
   (a) East
   (b) North
   is he from his starting point?

4 In the diagram, *ACD* and *BCD* are right-angled triangles.

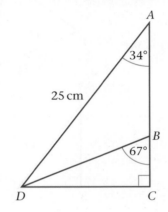

   Calculate
   (a) *DC*   (b) *AC*   (c) *AB*
   (d) angle *BDC*   (e) angle *ADB*

5 A cuboid has sides of 6 cm, 8 cm and 10 cm.

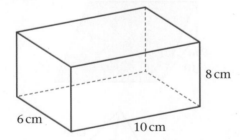

   Calculate the angle between one of the cuboid's longest diagonals
   and its base.

13.7 Angle between a line and a plane

21 Trigonometry in 3-D

- To find the angle between a line and a plane, draw a perpendicular
  from a point on the line down to the plane.
  Then use Pythagoras' theorem and trigonometry in the resulting
  right-angled triangle.

Example 15

In the shape below, A is 1 m horizontally from M (i.e. $MX = 1$ m), the midpoint of PQ. Find the angle that AQ makes with the horizontal.

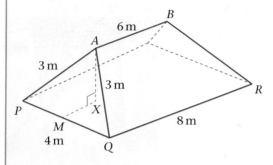

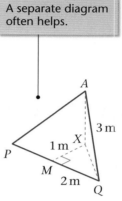

A separate diagram often helps.

In triangle XMQ, $MQ = 2$, $MX = 1$, angle $XMQ = 90°$.

So by Pythagoras $XQ^2 = (2^2 + 1^2) = 5$

$$XQ = \sqrt{5}$$

In triangle AXQ, angle AXQ is $90°$.

So $\cos AQX = \dfrac{\sqrt{5}}{3}$

angle $AQX = 41.8°$ (1 d.p.)

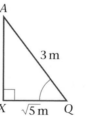

Exercise 13G

1 By travelling diagonally across the road, the steepness is reduced. Work out the angle that AB makes with the horizontal.

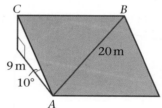

2 This shape is a square-based pyramid. Work out the angle that an edge makes with the horizontal face.

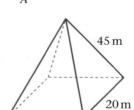

3 A vertical flagpole stands at the corner of a rectangular parade ground. Work out the angle of elevation of the top of the flagpole from the corner P.

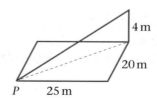

13.8 Area of a triangle

- Area of a triangle $= \frac{1}{2}ab \sin C$

  The formula works for acute- and obtuse-angled triangles.

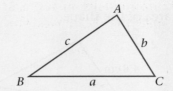

Side a is opposite angle A.
Side b is opposite angle B.
Side c is opposite angle C.
Angle C is between the two sides used in the formula.

Example 16

Calculate the area of this triangle.

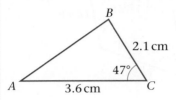

Area $= \frac{1}{2}ab \sin C$

$= \frac{1}{2} \times 2.1 \times 3.6 \times \sin 47°$

Area $= 2.76 \, \text{cm}^2$ (to 3 s.f.)

$a = 2.1 \, \text{cm}$
$b = 3.6 \, \text{cm}$
$C = 47°$

- For angles between 90° and 180°
  - $\sin x = \sin(180° - x)$
  - $\cos x = -\cos(180° - x)$

  For example, $\sin 127° = \sin(180° - 127°) = \sin 53°$
  and $\cos 127° = -\cos(180° - 127°) = -\cos 53°$.

Example 17

The area of triangle PQR is $28.6 \, \text{cm}^2$.
Sides PQ and PR are $10.9 \, \text{cm}$ and $8.5 \, \text{cm}$ respectively.
Find angle P.

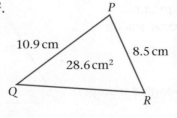

Area $= \frac{1}{2}PQ \times PR \sin P$

$28.6 = \frac{1}{2} \times 10.9 \times 8.5 \sin P$

So $\sin P = \dfrac{28.6 \times 2}{10.9 \times 8.5} = 0.6174\ldots$

angle $P = 38.1°$ (to 3 s.f.)

But $\sin x = \sin(180° - x)$, so angle $P = 180° - 38.1° = 141.9°$ is also a correct solution.

There are two possible triangles with area $28.6 \, \text{cm}^2$ and the two sides given:

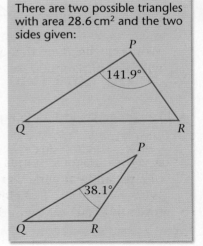

Exercise 13H

In questions **1–8** work out the area of the shape.

1

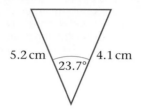

2

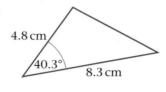

3

4

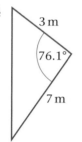

5

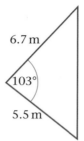

6

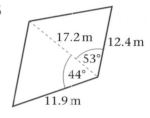

7

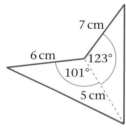

8

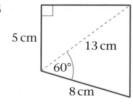

9 The area of triangle ABC is $70\,\text{cm}^2$.
Find angle A (there are two possible answers).

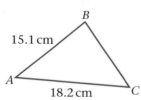

13.9 The sine rule

- In any triangle, including right-angled triangles,
  $$\frac{a}{\sin A} = \frac{b}{\sin B} = \frac{c}{\sin C}$$
  or
  $$\frac{\sin A}{a} = \frac{\sin B}{b} = \frac{\sin C}{c}$$
- $\sin x = \sin(180° - x)$

Example 18

Find BC.

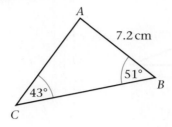

Angle $A = 180° - 43° - 51° = 86°$

So $\dfrac{BC}{\sin 86°} = \dfrac{7.2}{\sin 43°}$ $\qquad \boxed{\dfrac{a}{\sin A} = \dfrac{c}{\sin C}}$

$BC = \dfrac{7.2 \sin 86°}{\sin 43°} = 10.53 \text{ cm (2 d.p.)}$

Exercise 13I

In each question, work out the value of the length or angle marked with a letter.

1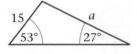

2

3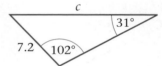

4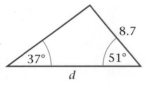

5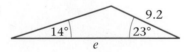

6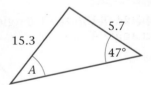

7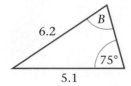

8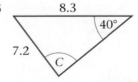

There are two possible angles.

13.10 The cosine rule

- $a^2 = b^2 + c^2 - 2bc \cos A$
  or $\cos A = \dfrac{b^2 + c^2 - a^2}{2bc}$
- $\cos x = -\cos(180° - x)$

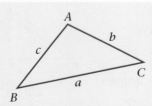

Example 19

In the diagram, work out
(a) BC and (b) angle B.

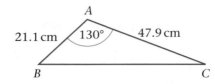

(a) $a^2 = b^2 + c^2 - 2bc \cos A$
$BC^2 = 21.1^2 + 47.9^2 - 2 \times 21.1 \times 47.9 \times \cos 130°$
$= 445.21 + 2294.41 - 2021.38 \cos 130°$
$= 4038.938...$
$BC = 63.55$ cm to 2 d.p.

(b) Using the sine rule:
$$\frac{\sin 130°}{63.55} = \frac{\sin B}{47.9}$$
$$\sin B = \frac{47.9 \sin 130°}{63.55} = 0.5773...$$
angle $B = 35.3°$ (1 d.p.)

- In any triangle, the smallest angle is opposite the smallest side.

Example 20

Find the angles in the triangle.

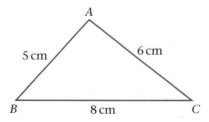

Angle C is the smallest angle. It must be acute.

$$\cos C = \frac{8^2 + 6^2 - 5^2}{2 \times 8 \times 6} = 0.7812...$$

angle $C = 38.6°$ to 1 d.p.

$$\cos A = \frac{6^2 + 5^2 - 8^2}{2 \times 6 \times 5} = -0.05$$

angle $A = 92.9°$ to 1 d.p.

angle $B = 180° - $ angle $A - $ angle C
$= 48.5°$ to 1 d.p.

$$\cos C = \frac{a^2 + b^2 - c^2}{2ab}$$

$$\cos A = \frac{b^2 + c^2 - a^2}{2bc}$$

Exercise 13J

In questions **1–6**, work out the third side and the other angles.

1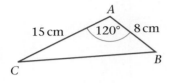

2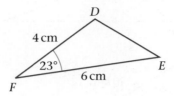

3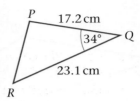

4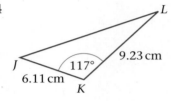

5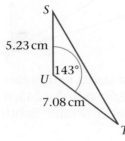

6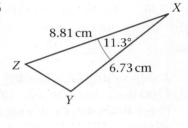

In questions **7–10**, work out the sizes of the angles in the triangle.

7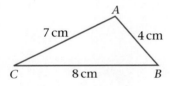

8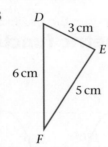

9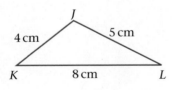

10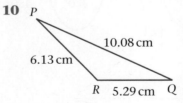

11 (a) Calculate the length of *AB*.
Give your answer correct to 3 significant figures.
(b) Calculate the size of angle *ABC*.
Give your answer correct to 3 significant figures.   [E]

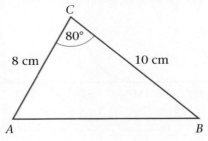

12 A plane flies on a bearing of 037° for 200 km before changing to a heading of 083° for a distance of 300 km.
Calculate its distance and bearing from its starting point.

13

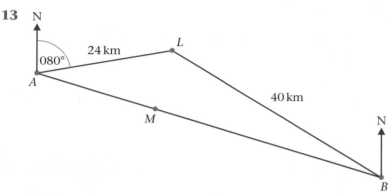

A ship sailing on a bearing of 140° first sights lighthouse *L* at 1100 hours on a bearing of 080°. It is known to be 24 km away. Three hours later the ship, now at *B*, sees the same lighthouse at a distance of 40 km.

(a) Work out the ship's average speed.

(b) *M* is the closest the ship gets to the lighthouse.
Work out the distance *LM*.

13.11 Graphs of trigonometric functions

• The graph of $y = \sin x$ is:

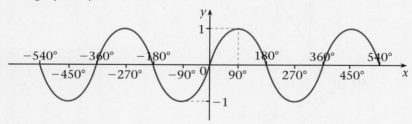

• The graph of $y = \cos x$ is:

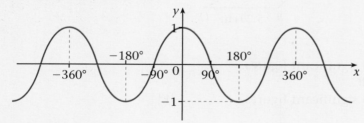

• The graph of $y = \tan x$ is:

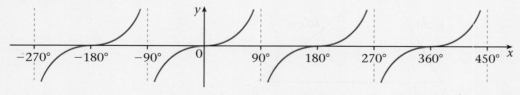

Example 21

Sketch the graph of $y = 2\sin x$.

The maximum and minimum values of $\sin x$ are $+1$ and -1.
For $2\sin x$ the maximum and minimum values are $+2$ and -2.
The intercepts on the x-axis are unchanged.

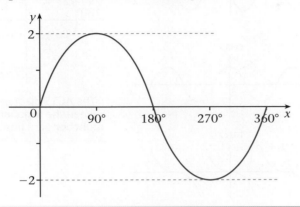

The function $2\sin x$ stretches the function $\sin x$ in the y-direction by scale factor 2.

Example 22

Sketch the graph of $y = \sin 2x$.

$\sin 2x$ has the same maximum and minimum as $\sin x$.
In the x-direction, $\sin 2x$ completes a complete cycle in $180°$ instead of $360°$.

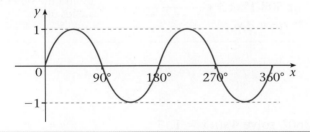

The function $\sin 2x$ stretches the function $\sin x$ in the x-direction by scale factor $\frac{1}{2}$.

Similar results can be deduced for cosine and tangent functions.

Exercise 13K

Draw sketches for x from $-360°$ to $+360°$ for the following functions.

1 $4\sin x$ **2** $3\tan x$ **3** $2\cos x$ **4** $-2\sin x$

5 $-\tan x$ **6** $-3\sin x$ **7** $\cos 2x$ **8** $\sin\frac{1}{2}x$

9 $2\sin 3x$ **10** $5\cos 2x$

13.12 Solving trigonometric equations

- The following results can be seen from the symmetry of the trigonometric graphs.

  - $\sin(-x) = -\sin x$
    $\sin(180° - x) = \sin x$
    $\sin(360° + x) = \sin x$

    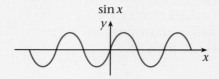

  - $\cos(-x) = \cos x$
    $\cos(180° - x) = -\cos x$
    $\cos(360° + x) = \cos x$

    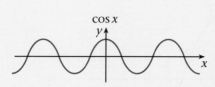

  - $\tan(-x) = -\tan x$
    $\tan(180° - x) = -\tan x$
    $\tan(360° + x) = \tan x$

    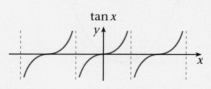

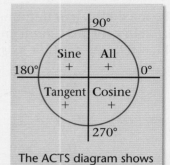

The ACTS diagram shows when the trigonometric functions are positive.

Example 23

Solve the equation $5 \sin 3x - 3 = 0$ for $0° \leqslant x \leqslant 180°$.

$$5 \sin 3x = 3$$
$$\sin 3x = \tfrac{3}{5} = 0.6 \quad \boxed{\text{Using a calculator.}}$$
$$3x = 36.9°$$

Hence $3x = 36.9°$ or $143.1°$ or $396.9°$ or $503.1°$ etc. $\boxed{\text{Using the results above to find the other possible values of } 3x.}$

$$x = 12.3°, 47.7°, 132.3°, 167.7° \text{ (to 1 d.p.)}$$

Exercise 13L

1 For values of x in the range $0°$ to $360°$, solve $4 \sin x = 1$.

2 For values of x in the range $0°$ to $360°$, solve $2 \tan x = 3$.

3 For values of x in the range $0°$ to $360°$, solve $2 \cos 2x = 1$.

4 For values of x in the range $0°$ to $180°$, solve $5 \cos 2x = 2$.

5 For values of x in the range $0°$ to $720°$, solve $2 \tan 3x = 10$.

6 For values of x in the range $-180°$ to $180°$, solve $3 \sin x + 1 = 0$.

7 For values of x in the range $-180°$ to $180°$, solve $5 \sin 2x + 1 = 0$.

8 For values of x in the range $-180°$ to $180°$, solve $4 \tan 2x + 6 = 0$.

Mixed exercise 13

1 Calculate the distance between the points

(a) (5, 2) and (11, 6)

(b) (−2, −5) and (3, 0).

2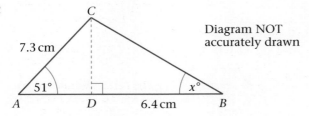

The diagram shows a triangle *ABC*.
The line *CD* is perpendicular to the line *AB*.
AC = 7.3 cm, *BD* = 6.4 cm and angle *BAC* = 51°.
Calculate the size of the angle marked *x*°.
Give your answer correct to 1 decimal place. [E]

3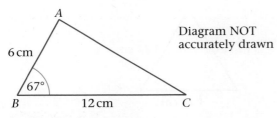

The diagram shows a triangle *ABC*.
AB = 6 cm, *BC* = 12 cm, angle *B* = 67°.
Calculate the length *AC*.
Give your answer correct to 3 significant figures. [E]

4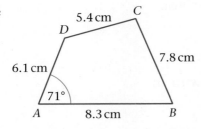

The diagram shows a quadrilateral *ABCD*.
AB = 8.3 cm, *BC* = 7.8 cm, *CD* = 5.4 cm and *AD* = 6.1 cm.
Angle *BAD* = 71°.

(a) Calculate the area of triangle *ABD*.
Give your answer correct to 3 significant figures.

(b) Calculate the size of angle *BCD*.
Give your answer correct to 1 decimal place. [E]

5

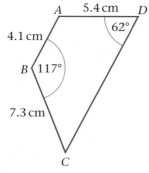

The diagram shows a quadrilateral $ABCD$.

$$AB = 4.1 \text{ cm}$$
$$BC = 7.3 \text{ cm}$$
$$AD = 5.4 \text{ cm}$$

Angle $ABC = 117°$
Angle $ADC = 62°$

(a) Calculate the length of AC.
Give your answer correct to 3 significant figures.

(b) Calculate the area of triangle ABC.

(c) Calculate the area of quadrilateral $ABCD$. [E]

6 The diagram represents an isosceles triangle.

(a) Calculate the vertical height of
the triangle.

(b) Calculate the area of the triangle.

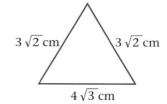

7 $VPQRS$ is a square-based pyramid.
Calculate

(a) PR

(b) VM (M is the midpoint of PR)

(c) angle VQM

(d) angle PVR

(e) the angle between VR and the base $PQRS$.

8 A tower is 92 metres high.
From the top of the tower, point A is on a bearing of 063° with an
angle of depression of 53°.
From the same point at the top of the tower, point B is on a
bearing of 140° with an angle of depression of 71°.
Calculate the distance AB.

9 A motorway runs in a North-easterly direction (its bearing is 045°).
Peter is 200 m due East of a point on the motorway.
He sees a kestrel hovering above the motorway on a bearing of 020°.
The angle of elevation of the kestrel is 36°.
Calculate the height of the kestrel.

10 In the diagram *PT* and *PS* are tangents
to the circle.
Calculate *SO*.

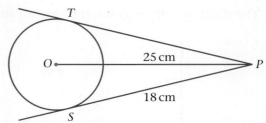

11 *PR* and *PQ* are tangents to the circle.
Calculate angle *POR*.

> Tangents meet radii at
> 90°. See page 245.

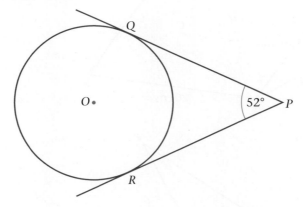

12 *PR* and *PQ* are tangents to the circle.
Calculate angle *POQ*.

13 The rise and fall of a tide can be modelled by the function
$$f(t) = 10\cos(30t)° + 25$$
This gives the height in feet when *t* is the time on the 24-hour clock.
(a) Write down the height of low tide.
(b) Write down the height of high tide.
(c) Work out the number of hours between high and low tide.

14 The depth of water, *d* metres, at the entrance to a harbour is
given by the formula
$$d = 5 - 4\sin(30t)°$$
where *t* is the time in hours after midnight on one day.
(a) Draw the graph of *d* against *t* for $0 < t < 12$.
(b) Find two values of *t*, where $0 < t < 24$, when the depth is
least.

[E]

15 The diagram shows a sketch of part of the curve $y = f(x) = \cos x°$.

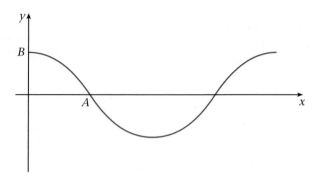

(a) Write down the coordinates of the points A and B.

(b) Draw this function and, on the same diagram, sketch the graph of $y = f(2x)$.   [E]

16 This is a wedge. Faces *EFBA*, *EFCD* and *DCBA* are rectangles. Calculate

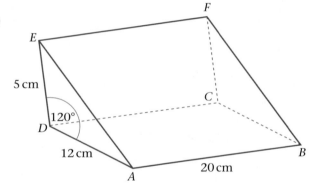

(a) length *EA*

(b) length *EB*

(c) angle *EBD*.

17 The diagram shows two rectangular pieces of card joined at *VT*, at an angle of 80°. Calculate

(a) the length *SP*

(b) the angle *PRQ*

(c) the length *SQ*.

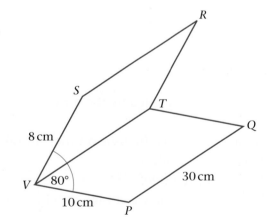

Summary of key points

1 Pythagoras' theorem states that in a right-angled triangle the square on the hypotenuse is equal to the sum of the squares on the other two sides.
$$a^2 + b^2 = c^2$$
or $c^2 = a^2 + b^2$

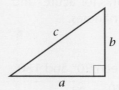

2 Given the coordinates $A(x_1, y_1)$ and $B(x_2, y_2)$, the length
$$AB = \sqrt{(x_2 - x_1)^2 + (y_2 - y_1)^2}$$

3 To calculate one of the shorter sides in a right-angled triangle, use
$a^2 = c^2 - b^2$ or $b^2 = c^2 - a^2$

4 *AG* is one of the **longest diagonals** of this cuboid *ABCDEFGH*. The others are *BH*, *CE* and *DF*.

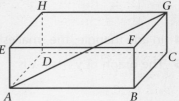

5 The **tangent** ratio for any right-angled triangle is
$$\tan \theta = \frac{\text{opp}}{\text{adj}}$$

6 The **sine** ratio for a right-angled triangle is
$$\sin \theta = \frac{\text{opp}}{\text{hyp}}$$

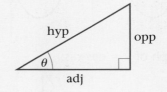

7 The **cosine** ratio for a right-angled triangle is
$$\cos \theta = \frac{\text{adj}}{\text{hyp}}$$

8 The **angle of elevation** is measured from the horizontal upwards.

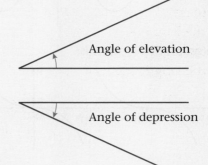

Angle of elevation

9 The **angle of depression** is measured from the horizontal downwards.

Angle of depression

10 To find the angle between a line and a plane, draw a perpendicular from a point on the line down to the plane.
Then use Pythagoras' theorem and trigonometry in the resulting right-angled triangle.

11 Area of a triangle $= \frac{1}{2}ab \sin C$

The formula works for acute- and obtuse-angled triangles.

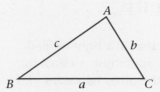

12 For angles between 90° and 180°

- ○ $\sin x = \sin(180° - x)$
- ○ $\cos x = -\cos(180° - x)$

13 In any triangle, including right-angled triangles,

- ○ $\dfrac{a}{\sin A} = \dfrac{b}{\sin B} = \dfrac{c}{\sin C}$
- ○ $a^2 = b^2 + c^2 - 2bc \cos A$ or $\cos A = \dfrac{b^2 + c^2 - a^2}{2bc}$

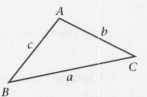

14 In any triangle, the smallest angle is opposite the shortest side.

15 The graph of $y = \sin x$ is:

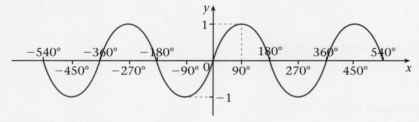

16 The graph of $y = \cos x$ is:

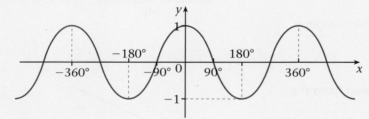

17 The graph of $y = \tan x$ is:

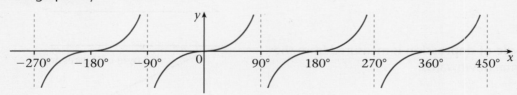

18
- ○ $\sin(-x) = -\sin x$
  $\sin(180° - x) = \sin x$
  $\sin(360° + x) = \sin x$
- ○ $\cos(-x) = \cos x$
  $\cos(180° - x) = -\cos x$
  $\cos(360° + x) = \cos x$
- ○ $\tan(-x) = -\tan x$
  $\tan(180° - x) = -\tan x$
  $\tan(360° + x) = \tan x$

14 Circle theorems

14.1 Tangents, chords and angles

- The angle between a tangent and a radius is 90°.

  $O\hat{Q}R = 90°$

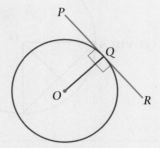

- The lengths of the two tangents from a point to a circle are equal.

  $TP = TQ$

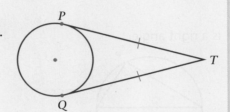

- A line drawn from the centre of a circle to the midpoint of a chord is perpendicular to the chord.

  Angle $ABO = 90°$

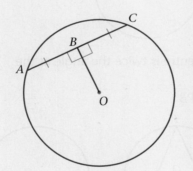

- A line drawn from the centre of a circle perpendicular to a chord bisects the chord.

  $AB = BC$

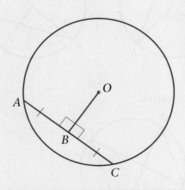

Example 1

Show why the perpendicular from the centre of a circle to a chord bisects the chord.

OB is perpendicular to AC.
For triangles OBC and OBA:

    OB is common

    OA = OC (radii)

    angle OBA = angle OBC = 90° (given)

So triangles OBC and OBA are congruent.

So AB = BC, hence OB bisects AC.

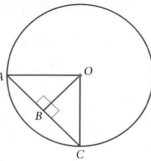

- The angle in a semicircle is a right angle.

    Angle APB = 90°

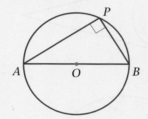

- The angle subtended at the centre is twice the angle at the circumference.

    Angle AOB = 2 × angle APB

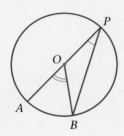 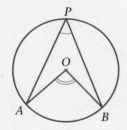 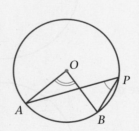

- Angles in the same segment are equal.

    Angle APB = angle AQB

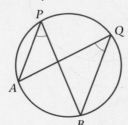

Example 2

Angle $APB = 38°$.
Find angles AQB and AOB.
Give reasons for your answers.

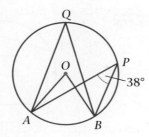

Angle AQB = angle $APB = 38°$ (angles in the same segment)
Angle $AOB = 2 ×$ angle $APB = 76°$ (angle at centre = $2 ×$ angle at circumference)

Exercise 14A

In each question, work out the angles marked by a letter.
Where marked, O is the centre of the circle.

1

2

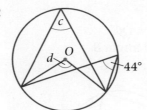

3

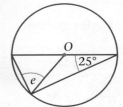

4

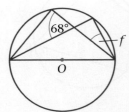

5

6

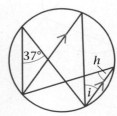

7

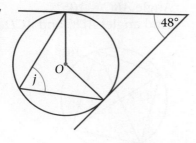

8

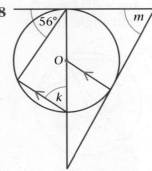

14.2 Cyclic quadrilaterals

⊙ **26** Opposite angles of a cyclic quadrilateral

- Opposite angles in a cyclic quadrilateral add up to 180°.

  Angle A + angle C = 180°
  Angle B + angle D = 180°

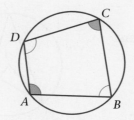

Example 3

OQ is parallel to BP. Angle QOP = 63°.
Find angle AXB.
Give reasons for your answer.

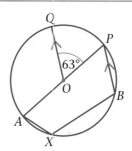

Angle OPB = angle QOP = 63°   (alternate angles)
Angle AXB = 180° − angle APB (opposite angles in a
                                     cyclic quadrilateral)
             = 180° − 63° = 117°

Exercise 14B

1 Find the angles marked a and b.

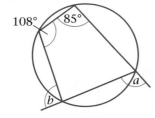

2 $AD = DC$.
Find angle B.

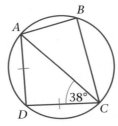

3 $AC = CB$.
Angle C = 54°.
Find angle XTY.

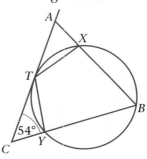

4 PT and PS are tangents.
O is the centre.
Find angle TYS.

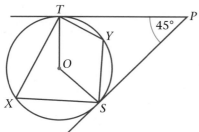

5 Angle BAC = 26°.
Angle BDA = 30°.
Find angle ABC.

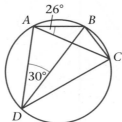

6 Angle DAC = 42°.
Angle ABC = 105°.
Find angles ADC and ACD.

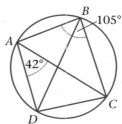

7

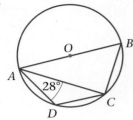

$AD = DC$.
AOB is a diameter.
Find angles ABC and BAC.

8 A, B, C and D are points on the circumference of a circle centre O.
A tangent is drawn from E to touch the circle at C.
Angle $AEC = 36°$. EAO is a straight line.

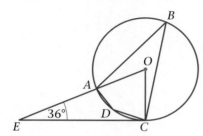

Diagram NOT
accurately drawn

(a) Calculate the size of angle ABC.
Give reasons for your answer.

(b) Calculate the size of angle ADC.
Give a reason for your answer. [E]

14.3 The alternate segment theorem

26 Alternate segment
theorem

• The angle between a tangent and
its chord is equal to the angle in the
alternate segment.

Angle RQX = angle QYX

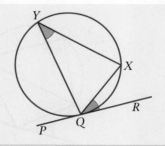

Example 4

Angle $ABC = 73°$.
Angle $CTQ = 40°$.
TQ is a tangent.
Find angle ACT.
Give reasons for your answer.

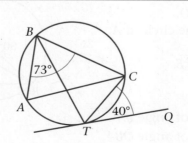

Angle $CBT = 40°$ (alternate segment)
Angle $ABT = 73° - 40° = 33°$
Angle ACT = angle $ABT = 33°$ (angles in same segment)

Exercise 14C

1 Find angle *TBA*.

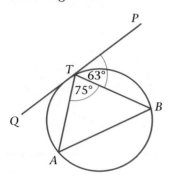

2 Find angles *ABT* and *BTC*.

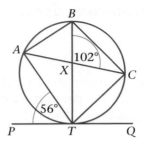

3 *PTQ* is a tangent.
 AB = *AT*.
 Find angle *ABT*.

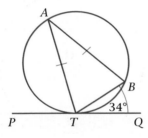

4 *PTQ* is a tangent.
 AB is parallel to *TS*.
 Find angle *BTA*.

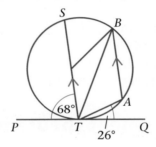

5 *PTQ* is a tangent.
 Find angle *CBT*.

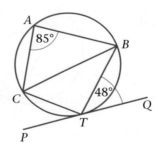

6 Points *A*, *B* and *C* lie on the circumference
 of a circle with centre *O*.
 DA is the tangent to the circle at *A*.
 BCD is a straight line.
 OC and *AB* intersect at *E*.
 Angle *BOC* = 80°.
 Angle *CAD* = 38°.

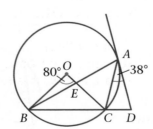

 (a) Calculate the size of angle *BAC*.

 (b) Calculate the size of angle *OBA*.

 (c) Give a reason why it is not possible to draw a circle with
  diameter *ED* through the point *A*. [E]

14.4 Proofs of circle and geometrical theorems

Proof 1

The lengths of the two tangents from a point to a circle are equal.

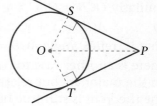

In triangles OPS and OPT:

$\qquad OS = OT$ $\qquad\qquad\qquad$ (radii)

$\qquad OP$ is common to both.

$\qquad$ Angle OSP = angle OTP = 90° $\qquad$ (tangent and radii)

So triangles OPS and OPT are congruent. $\quad$ (RHS)

So $\quad PS = PT$

Proof 2

The line from the centre of a circle to the mid-point of a chord is perpendicular to the chord.

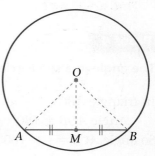

M is the mid-point of the chord AB.

In triangles OAM and OBM:

$\qquad OA = OB$ $\qquad\qquad\qquad$ (radii)

$\qquad OM$ is common to both.

$\qquad AM = MB$ $\qquad\qquad\qquad$ (M is the mid-point of AB)

So triangles OAM and OBM are congruent. (SSS)

So angle OMA = angle OMB = 90°.

Proof 3

The angle subtended at the centre of a circle is twice the angle at the circumference.

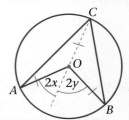

You need to prove that $A\hat{O}B = 2 \times A\hat{C}B$.

Call the two parts of $A\hat{O}B$ $2x$ and $2y$, as shown.

So $\quad A\hat{O}B = 2x + 2y$

Now $A\hat{O}C = 180° - 2x$ $\qquad$ (straight line)

$\qquad O\hat{A}C + O\hat{C}A = 2x$ $\qquad$ (exterior angle of triangle = sum of two interior opposite angles)

$\qquad O\hat{A}C = O\hat{C}A = x$ $\qquad$ (triangle AOC is isosceles)

Similarly, $O\hat{B}C = O\hat{C}B = y$

So $\quad A\hat{C}B = x + y$

That is, $A\hat{O}B = 2 \times A\hat{C}B$

Since nothing has been assumed about the values of x and y, this result must be generally true for all diagrams like the one above.

The theorem is also true if C is on the minor arc, as shown on the right. To prove this, call the two parts of the reflex angle AOB $2x$ and $2y$, as before.

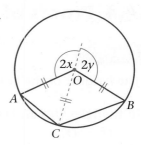

$$A\hat{O}C = 180° - 2x \qquad \text{(straight line)}$$

So $\quad O\hat{A}C = O\hat{C}A = x \qquad$ (triangle OAC is isosceles)

Similarly $O\hat{C}B = O\hat{B}C = y$

So $\quad A\hat{C}B = x + y$

That is, reflex angle $AOB = 2 \times A\hat{C}B$

There is another case to consider. Here C is on the major arc but relatively close to B. The theorem is still true but the proof is not demonstrated here.

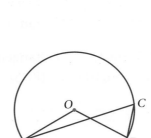

Proof 4

The angle in a semicircle is a right angle.

In triangle ABC:

$\qquad$ Angle $AOB = 180° \qquad$ (straight line)

So angle $ACB = \frac{1}{2} \times 180° \qquad$ (angle at centre is twice angle

$\qquad\qquad = 90° \qquad\qquad$ at circumference)

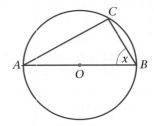

Proof 5

Angles in the same segment are equal.

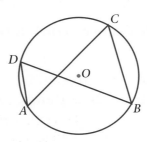

Join AO and OB.

$\qquad$ Angle $ACB = \frac{1}{2}$ angle $AOB \qquad$ (angle at centre is twice angle

and $\quad$ angle $ADB = \frac{1}{2}$ angle $AOB \qquad$ at circumference)

So $\quad$ angle $ACB = $ angle ADB

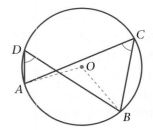

Proof 6

Opposite angles of a cyclic quadrilateral add up to 180°.

$2x + 2y = 360°$

So $x + y = 180°$

       Angle $BAD = x$ (angle at centre is twice angle
                            at circumference)

and   angle $BCD = y$

So   angle BAD + angle $BCD = x + y = 180°$

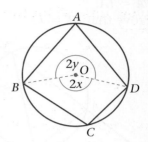

> You can show that $A\hat{B}C + C\hat{D}A = 180°$
> by drawing AO and CO.

Proof 7

The angle between a tangent and a chord is equal to the angle in the alternate segment.

TD is a diameter of the circle, so $T\hat{X}D = 90°$.
                                (angle in a semicircle is a right angle)

$T\hat{D}X + D\hat{T}X = 90°$ **(1)**   (angle sum of triangle is 180°)

PT is a tangent, so PTD is 90°.

Thus $P\hat{T}X + D\hat{T}X = 90°$ **(2)**

Comparing **(1)** and **(2)**:

$T\hat{D}X = P\hat{T}X$

C is any other point on the circumference

so $T\hat{C}X = T\hat{D}X$ (angles in the same segment)

and $P\hat{T}X = T\hat{C}X$

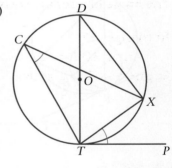

Exercise 14D

1 Prove that triangles BXA and CXD are similar.

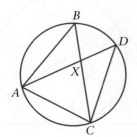

2 AB is parallel to CD. Prove that triangle CXD is isosceles.

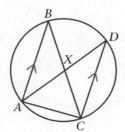

3 PTQ is a tangent. Prove that PAT and PTB are similar triangles.

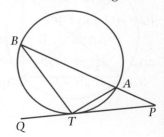

4 *PT* is a tangent.
PA = *TA*.
Prove that *PT* = *TX*.

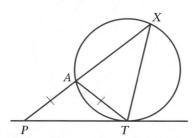

5 Prove that triangles *APS* and
AQR are similar.

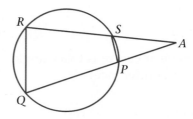

6 *RPT* is a tangent to the circles
at the point of contact.
PAX and *PBY* are straight lines.
Prove that *AB* is parallel to *XY*.

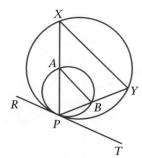

7 *PTR* and *RSQ* are tangents.
O is the centre.
XY is parallel to *OS*.
Prove that triangles *TXY* and
TRQ are similar.
Hence show that *TX* is
parallel to *RQ*.

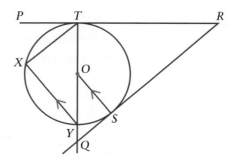

Mixed exercise 14

In each question find the angle marked by a letter.
Give full reasons for each step in your working.
Where marked, *O* is the centre of the circle.

1

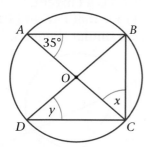

2

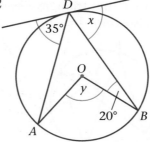

3

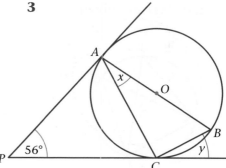

4

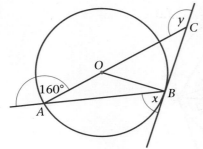

5

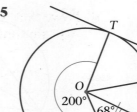

6

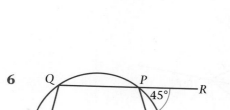

7

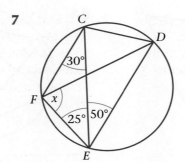

8

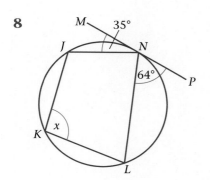

9

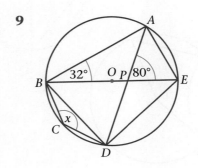

10

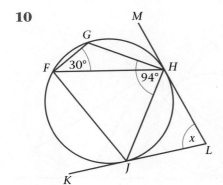

11

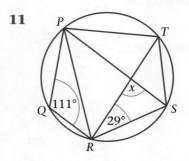

12

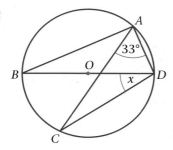

13

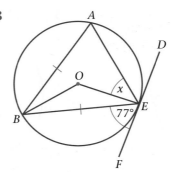

14

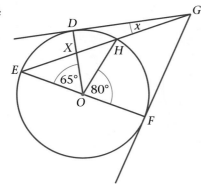

15

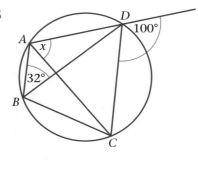

16

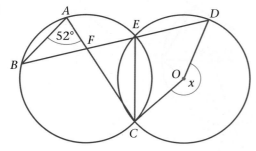

Summary of key points

1 The angle between a tangent and
   a radius is 90°.

   $O\hat{Q}R = 90°$

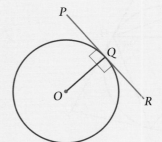

2 The lengths of the two tangents
from a point to a circle are equal.

$TP = TQ$

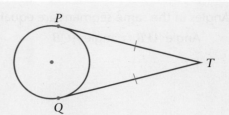

3 A line drawn from the centre of a circle to the
midpoint of a chord is perpendicular to the chord.

Angle $ABO = 90°$

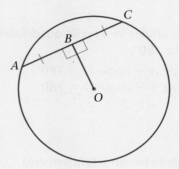

4 A line drawn from the centre of a circle perpendicular
to a chord bisects the chord.

$AB = BC$

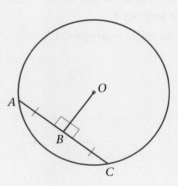

5 The angle in a semicircle is a right angle.

Angle $APB = 90°$

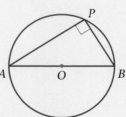

6 The angle subtended at the centre is twice the angle at the circumference.

Angle $AOB = 2 \times$ angle APB

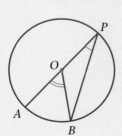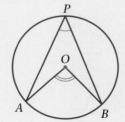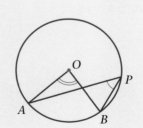

7 Angles in the same segment are equal.

Angle *APB* = angle *AQB*

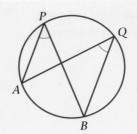

8 Opposite angles in a cyclic quadrilateral add up to 180°.

Angle *A* + angle *C* = 180°
Angle *B* + angle *D* = 180°

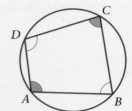

9 The angle between a tangent and its chord is equal to the angle in the alternate segment.

Angle *RQX* = angle *QYX*

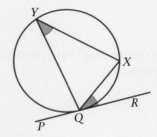

15 2-D and 3-D shapes

15.1 Area and circumference of circles

- Area of a circle = πr^2
- Circumference of a circle = $2\pi r$ (or πd)

Example 1

Work out the area and circumference of a circle diameter 10 cm.

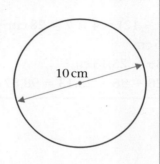

10 cm

Radius is half the diameter.

Area = πr^2
  = $\pi \times 5 \times 5$
  = 78.5 cm² to 3 s.f.
Circumference = πd
  = $\pi \times 10$
  = 31.4 cm to 3 s.f.

Use the π button on your calculator or 3.14.

Example 2

Work out the area and perimeter of this pond.
The pond is a semicircle.
Give your answer for the perimeter
(i) in terms of π (ii) numerically.

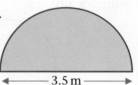

← 3.5 m →

Area of pond = $\frac{1}{2} \times \pi r^2$
  = $\frac{1}{2} \times \pi \times 1.75 \times 1.75$
  = 4.81 m² to 3 s.f.

Perimeter of pond = diameter + half circumference of circle
  = $d + \frac{1}{2}\pi d$
  = $3.5 + \frac{1}{2} \times \pi \times 3.5$
(i) = $3.5 + 1.75\pi$
(ii) = 9.00 m to 3 s.f.

Area of a semicircle is half the area of a circle.

You may be asked to leave your answer in terms of π in the examination.

Using a calculator.

Example 3

The area of a circle is 10π.
Find the length of a radius. Give your answer in surd form.

$\pi r^2 = 10\pi$
$r^2 = 10$
So $r = \sqrt{10}$

Example 4

Work out the area of the shape shown.

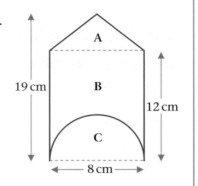

Area **A** = $\frac{1}{2} \times 8 \times (19 - 12) = 4 \times 7 = 28 \, \text{cm}^2$
Area **B** = $8 \times 12 = 96 \, \text{cm}^2$
Area **C** = $\frac{1}{2}\pi \times 4^2 = 8\pi = 25.13 \, \text{cm}^2$
Area of the shape = $28 + 96 - 25.13 = 98.87 \, \text{cm}^2$ to 2 d.p.

Area = area of triangle **A**
+ area of rectangle **B**
− area of semicircle **C**.

Exercise 15A

1 Work out the area and circumference of these circles.
Give your answers
(i) in terms of π (ii) numerically.

(a)

radius 16 cm

(b)
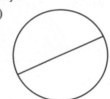
diameter 24 mm

(c)
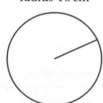
radius 2.62 m

(d)
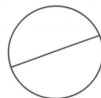
diameter 56.32 m

2 The diameter of a bicycle wheel is 700 mm.
Work out how far it travels in
(a) 1 revolution   (b) 50 revolutions.

3 The diameter of a circular pipe is 15.2 cm.
Work out the area of its cross-section.

4 A circus ring has radius 17 m.
Work out its area and circumference.

5 The circumference of a circular pond is 83 metres.
Work out its diameter.

6 The cross-sectional area of a circular pipe is 2.35 cm².
Work out its diameter.

7 Work out the area and perimeter of these semicircles.
Give your answers
    (i) in terms of π
    (ii) numerically.

(a)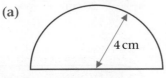

(b)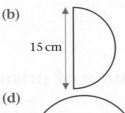

15 cm

(c)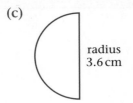

radius
3.6 cm

(d)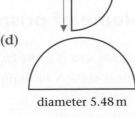

diameter 5.48 m

8 A semicircular pond has a radius of 2.5 m.
Work out the area and perimeter of the pond.

9 A semicircular gutter pipe has a cross-sectional area of 14.135 cm².
Work out the radius of the pipe.

10 A patio is built in the shape of a quarter circle,
radius 1.3 metres.
Work out the area and perimeter of the patio.

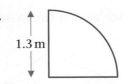

1.3 m

11 Work out the area and perimeter of these shapes.

(a)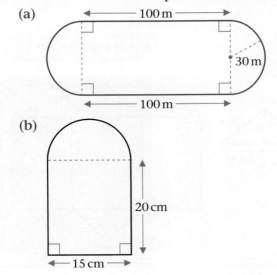

← 100 m →

30 m

← 100 m →

The shapes are made
up of rectangles and
semicircles.

(b)

20 cm

← 15 cm →

12 In each part work out the area.

(a)

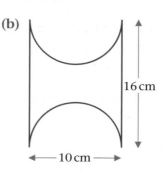

16 cm

12 cm

(b)

16 cm

10 cm

(c)

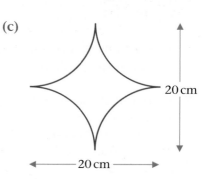

20 cm

20 cm

15.2 Surface area and volume of prisms

⊙ 22 Cross-section checker

- The surface area of a solid shape is the total area of all its faces.
- A **prism** is a 3-D shape with the same cross-section all along its length.
- Volume of a prism = area of cross-section × length

Example 5

Find the volume and surface area of the isosceles triangular prism shown.

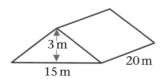

3 m

20 m

15 m

Area of cross-section = $\frac{1}{2} \times 15 \times 3 = 22.5\,\text{m}^2$

Volume = $22.5 \times 20 = 450\,\text{m}^3$

Area of triangular ends = $2 \times 22.5 = 45\,\text{m}^2$

Area of base = $20 \times 15 = 300\,\text{m}^2$

For the sloping faces use Pythagoras to find the width.

$w = \sqrt{7.5^2 + 3^2} = 8.077\ldots$

Area of sloping faces = $2 \times 20 \times 8.077\ldots$

$= 323.110\ldots$

Total surface area = $45 + 300 + 323.110\ldots$

$= 668.1$ (1 d.p.)

Area of triangle = $\frac{1}{2}bh$

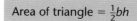

3 m

w

7.5 m

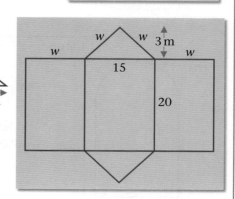

Example 6

Work out the total surface area (not including the floor) of the shed shown. The height of the shed is $3\frac{1}{2}$ m.

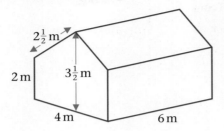

Total surface area = 2 end sections + roof + 2 sides

Shaded area = $\frac{1}{2}(2 + 3\frac{1}{2}) \times 2 = 5\frac{1}{2}$ m^2 | Area of trapezium = $\frac{1}{2}(a + b)h$ |

Area of one end = $2 \times 5\frac{1}{2} = 11$ m^2

Area of roof = $(2\frac{1}{2} \times 6) \times 2 = 30$ m^2

Area of two sides = $(2 \times 6) \times 2 = 24$ m^2

Total area (not including the floor) = $22 + 30 + 24 = 76$ m^2

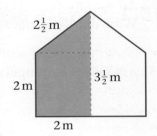

Exercise 15B

In questions **1–3** work out the total surface area.

1

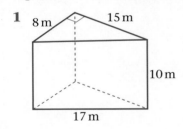

2

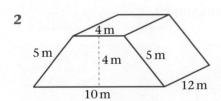

3

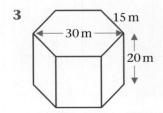

The shape is a prism with a regular hexagon as its cross-section.

4 *ABCDEF* is a triangular-based prism.

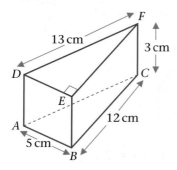

Angle *ABC* = 90°.
AB = 5 cm, *BC* = 12 cm, *CF* = 3 cm, *AC* = 13 cm.
Work out the surface area and volume.

5 *ABCDEF* is a triangular-based prism.

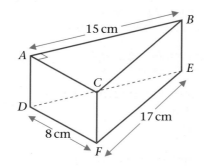

Angle *FDE* = 90°.
DF = 8 cm, *DE* = 15 cm, *EF* = 17 cm.
Volume = 300 cm³.
Work out *BE* and the total surface area.

6 Calculate the volume and total surface area of the two prisms shown.

(a)

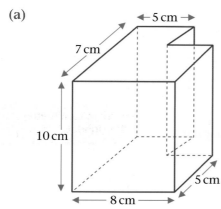

(b)

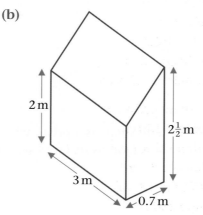

7   Work out the surface area
    and volume of this storage
    shed. The surface area
    should not include the
    base.

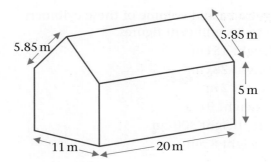

15.3 Surface area and volume of cylinders

- For a cylinder of height h with a
  base of radius r:
    ○ surface area $= 2\pi rh + 2\pi r^2$
    ○ volume $= \pi r^2 h$

Example 7

Find the total surface area of a cylinder which has diameter 8 mm
and height 32 cm.

Work in cm. 8 mm = 0.8 cm

Radius $= 0.4$ cm
Volume $= \pi \times (0.4)^2 \times 32 = 5.12\pi$ cm^3 (answer in terms of π)
$\qquad\qquad = 16.08$ cm^3 (1 d.p.)
Surface area $= 2\pi r^2 + 2\pi rh$
$\qquad\qquad = 2\pi \times (0.4)^2 + 2\pi \times 0.4 \times 32$
$\qquad\qquad = 0.32\pi + 25.6\pi = 25.92\pi$ cm^2 (in terms of π)
$\qquad\qquad\qquad = 81.4$ cm^2 (1 d.p.)

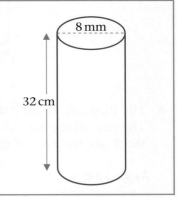

Exercise 15C

1   Work out the volume of these cylinders.
    Give your answers in terms of π.
    (a) radius 5 cm, height 12 cm
    (b) radius 8 cm, height 8 cm
    (c) radius 3 cm, height 20 cm
    (d) diameter 80 mm, height 2 m
    (e) diameter 0.46 m, height 1.2 mm

2   Work out the radii of these cylinders.
    (a) height 20 cm, volume 150 cm^3
    (b) height 15 cm, volume 200 cm^3
    (c) height 8 cm, volume 170 cm^3
    (d) height 15 mm, volume 10 cm^3
    (e) height 2 m, volume 2300 cm^3

Work in centimetres
throughout.

3 Work out the surface area and volume of these cylinders.
Give your answers to 3 significant figures.
- **(a)** radius 4 cm, height 15 cm
- **(b)** radius 6 cm, height 28 cm
- **(c)** radius 5 cm, height 2 m
- **(d)** radius 15 mm, height 9 cm
- **(e)** diameter 50 mm, height 300 cm
- **(f)** diameter 6 m, height 8 mm

4 Work out the volume of the tunnel.

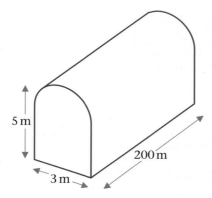

5 The diagram shows a skateboard ramp.
The curved surface has two edges which are quarter circles.
Work out the area of the curved surface.

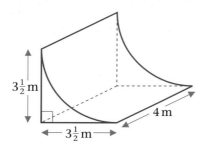

6 Work out the volume and surface area of this wedge.
The curved edges are quarter circles.

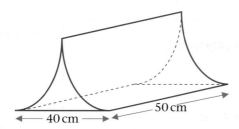

15.4 Converting units of area and volume

Area

- $1\,m^2 = 100 \times 100\,cm^2 = 10\,000\,cm^2$

- $1\,cm^2 = 10 \times 10\,mm^2 = 100\,mm^2$

Volume

- $1\,m^3 = 100 \times 100 \times 100\,cm^3 = 1\,000\,000\,cm^3$

- $1\,cm^3 = 10 \times 10 \times 10\,mm^3 = 1000\,mm^3$

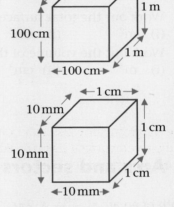

Example 8

The area of a stamp is $12\,cm^2$.
Write down its area in mm^2.

$1\,cm^2 = 100\,mm^2$
So $12\,cm^2 = 12 \times 100\,mm^2 = 1200\,mm^2$

Example 9

The volume of liquid in a small bottle is $35\,400\,mm^3$.
Write down the volume in cm^3.

$1\,cm^3 = 1000\,mm^3$
So $35\,400\,mm^3 = 35\,400 \div 1000\,cm^3 = 35.4\,cm^3$

Exercise 15D

1 Work out the number of

(a) cm² in 5 m²   (b) cm² in 28 m²

(c) cm² in 1.2 m²   (d) cm² in 105 m²

(e) m² in 26 000 cm²   (f) m² in 3400 cm²

(g) mm² in 8 cm²   (h) mm² in 22 cm²

(i) cm² in 2400 mm²   (j) cm² in 36 200 mm²

2 Work out the number of

(a) cm³ in 2.3 m³   (b) cm³ in 0.04 m³

(c) cm³ in 0.304 m³   (d) m³ in 7 000 000 cm³

(e) m³ in 530 000 cm³   (f) m³ in 26 500 cm³

(g) mm³ in 4 cm³   (h) mm³ in 13.05 cm³

(i) cm³ in 8400 mm³   (j) cm³ in 430 mm³

3 (a) Work out the total surface area of the cuboid in

   (i) m²   (ii) cm²

(b) Work out the volume of the cuboid in

   (i) m³   (ii) cm³

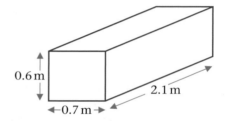

0.6 m   0.7 m   2.1 m

15.5 Arcs and sectors

22 Circle tool

- Length of an arc = $\dfrac{\theta}{360°} \times 2\pi r$

- Area of a sector = $\dfrac{\theta}{360°} \times \pi r^2$ or $\dfrac{\pi r^2 \theta}{360°}$

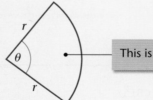

This is $\dfrac{\theta}{360°}$ of a full circle.

Example 10

Calculate **(a)** the area and **(b)** the perimeter of the sector shown.

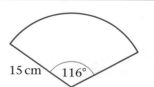

15 cm   116°

(a) Area = $\dfrac{116}{360} \times \pi \times 15^2 = 72.5\pi = 228$ cm² (3 s.f.)

(b) Arc length = $\dfrac{116}{360} \times 2\pi \times 15 = \dfrac{3480\pi}{360} = 30.4$ cm (3 s.f.)

Perimeter = $15 + 15 + 30.4 = 60.4$ cm (3 s.f.)

Exercise 15E

In questions **1** and **2** calculate
(i)   the length of the arcs
(ii) the perimeters and
(iii) the areas of the sectors shown.

1 Give your answers in terms of π.

(a)

(b)

(c)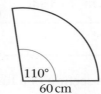

(d)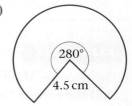

2 Give your answers to 1 decimal place.

(a)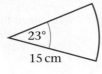

(b)

(c)

(d)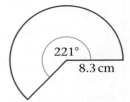

3 Work out the angles marked with a letter.

(a)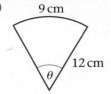

(b)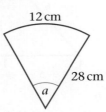

(c)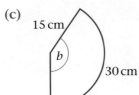

(d)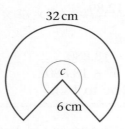

15.6 Area of a segment

- Area of a segment $= \dfrac{\pi r^2 \theta}{360°} - \dfrac{1}{2} r^2 \sin \theta$

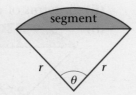

Example 11

Calculate the area of the segment shown.

Area of a segment $= \dfrac{\pi r^2 \theta}{360°} - \dfrac{1}{2}r^2 \sin \theta$

$$= \dfrac{\pi \times 8^2 \times 80}{360} - \dfrac{1}{2} \times 8^2 \times \sin 80°$$

$$= 44.680... - 31.513...$$

$$= 13.2 \text{ cm}^2 \text{ to 3 s.f.}$$

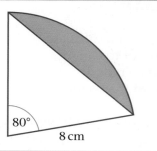

Example 12

The diagram shows a cross-section of a tunnel.
Find the area of the cross-section.

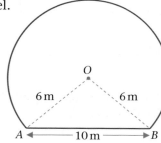

> The cross-section is a circle radius 6 m with a segment removed.
> You need to find the area of the missing segment.

First find the angle at the centre:

Using $\sin x = \dfrac{\text{opp}}{\text{hyp}}$

$$\sin x = \dfrac{5}{6}$$

$$x = 56.44...°$$

So angle of segment $= 2 \times x$

$$= 112.89...°$$

> This can also be done by adding the area of triangle *AOB* to the area of major sector *AOB*.

Area of segment $= \dfrac{\pi r^2 \theta}{360°} - \dfrac{1}{2}r^2 \sin \theta$

$$= \dfrac{\pi \times 6^2 \times 112.89...}{360} - \dfrac{1}{2} \times 6^2 \times \sin 112.89...°$$

$$= 18.880... \text{ cm}^2$$

So area of cross-section $= \pi r^2 - 18.880...$

$$= \pi \times 6^2 - 18.880...$$

$$= 94.2 \text{ m}^2 \text{ to 3 s.f.}$$

Exercise 15F

1 Calculate the area of each shaded segment, giving your answer.
   (i) to 3 significant figures   (ii) in terms of π.
   (a)   (b)

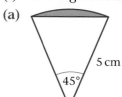

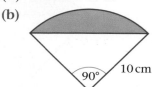

(c)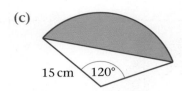

15 cm 120°

(d)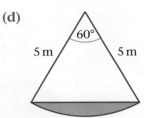

60°

5 m 5 m

2 The diagram shows a cross-section of a tunnel.

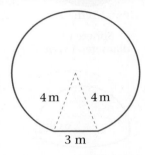

4 m 4 m

3 m

Calculate the area of the cross-section of this tunnel, which is a major segment of a circle radius 4 m.

15.7 More surface areas

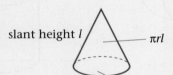

- Surface area of a cone $= \pi r l + \pi r^2$ slant height l $\pi r l$
- Surface area of a sphere $= 4\pi r^2$

πr^2

Example 13

A cone has base circumference 36 cm and height 10 cm. Work out its total surface area.

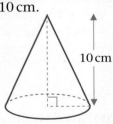

10 cm

To find the base radius:
$$2\pi r = 36$$
$$r = 5.73 \text{ cm (2 d.p.)}$$

To find the slant height:
$$l^2 = 10^2 + 5.73^2 \quad \text{(by Pythagoras)}$$
$$l = 11.525\ldots \text{ cm}$$

Surface area $= \pi r^2 + \pi r l$
$$= \pi(5.73\ldots)^2 + \pi \times 5.73\ldots \times 11.525\ldots$$
$$= 98.9\pi \quad \text{(1 d.p.)}$$
$$= 310.6 \text{ cm}^2 \text{ (1 d.p.)}$$

Exercise 15G

In these questions work out the total surface area.

1

8 cm

Sphere of
radius 8 cm

2

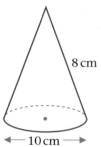

8 cm

10 cm

3

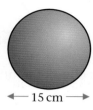

15 cm

Sphere of
diameter 15 cm

4

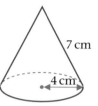

7 cm

4 cm

5

6 cm

6

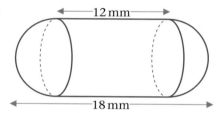

12 mm

18 mm

7

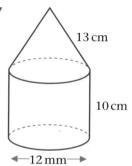

13 cm

10 cm

12 mm

15.8 Volumes of pyramids, cones and spheres

- Volume of a pyramid $= \frac{1}{3} \times$ base area $\times$ vertical height
- Volume of a cone $= \frac{1}{3} \times$ base area $\times$ vertical height
  $$= \frac{1}{3}\pi r^2 h$$
- Volume of a sphere $= \frac{4}{3}\pi r^3$

Example 14

The volume of a sphere is $500 \, \text{cm}^3$.
Find the radius of the sphere, to 3 significant figures.

$$\frac{4}{3}\pi r^3 = 500$$
$$r^3 = 500 \times \frac{3}{4\pi} = 119.366...$$
$$r = \sqrt[3]{119.366} = 4.92 \, \text{cm} \text{ (to 3 s.f.)}$$

Example 15

Steel ball bearings are cast from 3000 cm³ of molten metal.
Each ball bearing has a diameter of 4 mm.
How many can be made?

$$\text{Volume of 1 ball bearing} = \tfrac{4}{3}\pi r^3$$
$$= \tfrac{4}{3}\pi \times (0.2)^3$$
$$= 0.0335103\ldots \text{cm}^3$$

$$\text{Number of ball bearings cast} = 3000 \div 0.0335103\ldots$$
$$= 89\,524\ldots$$

A sensible answer would be 89 500 (or 90 000).

> As the volume is in cm³ it is easiest to work in cm. 4 mm = 0.4 cm and the radius is 0.2 cm.

> The answer must be a whole number, so round down.

Exercise 15H

In questions **1–6**, work out the volume.

1
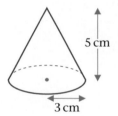
5 cm
3 cm

2
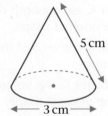
5 cm
3 cm

3
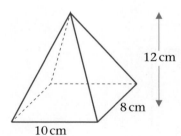
12 cm
8 cm
10 cm

4

A sphere, radius 18 cm

5
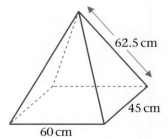
62.5 cm
45 cm
60 cm

6

A sphere, diameter 12 cm

7 A grain silo is in the shape of a cylinder on top of an inverted cone as shown.

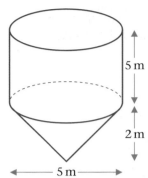

(a) How much grain does it hold when full?

(b) If 1 litre of paint covers about 15 m², how much paint would be required to paint the outside of the silo?

> The grain silo has no top.

15.9 Area and volume of similar shapes

- When a shape is enlarged by scale factor k, each length on the enlarged shape is $k \times$ the length on the original shape.
- When a shape is enlarged by scale factor k, the area of the enlarged shape is $k^2 \times$ the area of the original shape.
- When a 3-D shape is enlarged by scale factor k, the volume of the enlarged shape is $k^3 \times$ the volume of the original shape.

Example 16

A food manufacturer makes two similar boxes, regular and king-size.
The regular box has a height of 15 cm, and a volume of 1000 cm³.
The king-size box has a volume of 2500 cm³.
Calculate the height of the king-size box.

As they are similar:

$$\text{volume of king-size} = k^3 \times \text{volume of regular}$$

$$k^3 = \frac{\text{volume of king-size}}{\text{volume of regular}}$$

$$= \frac{2500}{1000}$$

$$= 2.5$$

$$k = \sqrt[3]{2.5} = 1.3572\ldots$$

So height of king-size = $k \times$ height of regular

$$= 1.3572\ldots \times 15$$

$$\text{height} = 20.36 \text{ cm to 2 d.p.}$$

Exercise 15I

1   Lemonade is sold in two sizes of similar bottles, small and giant.
    The volume of the small bottle is $500\,\text{cm}^3$, and it has height
    $10\,\text{cm}$.
    The volume of the giant bottle is 2 litres.
    Calculate the height of the giant bottle.

2   Two similar tins of food have heights $5\,\text{cm}$ and $12\,\text{cm}$.
    (a) The volume of the smaller tin is $80\,\text{cm}^3$.
        Calculate the volume of the larger tin.
    (b) The area of the label on the larger tin is $25\,\text{cm}^2$.
        Calculate the area of the label on the smaller tin.

3   A model aeroplane is built on a scale of $1:50$.
    Copy and complete this table.

Measurement	Aeroplane	Model of aeroplane
Area of roundel	$3\,\text{m}^2$	$\ldots\,\text{cm}^2$
Number of wheels	4	$\ldots$
Width	$\ldots\,\text{m}$	$6.5\,\text{cm}$
Volume of cabin	$\ldots\,\text{m}^3$	$1600\,\text{cm}^3$

4   The heights of two similar cones are in the ratio $2:5$.
    Calculate the ratio of
    (a) the surface areas of the cones
    (b) the volumes of the cones.

5   A model of a factory is built on a scale of $1:60$.
    Calculate the ratio of the volume of the real factory to the
    volume of the model factory.

15.10 Compound solids

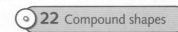 22 Compound shapes

Example 17

Find the volume of this concrete block.
It is made from the bottom part of a cone.

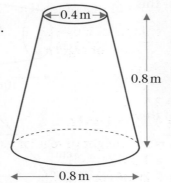

The proper name for this shape is a 'frustum'. The frustum of a cone is the part of a cone cut off between the base and a plane parallel to the base.

The block is part of a cone, height h.
Find h by similar triangles.
Triangles ABC and AED are similar.

So $\quad \dfrac{h}{0.4} = \dfrac{0.8}{0.2}$

$\qquad h = \dfrac{0.4 \times 0.8}{0.2}$

$\qquad \quad = 1.6\,\text{m}$

Volume of concrete block

$\quad$ = volume of large cone − volume of small top cone

$\quad = \frac{1}{3}\pi \times 0.4^2 \times 1.6 - \frac{1}{3}\pi \times 0.2^2 \times 0.8$

$\quad = \dfrac{0.256\pi}{3} - \dfrac{0.032\pi}{3}$

$\quad = \dfrac{0.224\pi}{3}\,\text{m}^3$

$\quad = 0.235\,\text{m}^3$ to 3 s.f.

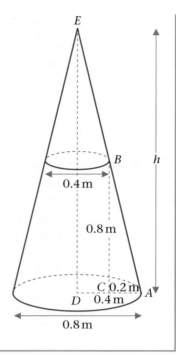

Remember:
volume of a cone = $\frac{1}{3}\pi r^2 h$

You may be asked to leave your answer in terms of π.

Exercise 15J

1 (a) Find the volume of this frustum.
Give your answer
(i) correct to 3 s.f.
(ii) in terms of π.

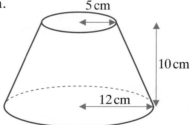

(b) Find the volume of this truncated cone.

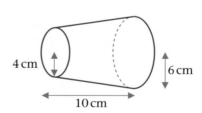

(c) Find the volume of this truncated pyramid.

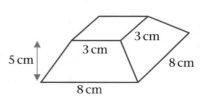

Volume of a pyramid
= $\frac{1}{3} \times$ area of base $\times$ vertical height

(d) Find the volume of
this frustum.

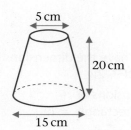

2 The solid is made up from a cone
and a hemisphere.
Calculate the volume to 2 d.p.

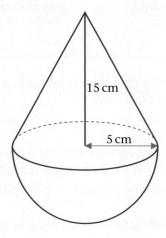

3

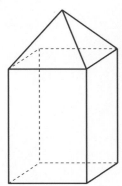

Calculate the volume of this church tower.
It is made of a cuboid 5 m × 5 m × 15 m
and a square-based pyramid of height
10 m.

4 Calculate the volume of this truncated pyramid correct
to 2 d.p.

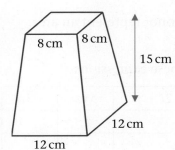

15.11 Dimensions

- All formulae for **length** or **distance** have the dimensions of length,
  e.g. perimeter of a rectangle $= 2l + 2w$
- All formulae for **area** have the dimensions of
  length $\times$ length,   e.g. area of a rectangle $= lw$
- All formulae for **volume** have the dimensions of
  length $\times$ length $\times$ length,   e.g. volume of cuboid $= lwh$

> Numbers (e.g. 5, π, $\sqrt{3}$) have no dimensions. They are dimensionless.

> l = length
> w = width
> h = height

Example 18

Write down whether each expression represents a length, an area or a volume, and explain your answer.

(a) $2\pi r$ 　　　　　(b) s^3 　　　　　(c) $\frac{1}{2}(a + b)h$

(a) Length 　　2 and π are numbers and r is a length.
　　　　　　　　Therefore it is a number $\times$ a length, giving a length.
(b) Volume 　　s^3 is a length $\times$ a length $\times$ a length, so it gives a
　　　　　　　　volume.
(c) Area 　　　$\frac{1}{2}$ is a number, $(a + b)$ is a length, and h is a length.
　　　　　　　　Number $\times$ length $\times$ length gives an area.

Exercise 15K

In this exercise all the letters represent lengths; π and all other numbers have no dimension.

1 For each of these expressions write down whether it represents a length, an area or a volume. Explain your answer.

(a) $\pi r^2 h$ 　　(b) πdh 　　　(c) x^3 　　　　(d) $l + w$

(e) $\frac{1}{2}bh$ 　　(f) $\frac{1}{3}\pi r^2 h$ 　(g) $6abc$ 　　　(h) $\frac{1}{2}\pi dl$

(i) $a(p + q)$ 　(j) $\dfrac{ab + cd}{w}$ 　(k) $pq(w + v)$ 　(l) $\dfrac{ab(c + d)}{e}$

2 Explain why the expression $a^2 + b^2 + c$ cannot represent an area.

3 Copy the table.
Tick ($\checkmark$) the box that applies for each of these expressions.

Expression	$a + b + 2c$	πr^2	$2l + w^2$	xyz	$\sqrt{3}a$	$mnpq$	$6s^2$
Length							
Area							
Volume							
None of these							

4 State whether each of the following expressions represents a length, an area or a volume, giving your reasons.

(a) $\frac{4}{3}\pi r^3$ (b) $\pi r^2 h$ (c) πd

(d) $\frac{1}{2}(a + b)h$ (e) $2l + 2w$ (f) $\pi r l$

(g) $\frac{\pi r^2 h + \pi dlh}{h}$ (h) $\frac{\pi r^2 + 2r^2}{r}$

5 In the following expressions, λ is dimensionless and x, y and z have dimensions of length. Explain whether each expression represents a length, an area or a volume.

(a) λxy (b) λxyz (c) λy^2

(d) $\lambda^2 x^2$ (e) $\lambda(x + y + z)$

Mixed exercise 15

1 Explain why the expression $\pi r^2 + \pi r^2 h$ cannot represent a volume.

2 Work out the volume of a ramp, 1 metre long with this cross-section.

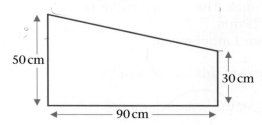

3 A cylindrical can has a diameter of 8 cm and height 15 cm.
(a) Calculate the volume of the can.
(b) Work out the total surface area of the can.

4 A bicycle wheel has a diameter of 28″ (28 inches) and a width of 1.5″.
Calculate the area the bicycle wheel covers in 50 revolutions.

5 Calculate the volume and total surface area of this metal ingot.

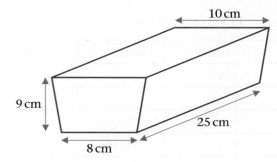

6 Work out the area of the bath mats shown.

(a)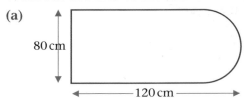

(b)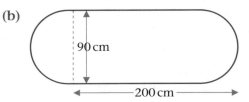

7 Find **(a)** the surface area
(b) the volume
of this pyramid.

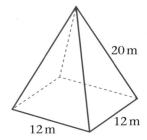

8 A spherical container is completely filled with exactly 1 litre
of water.
What is the radius of the sphere?

9 A country mints a coin which is circular with a circular hole
in the middle. The coins are 1 mm thick. The internal radius is
5 mm and the external diameter is 25 mm.
How many coins can be minted from 1 m³ of metal?

10 Work out the volume and surface area of this loaf of bread.

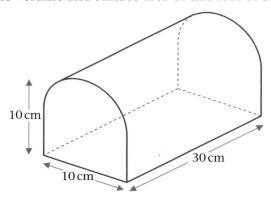

11 The table gives measurements of some planks of wood,
using mixed units, mm, cm, and m.
Copy and complete the table.

Thickness	Length	Width	Volume
12 mm	1.8 m	5 cm	
9 mm	2.4 m	8 cm	
15 mm	3.0 m		9000 cm³
5 cm		5 cm	0.02 m³

12 Here is the sector of a circle *OABC* with centre *O*. Calculate

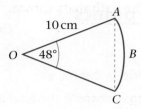

(a) the arc length *ABC*

(b) the chord length *AC*

(c) the area of the segment *ABC*.

13 In the expression λah^2, λ is dimensionless and *a* and *h* have dimensions of length.

Explain whether the expression represents a length, an area or a volume.

14 The widths and heights of two square-based pyramids are in the ratio 3:7.

Calculate the ratio of

(a) the surface areas of the pyramids

(b) the volumes of the pyramids.

15 Calculate the volume of this shape made up of a sphere, a truncated cone and a cylinder. Give your answer in terms of π.

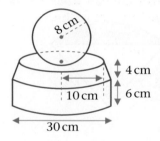

16 The diagram shows a sector *OABC* of a circle with centre *O*.

OA = *OC* = 10.4 cm.

Angle *AOC* = 120°.

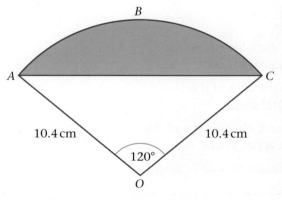

Diagram NOT accurately drawn

(a) Calculate the length of the arc *ABC* of the sector.
Give your answer correct to 3 significant figures.

(b) Calculate the area of the shaded segment *ABC*.
Give your answer correct to 3 significant figures. **[E]**

Summary of key points

1 Area of a circle $= \pi r^2$

2 Circumference of a circle $= 2\pi r$ (or πd)

3 The surface area of a solid shape is the total area of all its faces.

4 A **prism** is a 3-D shape with the same cross-section all along its length.

5 Volume of a prism $=$ area of cross-section $\times$ length

6 For a cylinder of height h with a base of radius r:
- surface area $= 2\pi rh + 2\pi r^2$
- volume $= \pi r^2 h$

7 $1\,\text{m}^2 = 10\,000\,\text{cm}^2$

8 $1\,\text{cm}^2 = 100\,\text{mm}^2$

9 $1\,\text{m}^3 = 1\,000\,000\,\text{cm}^3$

10 $1\,\text{cm}^3 = 1000\,\text{mm}^3$

11 Length of an arc $= \dfrac{\theta}{360°} \times 2\pi r$

12 Area of a sector $= \dfrac{\theta}{360°} \times \pi r^2$ or $\dfrac{\pi r^2 \theta}{360°}$

13 Area of a segment $= \dfrac{\pi r^2 \theta}{360°} - \dfrac{1}{2}r^2 \sin \theta$

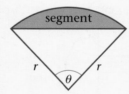

14 Surface area of a cone $= \pi rl + \pi r^2$

15 Surface area of a sphere $= 4\pi r^2$

16 Volume of a pyramid $= \dfrac{1}{3} \times$ base area $\times$ vertical height

17 Volume of a cone $= \dfrac{1}{3} \times$ base area $\times$ vertical height
$$= \tfrac{1}{3}\pi r^2 h$$

18 Volume of a sphere $= \dfrac{4}{3}\pi r^3$

19 When a shape is enlarged by scale factor k, each length on the enlarged shape is $k \times$ the length on the original shape.

20 When a shape is enlarged by scale factor k, the area of the enlarged shape is $k^2 \times$ the area of the original shape.

21 When a 3-D shape is enlarged by scale factor k, the volume of the enlarged shape is $k^3 \times$ the volume of the original shape.

22 All formulae for **length** or **distance** have the dimensions of length.

23 All formulae for **area** have the dimensions of
length $\times$ length.

24 All formulae for **volume** have the dimensions of
length $\times$ length $\times$ length.

16 Vectors

16.1 Vector facts

- A **vector** defined as 'a' has a unique length and direction.

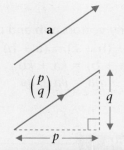

- Vectors can be used to describe translations.
  For example $\begin{pmatrix} p \\ q \end{pmatrix}$ is a translation of displacement p in the x-direction and q in the y-direction.

- You can multiply a vector by a **scalar**.
  For example
  $$2 \times \mathbf{a} = 2\mathbf{a}$$

  > A **scalar** is a number.

- A vector $k\mathbf{a}$ is parallel to $\mathbf{a}$ with length $k \times$ length of $\mathbf{a}$.

  > k is a scalar.

  For example $k \times \begin{pmatrix} p \\ q \end{pmatrix} = \begin{pmatrix} kp \\ kq \end{pmatrix}$ or $4\begin{pmatrix} 1 \\ 2 \end{pmatrix} = \begin{pmatrix} 4 \times 1 \\ 4 \times 2 \end{pmatrix} = \begin{pmatrix} 4 \\ 8 \end{pmatrix}$

- If two vectors $\mathbf{a}$ and $\mathbf{b}$ are parallel, then $\mathbf{a} = k\mathbf{b}$ for some scalar k.
- $\mathbf{a} + \mathbf{b} = \mathbf{b} + \mathbf{a}$
- The **resultant** of the vectors $\mathbf{a}$ and $\mathbf{b}$ is the vector $\mathbf{a} + \mathbf{b}$.

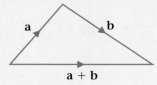

For example
$$\begin{pmatrix} 3 \\ 2 \end{pmatrix} + \begin{pmatrix} 4 \\ -3 \end{pmatrix} = \begin{pmatrix} 7 \\ -1 \end{pmatrix}$$

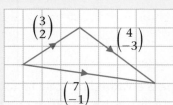

- You can subtract vectors.
  $\mathbf{p} - \mathbf{q}$ is the same as $\mathbf{p} + (-\mathbf{q})$.

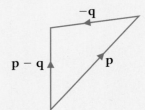

For example
$$\begin{pmatrix} 4 \\ 5 \end{pmatrix} - \begin{pmatrix} 2 \\ 4 \end{pmatrix} = \begin{pmatrix} 4 \\ 5 \end{pmatrix} + \begin{pmatrix} -2 \\ -4 \end{pmatrix} = \begin{pmatrix} 4 - 2 \\ 5 - 4 \end{pmatrix} = \begin{pmatrix} 2 \\ 1 \end{pmatrix}$$

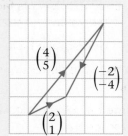

- You can use the **parallelogram rule** to add and subtract vectors.

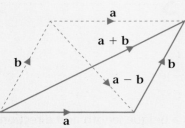

- For any vectors **a**, **b** and **c** and any scalars p, q and k:
  - $\mathbf{a} + (\mathbf{b} + \mathbf{c}) = (\mathbf{a} + \mathbf{b}) + \mathbf{c}$
  - $k(\mathbf{a} + \mathbf{b}) = k\mathbf{a} + k\mathbf{b}$
  - $(p + q)\mathbf{a} = p\mathbf{a} + q\mathbf{a}$

Example 1

A is the point $(3, -1)$ and B the point $(5, 3)$.

$\overrightarrow{AC} = \begin{pmatrix} 1 \\ 3 \end{pmatrix}$

Write down the column vector

(a) $\overrightarrow{AB}$

(b) $\overrightarrow{BA}$

(c) Write down the coordinates of C.

> $\overrightarrow{AC}$ is another way of writing down the vector that starts at A and finishes at C.

(a) $\overrightarrow{AB} = \begin{pmatrix} 2 \\ 4 \end{pmatrix}$

(b) $\overrightarrow{BA} = -\overrightarrow{AB} = \begin{pmatrix} -2 \\ -4 \end{pmatrix}$

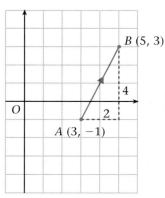

$\overrightarrow{AB} = \begin{pmatrix} 5 \\ 3 \end{pmatrix} - \begin{pmatrix} 3 \\ -1 \end{pmatrix} = \begin{pmatrix} 2 \\ 4 \end{pmatrix}$

(c)

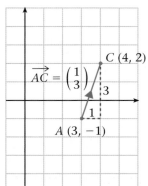

$C = \begin{pmatrix} 3 + 1 \\ -1 + 3 \end{pmatrix} = \begin{pmatrix} 4 \\ 2 \end{pmatrix}$

C is the point $(4, 2)$

Example 2

$\mathbf{m} = \begin{pmatrix} 2 \\ -1 \end{pmatrix}, \mathbf{n} = \begin{pmatrix} 3 \\ -4 \end{pmatrix}$

(a) Write as column vectors
    (i) $\mathbf{m} + \mathbf{n}$ (ii) $\mathbf{m} - \mathbf{n}$ (iii) $3\mathbf{n}$ (iv) $2\mathbf{m} - 3\mathbf{n}$

(b) Find the vector $\mathbf{y}$ such that $\mathbf{m} + 2\mathbf{y} = \mathbf{n}$

(a) (i) $\mathbf{m} + \mathbf{n} = \begin{pmatrix} 2 \\ -1 \end{pmatrix} + \begin{pmatrix} 3 \\ -4 \end{pmatrix} = \begin{pmatrix} 2 + 3 \\ -1 + -4 \end{pmatrix} = \begin{pmatrix} 5 \\ -5 \end{pmatrix}$

    (ii) $\mathbf{m} - \mathbf{n} = \begin{pmatrix} 2 \\ -1 \end{pmatrix} - \begin{pmatrix} 3 \\ -4 \end{pmatrix} = \begin{pmatrix} 2 - 3 \\ -1 - -4 \end{pmatrix} = \begin{pmatrix} -1 \\ 3 \end{pmatrix}$

    (iii) $3\mathbf{n} = 3 \times \begin{pmatrix} 3 \\ -4 \end{pmatrix} = \begin{pmatrix} 9 \\ -12 \end{pmatrix}$

    (iv) $2\mathbf{m} - 3\mathbf{n} = 2 \times \begin{pmatrix} 2 \\ -1 \end{pmatrix} - \begin{pmatrix} 9 \\ -12 \end{pmatrix} = \begin{pmatrix} 4 \\ -2 \end{pmatrix} - \begin{pmatrix} 9 \\ -12 \end{pmatrix}$

             $= \begin{pmatrix} 4 - 9 \\ -2 - -12 \end{pmatrix} = \begin{pmatrix} -5 \\ 10 \end{pmatrix}$

(b) $\mathbf{m} + 2\mathbf{y} = \mathbf{n}$
   So $2\mathbf{y} = \mathbf{n} - \mathbf{m}$

          $= \begin{pmatrix} 3 \\ -4 \end{pmatrix} - \begin{pmatrix} 2 \\ -1 \end{pmatrix} = \begin{pmatrix} 3 - 2 \\ -4 - -1 \end{pmatrix} = \begin{pmatrix} 1 \\ -3 \end{pmatrix}$

   So $\mathbf{y} = \frac{1}{2}\begin{pmatrix} 1 \\ -3 \end{pmatrix} = \begin{pmatrix} \frac{1}{2} \\ -1\frac{1}{2} \end{pmatrix}$

Exercise 16A

1 A is the point $(2, 4)$, B is the point $(-1, 5)$ and C is the point $(-2, -4)$.
Write down the column vectors
    (a) $\overrightarrow{AB}$ (b) $\overrightarrow{BA}$ (c) $\overrightarrow{AC}$ (d) $\overrightarrow{BC}$

2 A is the point $(0, 3)$ and B is the point $(-2, 5)$. $\overrightarrow{AC} = \begin{pmatrix} 2 \\ 5 \end{pmatrix}$.
    (a) Write down the column vectors
        (i) $\overrightarrow{AB}$ (ii) $\overrightarrow{BA}$
    (b) Write down the coordinates of C.

3 $\overrightarrow{AB}$ is the vector $\begin{pmatrix} 5 \\ -1 \end{pmatrix}$ and $\overrightarrow{BC}$ is the vector $\begin{pmatrix} 2 \\ 3 \end{pmatrix}$.
    (a) Work out the vector $\overrightarrow{AC}$.
    (b) Draw a diagram to illustrate your answer.

4 $\mathbf{m} = \begin{pmatrix} 3 \\ 2 \end{pmatrix}$ $\mathbf{n} = \begin{pmatrix} 2 \\ -5 \end{pmatrix}$
Work out these vector calculations, showing the resultant vectors on a coordinate grid.
    (a) $\mathbf{m} + \mathbf{n}$ (b) $\mathbf{m} - \mathbf{n}$ (c) $3\mathbf{m}$ (d) $2\mathbf{n}$ (e) $3\mathbf{m} - 2\mathbf{n}$

5 $\mathbf{a} = \begin{pmatrix} 1 \\ 3 \end{pmatrix}$ $\mathbf{b} = \begin{pmatrix} 3 \\ 2 \end{pmatrix}$

Work out the resultant vectors of

(a) $3\mathbf{a} - 2\mathbf{b}$

(b) $2\mathbf{b} - 3\mathbf{a}$

(c) Find the vector $\mathbf{x}$ such that $\mathbf{a} + 2\mathbf{x} = \mathbf{b}$

6 $\mathbf{a} = \begin{pmatrix} 2 \\ 5 \end{pmatrix}$ $\mathbf{b} = \begin{pmatrix} 1 \\ 1 \end{pmatrix}$

Draw a diagram to show that

(a) $3(\mathbf{a} + \mathbf{b}) = 3\mathbf{a} + 3\mathbf{b}$

(b) $(3 + 4)\mathbf{a} = 3\mathbf{a} + 4\mathbf{a}$

16.2 Linear combinations of vectors

- Combinations of the vectors **a** and **b** of the form $p\mathbf{a} + q\mathbf{b}$, where p and q are scalars, are called **linear combinations** of the vectors **a** and **b**.

- Vectors parallel to the x-axis have y-component zero: for example $\begin{pmatrix} a \\ 0 \end{pmatrix}$ or $m\mathbf{a}$.

- Vectors parallel to the y-axis have x-component zero: for example $\begin{pmatrix} 0 \\ b \end{pmatrix}$ or $n\mathbf{b}$.

Example 3

$\mathbf{a} = \begin{pmatrix} 1 \\ 5 \end{pmatrix}$ $\mathbf{b} = \begin{pmatrix} 3 \\ 2 \end{pmatrix}$

(a) Find scalars p and q such that $p\mathbf{a} + q\mathbf{b}$ is parallel to the x-axis.

(b) Find scalars m and n such that $m\mathbf{a} + n\mathbf{b}$ is parallel to the y-axis.

(a) $p\mathbf{a} + q\mathbf{b} = p\begin{pmatrix} 1 \\ 5 \end{pmatrix} + q\begin{pmatrix} 3 \\ 2 \end{pmatrix}$

To be parallel to the x-axis, the y-component of the vector must be zero.

So $p\begin{pmatrix} 1 \\ 5 \end{pmatrix} + q\begin{pmatrix} 3 \\ 2 \end{pmatrix} = \begin{pmatrix} \text{some value, say } x \\ 0 \end{pmatrix}$

$\begin{pmatrix} p + 3q \\ 5p + 2q \end{pmatrix} = \begin{pmatrix} x \\ 0 \end{pmatrix}$

Then $5p + 2q = 0$

Two possible values are $p = 2$, $q = -5$

So $2\mathbf{a} - 5\mathbf{b}$ is parallel to the x-axis.

There are many other possible values.

(b) $ma + nb = m\begin{pmatrix} 1 \\ 5 \end{pmatrix} + n\begin{pmatrix} 3 \\ 2 \end{pmatrix}$

To be parallel to the y-axis, the x-component of the vector must be zero.

So $m\begin{pmatrix} 1 \\ 5 \end{pmatrix} + n\begin{pmatrix} 3 \\ 2 \end{pmatrix} = \begin{pmatrix} 0 \\ y \end{pmatrix}$

$\begin{pmatrix} m + 3n \\ 5m + 2n \end{pmatrix} = \begin{pmatrix} 0 \\ y \end{pmatrix}$

Then $m + 3n = 0$

Two possible values are $m = 3$ and $n = -1$.

So $3a - b$ is parallel to the y-axis.

> y is some value.

Example 4

Find the values of the scalars p and q when $p\begin{pmatrix} 5 \\ 2 \end{pmatrix} + q\begin{pmatrix} -1 \\ 4 \end{pmatrix} = \begin{pmatrix} 7 \\ 16 \end{pmatrix}$

$\begin{pmatrix} 5p \\ 2p \end{pmatrix} + \begin{pmatrix} -q \\ 4q \end{pmatrix} = \begin{pmatrix} 7 \\ 16 \end{pmatrix}$

So

$5p - q = 7$ (1)

$2p + 4q = 16$ (2)

$20p - 4q = 28$ •——— $4 \times (1)$ (3)

$22p = 44$ •

$p = 2$ $(3) + (2)$

Substitute $p = 2$ into (1):

$5 \times 2 - q = 7$

$q = 3$

So $p = 2$ and $q = 3$.

> Solve these two simultaneous equations for p and q.

Exercise 16B

1   $a = \begin{pmatrix} 2 \\ -1 \end{pmatrix}$ and $b = \begin{pmatrix} 6 \\ 2 \end{pmatrix}$; calculate x, given that $a + x = b$

2   $m = \begin{pmatrix} 3 \\ -1 \end{pmatrix}$ and $n = \begin{pmatrix} 2 \\ -5 \end{pmatrix}$; calculate y, given that $m + 3y = n$

3   $r = \begin{pmatrix} 5 \\ -2 \end{pmatrix}$ and $s = \begin{pmatrix} -1 \\ 3 \end{pmatrix}$; calculate z, given that $2r + z = s$

4   $a = \begin{pmatrix} 2 \\ 3 \end{pmatrix}$ $b = \begin{pmatrix} 3 \\ 5 \end{pmatrix}$

    (a) Find scalars p and q such that $pa + qb$ is parallel to the x-axis.

    (b) Find scalars r and s such that $ra + sb$ is parallel to the y-axis.

5   $a = \begin{pmatrix} 4 \\ -1 \end{pmatrix}$ $b = \begin{pmatrix} 2 \\ 1 \end{pmatrix}$

    Given that $a + pb$ is parallel to the y-axis, find the value of p.

6 Find values of p and q when $p\begin{pmatrix}2\\1\end{pmatrix} + q\begin{pmatrix}3\\-1\end{pmatrix} = \begin{pmatrix}8\\1\end{pmatrix}$.

7 Find a linear combination of vectors $\mathbf{a} = \begin{pmatrix}2\\3\end{pmatrix}$ and $\mathbf{b} = \begin{pmatrix}-1\\2\end{pmatrix}$
which is equal to the vector $\begin{pmatrix}2\\5\end{pmatrix}$.

16.3 Position vectors

- The **position vector** of a point P is OP, where O is usually the origin.

  For example

  $\overrightarrow{OP}$ is position vector $\begin{pmatrix}2\\3\end{pmatrix}$

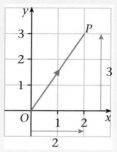

Example 5

A is the point $(2, 1)$ and B is the point $(4, 7)$.
Calculate the position vector of the midpoint of AB.

Let the midpoint of $AB = M$.
$\overrightarrow{OM}$ is the position vector of M.

$$\overrightarrow{OA} + \overrightarrow{AM} = \overrightarrow{OM}$$
$$\overrightarrow{OA} + \tfrac{1}{2}\overrightarrow{AB} = \overrightarrow{OM}$$

So $\begin{pmatrix}2\\1\end{pmatrix} + \tfrac{1}{2}\begin{pmatrix}2\\6\end{pmatrix} = \overrightarrow{OM}$

$$\begin{pmatrix}2\\1\end{pmatrix} + \begin{pmatrix}1\\3\end{pmatrix} = \overrightarrow{OM}$$

$$\overrightarrow{OM} = \begin{pmatrix}3\\4\end{pmatrix}$$

$\overrightarrow{AB} = \begin{pmatrix}4\\7\end{pmatrix} - \begin{pmatrix}2\\1\end{pmatrix} = \begin{pmatrix}2\\6\end{pmatrix}$
$\overrightarrow{AM} = \tfrac{1}{2}\overrightarrow{AB} = \tfrac{1}{2}\begin{pmatrix}2\\6\end{pmatrix}$

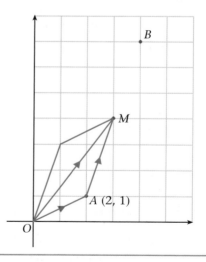

- If A and B have position vectors
  $\mathbf{a}$ and $\mathbf{b}$, then the position vector of
  the midpoint, M, of the line joining
  A to B is

  $$\overrightarrow{OM} = \mathbf{m} = \tfrac{1}{2}(\mathbf{a} + \mathbf{b})$$

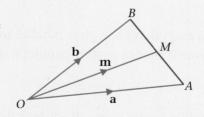

- If A and B have position vectors
  a and **b** respectively, then the vector

  $$\overrightarrow{AB} = \mathbf{b} - \mathbf{a}$$

  This is called the **triangle rule**.

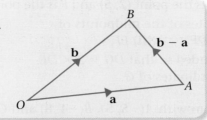

Example 6

The position vector of $A = \mathbf{a}$.
The position vector of $B = \mathbf{b}$.
C lies on the line AB and $AC = \frac{1}{3}CB$.
Find the position vector of C.

Draw a
diagram.

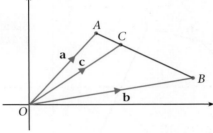

$$\overrightarrow{OC} = \overrightarrow{OA} + \overrightarrow{AC}$$
$$AC = \tfrac{1}{3}CB, \text{ so } \overrightarrow{AC} = \tfrac{1}{4}\overrightarrow{AB}$$
$$\overrightarrow{AB} = \mathbf{b} - \mathbf{a}$$

Using the parallelogram rule.

So $\quad \overrightarrow{AC} = \tfrac{1}{4}(\mathbf{b} - \mathbf{a})$
$$\overrightarrow{OC} = \overrightarrow{OA} + \overrightarrow{AC}$$
$$= \mathbf{a} + \tfrac{1}{4}(\mathbf{b} - \mathbf{a})$$
$$= \tfrac{3}{4}\mathbf{a} + \tfrac{1}{4}\mathbf{b}$$

Exercise 16C

1 A is the point $(2, 3)$ and B is the point $(8, 7)$.
   Calculate the position vector of the midpoint of AB.

2 The position vector of $A = \mathbf{a}$.
   The position vector of $B = \mathbf{b}$.
   C lies on the line AB and $AC = \frac{1}{4}CB$.
   Find the position vector of C.

3 A is the point $(3, -3)$ and B is the point $(9, 3)$.
   C lies on the line AB, such that $AC = \frac{1}{2}CB$.
   Calculate the coordinates of C.

4 *D* is the point (3, 2), *E* is the point (2, 5) and *F* is the point (−1, −1).

    (a) Find the coordinates of the midpoints of
        (i) *DE*   **(ii)** *DF*   **(iii)** *EF*

    (b) *G* lies on *DE* extended so that *DG* = 2 × *DE*.
        Calculate the coordinates of *G*.

5 *ABCD* is a parallelogram with *A*(−5, 5), *B*(−4, 8) and *C*(−4, 2).
    Write down the position vector of *D* and the midpoint of *BD*.

16.4 Proving geometrical results

Example 7

Prove that when the midpoints of the sides of a quadrilateral are joined, the shape formed is a parallelogram.

OABC is a quadrilateral.
$$\vec{OA} = \mathbf{a}$$
$$\vec{AB} = \mathbf{b}$$
$$\vec{OC} = \mathbf{c}$$

P, *Q*, *R*, *S* are the midpoints of *OA*, *AB*, *BC* and *OC* respectively.

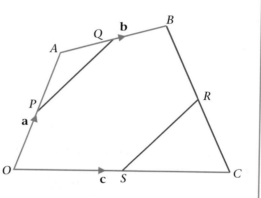

Sketch any quadrilateral *OABC*.

$$\vec{PQ} = \vec{PA} + \vec{AQ}$$
$$= \tfrac{1}{2}\mathbf{a} + \tfrac{1}{2}\mathbf{b}$$
$$\vec{SR} = \vec{SO} + \vec{OA} + \vec{AB} + \vec{BR}$$
$$= -\tfrac{1}{2}\mathbf{c} + \mathbf{a} + \mathbf{b} + \vec{BR}$$
$$= -\tfrac{1}{2}\mathbf{c} + \mathbf{a} + \mathbf{b} + \tfrac{1}{2}(-\mathbf{b} - \mathbf{a} + \mathbf{c})$$
$$= -\tfrac{1}{2}\mathbf{c} + \mathbf{a} + \mathbf{b} - \tfrac{1}{2}\mathbf{b} - \tfrac{1}{2}\mathbf{a} + \tfrac{1}{2}\mathbf{c}$$
$$= \tfrac{1}{2}\mathbf{a} + \tfrac{1}{2}\mathbf{b}$$
$$= \vec{PQ}$$

So *PQ* and *SR* are parallel.
$$\vec{QR} = \vec{QB} + \vec{BR}$$
$$= \tfrac{1}{2}\vec{AB} + \vec{BR}$$
$$= \tfrac{1}{2}\mathbf{b} + \tfrac{1}{2}(-\mathbf{b} - \mathbf{a} + \mathbf{c})$$
$$= -\tfrac{1}{2}\mathbf{a} + \tfrac{1}{2}\mathbf{c}$$
$$\vec{PS} = \tfrac{1}{2}\vec{AO} + \tfrac{1}{2}\vec{OC}$$
$$= -\tfrac{1}{2}\mathbf{a} + \tfrac{1}{2}\mathbf{c}$$
$$= \vec{QR}$$

So *PS* is parallel to *QR*.
Hence *PQRS* is a parallelogram.

To show that *PQRS* is a parallelogram you need to show that *PQ* and *SR* are parallel, and that *QR* and *PS* are parallel.

$$\vec{BR} = \tfrac{1}{2}\vec{BC}$$
$$= \tfrac{1}{2}(\vec{BA} + \vec{AO} + \vec{OC})$$
$$= \tfrac{1}{2}(-\mathbf{b} - \mathbf{a} + \mathbf{c})$$

Example 8

Prove that the diagonals of a rhombus bisect each other.

In rhombus $OACB$

$$\overrightarrow{OA} = \mathbf{a}$$
$$\overrightarrow{OB} = \mathbf{b}$$

Opposite sides are parallel and equal so

$$\overrightarrow{BC} = \mathbf{a}$$
$$\overrightarrow{AC} = \mathbf{b}$$

So

$$\overrightarrow{OC} = \overrightarrow{OA} + \overrightarrow{AC}$$
$$= \mathbf{a} + \mathbf{b}$$

Let M be the midpoint of $\overrightarrow{OC}$.

$$\overrightarrow{OM} = \tfrac{1}{2}\overrightarrow{OC}$$
$$= \tfrac{1}{2}(\mathbf{a} + \mathbf{b})$$

But $\tfrac{1}{2}(\mathbf{a} + \mathbf{b})$ is the position vector of the midpoint of AB.

So OC bisects AB and AB bisects OC.

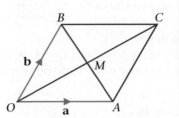

> A rhombus has
> 4 equal sides
> 2 pairs of parallel sides.

Mixed exercise 16

1 A is the point $(1, 3)$, B is the point $(-2, 4)$ and C is the point $(5, -7)$.
Write down the column vectors
  (a) $\overrightarrow{AB}$ (b) $\overrightarrow{AC}$ (c) $\overrightarrow{CA}$ (d) $\overrightarrow{BC}$

2 $\mathbf{a} = \begin{pmatrix} 5 \\ 3 \end{pmatrix}$ $\mathbf{b} = \begin{pmatrix} -2 \\ 3 \end{pmatrix}$
Work out
  (a) $\mathbf{a} + \mathbf{b}$ (b) $\mathbf{b} - \mathbf{a}$ (c) $3\mathbf{b}$ (d) $2\mathbf{a} - 3\mathbf{b}$

3 $\mathbf{a} = \begin{pmatrix} 3 \\ 1 \end{pmatrix}$ $\mathbf{b} = \begin{pmatrix} 4 \\ 3 \end{pmatrix}$
Work out
  (a) $3\mathbf{a} - 2\mathbf{b}$
  (b) $4\mathbf{b} - \mathbf{a}$
  (c) Find the vector x such that $\mathbf{a} + 2\mathbf{x} = \mathbf{b}$

4 $\mathbf{a} = \begin{pmatrix} 3 \\ -2 \end{pmatrix}$ and $\mathbf{b} = \begin{pmatrix} -1 \\ 3 \end{pmatrix}$; calculate x given that $\mathbf{a} + \mathbf{x} = \mathbf{b}$

5 $\mathbf{a} = \begin{pmatrix} 5 \\ -2 \end{pmatrix}$ $\mathbf{b} = \begin{pmatrix} 5 \\ 3 \end{pmatrix}$
Find scalars p and q such that $p\mathbf{a} + q\mathbf{b}$ is parallel to the y-axis.

6 Find values of p and q such that
$$p\begin{pmatrix} -1 \\ 2 \end{pmatrix} + q\begin{pmatrix} 2 \\ 3 \end{pmatrix} = \begin{pmatrix} 4 \\ 13 \end{pmatrix}$$

7 $OABC$ is a parallelogram.
$\overrightarrow{OA} = \mathbf{a}$
$\overrightarrow{OC} = \mathbf{c}$
Work out

(a) $\overrightarrow{OB}$ (b) $\overrightarrow{AC}$

Express your answers in terms of $\mathbf{a}$ and $\mathbf{c}$.

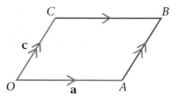

8 The position vector of $A = \mathbf{a}$.
The position vector of $B = \mathbf{b}$.
C is a point on AB such that $AC = \frac{1}{2}CB$.
Find the position vector of C.

9 M and N are the midpoints of the sides OA and OB of a triangle. Prove that the line AB is parallel to the line MN and equal to twice the length of MN.

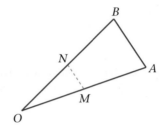

10 In triangle ABC, M is the midpoint of BC and N is the midpoint of AC.
$\overrightarrow{AB} = \mathbf{b}$ and $\overrightarrow{BC} = \mathbf{c}$.
BN is produced to a point D so that $BD:BN = 4:3$.

(a) Write $\overrightarrow{AM}$ and $\overrightarrow{DC}$ in terms of $\mathbf{b}$ and $\mathbf{c}$.

(b) Prove that AM is parallel to DC and $AM:DC = 3:2$.

11

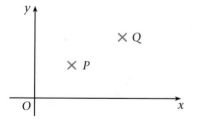

Diagram NOT accurately drawn

The diagram is a sketch.
P is the point $(2, 3)$.
Q is the point $(6, 6)$.

(a) Write down the vector $\overrightarrow{PQ}$

     Write your answer as a column vector $\begin{pmatrix} x \\ y \end{pmatrix}$

$PQRS$ is a parallelogram.
$\overrightarrow{PR} = \begin{pmatrix} 4 \\ 7 \end{pmatrix}$

(b) Find the vector $\overrightarrow{QS}$

     Write your answer as a column vector $\begin{pmatrix} x \\ y \end{pmatrix}$ [E]

12

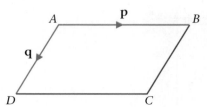

Diagram NOT
accurately drawn

$ABCD$ is a parallelogram.
AB is parallel to DC.
AD is parallel to BC.
$\overrightarrow{AB} = \mathbf{p}$
$\overrightarrow{AD} = \mathbf{q}$

Express, in terms of $\mathbf{p}$ and $\mathbf{q}$

(a) $\overrightarrow{AC}$
(b) $\overrightarrow{BD}$

13

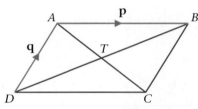

Diagram NOT
accurately drawn

AC and BD are diagonals of parallelogram $ABCD$.
AC and BD intersect at T.

Express $\overrightarrow{AT}$ in terms of $\mathbf{p}$ and $\mathbf{q}$.

Summary of key points

1 A **vector** defined as 'a' has a unique length and direction.

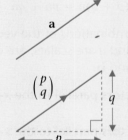

2 Vectors can be used to describe translations.
For example $\begin{pmatrix} p \\ q \end{pmatrix}$ is a translation of displacement p in the
x-direction and q in the y-direction.

3 You can multiply a vector by a **scalar**. | A **scalar** is a number. |
For example
$$2 \times \mathbf{a} = 2\mathbf{a}$$

4 A vector $k\mathbf{a}$ is parallel to $\mathbf{a}$ with length $k \times$ length of $\mathbf{a}$. | k is a scalar. |
For example $k \times \begin{pmatrix} p \\ q \end{pmatrix} = \begin{pmatrix} kp \\ kq \end{pmatrix}$ or $4\begin{pmatrix} 1 \\ 2 \end{pmatrix} = \begin{pmatrix} 4 \times 1 \\ 4 \times 2 \end{pmatrix} = \begin{pmatrix} 4 \\ 8 \end{pmatrix}$

5 If two vectors **a** and **b** are parallel, then **a** = k**b** for some scalar k.

6 **a** + **b** = **b** + **a**.

7 The **resultant** of the vectors **a** and **b** is the vector **a** + **b**.

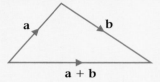

8 You can subtract vectors.
p − **q** is the same as **p** + (−**q**).

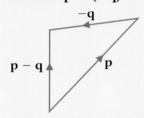

9 You can use the **parallelogram rule** to add and subtract vectors.

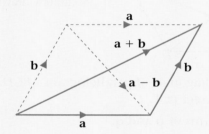

10 For any vectors **a**, **b** and **c** and any scalars p, q and k:
   ○ **a** + (**b** + **c**) = (**a** + **b**) + **c**
   ○ k(**a** + **b**) = k**a** + k**b**
   ○ (p + q)**a** = p**a** + q**a**

11 Combinations of the vectors **a** and **b** of the form p**a** + q**b**, where p and q are scalars, are called **linear combinations** of the vectors **a** and **b**.

12 Vectors parallel to the x-axis have y-component zero: for example $\begin{pmatrix} a \\ 0 \end{pmatrix}$ or m**a**.

13 Vectors parallel to the y-axis have x-component zero: for example $\begin{pmatrix} 0 \\ b \end{pmatrix}$ or n**b**.

14 The **position vector** of a point P is OP, where O is usually the origin.

15 If A and B have position vectors **a** and **b**, then the position vector of the midpoint, M, of the line joining A to B is

$$\overrightarrow{OM} = \mathbf{m} = \tfrac{1}{2}(\mathbf{a} + \mathbf{b})$$

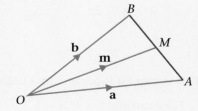

16 If A and B have position vectors **a** and **b** respectively, then the vector

$$\overrightarrow{AB} = \mathbf{b} - \mathbf{a}$$

This is called the **triangle rule**.

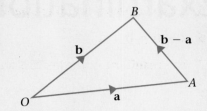

Examination practice paper

Section A (calculator)

1   Mark, Anne and Barbara share £7200 in the ratio 4 : 3 : 2.
    Work out how much each person receives.   **(3 marks)**

2   (a)   A shop sells a television for £800 plus $17\frac{1}{2}$% VAT.
          What is the total cost of the television?   **(3 marks)**

    (b)   In one week the shop sells 40 televisions.
          Of these, 5 are HD televisions.
          What percentage of the televisions are HD televisions?
                                                               (2 marks)

    (c)   A television is sold for £510 in a 15% sale.
          What was the original price of the television?   **(3 marks)**

3   Find the area of a circle of diameter 14 cm.
    Give your answer correct to 3 significant figures.   **(2 marks)**

4   Use the method of trial and improvement to solve the equation
        $x^3 - 2x = 37$.
    Give your answer correct to 2 decimal places.   **(4 marks)**

5   (a)   Solve $7 < 2n < 14$.   **(2 marks)**

    (b) x is an integer. Write down all the possible values
          of x if $-3 < x < 2$.   **(2 marks)**

6   A piece of machinery has a value of £5000 when new.
    Its value depreciates by 18% each year.
    What will its value be after 3 years?   **(3 marks)**

7   A cylinder has a diameter of 8 cm and
    a height of 10 cm.
    Calculate the total surface area of
    the cylinder.
    Give your answer correct to
    3 significant figures.

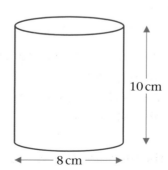

10 cm

(4 marks)   ← 8 cm →

8 Calculate the length of *AC*.
Give your answer correct to 3 significant figures.

(3 marks)

9 *BC* is parallel to *DE*.
Find the length of *CE*.

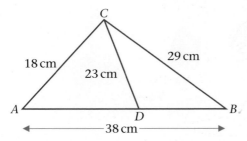

(3 marks)

10 A manufacturer claims that his 200 g jar of milk shake powder
will make approximately 110 glasses of milk shake.
The 200 g is correct to 3 significant figures.
The 110 glasses is correct to 2 significant figures.

(a) Write down the upper and lower bound for
(i) the 200 g (ii) the 110 glasses. **(4 marks)**

(b) Calculate the upper bound for the mean weight of
milk shake powder in each glass. **(2 marks)**

11

In the triangle *ABC*, *AB* = 38 cm, *BC* = 29 cm and *AC* = 18 cm.

(a) Calculate the size of angle *BAC*. **(3 marks)**

(b) *D* is a point on *AB* with *CD* = 23 cm.
Calculate the size of angle *ADC*. **(3 marks)**

12 Make *t* the subject of the formula $5(t + y) = 3y + 7$. **(3 marks)**

13 (a) y is directly proportional to x, and $y = 8$ when $x = 5$.
Calculate the value of y when $x = 7$. **(2 marks)**

(b) w is inversely proportional to the square of u, and $w = 12$
when $u = 5$.
Calculate the value of u when $w = 27$. **(3 marks)**

14 Solve $x^2 - 10x + 18 = 0$.
Give your answers correct to 2 decimal places. **(3 marks)**

15 The sketch graph shows a curve with equation $y = pq^x$,
where $q > 0$.
The curve passes through the points $(1, 10)$ and $(3, 160)$.
Calculate the values of p and q.

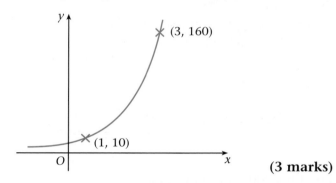

(3 marks)

Total for Section A: 60 marks

Section B (non-calculator)

1 Work out (a) $\frac{7}{8} - \frac{3}{5}$ (b) $1\frac{2}{3} \div \frac{1}{4}$ **(4 marks)**

2 (a) The price of a coat is reduced by 20% on Monday.
It is reduced by 20% again on Tuesday.
Explain why this is not a reduction of 40%. **(2 marks)**

(b) Another coat is reduced from £80 to £60.
Work out the percentage reduction. **(3 marks)**

3 Jane used these ingredients to make 24 cakes:

100 g butter, 80 g sugar, 2 eggs, 90 g flour, 30 ml milk

Write down how much of each ingredient Jane will need
to make 36 cakes. **(3 marks)**

4 For a cone, draw a sketch of (a) the plan (b) the front elevation.
(4 marks)

5

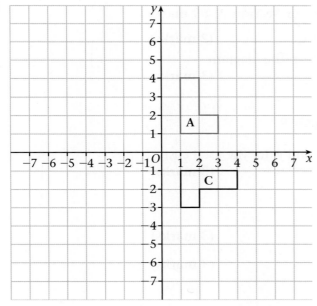

(a) Reflect shape **A** in the line $x = -1$. Label the image **B**.
(2 marks)

(b) Shape **A** has been mapped to shape **C**.
Describe the transformation from **A** to **C**. **(2 marks)**

(c) Enlarge shape **A** by a scale factor 2 from the point $(3, 5)$.
Label the image **D**. **(2 marks)**

6

(a) Use ruler and compasses only to construct the bisector of angle ABC. **(2 marks)**

(b) Draw the locus of points that are 2 cm from AB. **(2 marks)**

(c) Shade all the points that are no more than 2 cm from point C. **(2 marks)**

7 Here are some expressions:

$$\frac{ab}{2c}, \quad 2\pi ab^2, \quad c(a + b), \quad 2\pi a^3, \quad \pi abc, \quad 2(a^2 + b^2)$$

The letters all represent length and π and 2 are numbers that have no dimensions. Write **two** expressions that could represent areas. **(2 marks)**

8

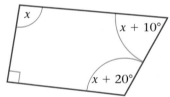

(a) Write down an equation in terms of x. **(2 marks)**

(b) Calculate the size of the largest angle in the diagram. **(3 marks)**

9 A pen costs 50 pence. A pencil costs 10 pence.
Martin buys x pens and y pencils.
Write down an expression, in terms of x and y, for the total cost, in pence. **(3 marks)**

10 Solve
(a) $3(x - 4) = 30$ **(3 marks)**

(b) $\dfrac{17 - x}{4} = 2 - x$ **(3 marks)**

11 Solve the simultaneous equations $2x + 5y = -1$ and $6x - y = 5$. **(4 marks)**

12 Two cans have heights of 8 cm and 16 cm.
The cans are mathematically similar.
The first can has a weight of 200 g.
What is the weight of the second can? **(2 marks)**

13 D is the midpoint of AB,
   E is the midpoint of DC.
   $\overrightarrow{AB}$ is the vector **a**.
   $\overrightarrow{BC}$ is the vector **b**.
   Write down an expression,
   in terms of **a** and **b**, for the
   vector $\overrightarrow{AE}$.

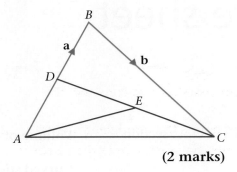

(2 marks)

14 Evaluate $(1 + \sqrt{3})^2$. Give your answer in the form $a + b\sqrt{3}$.

(2 marks)

15 A line L has an equation of the form $y = mx + c$.
   Line L passes through the points $(0, 2)$ and $(4, 14)$.
   Find the equation of line L.   **(3 marks)**

16 A cylinder has a radius of x cm and a height of $2x$ cm.
   A sphere has a radius of r cm.
   The surface area of the cylinder is the same as the surface
   area of the sphere.
   Show that $r = \sqrt{\dfrac{3}{2}}x$.   **(3 marks)**

Total for Section B: 60 marks

Formulae sheet

Volume of a prism = area of cross-section × length

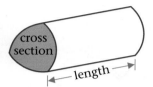

Volume of sphere = $\frac{4}{3}\pi r^3$

Surface area of sphere = $4\pi r^2$

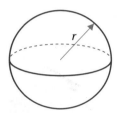

In any triangle ABC

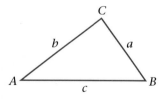

Sine rule $\dfrac{a}{\sin A} = \dfrac{b}{\sin B} = \dfrac{c}{\sin C}$

Cosine rule $a^2 = b^2 + c^2 - 2bc\cos A$

Area of triangle = $\frac{1}{2}ab\sin C$

Volume of cone = $\frac{1}{3}\pi r^2 h$

Curved surface area of cone = πrl

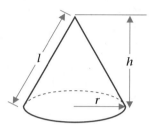

The quadratic equation
The solutions of $ax^2 + bx + c = 0$, where $a \neq 0$, are given by

$$x = \frac{-b \pm \sqrt{(b^2 - 4ac)}}{2a}$$

Answers

Exercise 1A

1 13.172 **2** 1.4288 **3** 12.15 **4** 151.36
5 361 **6** 453 **7** 893 **8** 5.6
9 57.1 **10** 11.9232 **11** £94.96

Exercise 1B

1 (a) $\frac{1}{5}$ (b) $\frac{1}{6}$ (c) $\frac{1}{9}$
(d) $\frac{1}{3}$ (e) $\frac{1}{10}$ (f) $\frac{1}{18}$
2 (a) 5 (b) $\frac{10}{7}$ or $1\frac{3}{7}$ (c) $\frac{4}{3}$ or $1\frac{1}{3}$
(d) $\frac{10}{6}$ or $1\frac{2}{3}$ (e) 20 (f) 8
3 (a) $2\frac{1}{2}$ (b) $1\frac{3}{4}$ (c) $1\frac{1}{3}$
(d) $2\frac{2}{3}$ (e) $3\frac{3}{4}$ (f) $1\frac{3}{7}$
4 (a) $\frac{1}{n}$ (b) $\frac{1}{m^3}$ (c) y (d) x^2

Exercise 1C

1 (a) -8 (b) 15 (c) 20 (d) -18 (e) -3
(f) 5 (g) 1 (h) 56 (i) -9
2 (a)

$\div$	12	-16	48
-2	-6	8	-24
$+4$	3	-4	12
-8	$-1\frac{1}{2}$	-2	-6

(b)

$\times$	-3	5	-13
11	-33	55	-143
-7	21	-35	91
-3	9	-15	39

Exercise 1D

1 (a) $\frac{1}{81}$ (b) $\frac{1}{9}$ (c) $\frac{1}{125}$ (d) $\frac{1}{81}$ (e) 7
(f) $\frac{1}{10000}$ (g) 2 (h) 100 (i) $\frac{1}{8}$ (j) $\frac{1}{6}$
(k) $\frac{1}{5}$ (l) 1 (m) 25 (n) 243 (o) 343
(p) $\frac{1}{216}$ (q) $\frac{1}{243}$
2 (a) $\frac{1}{2}$ (b) 9 (c) 4 (d) 4 (e) $\frac{1}{36}$
(f) 1 (g) 64 (h) 2 (i) $\frac{1}{64}$ (j) $\frac{1}{27}$
(k) $\frac{5}{49}$ (l) 16 (m) $\frac{1}{9}$

Exercise 1E

1 (a) $\frac{1}{6}$ (b) $\frac{3}{10}$ (c) $\frac{5}{12}$
2 $\frac{9}{40}$
3 (a) $1\frac{1}{4}$ (b) $\frac{1}{8}$ (c) $1\frac{5}{6}$ (d) $1\frac{11}{20}$
(e) $1\frac{3}{8}$ (f) $5\frac{7}{8}$ (g) $1\frac{8}{15}$ (h) $4\frac{5}{24}$
4 (a) $26\frac{3}{5}$ (b) $\frac{1}{2}$ (c) $8\frac{1}{4}$ (d) 35
(e) 8 (f) $3\frac{3}{5}$ (g) $3\frac{3}{7}$ (h) $10\frac{1}{4}$
(i) 24 (j) 3 (k) 7 (l) $3\frac{4}{5}$
(m) 2 (n) $1\frac{1}{2}$ (o) $2\frac{1}{4}$ (p) $\frac{5}{8}$
(q) 28 (r) $\frac{5}{12}$ (s) $2\frac{1}{7}$ (t) $\frac{7}{8}$

Exercise 1F

1 (a) 0.375 (b) 0.109375
(c) 0.68 (d) 0.776
(e) 0.3472 (f) 0.291$\dot{6}$
(g) 0.2$\dot{4}$ (h) 0.$\dot{5}$384$\dot{6}\dot{1}$
(i) 0.13$\dot{6}$ (j) 0.$\dot{6}\dot{3}$
(k) 0.27$\dot{1}$ (l) 0.$\dot{3}$5897$\dot{4}$
2 $\frac{3}{4}, \frac{7}{10}, \frac{9}{50}, \frac{3}{15}$

Mixed exercise 1

1 (a) 9.5256 (b) 456
2 (a) $\frac{1}{9}$ (b) $\frac{1}{8}$ (c) 2 (d) $\frac{8}{5}$ or $1\frac{3}{5}$
(e) $\frac{5}{4}$ or $1\frac{1}{4}$ (f) $\frac{7}{5}$ or $1\frac{2}{5}$ (g) $\frac{1}{m}$ (h) y
3 (a) -8 (b) 40 (c) -21
(d) $\frac{1}{2}$ (e) -143 (f) -2
4 (a) $\frac{11}{15}$ (b) $2\frac{1}{6}$ (c) $2\frac{7}{8}$
(d) $5\frac{1}{2}$ (e) $3\frac{4}{7}$ (f) $3\frac{3}{10}$
5 (a) $\frac{9}{40}$ (b) $\frac{13}{20}$
6 (a) 0.875 (b) 0.58$\dot{3}$ (c) 0.894…
7 $\frac{14}{20}, \frac{7}{8}, \frac{9}{25}$

Exercise 2A

1 (a) (i) 0.75 (ii) $\frac{3}{4}$
(b) (i) 0.3 (ii) $\frac{3}{10}$
(c) (i) 0.65 (ii) $\frac{13}{20}$
(d) (i) 0.48 (ii) $\frac{12}{25}$
(e) (i) 0.64 (ii) $\frac{16}{25}$
(f) (i) 0.325 (ii) $\frac{13}{40}$
(g) (i) 0.875 (ii) $\frac{7}{8}$
(h) (i) 0.$\dot{6}$ (ii) $\frac{2}{3}$
(1) (i) 0.$\dot{3}$ (ii) $\frac{1}{3}$
2 (a) 75% (b) 80% (c) 28% (d) 85%
(e) 95% (f) 70% (g) $67\frac{1}{2}$% (h) $47\frac{1}{2}$%
(i) $22\frac{1}{2}$% (j) $41\frac{2}{3}$%
3

Fraction	Decimal	Percentage
$\frac{1}{20}$	0.05	5%
$\frac{3}{10}$	0.3	30%
$\frac{16}{25}$	0.64	64%
$\frac{15}{16}$	0.9375	$93\frac{3}{4}$%
$\frac{5}{6}$	0.8$\dot{3}$	$83\frac{1}{3}$%

4 Art (80%)

Exercise 2B

1 (a) 57   (b) 420   (c) 121   (d) 84
   (e) £19.26   (f) £91.80   (g) £87.50   (h) 787.5 kg
   (i) 100 g   (j) £53.73
2 (a) 130   (b) 120
3 5.25 g
4 £4510
5 84 pages
6 £8
7 £2.25

Exercise 2C

1 (a) £350   (b) £131.25
   (c) £196.88 (to nearest penny)
2 (a) £14 040   (b) £17 992   (c) £25 688
3 (a) £250   (b) £500   (c) £2500
4 Ladder: £96.35
   Tin of paint: £7.05
   Electric drill: £44.06 (to nearest penny)
5 (a) 440 g   (b) 1.65 kg   (c) 247.5 g
6 (a) £678 950   (b) £1 322 750
   (c) £2 127 500   (d) £334 800
7 £3055.50
8 £77.51 (to nearest penny)
9 £33 600

Exercise 2D

1 (a) 60p   (b) £3.20   (c) £1.00
2 £15 000   3 £100 000
4 £120   5 £120 000
6 £20 872 (to nearest pound)   7 261 g (to nearest g)
8 £12.50   9 £10
10 £19 231 (to nearest pound)   11 70 g

Exercise 2E

1 90%   2 80%
3 (a) 26%   (b) 38.4%   (c) 35.6%
4 (a) $66\frac{2}{3}$%   (b) $33\frac{1}{3}$%
5 20%   6 17.5%
7 25%   8 20%

Exercise 2F

1 (a) £531.50
   (b) £600.58 (to nearest penny)
   (c) £678.64 (to nearest penny)
2 £544.54 (nearest penny)
3 £14 599.83 (nearest penny)
4 5 yrs (after 9 yrs she is 50p short)
5 £1172.54 (nearest penny)
6 £336.17 (to nearest penny)

Mixed exercise 2

1 (a) 75%   (b) 87.5%   (c) 40%
   (d) 45%   (e) 27.5%   (f) $91\frac{2}{3}$%
2 $\frac{75}{110}$
3 (a) £9   (b) 0.375 kg   (c) £32.50   (d) 3.5 m
4 £900
5 £3.75
6 Bath: £94
   Tap: £12.34 (to nearest penny)
   Tiles: £14.10 per dozen

7 (a) £29.33 (to nearest penny)
   (b) £123.25   (c) £51
8 £78 788 (to nearest pound)
9 (a) 68   (b) 12
10 £423
11 £37.40
12 80%
13 No, the increase is $12\frac{1}{2}$%
14 £511.13 (nearest penny)
15 348 cm²
16 15%
17 22% (nearest %)
18 £192.86 (nearest penny)
19 £214.87 (nearest penny)
20 4 years
21 (a) £192 × $\frac{120}{100}$ = £230.40 (not £240)
   (b) £200
22 24.72 litres

Exercise 3A

1 (a) (i) 2:1   (ii) $1:\frac{1}{2}$ (iii) 2:1
   (b) (i) 3:1   (ii) $1:\frac{1}{3}$ (iii) 3:1
   (c) (i) 4:1   (ii) $1:\frac{1}{4}$ (iii) 4:1
   (d) (i) 1:2   (ii) 1:2   (iii) $\frac{1}{2}$:1
   (e) (i) 5:1   (ii) $1:\frac{1}{5}$ (iii) 5:1
   (f) (i) 3:2   (ii) $1:\frac{2}{3}$ (iii) 1.5:1
2 (a) (i) 8:3   (ii) $1:\frac{3}{8}$ (iii) $2\frac{2}{3}$:1
   (b) (i) 24:5   (ii) $1:\frac{5}{24}$ (iii) 4.8:1
   (c) (i) 3:7   (ii) $1:2\frac{1}{3}$ (iii) $\frac{3}{7}$:1
   (d) (i) 11:24   (ii) $1:2\frac{2}{11}$ (iii) $\frac{11}{24}$:1
   (e) (i) 16:25   (ii) $1:1\frac{9}{16}$ (iii) $\frac{16}{25}$:1
   (f) (i) 7:20   (ii) $1:2\frac{6}{7}$ (iii) $\frac{7}{20}$:1
3 (a) (i) 8:3   (ii) $1:\frac{3}{8}$ (iii) $2\frac{2}{3}$:1
   (b) (i) 4:1   (ii) 1:0.25   (iii) 4:1
   (c) (i) 12:1   (ii) $1:\frac{1}{12}$ (iii) 12:1
   (d) (i) 4:1   (ii) 1:0.25   (iii) 4:1
   (e) (i) 2:1   (ii) 1:0.5   (iii) 2:1
   (f) (i) 8:7   (ii) $1:\frac{7}{8}$ (iii) $1\frac{1}{7}$:1
4 (a) 1:2:3   (b) 4:2:1   (c) 5:3:2
   (d) 5:3:1   (e) 6:4:1   (f) 8:6:1
5 4 times   6 1:4   7 3:5

Exercise 3B

1 (a) 1   (b) 4   (c) 2   (d) 2
   (e) 3   (f) 18   (g) 12   (h) 40
2 9 women
3 28 cm
4 30 raisins
5 9.6 cm
6 £216.80
7 20 000 cm² or 2 m²

Exercise 3C

1 (a) 15:10   (b) 70:30
   (c) £24:£6   (d) £14.35:£10.25
   (e) 200:100:50   (f) 90 cm:30 cm:30 cm
   (g) £120:£90:£30   (h) £20.50:£12.30:£4.10

2 Juan £96, Gabrielle £64, Kwame £40
3 800 women
4 $\frac{4}{7}$
5 17.5 cm
6 (a) $\frac{1}{5}$ (b) 140 g
7 George £30, Charlie £18, Ryan £12
8 (a) $\frac{1}{3}$ (b) $\frac{1}{9}$ (c) 1000
9 (a) $\frac{1}{3}$ (b) 21
10 (a) 40 (b) $\frac{2}{11}$

Exercise 3D

1 150 g haddock, 75 g prawns
2 (a) £20 (b) £130
3 (a) 9.1 mg (b) 18.2 mg
4 (a) $\frac{3}{20}$ (b) 5 : 12 : 3 (c) 36 blue, 9 green
5 (a) 2 (b) Douglas £100, Gillian £400

Exercise 3E

1 (a) 100 km (b) 250 km (c) 25 km
2 (a) 3 h (b) 5 h 50 min (c) 2 h 20 min
3 (a) £1.50 (b) £19.50
4 (a) £3.74 (b) £41.14
5 (a) 6000 (b) 333 (c) 1667 (to nearest word)
6 9.375 or $9\frac{3}{8}$ min
7 3.75 m
8 £21.30
9 (a) 100 days (b) 25 days
10 3 days
11 10 oz flour, 5 oz butter, $2\frac{1}{2}$ oz sugar
12 5 hours
13 6 days
14 9 days
15 £3.04
16 4 h 40 min
17 (a) 8.78 volts (b) 5.70 amps (to 2 d.p.)
18 (a) 161.29 miles (b) 5.58 litres

Exercise 3F

1 3.54 kg (to 2 d.p.) 2 £76 095 (nearest pound)
3 32.8 cm (to 1 d.p.) 4 17 294
5 £54 698 (nearest pound) 6 41 rabbits
7 84 hamsters 8 9 years

Exercise 3G

1 0.55 kg
2 (a) $V = \frac{10.9}{6.2} I$ (b) 7.56 volts (3 s.f.)
3 (a) $C = \frac{37.7}{6} r$ or $C = 2\pi r$ (b) 50.3 cm (3 s.f.)
4 (a) $m = 0.003 v$ (b) 1.275 kg (3 s.f.)
5 (a) $h = 1.5 s$
   (b) Length of shadow = 6.4 m
   (c) Height of tree = 18.9 m
6

x	4	6	10
y	15	10	6

7 5 drinks 8 18 cm

Mixed exercise 3

1 (a) 4 : 1 (b) 4 : 2 : 1 (c) 5 : 12
   (d) 4 : 5 (e) 6 : 1 (f) 5 : 8

2 (a) 8 (b) 4
3 5 cm
4 £70
5 3 : 2
6 £1.95
7 7.5 m
8 625 g flour, 250 g fat, 125 g sugar
9 990 g (nearest g)
10 35.6 cm (to 1 d.p.)
11 £535.29
12 £57.30 (to nearest penny)
13 7 years
14 between 7 and 8 years
15 $(1.015)^{50}$
16 (a) $\frac{1}{3}$ (b) £2400
17 Amy 8, Beth 12, Colin 16
18 (a) 2 : 3 : 4 (b) 200 ml
19 6 days
20 £3.00
21 (a) 960 s (b) 560 s
22

a	25	15	9
b	36	60	100

23 (a) 18 414 (b) 1 491 534

Exercise 4A

1 (a) 1.5×10^8 (b) 1.05×10^0 (c) 3.6×10^3
   (d) 3.84×10^6 (e) 3×10^{-7} (f) 4×10^3
   (g) 5×10^1 (h) 9×10^{-10}
2 (a) 210 000 000 (b) 368 (c) 0.000 003 04
   (d) 15.5 (e) 0.000 000 08 (f) 0.0071
3 (a) 2 800 000 (b) 2.7 (c) 3600
   (d) 0.0024 (e) 20 000 (f) 500
   (g) 2250 (h) 0.04
4 30 times
5 236 people per km^2
6 8.375×10^{-18}

Exercise 4B

1 3.655 55 (or better)
2 41.2 (1 d.p.)
3 (a) £360 (b) £288.26 (nearest penny)
4 £222 797.15 (nearest penny)
5 2.6 (1 d.p.)
6 1.77 (3 s.f.)
7 £2877.08 (nearest penny)

Exercise 4C

1 (a) 128 grains (b) 32 768 grains
2 (a) 16 777 216 cells (b) 3.74×10^{50} cells (3 s.f.)
3 43 680
4 1220 m^3 (3 s.f.)
5 (a) 58 320 (b) 1 574 640 (c) 3.83×10^8 (3 s.f.)
6 4.7×10^7 (2 s.f.)

Exercise 4D

1 (a) $2\sqrt{7}$ (b) $3\sqrt{5}$ (c) $2\sqrt{2}$
   (d) $3\sqrt{3}$ (e) $2\sqrt{15}$ (f) $2\sqrt{3}$
   (g) $\frac{2}{3}\sqrt{3}$ (h) $\frac{\sqrt{6}}{2}$ (i) $\frac{3}{5}\sqrt{3}$

2 Area = $6\sqrt{2}$
3 Area = 36π cm^2, circumference = 12π cm
4 (a) Radius = $2\sqrt{3}$ cm (b) Circumference = $4\sqrt{3}\pi$ cm

Exercise 4E

1 (a) $\pm 2\sqrt{5}$ (b) $\pm 3\sqrt{2}$ (c) $\pm\sqrt{2}$

2 (a) $\dfrac{\sqrt{5}}{5}$ (b) $\dfrac{2\sqrt{3}}{3}$ (c) $2\sqrt{7}$ (d) $4\sqrt{5}$

3 (a) $19 + 8\sqrt{3}$ (b) 23 (c) $54 - 14\sqrt{5}$

4 (a) (i) $m = \frac{7}{2}$ (ii) $n = 1$ (b) $t = 3$

5 $\dfrac{67 - 42\sqrt{2}}{7}$

6 $x = \pm 6\sqrt{2}$ 7 $4 + 2\sqrt{3}$ 8 $2 + \frac{5}{3}\sqrt{3}$

Exercise 4F

1 (a) Smallest 11.5 cm
    Largest 12.5 cm
  (b) Smallest 10.015 m
    Largest 10.025 m
  (c) Smallest 5.5 cm
    Largest 6.5 cm
  (d) Smallest 9.005 m
    Largest 9.015 m
  (e) Smallest 7.995 m
    Largest 8.005 m

2 Between 22.5 km and 23.5 km

3 (a) Minimum 175
    Maximum 185
  (b) Minimum 530 050
    Maximum 530 150
  (c) Minimum 0.0015
    Maximum 0.0025
  (d) Minimum 0.003 15
    Maximum 0.003 25

4 upper bound 12.35 seconds
  lower bound 12.25 seconds

5 (a) 2.45 cm, 4.55 cm, 6.85 cm
  (b) 2.35 cm, 4.45 cm, 6.75 cm

Exercise 4G

1 upper bound $= 14.3325$ cm^2
  lower bound $= 13.5125$ cm^2
2 upper bound $= 30.25\pi$ cm^2
  lower bound $= 20.25\pi$ cm^2
3 upper bound $= 9.56$ cm (3 s.f.)
  lower bound $= 9.33$ cm (3 s.f.)
4 upper bound $= 41.5$ cm
  lower bound $= 38.5$ cm
5 upper bound $= 8.66$ m/s (3 s.f.)
  lower bound $= 8.58$ m/s (3 s.f.)
6 upper bound $= 15\,°C$
  lower bound $= 13\,°C$
7 upper bound $= 0.47\pi$ m
  lower bound $= 0.45\pi$ m
8 upper bound $= 3.21$ g/cm^3 (3 s.f.)
  lower bound $= 2.82$ g/cm^3 (3 s.f.)
9 upper bound $= 1.35$ (3 s.f.)
  lower bound $= 1.27$ (3 s.f.)
10 upper bound $= 70$
  lower bound $= 23.4$ (3 s.f.)

Mixed exercise 4

1 (a) $\frac{1}{9}$ (b) $\frac{1}{7}$ (c) 243
  (d) 125 (e) 0.001 (f) 512
2 (a) 1.15×10^7 (b) 1.24×10^2
  (c) 4×10^6 (d) 4.5×10
3 (a) 3600 (b) $0.000\,24$
  (c) $30\,000$ (d) $0.000\,000\,000\,225$

4 7.344×10^{19} kg

5 (a) $2\sqrt{5}$ (b) $3\sqrt{7}$ (c) $4\sqrt{3}$ (d) $\dfrac{\sqrt{3}}{2}$

6 Length $= 3\sqrt{3}$ cm

7 Area $= (112 + 8\pi)$ cm^2

8 (a) $\dfrac{\sqrt{13}}{13}$ (b) $7\sqrt{6}$

9 $9 + 4\sqrt{5}$

10 (a) Length $= 13.95$ cm,   Width $= 7.95$ cm
  (b) Length $= 14.05$ cm,   Width $= 8.05$ cm

11 (a) 99.5 m
  (b) (i) 14.75 s   (ii) 14.85 s
  (c) (i) $6.700\,336\,7$ m/s
      (ii) $6.813\,559\,3$ m/s
  (d) (i) 6.76 m/s
      (ii) mean of the lower and upper bounds

12 (a) $8\,450\,000$ and $8\,550\,000$ km^2
  (b) 21.83 and 21.46 people/km^2

13 upper bound 5775, lower bound 1575

14 $0.034\,340$ (to 5 s.f.)

15 (a) 4 (b) 2 (c) $83.\dot{3}\%$

16 (a) 2 (b) $\frac{3}{2}$ (c) $16\sqrt{2}$ (d) $\dfrac{\sqrt{2}}{32}$

Exercise 5A

1 $x = 3$ 2 $x = 7$
3 $x = 6$ 4 $x = 7$
5 $x = 16$ 6 $x = 20$
7 $x = \frac{1}{3}$ 8 $x = -3$
9 $x = 3\frac{1}{2}$ 10 $x = 0$
11 $x = -12$ 12 $x = -1\frac{2}{3}$
13 $x = 2\frac{3}{4}$ 14 $x = -4$
15 $x = 0$ 16 $x = 18$
17 $x = \frac{5}{6}$ 18 $x = 3\frac{1}{4}$
19 $x = -6$ 20 $x = -\frac{2}{3}$

Exercise 5B

1 $x = 5$ 2 $x = \frac{1}{2}$
3 $x = 6$ 4 $x = 7$
5 $x = -3$ 6 $x = 0$
7 $x = 4\frac{1}{3}$ 8 $x = \frac{3}{4}$
9 $x = 8\frac{1}{2}$ 10 $x = -2$
11 $x = -\frac{2}{3}$ 12 $x = 8$
13 $x = -4\frac{3}{4}$ 14 $x = -3$
15 $x = 2$

Exercise 5C

1 $x = 2$ 2 $x = -3$
3 $x = 3\frac{1}{4}$ 4 $x = \frac{4}{5}$
5 $x = 1\frac{1}{4}$ 6 $x = \frac{3}{10}$
7 $x = \frac{2}{3}$ 8 $x = -\frac{7}{10}$
9 $x = 2\frac{1}{2}$ 10 $x = -1\frac{1}{2}$
11 $x = 1\frac{3}{4}$ 12 $x = -\frac{1}{4}$
13 $x = 1\frac{1}{3}$ 14 $x = -\frac{1}{2}$
15 $x = 0$ 16 $x = 6$
17 $x = 1\frac{2}{5}$ 18 $x = 6$
19 $x = -1$ 20 $x = -\frac{4}{5}$

Exercise 5D

1 $7n$ **2** $5a$ cm **3** $56f + 64g$
4 $25 - n$ **5** $\dfrac{36}{y}$
6 (a) $x = 5$
  (b) Identity. Simplifying on the left gives $4x - 3$.
  (c) Identity. Expanding the left gives $7x - 21$.
  (d) $x = -3$
  (e) Identity. Expanding each side gives $6x - 30$.
  (f) $x = 10$
  (g) $x = 3$
  (h) Identity. Simplifying the left gives $2x + 1$.
  (i) Identity. Simplifying the left gives $5x$.
  (j) $x = 0$

Exercise 5E

1 angle $DBE = 67°$ **2** angle $PQR = 48°$
3 $49°$ **4** 16 cm, 17 cm, 31 cm
5 Number is 24 **6** $y = 8.5$
7 Numbers are 38, 5 and 14 **8** Rashid is 51
9 Length is 17 cm **10** Number is 13
11 Numbers are 17 and 29 **12** Mrs Banerji is 41
13 Largest number is 33 **14** $x = 8$, $y = 7$
15 She had 14 20p coins

Exercise 5F

1 $x = 12$ **2** $x = 24$
3 $x = 23$ **4** $x = 20$
5 $x = 11$ **6** $x = 2\frac{2}{3}$
7 $x = -4$ **8** $x = 24$
9 $x = 1\frac{1}{2}$ **10** $x = 23$
11 $x = 1\frac{1}{2}$ **12** $x = -\frac{2}{5}$
13 $x = 2\frac{1}{3}$ **14** $x = 6\frac{1}{2}$
15 $x = -2\frac{2}{3}$ **16** $x = 6\frac{3}{5}$
17 $x = -2$ **18** $x = 4$
19 $x = 2\frac{1}{2}$ **20** $x = -4\frac{1}{2}$
21 $x = 1$ **22** $x = \frac{1}{2}$
23 $x = 12$ **24** $x = 10\frac{1}{2}$
25 $x = 47$ **26** $x = 6\frac{1}{4}$
27 $x = -4$ **28** $x = -13$
29 $x = -\frac{1}{8}$ **30** $x = -4\frac{2}{5}$

Exercise 5G

1 $x = 9$ **2** $x = \frac{5}{8}$ **3** $x = 1\frac{3}{5}$
4 $x = \frac{1}{6}$ **5** $x = \frac{3}{10}$ **6** $x = 2\frac{1}{6}$
7 $x = 2\frac{2}{5}$ **8** $x = \frac{1}{24}$ **9** $x = 3\frac{2}{5}$
10 $x = -1\frac{1}{2}$ **11** $x = \frac{3}{4}$ **12** $x = -\frac{7}{8}$
13 $x = 3\frac{1}{6}$ **14** $x = -1$ **15** $x = 4\frac{2}{3}$
16 $x = 0$ **17** $x = 2\frac{1}{2}$ **18** $x = -\frac{2}{3}$
19 $x = \frac{1}{4}$ **20** $x = -24\frac{1}{2}$ **21** $x = -1\frac{2}{11}$

Exercise 5H

1 x^9 **2** x^3 **3** x^{10}
4 $14x^8$ **5** $40x^6$ **6** $30x^{13}$
7 $6x^3$ **8** $5x$ **9** $4x^5$

10 $3x^8$ **11** $64x^3$ **12** $21x^6y^7$
13 $20x^9y^5$ **14** $56x^8y^6$ **15** $30x^9y^8$
16 $7x^3y^3$ **17** $3x^4y^7$ **18** $\frac{3}{5}x^5$
19 $4x^3$ **20** $80x^{10}$ **21** $16x^8y^{10}$
22 $40x^{13}y^6$ **23** $3x^2$ **24** $2x^4$
25 $8x^6y^2$

Exercise 5I

1 (a) 9 (b) $1\frac{1}{2}$ (c) $\frac{1}{2}$ (d) 1 (e) 4
2 (a) $\dfrac{1}{x^3} = x^{-3}$ (b) $x^{-8} = \dfrac{1}{x^8}$
3 (a) x^{-3} (b) x^{-5} (c) $20x^2$
  (d) x^{-3} (e) x^{-5} (f) x^6
  (g) $4x^{-3}$ (h) $8x^{-3}$ (i) x^{-8}
  (j) x^{15} (k) $\frac{1}{9}x^{-8}$ (l) x^3y^{-3}
  (m) 2 (n) $5y$

Exercise 5J

1 (a) 100 (b) 50 (c) 149 (d) 1
  (e) 5 (f) 9 (g) 9 (h) 125
2 (a) 18 (b) 50 (c) -36 (d) 192
  (e) -4 (f) 64
3 (a) -15 (b) $-7\frac{1}{5}$ (c) 1 (d) $-\frac{5}{9}$
  (e) 120 (f) $506\frac{1}{4}$

Mixed exercise 5

1 $x = 2\frac{2}{3}$ **2** $x = \frac{3}{5}$
3 $x = 5\frac{3}{4}$ **4** $x = -1\frac{1}{6}$
5 $x = 1\frac{1}{2}$ **6** $x = -3$
7 $x = 3$ **8** $x = -1$
9 $x = -\frac{3}{5}$ **10** $x = \frac{2}{3}$
11 $x = 1$ **12** $x = -\frac{1}{2}$
13 $x = \frac{4}{5}$ **14** $x = -1\frac{1}{2}$
15 $x = 4\frac{4}{5}$ **16** $x = -\frac{3}{4}$
17 $x = 1$ **18** $x = \frac{1}{8}$
19 $x = -2$ **20** $x = \frac{5}{9}$
21 $x = 1\frac{3}{8}$ **22** $x = -\frac{1}{3}$
23 $x = -1\frac{7}{10}$
24 Equal angles are 72°, other angle is 36°
25 Number is 17
26 (a) Identity (b) Identity (c) $x = 4$
  (d) $x = -1$ (e) Identity (f) Identity
27 (a) x^8 (b) x^5 (c) x^{15}
  (d) $6x^{10}$ (e) $8x^5$ (f) $32x^{15}$
  (g) $20x^9y^5$ (h) $8x$ (i) $3x^4$
28 (a) 1 (b) 3 (c) 1
29 (a) x^{-1} (b) $15x^{-9}$ (c) x^{-4}
  (d) $3x^5$ (e) $3x^{-5}$ (f) x^{-6}
  (g) x^{12} (h) $\frac{1}{8}x^{-15}$
30 $180° - 2a°$
31 (a) 6 (b) 86 (c) 11.25
32 (a) -66 (b) -2 (c) 80
  (d) 75 (e) 64 (f) 31

Exercise 6A

1 $d = vt$

2 $T = 30W + 30$

3 $C = F + 0.4m$

4 $P = 6h$

5 $v = \dfrac{d}{t}$

6 $A = \frac{1}{2}bh$

7 $C = 500 - 47n$

Exercise 6B

1 $y = -5$

2 $V = 240$

3 $A = 209$

4 $s = 6.6$

5 $F = -40$

6 $A = 37.5$

7 $A = 670$

8 $v = -13$

9 $d = 5.35$

10 $A = 59.4$

11 $y = 7$

12 $s = 67.5$

13 $d = 125.05$

14 $D = 54$

15 $H = 10.5$

16 $E = -127.5$

17 $A = 147$

18 $y = -4$

19 $v = -3.9$

20 $F = 304.2$

21 $V = 12\,200$

22 $d = 270$

23 $P = 28.5$

24 $R = 0.0021$

25 $A = 2260$

26 $v = 21.6$

27 $D = 16$

28 $T = 14.3$

29 $v = 13.8$

30 $v = 160$

Exercise 6C

1 $x = -2$

2 $R = 48$

3 $r = 3.45$ (3 s.f.)

4 $a = 9.3$

5 $C = 35$

6 $b = 19$

7 $r = 3.45$ (3 s.f.)

8 $t = 3.6$

9 $C = 18.5$ (3 s.f.)

10 $d = 10.4$ (3 s.f.)

11 $x = \pm 4$

12 $u = 9$

13 $A = 9$

14 $u = 7$

15 $x = -3$

16 $v = 5$

17 $r = 3.63$ (3 s.f.)

18 $h = 3.2$

19 $h = 5.78$

20 $x = 15$

Exercise 6D

1 $I = \dfrac{P}{V}$

2 $r = \dfrac{A}{\pi l}$

3 $x = \dfrac{y + 3}{4}$

4 $n = \dfrac{t - 5}{3}$

5 $y = P - 2x$

6 $x = \dfrac{P - y}{2}$

7 $u = v + gt$

8 $t = \dfrac{u - v}{g}$

9 $b = \dfrac{2A}{h}$

10 $a = 2s - b - c$ **11** $M = VD$

12 $V = \dfrac{M}{D}$

13 $v = \dfrac{I + mu}{m}$

14 $u = \dfrac{mv - I}{m}$

15 $h = \dfrac{2A}{a + b}$

16 $b = \dfrac{2A - ah}{h}$

17 $x = 3(y + 2)$

18 $x = \dfrac{v + 2}{2}$

19 $y = \dfrac{x - 6}{3}$

20 $A = 2(17 - H)$ **21** $x = 5 - 2y$

22 $x = \dfrac{2y + 6}{3}$

23 $y = \dfrac{3x - 6}{2}$

24 $V = \dfrac{mv}{m + M}$

25 $c = \pm\sqrt{\dfrac{E}{m}}$

26 $a = \pm\sqrt{c^2 - b^2}$ **27** $v = \pm 10\sqrt{d}$

28 $R = \pm\sqrt{\dfrac{A + \pi r^2}{\pi}}$ **29** $t = \dfrac{d - L}{La}$

30 $a = \dfrac{kL - T}{k}$

31 $a = \pm\sqrt{\dfrac{3I}{4M}}$

32 $x = \pm\sqrt{\dfrac{2aE}{L}}$

33 $x = a(y - b)$

34 $f = \dfrac{uv}{u + v}$

35 $u = \dfrac{vf}{v - f}$

36 $x = \pm\sqrt{2(y + 5)}$

37 $m = \dfrac{2E}{v^2 - u^2}$

38 $a = \pm\sqrt{\dfrac{3I - Mb^2}{M}}$

39 $R = \dfrac{100(A - P)}{PT}$

40 $P = \dfrac{100A}{RT + 100}$

41 $a = \dfrac{bx}{b - y}$

42 $r = \pm\sqrt{\dfrac{GMm}{F}}$

43 $D = \sqrt[3]{\dfrac{6V}{\pi}}$

44 $L = \sqrt[3]{\dfrac{3EIx}{W}}$

45 $r = \pm\sqrt{\dfrac{12I - 4Ma^2}{3M}}$

46 $I = ma^2$

47 $h = \dfrac{v^2}{2g}$

48 $v = e - i^2R$

49 $h = \dfrac{2d^2}{25}$

50 $M = \dfrac{m}{R^2 - 3}$

51 $y = \dfrac{a - bc}{2b - 1}$

52 $x = \dfrac{y + 3}{y - 2}$

Exercise 6E

1 $s = \frac{1}{2}gt^2$

2 $A = \dfrac{\pi d^2}{4}$

3 $E = \frac{1}{2}kx^2$

4 $V = \frac{1}{2}rS$

5 (a) $A = \dfrac{P^2}{24}$ (b) $V = \left(\dfrac{P}{12}\right)^3$

Mixed exercise 6

1 $C = 6.35 + 0.0825x$

2 $S = 180(n - 2)$

3 (a) $T = 8x + 4h$

 (b) Rearranging gives $h = \dfrac{T - 8x}{4}$

 (c) $V = \dfrac{x^2(T - 8x)}{4}$

4 $A = 6d^2$

5 (a) $e = 53$ (b) $R = 9$

6 (a) $y = 17$ (b) $x = 7$

7 (a) $L = 64.2$ (3 s.f.) (b) $r = 3.4$ (2 s.f.)

8 (a) $I = 7.5$ (b) $d = 20$

9 (a) $r = 2.36$ (3 s.f.) (b) $A = 290$ (3 s.f.)

10 (a) $V = 1430$ (3 s.f.) (b) $R = 7.3$ (2 s.f.)

11 $A = 54$

12 (a) $h = \dfrac{E}{mg}$ (b) $D = VT$

 (c) $T = \dfrac{D}{V}$ (d) $I = \dfrac{V - e}{R}$

 (e) $n = \dfrac{2S}{a + l}$ (f) $l = \dfrac{2S - na}{n}$

13 (a) $y = b(a - c)$ (b) $y = \dfrac{c - ab}{a}$

 (c) $y = \pm\sqrt{\dfrac{ac}{b}}$ (d) $y = \pm\sqrt{\dfrac{a - c}{b}}$

 (e) $y = \dfrac{c}{a - b}$ (f) $y = \dfrac{c}{a + b}$

 (g) $y = \dfrac{ab - cd}{c - a}$ (h) $y = \pm\sqrt{\dfrac{a - bc}{b}}$

 (i) $y = \pm\sqrt{\dfrac{c}{a - b}}$ (j) $y = \pm\sqrt{\dfrac{b}{a + c}}$

 (k) $y = \sqrt[3]{\dfrac{ac}{b}}$ (l) $y = \dfrac{a - bc}{c - 1}$

14 $y = 10t + 3$

15 $a = r\omega^2$

16 $y = 2x + 5$

Exercise 7A

1 (a)

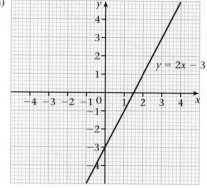

$y = 2x - 3$

(i) 2   **(ii)** $y = -3$

(b)

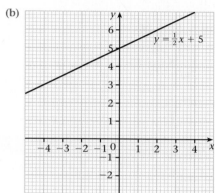

$y = \frac{1}{2}x + 5$

(i) $\frac{1}{2}$ **(ii)** $y = 5$

(c)

$y = 12 - 3x$

(i) -3 **(ii)** $y = 12$

(d)

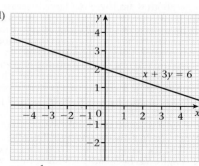

$x + 3y = 6$

(i) $-\frac{1}{3}$ **(ii)** $y = 2$

(e)

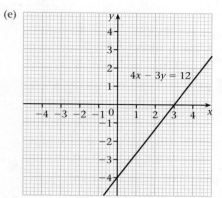

$4x - 3y = 12$

(i) $\frac{4}{3}$ **(ii)** $y = -4$

(f)

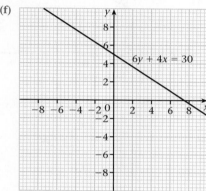

$6y + 4x = 30$

(i) $-\frac{2}{3}$ **(ii)** $y = 5$

2 $y = 4x - 22$

3 $y = -\frac{2}{3}x + 2\frac{2}{3}$

4 (a) $y = 5 - 2x$ **(b)** $y = -1 - 2x$

5 Gradient $= \frac{9}{4}$, intercept $= 6$

6 $y = 3x - 2$

7 (a) (i) and (iii), (ii) and (iv)
  (b) (ii) and (iv)
  (c) (i) and (ii)

8 (a) $y = 2x + 1$ **(b)** $y = 2x + 3$ **(c)** $y = 2x + 1$

9 (a) $2y + 3x - 15 = 0$
  (b) $2y + 3x - 7 = 0$
  (c) $2y + 3x - 6 = 0$

10 Equation of AC: $y = \frac{1}{2}x + \frac{1}{2}$

    Equation of BD: $y = \frac{7}{2} - \frac{1}{2}x$

11 $m = 45$, $c = 30$

Exercise 7B

1 (a) $-\frac{1}{2}$ **(b)** $\frac{1}{3}$

2 $y = -\frac{1}{2}x + 5$

3 (a) (i) 3   (ii) $-\frac{1}{3}$

  (b) (i) 1   (ii) -1

  (c) (i) $\frac{1}{2}$ (ii) -2

  (d) (i) $-\frac{3}{2}$ (ii) $\frac{2}{3}$

  (e) (i) $\frac{2}{5}$ (ii) $-\frac{5}{2}$

4 (a) $y = 3x - 3$ **(b)** $y = -\frac{1}{3}x - 2$

5 (a) (i) $-\frac{3}{5}$ (ii) (0, 3)

  (b) $5y + 3x = -20$ **(c)** $y = \frac{5x}{3} - 21$

6 $y = \frac{x}{5} - 3$

7 (a) B and F, D and E
(b) A is perpendicular to C.
B and F are perpendicular to D and E.

Exercise 7C

Equations will depend on chosen line of best fit.

1 (a)
(b)

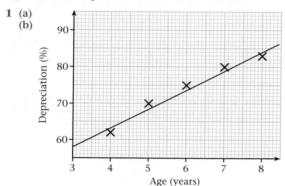

Age (years)

(c) $D = 5.2 + 58$

2 (a)
(b)

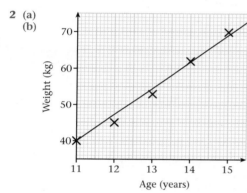

Age (years)

(c) $W = 7.1A + 40$

3 (a)
(b)

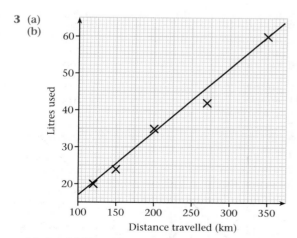

Distance travelled (km)

(c) $L = 0.17D + 17$

4 (a)
(b)

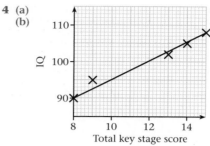

Total key stage score

(c) $I = 2.5 + 90$

5 (a)
(b)

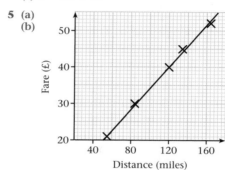

Distance (miles)

(c) $F = 0.3D + 4.5$

Exercise 7D

1 (a) 45 miles   (b) 11:00   (c) 30 min
(d) (i) 45 mph
(ii) 36 mph
(iii) 36 mph

2 (a) 24 m/s   (b) 12 s   (c) 432 m   (d) 3 s, 21.5 s

3 (a)

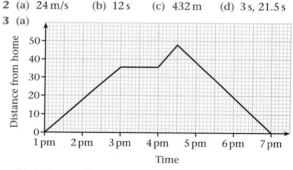

Time

(b) 16 km per hour

4 From 6 am to about 8 am there is a large increase
in the traffic flow (possibly due to people driving
to work). It then decreases until about 10 am (most
people will need to be at work for 9 am, so as more
people arrive at work, there will be less traffic on
the roads). During the rest of the morning and early
afternoon the traffic flow is at a constant rate. Then
at about 4 pm the flow increases to a peak at 6 pm,
similar to the morning (this could be because of people
driving home after work).

5 At first, as weight is added the spring extends at
a constant rate. In fact the extension is linearly
proportioned to the weight added. Then after a certain
amount of weight has been added, adding more weight
extends the spring by more for the same amount of
weight added, and this continues so that as we add on
more weight the spring extends at an increasing rate.

6 Prices steadily increase from 1980 to a peak about 1987 when suddenly the prices decrease at about the same rate as the increase. The decrease continues and slows to about 1995, when the prices being to increase again. The increase becomes faster up to the year 2000.

7 The car is travelling at a constant speed at the start of this part of the journey. It continues at this speed for a while and then slows down until it stops. The car is then at rest for a short period of time.

8 height

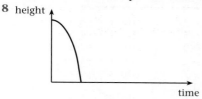

7

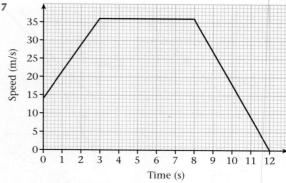

8 A4, B2, C5, D1, E3

9 Lester's speed increases quickly at first then steadies to a constant speed at about 2 seconds. After about 8 seconds his speed starts decreasing gradually.

10 h

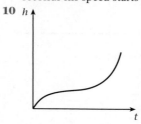

Mixed exercise 7

1 (a) $y = 2x + 5$
(b) $y = 2x - 2$
(c) $y = 2x - 6$
(d) $y = 2x + 7$

2 (a) gradient $\frac{2}{3}$, intercept -2
(b) gradient $-\frac{1}{2}$, intercept $1\frac{1}{2}$
(c) gradient $\frac{2}{3}$, intercept $2\frac{1}{3}$
(d) gradient -2, intercept $4\frac{1}{2}$

3 (a) $y = -\frac{1}{2}x + 6$
(b) $y = 2x + 1$

4 $3y + x = 8$

5 (a) (b)

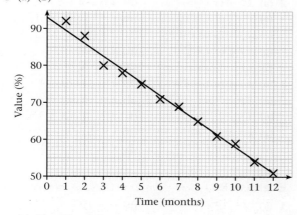

(c) $V = 93 - 3.5x$

6 (a) 70 miles
(b) 42 minutes
(c) 70 mph
(d) 10:30
(e) 60 mph

Exercise 8A

1 For example
(a) $x = 0$ $x = 3$ $x = 7$
$y = 7,$ $y = 4,$ $y = 0$
(b) $x = 3$ $x = 4$ $x = 5$
$y = 0,$ $y = 1,$ $y = 2$
(c) $x = 0$ $x = 1$ $x = 2$
$y = -3,$ $y = -1,$ $y = 1$
(d) $x = 0$ $x = 2$ $x = 8$
$y = 4,$ $y = 3,$ $y = 0$
(e) $x = 0$ $x = 1$ $x = 3$
$y = 3,$ $y = 2,$ $y = 0$
(f) $x = 0$ $x = 1$ $x = 2$
$y = 5,$ $y = 3,$ $y = 1$

2 (a) Yes   (b) No   (c) No
(d) Yes   (e) Yes   (f) No

3 (a) No   (b) Yes   (c) Yes
(d) No   (e) No   (f) Yes

4 (a) Yes   (b) Yes   (c) Yes
(d) No   (e) Yes   (f) Yes

5 (a) Yes   (b) No   (c) Yes
(d) Yes   (e) No   (f) Yes

6 $x = -1, y = 3$

7 $x = 3, y = 2$

8 (a)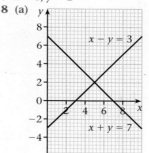

(b)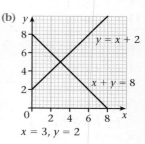

$x = 5, y = 2$

$x = 3, y = 2$

(c)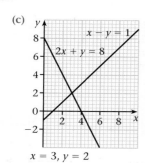

$x = 3, y = 2$

(d)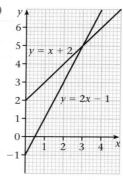

$x = 3, y = 5$

(e)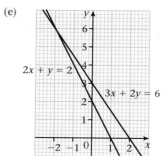

$x = -2, y = 6$

(f)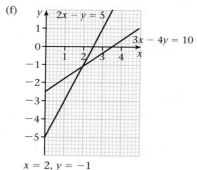

$x = 2, y = -1$

Exercise 8B

1 $x = 2, y = 1$ **2** $x = 3, y = 1$

3 $x = 5, y = 0$ **4** $x = 3, y = -1$

5 $x = -1, y = -4$ **6** $x = 4, y = 2$

7 $x = 3\frac{1}{2}, y = 1$ **8** $x = -4, y = 3$

9 $x = -3, y = 1\frac{1}{2}$ **10** $x = 1\frac{1}{2}, y = -\frac{1}{5}$

11 $x = 2\frac{2}{3}, y = -1$ **12** $x = -2, y = -5$

Exercise 8C

1 $x = 4, y = 1$ **2** $x = 2, y = 5$

3 $x = 4, y = 2$ **4** $x = 1\frac{1}{2}, y = 2$

5 $x = 2, y = -1$ **6** $x = -2, y = -3$

7 $x = 3, y = 4$ **8** $x = 2\frac{1}{2}, y = 3\frac{1}{2}$

9 $x = 4, y = -2$ **10** $x = 1\frac{1}{2}, y = -1$

11 $x = 3\frac{1}{2}, y = -2\frac{1}{2}$ **12** $x = -\frac{1}{2}, y = -1\frac{1}{2}$

13 $x = -1, y = -3$ **14** $x = 4, y = -3$

Exercise 8D

1 (a) $x = 2, x = 3$ (b) $x = -8, x = 5$

(c) $x = -8, x = -3$ (d) $x = 0, x = 2$

(e) $x = 7, x = -4$ (f) $x = -9, x = 9$

(g) $x = 6, x = -6$ (h) $x = 0, x = -8$

(i) $x = 7$ (j) $x = -5$

2 (a) $x = -2, x = 1$ (b) $x = 1, x = 2$

(c) $x = -3, x = -1$ (d) $x = -1, x = 5$

(e) $x = -2, x = 3$ (f) $x = -7, x = -1$

(g) $x = -4, x = 1$ (h) $x = -4, x = 2$

(i) $x = -2, x = 5$ (j) $x = -4, x = -3$

(k) $x = -2, x = 9$ (l) $x = -7, x = 2$

(m) $x = 2$ (n) $x = -4$

3 (a) $x = 0, x = -7$ (b) $x = 0, x = 5$

(c) $x = 0, x = 1$

4 (a) $x = -5, x = 5$ (b) $x = -1, x = 1$

(c) $x = -10, x = 10$ (d) $x = \pm 9$

(e) $x = \pm 5$ (f) $x = \pm\frac{5}{6}$

(g) $x = \pm 3\frac{1}{2}$

5 (a) $x = -2, x = 8$ (b) $x = -9, x = 1$

(c) $x = -2, x = 2$ (d) $x = -3, x = 5$

(e) $x = 0, x = 4$ (f) $x = -6, x = -2$

(g) $x = -3$ (h) $x = 0, x = -1$

(i) $x = -3, x = 8$ (j) $x = 6$

Exercise 8E

1 (a) $x = 1$ or $x = 2$ (b) $x = 6$ or $x = -4$

(c) $x = -1$ or $x = 1$ (d) $x = 0$ or $x = -6$

(e) $x = -3$ or $x = -4$ (f) $x = 2$

(g) $x = 0$ or $x = 7$ (h) $x = -5$

(i) $x = -5$ or $x = 5$ (j) $x = 9$ or $x = -2$

2 (a) $x = 2$ or $x = -\frac{3}{5}$ (b) $x = 3$ or $x = -2\frac{1}{2}$

(c) $x = \frac{1}{2}$ or $x = 1\frac{2}{3}$ (d) $x = 1\frac{1}{2}$ or $x = -1\frac{2}{5}$

(e) $x = -2\frac{1}{2}$ or $x = 2\frac{1}{2}$ (f) $x = \frac{2}{3}$

(g) $x = \frac{3}{4}$ or $x = \frac{2}{5}$ (h) $x = -3\frac{1}{2}$

(i) $x = -\frac{2}{3}$ or $x = \frac{2}{3}$ (j) $x = -3\frac{1}{2}$ or $x = \frac{3}{4}$

3 (a) $x = 0$ or $x = \frac{1}{2}$ (b) $x = -4$ or $x = 4$

(c) $x = -7$ or $x = 6$ (d) $x = -6$ or $x = 3$

(e) $x = -2$ (f) $x = -5$ or $x = 3$

(g) $x = 5$ (h) $x = \frac{1}{12}$ or $x = 1$

(i) $x = \frac{2}{3}$ or $x = 2\frac{1}{2}$ (j) $x = -\frac{4}{5}$ or $x = \frac{4}{5}$

Exercise 8F

1 (a) $(x + 3)^2 - 9$ (b) $(x - 1)^2 - 1$

(c) $\left(x + \frac{3}{2}\right)^2 - \frac{9}{4}$ (d) $(x + 4)^2 - 3$

(e) $(x - 2)^2 + 3$ (f) $(x + 6)^2 - 6$

(g) $(x - 5)^2 + 10$ (h) $(x + 10)^2 - 20$

(i) $\left(x - \frac{5}{2}\right)^2 - \frac{9}{4}$

2 (a) $2(x + 1)^2 - 2$ (b) $3(x - 5)^2 - 75$

(c) $5(x + 3)^2 - 45$ (d) $4(x - 2)^2 + 5$

(e) $6(x + 3)^2 - 7$ (f) $7(x - 1)^2 + 3$

(g) $3\left(x - \frac{1}{2}\right)^2 + \frac{1}{4}$ (h) $5\left(x + \frac{3}{2}\right)^2 - \frac{9}{4}$

(i) $6\left(x - \frac{5}{2}\right)^2 - \frac{1}{2}$

Exercise 8G

1 (a) $x = 2 + \sqrt{5}$ or $x = 2 - \sqrt{5}$
  (b) $x = -4 + \sqrt{11}$ or $x = -4 - \sqrt{11}$
  (c) $x = 5 + \sqrt{17}$ or $x = 5 - \sqrt{17}$
  (d) $x = -3 + \sqrt{10}$ or $x = -3 - \sqrt{10}$
  (e) $x = -3 + \sqrt{\frac{13}{2}}$ or $x = -3 - \sqrt{\frac{13}{2}}$
  (f) $x = 2 + \sqrt{\frac{19}{3}}$ or $x = 2 - \sqrt{\frac{19}{3}}$
  (g) $x = \frac{5 + \sqrt{13}}{2}$ or $x = \frac{5 - \sqrt{13}}{2}$
  (h) $x = \frac{-9 + \sqrt{97}}{2}$ or $x = \frac{-9 - \sqrt{97}}{2}$

2 (a) $x = 1.24$ or $x = -3.24$
  (b) $x = 6.65$ or $x = 1.35$
  (c) $x = 5.45$ or $x = 0.55$
  (d) $x = 1.16$ or $x = -5.16$
  (e) $x = 0.22$ or $x = -2.22$
  (f) $x = 3.90$ or $x = 0.10$
  (g) $x = 2.62$ or $x = 0.38$
  (h) $x = 0.27$ or $x = -7.27$

Exercise 8H

1 (a) $x = \frac{3 + \sqrt{5}}{2}$ or $x = \frac{3 - \sqrt{5}}{2}$
  (b) $x = \frac{-5 + \sqrt{13}}{2}$ or $x = \frac{-5 - \sqrt{13}}{2}$
  (c) $x = 3 + \sqrt{11}$ or $x = 3 - \sqrt{11}$
  (d) $x = \frac{-7 + \sqrt{69}}{2}$ or $x = \frac{-7 - \sqrt{69}}{2}$
  (e) $x = \frac{-3 + \sqrt{15}}{2}$ or $x = \frac{-3 - \sqrt{15}}{2}$
  (f) $x = \frac{9 + \sqrt{57}}{6}$ or $x = \frac{9 - \sqrt{57}}{6}$
  (g) $x = \frac{-7 + \sqrt{17}}{8}$ or $x = \frac{-7 - \sqrt{17}}{8}$
  (h) $x = \frac{2 + \sqrt{19}}{5}$ or $x = \frac{2 - \sqrt{19}}{5}$
  (i) $x = \frac{-4 + \sqrt{10}}{3}$ or $x = \frac{-4 - \sqrt{10}}{3}$
  (j) $x = \frac{5 + \sqrt{73}}{8}$ or $x = \frac{5 - \sqrt{73}}{8}$

2 (a) $x = 0.45$ or $x = -4.45$
  (b) $x = 3.54$ or $x = -2.54$
  (c) $x = -0.68$ or $x = -7.32$
  (d) $x = 6.37$ or $x = 0.63$
  (e) $x = 2.69$ or $x = -0.19$
  (f) $x = -0.57$ or $x = -1.77$
  (g) $x = 1.81$ or $x = 0.69$
  (h) $x = 0.64$ or $x = -1.24$
  (i) $x = 1.64$ or $x = -2.14$
  (j) $x = 1.54$ or $x = 0.26$

3 (a) $x = 0.54$ or $x = -5.54$
  (b) $x = 0.54$ or $x = -5.54$
  (c) $x = 4.37$ or $x = -1.37$
  (d) $x = 7.16$ or $x = 0.84$

(e) $x = 0.68$ or $x = -3.68$
(f) $x = -0.63$ or $x = -2.37$
(g) $x = 2.72$ or $x = 0.28$
(h) $x = 0.40$ or $x = -1.24$
(i) $x = 2.62$ or $x = 0.38$
(j) $x = 2.22$ or $x = 0.45$

Exercise 8I

1 $x \leqslant 1$ 2 $x > -1$ 3 $-1 \leqslant x < 2$
4 $-3 < x < 3$ 5 $-3 < x \leqslant -1$ 6 $-3 \leqslant x \leqslant 0$
7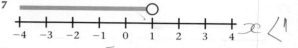
8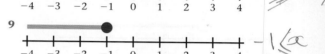
9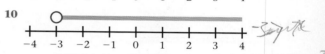
10
11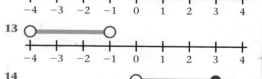
12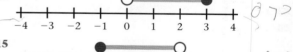
13
14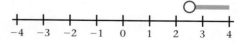
15

Exercise 8J

1 $x < 3$ 2 $x \geqslant \frac{1}{2}$ 3 $x > -5$
4 $x \leqslant -1$ 5 $x \leqslant -2$ 6 $x > 1$
7 $x > 2\frac{1}{2}$

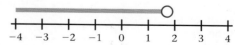

8 $x < 1\frac{3}{4}$

9 $x \geqslant \frac{2}{3}$

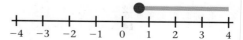

10 $x < -\frac{1}{2}$

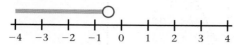

11 $x > 2\frac{1}{3}$

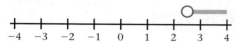

12 $x \leq 0$

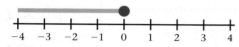

13 $x > -1\frac{1}{2}$

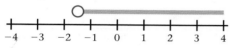

14 $x < 2\frac{2}{3}$

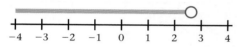

15 $x \geq -2\frac{1}{2}$

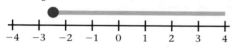

16 $x < 6\frac{1}{2}$ **17** $x \geq -1\frac{3}{4}$
18 $x > \frac{5}{7}$ **19** $x > -2$
20 $x \leq 1\frac{1}{2}$ **21** $x \leq -3\frac{2}{3}$
22 $x < \frac{3}{5}$ **23** $x \geq 2\frac{1}{5}$
24 $x > -\frac{2}{3}$

Exercise 8K

1 $-2, -1, 0, 1, 2$
2 $-2, -1, 0, 1$
3 $1, 2, 3$
4 $-3, -2, -1$
5 $-1, 0$
6 $0, 1, 2, 3$
7 $7, 8, 9$
8 $-6, -5$
9 $0, 1, 2$
10 $-5, -4, -3, -2$
11 $-3, -2, -1, 0, 1$
12 $-1, 0, 1, 2, 3$
13 Greatest integer is 0
14 Least integer is -1
15 Greatest integer is 1
16 (a) $1, 2$
  (b) $0, 1, 2, 3, 4, 5$
  (c) $-2, -1, 0, 1, 2, 3, 4, 5, 6, 7$

Exercise 8L

1

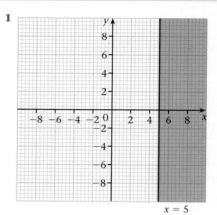

$x = 5$

2

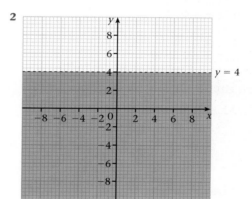

$y = 4$

3

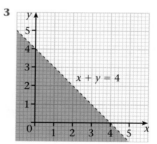

$x + y = 4$

4

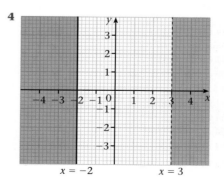

$x = -2$ $x = 3$

5

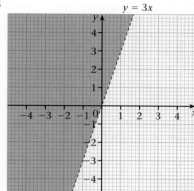

$y = 3x$

6

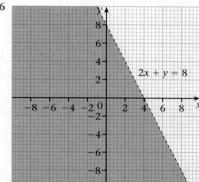

$2x + y = 8$

7

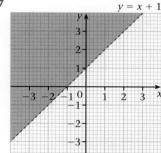

$y = x + 1$

8

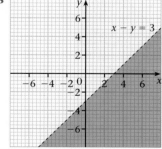

$x - y = 3$

9

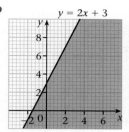

$y = 2x + 3$

10

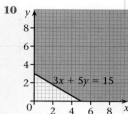

$3x + 5y = 15$

11

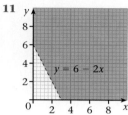

$y = 6 - 2x$

12

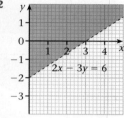

$2x - 3y = 6$

13 $y < 3$

14 $x + y \leqslant 2$

15 $y > x + 2$

16 $2x + 3y < 6$

17

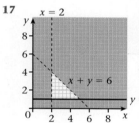

$x = 2$

$x + y = 6$

$y = 1$

18

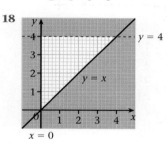

$y = 4$

$y = x$

$x = 0$

19

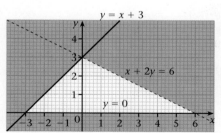

$y = x + 3$

$x + 2y = 6$

$y = 0$

20

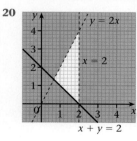

$y = 2x$

$x = 2$

$x + y = 2$

21

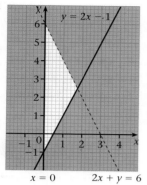

$y = 2x - 1$

$x = 0$ $2x + y = 6$

22

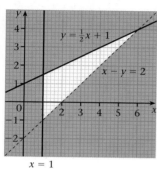

$y = \frac{1}{2}x + 1$

$x - y = 2$

$x = 1$

23

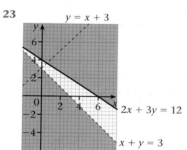

$y = x + 3$

$2x + 3y = 12$

$x + y = 3$

24

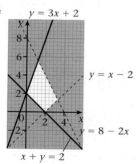

$y = 3x + 2$

$y = x - 2$

$y = 8 - 2x$

$x + y = 2$

25

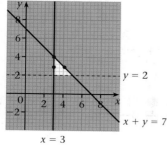

$y = 2$

$x + y = 7$

$x = 3$

26

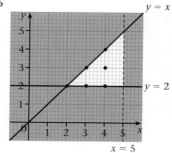

$y = x$

$y = 2$

$x = 5$

27

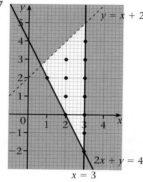

$y = x + 2$

$2x + y = 4$

$x = 3$

28

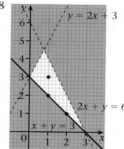

$y = 2x + 3$

$2x + y = 6$

$x + y = 3$

29

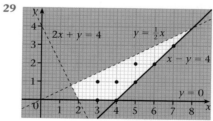

$2x + y = 4$ $y = \frac{1}{2}x$

$x - y = 4$

$y = 0$

30

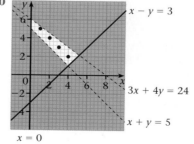

$x - y = 3$

$3x + 4y = 24$

$x + y = 5$

$x = 0$

Exercise 8M

1 $x = 2.6$ (1 d.p.) **2** $x = 3.7$ (1 d.p.)
3 $x = 1.77$ (2 d.p.) **4** $x = 3.44$ (2 d.p.)
5 $x = 2.35$ (2 d.p.) **6** $x = 3.76$ (2 d.p.)
7 $x = 4.55$ (2 d.p.) **8** $x = 4.27$ (2 d.p.)
9 (a) $x = 0.158$ (3 d.p.)
  (b) $x = 4.28$ (2 d.p.)
10 $x = 4.77$ (2 d.p.)

Mixed exercise 8

1 (a)
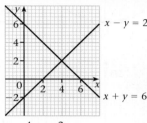
$x = 4, y = 2$

(b)
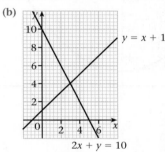
$x = 3, y = 4$

(c)
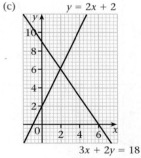
$x = 2, y = 6$

2 (a) $x = 4, y = 1$ (b) $x = 3, y = -2$
(c) $x = 1, y = 1\frac{1}{2}$ (d) $x = 3\frac{1}{2}, y = -1\frac{1}{2}$
(e) $x = 4, y = 3$ (f) $x = \frac{1}{2}, y = -3$

3 (a) $x = 4$ or $x = 5$ (b) $x = -3$ or $x = 8$
(c) $x = -8$ or $x = -1$ (d) $x = 0$ or $x = 6$
(e) $x = 7$ or $x = -2$ (f) $x = -9$ or $x = 9$
(g) $x = 0$ or $x = -2$ (h) $x = -6$ or $x = 4$
(i) $x = \frac{1}{2}$ or $x = \frac{2}{3}$ (j) $x = 2\frac{1}{2}$ or $x = -\frac{2}{5}$

4 (a) $x = 2$ or $x = 3$ (b) $x = 1$ or $x = -7$
(c) $x = -8$ or $x = -2$ (d) $x = 0$ or $x = 5$
(e) $x = -2$ or $x = 2$ (f) $x = 4$
(g) $x = 0$ or $x = -9$ (h) $x = 5$ or $x = -4$
(i) $x = -10$ or $x = 10$ (j) $x = -6$

5 (a) $x = -7$ or $x = 5$
(b) $x = 0$ or $x = 10$
(c) $x = -9$ or $x = 9$
(d) $x = -4\frac{1}{2}$ or $x = 1\frac{2}{3}$
(e) $x = -5 + 4\sqrt{2}$ or $x = -5 - 4\sqrt{2}$
(f) $x = \dfrac{7 + \sqrt{33}}{2}$ or $x = \dfrac{7 - \sqrt{33}}{2}$
(g) $x = -1 + 2\sqrt{2}$ or $x = -1 - 2\sqrt{2}$
(h) $x = -2 + \frac{1}{2}\sqrt{6}$ or $x = -2 - \frac{1}{2}\sqrt{6}$
(i) $x = \dfrac{1 + \sqrt{73}}{6}$ or $x = \dfrac{1 - \sqrt{73}}{6}$
(j) $x = \dfrac{-9 + \sqrt{33}}{8}$ or $x = \dfrac{-9 - \sqrt{33}}{8}$

6 (a) $x = 4.25$ (b) $x = 3.51$ (c) $x = 3.40$
7 309 cm
8 3.3 cm
9 $x = -4 \pm \sqrt{28}$
10 $x^2 - 20 = 0$

11 (a)
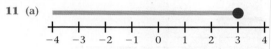

(b)
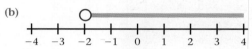

(c)
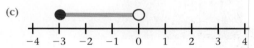

12 (a) $x \leqslant -1\frac{1}{2}$

(b) $x > 2\frac{1}{4}$

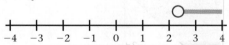

(c) $x \geqslant 0$
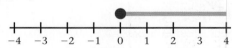

13 (a) $x < -\frac{4}{5}$ (b) $x \geqslant 3\frac{1}{2}$ (c) $x > \frac{2}{3}$

14 (a) $-3, -2, -1, 0$
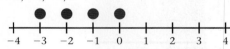

(b) $0, 1, 2$
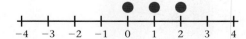

(c) $-2, -1, ..., 11$
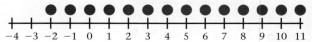

15 (a)

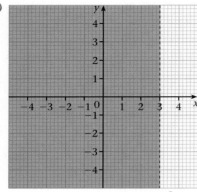

$x = 3$

(b)

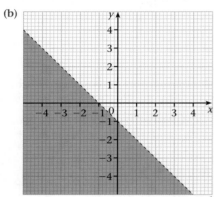

$x + y = -1$

(c)

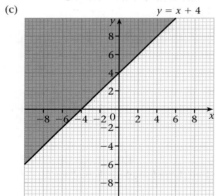

$y = x + 4$

16 (a) (b)

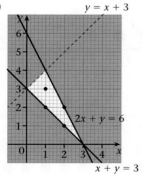

$y = x + 3$

$2x + y = 6$

$x + y = 3$

17 4.4

18 4.2

Exercise 9A

1

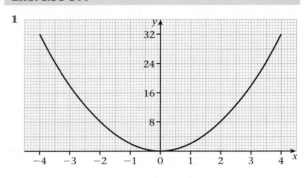

2

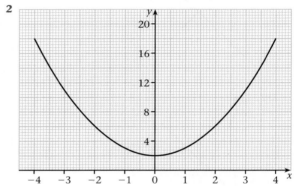

3

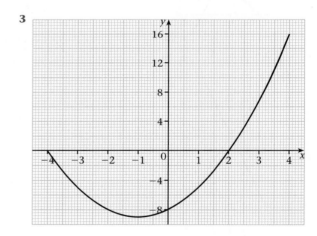

4

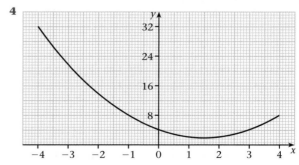

5

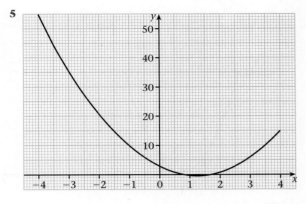

8

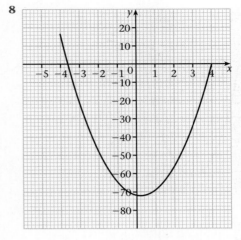

6

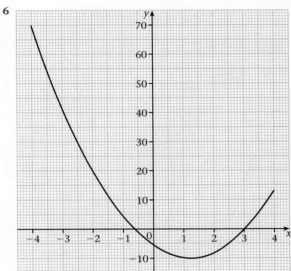

9

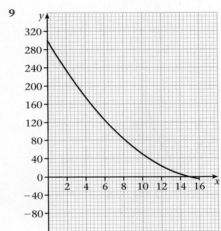

7

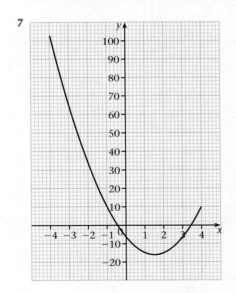

10

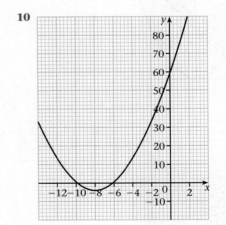

11

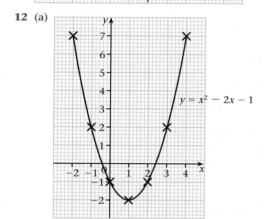

12 (a)

(b) Min. value of $y = -2$ and occurs at $x = 1$

13 (a)

$y = x^2 - 4x + 4$

(b) $x = 2$

14 (a)

x	-4	-3	-2	-1	0	1	2
y	11	1	-5	-7	-5	1	11

(b)

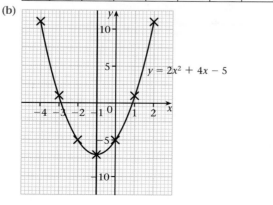

$y = 2x^2 + 4x - 5$

(c) $x = -1$
(d) Min. value of $y = -7$ and occurs at $x = -1$

15 (a)

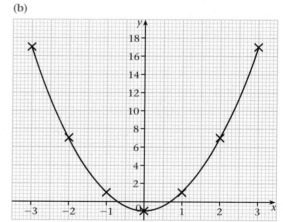

$y = 3x^2 - 6x - 1$

(b) $x = 1$
(c) Min. value of $y = -4$ and occurs at $x = 1$

Exercise 9B

1 (a)

x	-3	-2	-1	0	1	2	3
y	17	7	1	-1	1	7	17

(b)

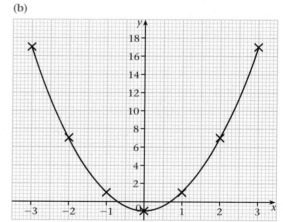

(c) (i) $x = 0.7$ and -0.7 (1 d.p.)
  (ii) $y = 11.5$
  (iii) $x = 2.6$ and -2.6

2 (a)

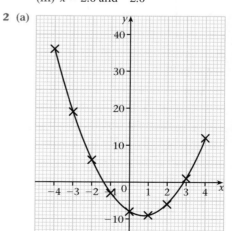

(b) $x = 2.9$ and -1.4 (1 d.p.)

3 (a)

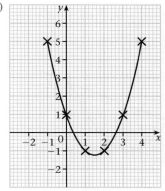

(b) $x = 0.4$ and 2.6 (1 d.p.)

4 (a)

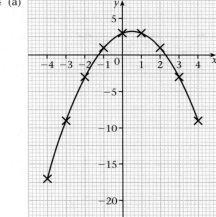

(b) $x = 2.3$ and -1.3 (1 d.p.)

Exercise 9C

1 (a) $(-1, 1)$ and $(2, 4)$

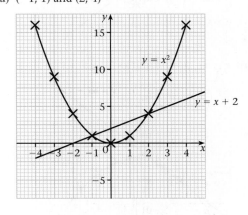

(b) $(1, 1)$ and $(3, 9)$

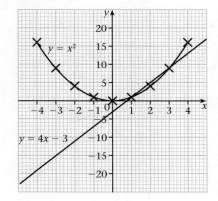

(c) $(-1, 5)$ and $(-3, 13)$

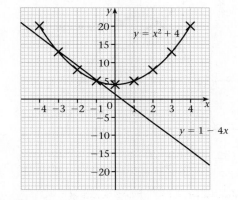

(d) $(-2, -2)$ and $(1, 1)$

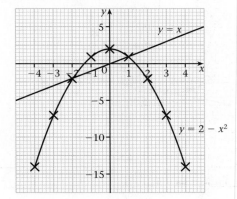

(e) $(-3, 11)$ and $(2, 6)$

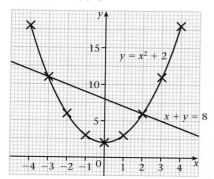

(f) $(-1, 8)$ and $(3, 0)$

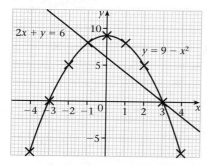

(g) $(-2, -3)$ and $(-1, -2)$

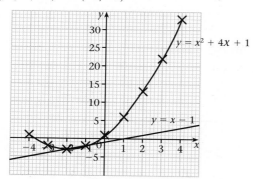

(h) $(-1, 4)$ and $(2, 1)$

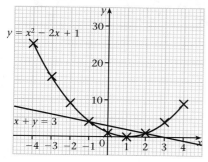

2 $x = 1.15$ or -2.15

3 (a) $x = -2, y = 4$ and $x = 3, y = 9$

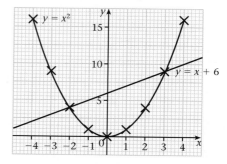

(b) $x = 1, y = 2$ and $x = 2, y = 5$

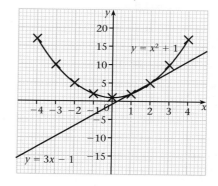

(c) $x = -3, y = 7$ and $x = 1, y = -1$

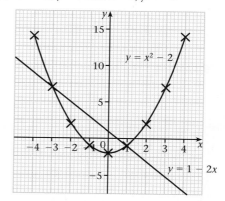

(d) $x = -3, y = -5$ and $x = -1, y = 3$

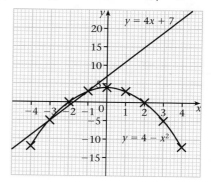

(e) $x = -1$, $y = 2$ and $x = 2$, $y = -1$

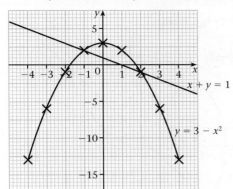

(h) $x = 2$, $y = 2$ and $x = 3$, $y = 1$

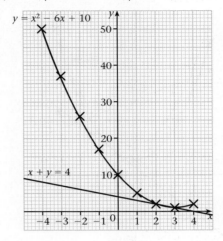

(f) $x = -2$, $y = 12$ and $x = -1$, $y = 9$

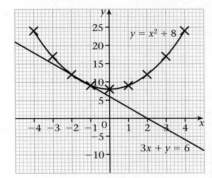

4 (a) (b)

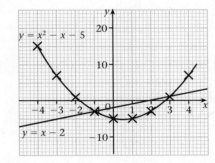

(b) $x = 3$, $x = -1$

5 (a) (b)

(g) $x = 1$, $y = -1$ and $x = 3$, $y = 3$

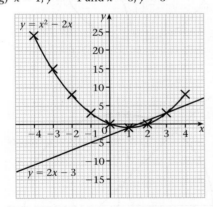

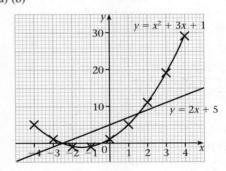

(b) $x = 1.6$, $x = -2.6$ (1 d.p.)

6 (a) (1, 3)

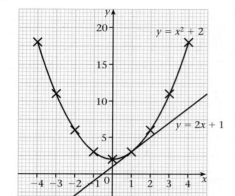

(b) $x = 1$, $y = 3$

Exercise 9D

1 (a) $x = 1$, $y = 1$ and $x = 4$, $y = 16$

  (b) $x = -1$, $y = 1$ and $x = 5$, $y = 25$

  (c) $x = -4$, $y = 17$ and $x = 2$, $y = 5$

  (d) $x = -5$, $y = 17$ and $x = 4$, $y = 8$

  (e) $x = -5$, $y = -16$ and $x = 2$, $y = 5$

  (f) $x = -6$, $y = 33$ and $x = 3$, $y = 6$

  (g) $x = -7$, $y = -10$ and $x = -1$, $y = -4$

  (h) $x = -7$, $y = 31$ and $x = 2$, $y = 4$

2 (a) $x = \frac{1}{2}$, $y = \frac{1}{2}$ and $x = 3$, $y = 18$

  (b) $x = -1$, $y = 3$ and $x = \frac{2}{3}$, $y = 1\frac{1}{3}$

  (c) $x = -\frac{3}{5}$, $y = 3\frac{4}{5}$ and $x = 1$, $y = 7$

  (d) $x = -2$, $y = 1$ and $x = 2\frac{1}{2}$, $y = 5\frac{1}{2}$

  (e) $x = -1\frac{1}{2}$, $y = -3$ and $x = \frac{1}{2}$, $y = 5$

  (f) $x = -\frac{3}{4}$, $y = 13\frac{3}{4}$ and $x = \frac{1}{3}$, $y = 8\frac{1}{3}$

  (g) $x = -\frac{1}{2}$, $y = 2$ and $x = 1\frac{1}{3}$, $y = 5\frac{2}{3}$

  (h) $x = -1\frac{1}{2}$, $y = 8$ and $x = 1\frac{1}{5}$, $y = 2\frac{3}{5}$

3 (a) (2, 10) and (5, 31)

  (b) (−9, −77) and (1, 3)

  (c) (−1, 2) and $(2\frac{1}{2}, 12\frac{1}{2})$

  (d) $(\frac{3}{5}, 3\frac{4}{5})$ and (3, 47)

  (e) $(\frac{1}{3}, 1)$ and (4, 23)

  (f) $(-\frac{2}{3}, 3\frac{2}{3})$ and $(-\frac{1}{2}, 3\frac{1}{2})$

  (g) $(-1\frac{2}{3}, 36\frac{2}{3})$ and $(\frac{3}{4}, 12\frac{1}{2})$

4 (3, 17)

5 $x = \frac{1}{2}$, $y = 8\frac{1}{2}$

Exercise 9E

1 (a) (−4, −3) and (3, 4)

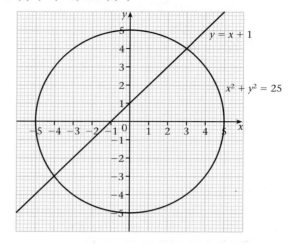

(b) (0, −10) and (6, 8)

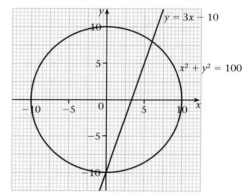

(c) (−3, 4) and (4, −3)

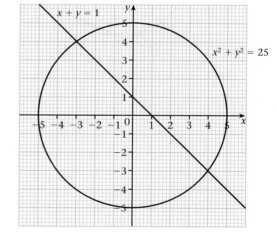

(d) (0, 10) and (8, 6)

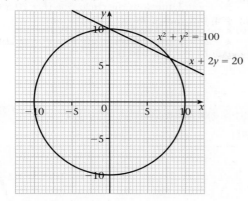

(e) (0, 3) and (3, 0)

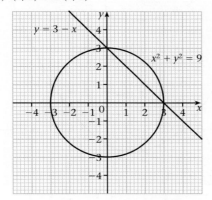

2 (a) $x = -6$, $y = -8$ and $x = 8$, $y = 6$

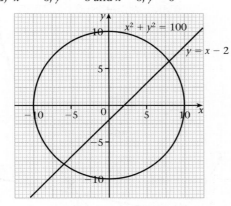

(b) $x = -3$, $y = -4$ and $x = 0$, $y = 5$

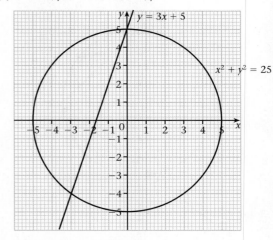

(c) $x = -4$, $y = 3$ and $x = 3$, $y = -4$

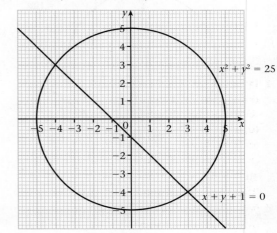
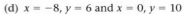

(d) $x = -8$, $y = 6$ and $x = 0$, $y = 10$

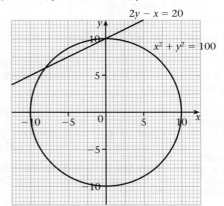

(e) $x = 0$, $y = 4$ and $x = 4$, $y = 0$

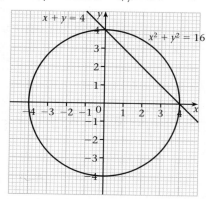

3 (a) $(6, -8)$

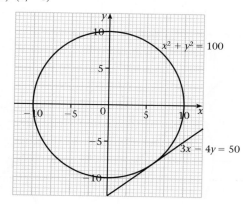

(b) $x = 6$, $y = -8$

Exercise 9F

1 (a) $x = -3$, $y = -2$ and $x = 2$, $y = 3$
(b) $x = -3$, $y = -5$ and $x = 5$, $y = 3$
(c) $x = -3$, $y = 6$ and $x = 6$, $y = -3$
(d) $x = 0$, $y = -7$ and $x = 7$, $y = 0$
(e) $x = \frac{2}{5}$, $y = -2\frac{1}{5}$ and $x = 2$, $y = 1$
(f) $x = -1$, $y = -1$ and $x = 1\frac{2}{5}$, $y = \frac{1}{5}$

2 (a) $x = -6$, $y = 2$ and $x = 6$, $y = 2$. The line $y = 2$ intersects the circle $x^2 + y^2 = 40$ at two points, $(-6, 2)$ and $(6, 2)$.
(b) $x = -7$, $y = -1$ and $x = 1$, $y = 7$. The line $y = x + 6$ intersects the circle $x^2 + y^2 = 50$ at two points, $(-7, -1)$ and $(1, 7)$.
(c) $x = 1$, $y = -4$ and $x = 4$, $y = -1$. The line $y = x - 5$ intersects the circle $x^2 + y^2 = 17$ at two points, $(1, -4)$ and $(4, -1)$.
(d) $x = -2$, $y = 2$. The line $y = x + 4$ intersects the circle $x^2 + y^2 = 8$ at one point, $(-2, 2)$. The line is a tangent to the circle.
(e) $x = -2$, $y = -5$ and $x = 1\frac{2}{5}$, $y = 5\frac{1}{5}$. The line $y = 3x + 1$ intersects the circle $x^2 + y^2 = 29$ at two points, $(-2, -5)$ and $(1\frac{2}{5}, 5\frac{1}{5})$.
(f) $x = 3$, $y = 3$. The line $x + y = 6$ intersects the circle $x^2 + y^2 = 18$ at one point, $(3, 3)$. The line is a tangent to the circle.

(g) $x = -\frac{4}{5}$, $y = 4\frac{2}{5}$ and $x = 2$, $y = -4$. The line $3x + y = 2$ intersects the circle $x^2 + y^2 = 20$ at two points, $(-\frac{4}{5}, 4\frac{2}{5})$ and $(2, -4)$.
(h) $x = -7$, $y = -4$ and $x = 7\frac{2}{5}$, $y = 3\frac{1}{5}$. The line $x - 2y = 1$ intersects the circle $x^2 + y^2 = 65$ at two points, $(-7, -4)$ and $(7\frac{2}{5}, 3\frac{1}{5})$.

3 $(2, 3)$

Mixed exercise 9

1 (a)

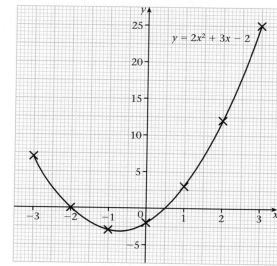

(b) (i) $x = -2$, $x = \frac{1}{2}$ (ii) $x = -2\frac{1}{2}$, $x = 1$

(c)

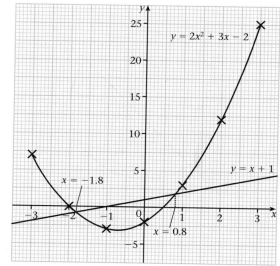

Approximate answers: $x = -1.8$, $x = 0.8$
(d) $2x^2 + 3x - 2 = x + 1$ can be simplified to
$2x^2 + 2x - 3 = 0$

2 (a)

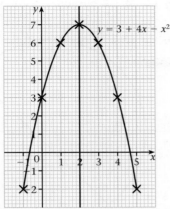

$y = 3 + 4x - x^2$

(b) $x = 2$
(c) Max. value of $y = 7$ and occurs at $x = 2$

3 (a) $x = -3, y = 1$ and $x = 4, y = 8$

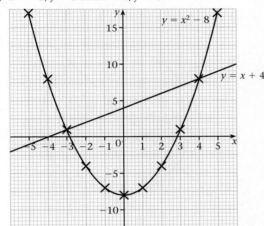

$y = x^2 - 8$

$y = x + 4$

(b) $x = -5, y = 27$ and $x = 1, y = 3$

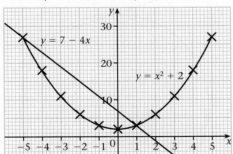

$y = 7 - 4x$

$y = x^2 + 2$

(c) $x = -4, y = -13$ and $x = 2, y = -1$

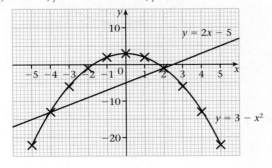

$y = 2x - 5$

$y = 3 - x^2$

(d) $x = -3, y = 5$ and $x = -1, y = 3$

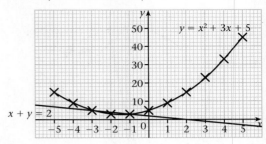

$y = x^2 + 3x + 5$

$x + y = 2$

(e) $x = -3, y = 11$ and $x = 2, y = 6$

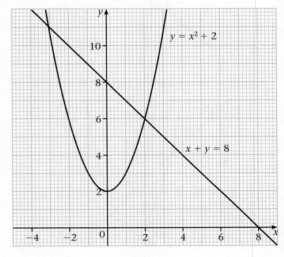

$y = x^2 + 2$

$x + y = 8$

(f) $x = -1, y = 8$ and $x = 3, y = 0$

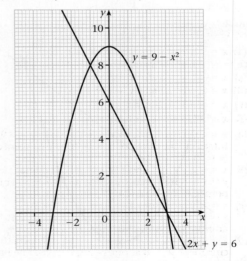

$y = 9 - x^2$

$2x + y = 6$

(g) $x = -2, y = -3$ and $x = -1, y = -2$

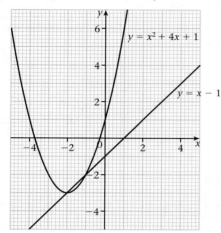

(h) $x = -1, y = 4$ and $x = 2, y = 1$

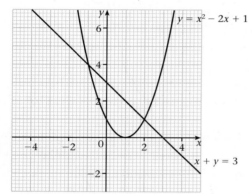

4 (a) (e)

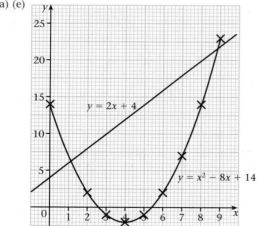

(b) -2
(c) $x = 2.6$ and $x = 5.4$
(d) $x = 0.8$ and $x = 7.2$
(e) $x = 1.1$ and $x = 8.9$

5 (a) $x = -3, y = -4$ and $x = 4, y = 3$

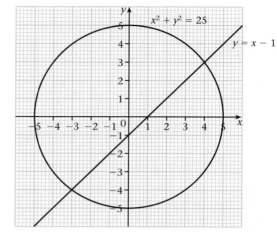

(b) $x = -8, y = -6$ and $x = 6, y = 8$

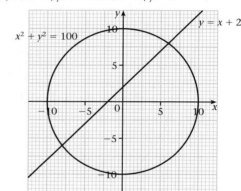

(c) $x = 0, y = 5$ and $x = 3, y = 4$

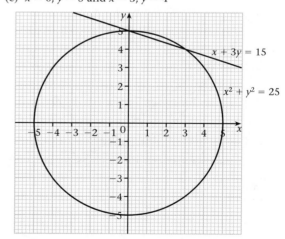

(d) $x = -8$, $y = 6$ and $x = 6$, $y = -8$

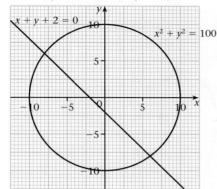

6 (a) $x = -2$, $y = -2$ and $x = 5$, $y = 19$
(b) $x = -6$, $y = 13$ and $x = 1$, $y = -1$
(c) $x = -2$, $y = 1$ and $x = 3$, $y = 11$
(d) $x = -5$, $y = 27$ and $x = 1$, $y = 3$
(e) $x = -3$, $y = -1$ and $x = -1$, $y = 3$
(f) $x = -3$, $y = 7$ and $x = 7$, $y = -3$
(g) $x = -4\frac{2}{5}$, $y = -\frac{4}{5}$ and $x = 4$, $y = 2$
(h) $x = -3$, $y = -8$ and $x = 8$, $y = 3$

7 (a) $x = -\frac{2}{3}$, $y = \frac{1}{3}$ and $x = 1$, $y = 2$. The line $y = x + 1$
intersects the parabola $y = 3x^2 - 1$ at two points,
$(-\frac{2}{3}, \frac{1}{3})$ and $(1, 2)$.
(b) $x = 2$, $y = -3$. The line $4x + y = 5$ intersects the
parabola $y = 1 - x^2$ at one point, $(2, -3)$. The line
is a tangent to the parabola.
(c) $x = 6$, $y = 2$. The line $3x + y = 20$ intersects the
circle $x^2 + y^2 = 40$ at one point, $(6, 2)$. The line is a
tangent to the circle.
(d) $x = 1\frac{3}{5}$, $y = -3\frac{4}{5}$ and $x = 4$, $y = 1$. The line
$y = 2x - 7$ intersects the circle $x^2 + y^2 = 17$ at two
points, $(1\frac{3}{5}, -3\frac{4}{5})$ and $(4, 1)$.

8 (a) (b) (c)

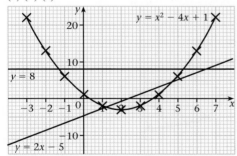

(b) $x = 5.3$, $x = -1.3$ (1 d.p.)
(c) $x = 4.7$, $x = 1.3$ (1 d.p.)

9 (a) $(4, 4)$
(b) Solving for x gives $x^2 + (c - x)^2 = r^2$, so
$2x^2 - 2cx + c^2 = r^2$
Rearranging gives $2x^2 - 2cx + c^2 - r^2 = 0$
We know the tangent only intersects the circle at
one point, so there can only be one solution to the
quadratic equation.
This means it must factorize like $(x - a)^2 = 0$ for
some a.
So completing the square:
$2x^2 - 2cx + c^2 - r^2 = 0$
$2(x - \frac{1}{2}c)^2 - \frac{1}{2}c^2 + c^2 - r^2 = 0$
$2(x - \frac{1}{2}c)^2 + \frac{1}{2}c^2 - r^2 = 0$

Then, we must have $\frac{1}{2}c^2 - r^2 = 0$ or $c^2 = 2r^2$.
OR – a quicker way:
By looking at a diagram, we see that, because of the
slope of the tangent, the x- and y-coordinates of
the intersection point must be the same.

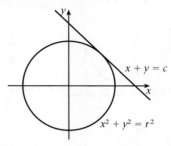

Suppose the point is (a, a). It must satisfy both
equations: $a + a = c$ and $a^2 + a^2 = r^2$.
So, $c^2 = (2a)^2 = 4a^2 = 2 \times 2a^2 = 2r^2$.

10 (a) $\angle ATO = 90°$
So, using Pythagoras' theorem
$(x + 8)^2 = (x + 5)^2 + x^2$
$x^2 + 16x + 64 = x^2 + 10x + 25 + x^2$
$x^2 - 6x - 39 = 0$
(b) $x = 9.93$

11 (a)

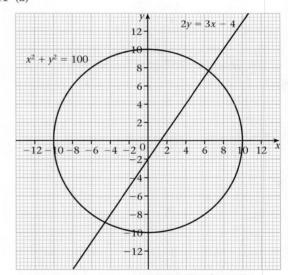

(b) $x = -4.6$, $y = -8.9$ and $x = 6.4$, $y = 7.6$
(c) $q = 9$
(d) $x = 3$, $y = 10$

Exercise 10A

1

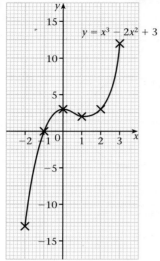

$y = x^3 - 2x^2 + 3$

$x = -1$

2

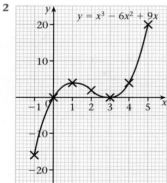

$y = x^3 - 6x^2 + 9x$

$x = 0, x = 3$

3

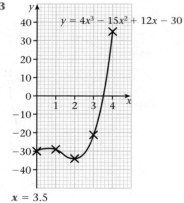

$y = 4x^3 - 15x^2 + 12x - 30$

$x = 3.5$

4

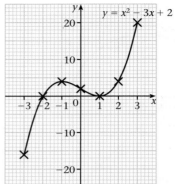

$y = x^2 - 3x + 2$

$x = -2, 1$

5

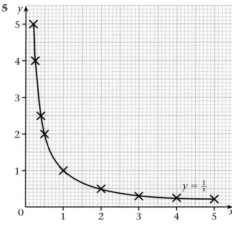

$y = \frac{1}{x}$

$x = 0.33$

6

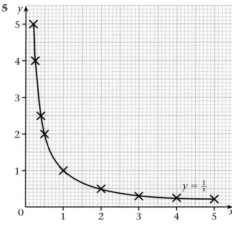

$y = \frac{2}{x} + 3$

No solution

7

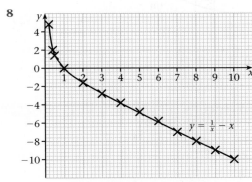

$y = 4 - \frac{1}{x}$

$x = 1$

8

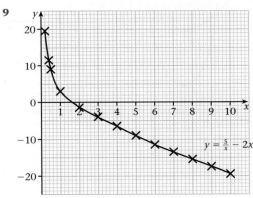

$y = \frac{1}{x} - x$

$x = 1$

9

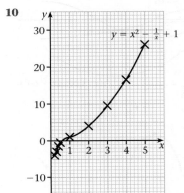

$y = \frac{5}{x} - 2x$

$x = 1.6$

10

$y = x^2 - \frac{1}{x} + 1$

$x = 0.7$

11 (i) $x = -1.2, 0, 3.2$
(ii) $x = -1, -0.3, 3.3$

Exercise 10B

1 $y = 5\sqrt{x}$

2 $y = \frac{30}{x}$

3 (a) $y = \frac{48}{x^2}$ (b) $y = \frac{48}{25}$ or $1\frac{23}{25}$ or 1.92

   (c) $x = \pm 2$

4 (a) $y = \frac{25}{3}$ or $8\frac{1}{3}$ (b) $x = \pm\sqrt{24}$, i.e. $\pm 2\sqrt{6}$

5

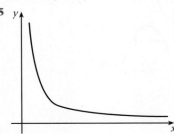

6 (a) $y = 5x^3$ (b) $y = 135$

7 $y = 1.5$

8 $y \propto \frac{1}{x}$ so $y = \frac{k}{x}$. $y = 3$ when $x = 2$ so $3 = \frac{k}{2}$ or $k = 6$

   Therefore, $y = \frac{6}{x}$ or $xy = 6$.

9 $y = 25$

10 (a) $s = 3$ (b) $t = \pm\sqrt{3}$

11 £90

12 (a) 500 g   (b) 10 cm

Exercise 10C

1

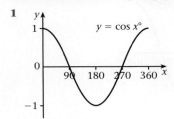

$y = \cos x°$

2

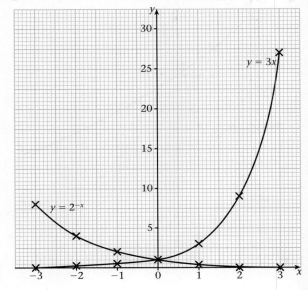

$y = 3x$

$y = 2^{-x}$

3 (a)

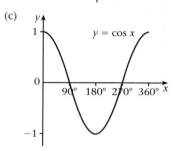

$y = \sin x$

(b)

$y = 3 \sin x$

(c)

$y = \cos x$

(d)

$y = 3 \cos x$

4

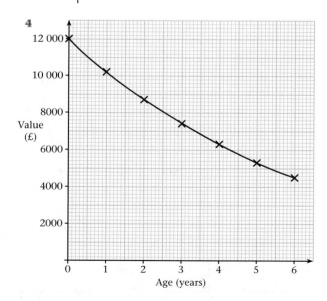

Value (£)

Age (years)

5 (a) $p = 4$, $q = 3$ \quad (b) (i) 324 \quad (ii) $1.\dot{3}$
6 A is $(90°, 0)$; B is $(0°, 1)$
7 P is $(90°, 1)$, Q is $(270°, -1)$
8 (a) $p = 2$, $q = 5$
   (b)

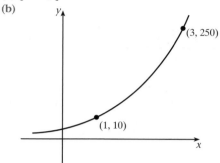

(3, 250)

(1, 10)

   (c) (i) $\frac{2}{25}$ \quad (ii) 50
   (d) 4

Exercise 10D

1 (a)

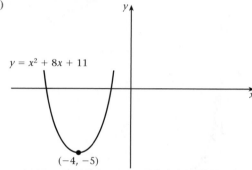

$y = x^2 + 8x + 11$

$(-4, -5)$

   (b) Minimum value of $y = -5$, value of x at this minimum $= -4$.

2 (a) (b) (c)

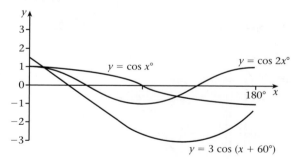

$y = \cos x°$

$y = \cos 2x°$

$y = 3 \cos (x + 60°)$

3 (a)

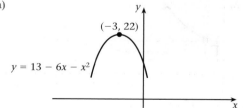

$(-3, 22)$

$y = 13 - 6x - x^2$

   (b) Maximum value is 22
   (c) $g(x) = -x^2 + 10x - 3$

4 (a) (2, 5)   (b) (6, 5)   (c) (3, 7)
(d) (−3, 5)   (e) (1½, 5)

5 (a) (i) $A = (90, 1)$ (ii) $B = (270, -1)$

(b)

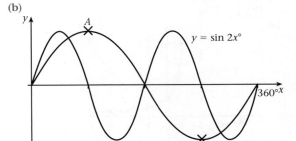

6 (a)

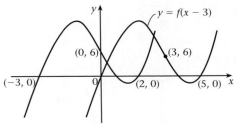

Diagram A

(b)

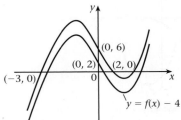

Diagram B

Mixed exercise 10

1 (a)

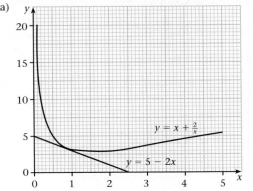

(b) $x = 0.6$ and $x = 3.4$
(c) $x = 1$ and $x = 2$
(d) $x = \frac{2}{3}$ and $x = 1$
$y = 5 - 2x$

2 (a)

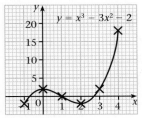

(b) $x = -0.7, x = 1, x = 2.7$
(c) $x = 3.2$ (d) $y = 2x + 1$

3 (a)

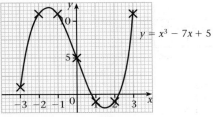

(b) $x = -3, x = 0.8, x = 2.2$
(c) $x = -2.4, x = -0.7, x = 3.1$

4 A

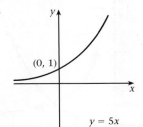

$y = 5x$

B

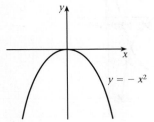

$y = -x^2$

C

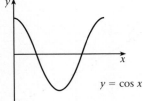

$y = \cos x$

D

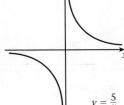

$y = \frac{5}{x}$

E

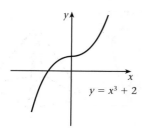

$y = x^3 + 2$

F

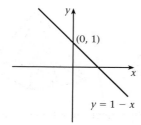

(0, 1)

$y = 1 - x$

5

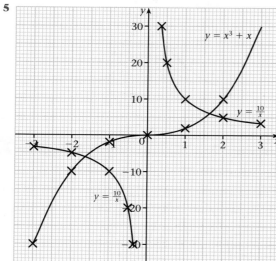

$y = x^3 + x$

$y = \frac{10}{x}$

$y = \frac{10}{x}$

6 $k = \frac{1}{2}$, $m = 3$

7

Cost per person

No. of people

8 (a) $d = 5t^2$
  (b) $d = 245$
  (c) $t = 3$

9 (a) $T = 960$
  (b) $T = 576$

10

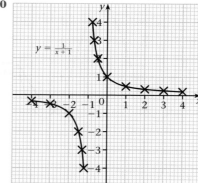

$y = \frac{1}{x+1}$

11 $y = 5 \sin x°$

12

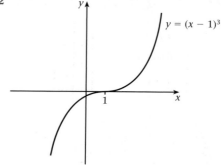

$y = (x - 1)^3$

13 $a = 20$, $b = 40$, $k = 3$

14 (a) 19
  (b) (0, 16)
  (c) (1, 32)
  (d) (i) $x = 6$ (ii) $x = -3$

Exercise 11A

1 Translation **A** to **B** is $\begin{pmatrix} -6 \\ -4 \end{pmatrix}$

  Translation **A** to **C** is $\begin{pmatrix} -1 \\ -4 \end{pmatrix}$

  Translation **A** to **D** is $\begin{pmatrix} -3 \\ -8 \end{pmatrix}$

  Translation **A** to **E** is $\begin{pmatrix} 2 \\ -10 \end{pmatrix}$

  Translation **A** to **F** is $\begin{pmatrix} 3 \\ 1 \end{pmatrix}$

  Translation **A** to **G** is $\begin{pmatrix} -5 \\ -10 \end{pmatrix}$

2

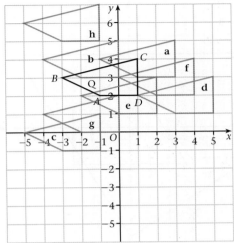

(b) There are 4 possible planes.

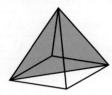
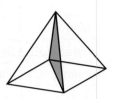

(c) There are an infinite number of possible plans. For example

Exercise 11B

1 (a)

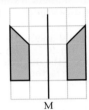

(b)

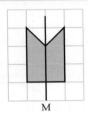

(c)

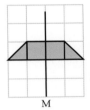

(d)

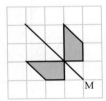

2 (a) Reflection in line $y = -x$
(b) Reflection in line $y = 0$
(c) Reflection in line $x = -1$
(d) Reflection in line $x = 1$

3 (a) $x = 0$
(b) $x = 3.5$
(c) $y = -x$
(d) $y = 0$

4 (a) There are 5 possible planes.

Exercise 11C

1

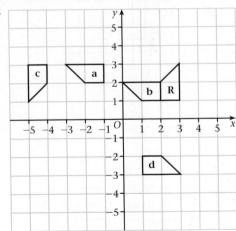

2 (a) Rotation centre $(\frac{1}{2}, -\frac{1}{2})$ through $-90°$
(b) Rotation centre $(0, 0)$ through $+180°$
(c) Rotation centre $(0, 3)$ through $-90°$
(d) Rotation centre $(3, 0)$ through $-90°$

3

Rotation	Transforms
centre (0, 0), 90°	point (1, 2) to (−2, 1)
centre (0, 0), −180°	point (3, 5) to (−3, −5)
centre (−1, 2), −90°	point (2, 3) to (0, −1)
centre (2, 4), 270°	point (2, −1) to (−3, 4)
centre (0, 0), −270°	point (−1, 4) to (−4, −1)

4 (a) 9   (b) 5   (c) 2   (d) 2

Exercise 11D

1
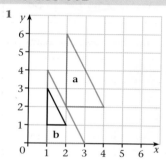

2
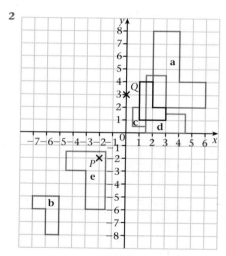

3 (a) Enlargement scale factor $3\frac{1}{2}$, centre $(\frac{3}{5}, \frac{1}{5})$
   (b) Enlargement scale factor −1, centre (0, 0)
   (c) Enlargement scale factor 2, centre (2, 0)
   (d) Enlargement scale factor 3, centre $(\frac{1}{2}, 4\frac{1}{2})$
   (e) Enlargement scale factor $-1\frac{1}{2}$, centre $(-1, 2\frac{2}{5})$

4
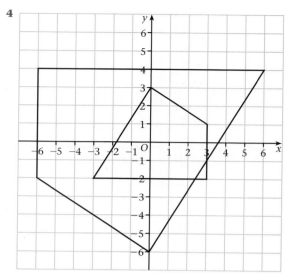

5 Perimeter of shape is 10. Perimeter of enlarged shapes:
   (a) 20   (b) 10   (c) 5   (d) 15   (e) 15
   Perimeter of enlarged shape is the numerical value of the scale factor multiplied by the perimeter of the original shape.

6 Area of shape is 4. Area of enlarged shapes:
   (a) 16   (b) 4   (c) 1   (d) 9   (e) 9
   Area of enlarged shape is the area of the original shape multiplied by the square of the scale factor.

Exercise 11E

1
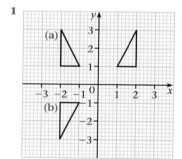

   (c) Roltation about the origin through 180°

2
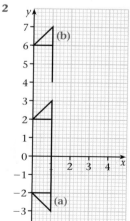
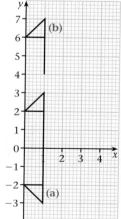

   (c) Translation by $\binom{0}{4}$

3

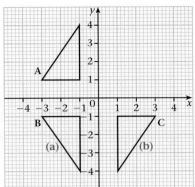

(c) Reflection in y-axis

4 (a)

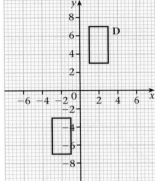

(b) Rotation about the origin through 180°

5

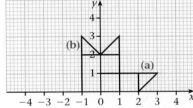

(b) Reflection in y-axis

6 (a)

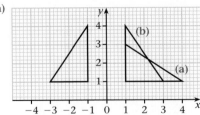

(b) Reflection in y-axis

Mixed exercise 11

1 9 planes (1 parallel to each pair of opposite faces = 3 and 1 through each pair of opposite edges = 6)

2 (a)

2 planes

(b)

2 planes

(c)

4 planes

3

	Reflection	Rotation	Translation	Enlargement
Sides stay the same length	Yes	Yes	Yes	No
Angles stay the same size	Yes	Yes	Yes	Yes
Orientation	No	No	Yes	Yes
Image Congruent	Yes	Yes	Yes	No
Image Similar	Yes	Yes	Yes	Yes

4 (a) Translation onto $\mathbf{A} = \begin{pmatrix} 5 \\ 3 \end{pmatrix}$

Translation onto $\mathbf{B} = \begin{pmatrix} 7 \\ -2 \end{pmatrix}$

Translation onto $\mathbf{C} = \begin{pmatrix} -7 \\ -5 \end{pmatrix}$

(b) $\begin{pmatrix} 14 \\ 3 \end{pmatrix}$ (c) $\begin{pmatrix} -14 \\ -3 \end{pmatrix}$

5

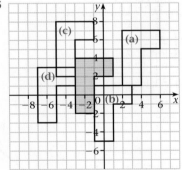

6

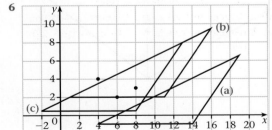

7

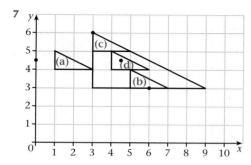

8 (a) Rotation by 180°, centre (0, 0)
   (b) Rotation by 90° clockwise, centre (0, 0)
   (c) Rotation by 270° clockwise, centre (6, 6)
   (d) Translation $\begin{pmatrix} 2 \\ -4 \end{pmatrix}$
   (e) Enlargement scale factor $1\frac{1}{2}$, centre (−3, 3)
   (f) Rotation by 180°, centre ($2\frac{1}{2}$, $2\frac{1}{2}$)

5

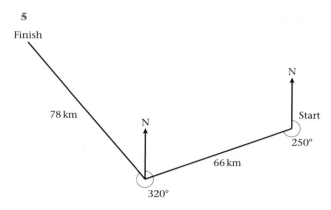

6 (a) Actual size is 25 m by 32.5 m
   (b) Measurements on map are 4 mm wide and 5 cm long

7 Real distance: Brownsea island is 2 km by 1.25 km
   Bournemouth pier is 225 m long

Exercise 12A

(allow ±1°)

1 (a) 058°   (b) 238°
2 (a) 034°   (b) 122°   (c) 256°   (d) 076°
3 (a) 092°   (b) 058°   (c) 041°   (d) 195°
   (e) 270°   (f) 293°   (g) 129°   (h) 163°

Exercise 12C

1

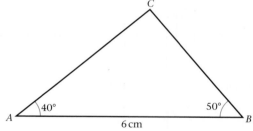

Exercise 12B

1 (a) 12 km   (b) 8 km   (c) 10 km
   (d) 5 km   (e) 8.4 km
2 (b) 45 km
3

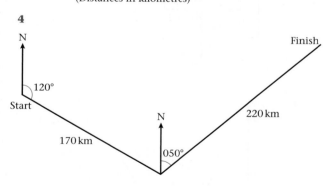

	Ramsey	Castletown	Douglas
Castletown	32		
Douglas	18.8	14.4	
Peel	22.4	16.4	15.6

(Distances in kilometres)

2

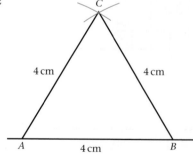

4

N
120°
Start
170 km
N
050°
Finish
220 km

3 (a)

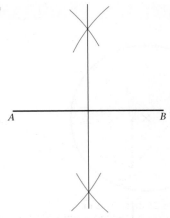

(b)

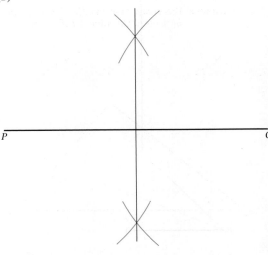

(c) Half size:

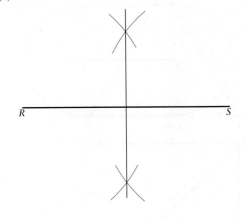

4 Half size:

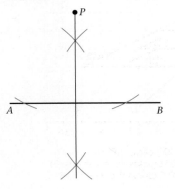

5 Half size:

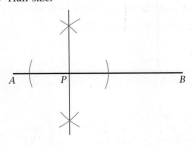

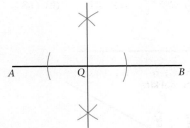

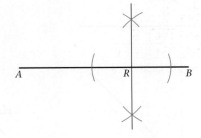

6

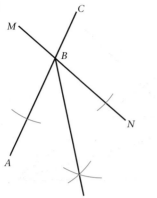

7 (a)

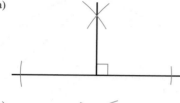

(b)

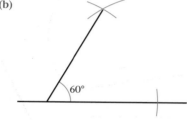

(c)

(d) (e)

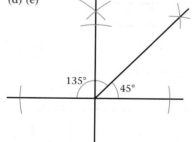

Exercise 12D

1 (a) Half size:

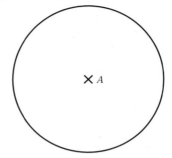

(b)

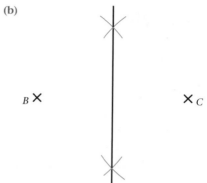

(c)

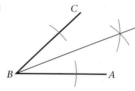

(d) Half size:

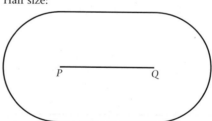

2

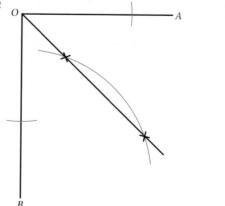

3 (a) (b) (c) Half size:

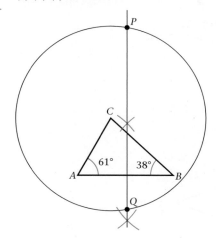

4 Half size:

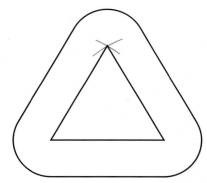

5

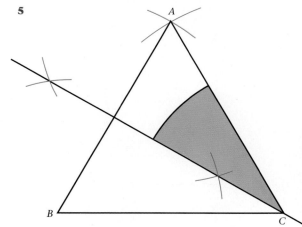

6

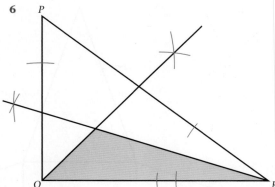

7 Half size:

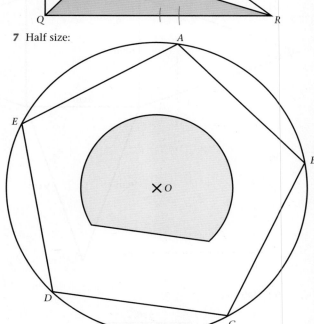

8 Half size:

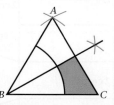

Exercise 12E

1 (a) Half size:

(b) Half size:

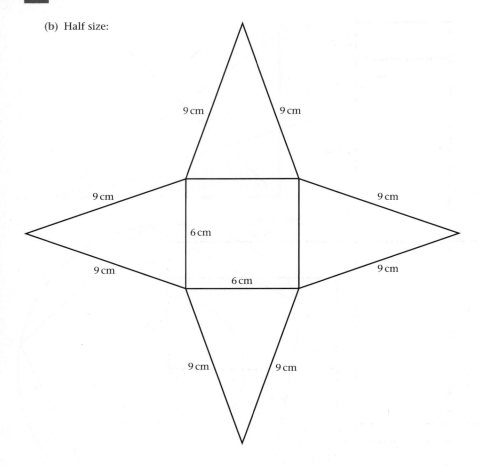

(c) Half size:

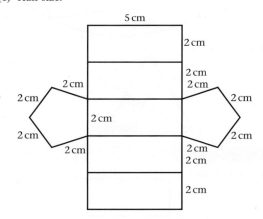

(d) Half size:

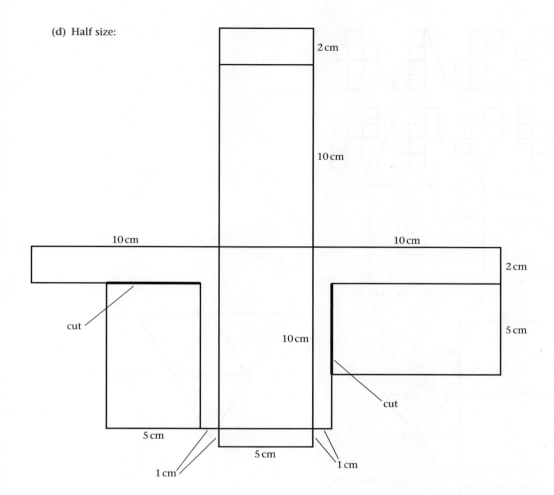

2 cm

10 cm

10 cm

10 cm

2 cm

cut

5 cm

10 cm

5 cm

cut

5 cm

5 cm

1 cm

1 cm

2 (a)

(b)

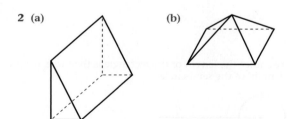

3

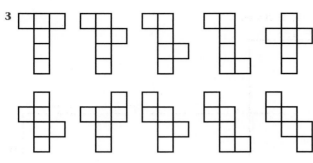

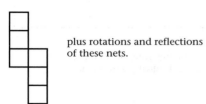

plus rotations and reflections
of these nets.

4

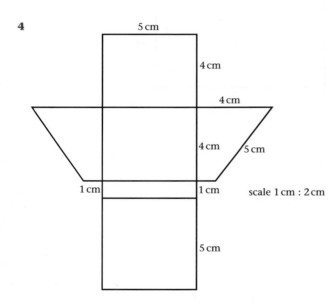

scale 1 cm : 2 cm

5

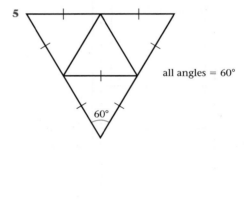

all angles = 60°

6

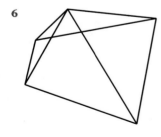

7 Yes, since the length of the rectangle is the same as the
'length' of the semi-circle.

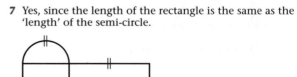

8 (a), (c), (e), (f)

9 (a) Half size:

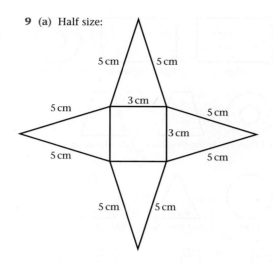

(b) Half size:

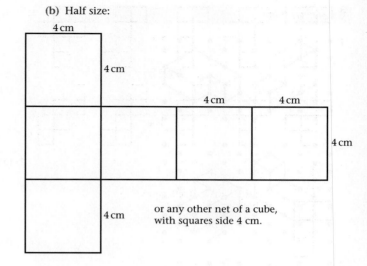

or any other net of a cube, with squares side 4 cm.

(c) Half size:

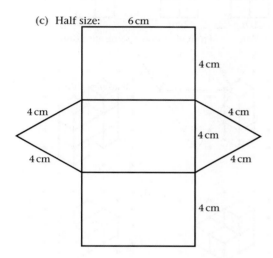

10 Possible answer:

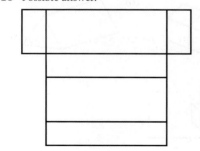

Exercise 12F

1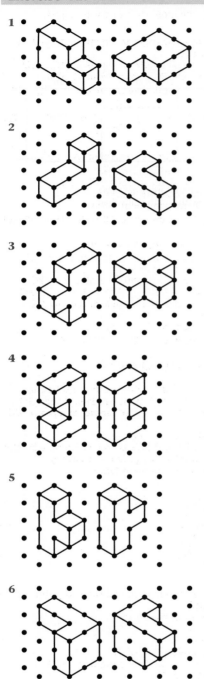

2

3

4

5

6

Exercise 12G

1 (a)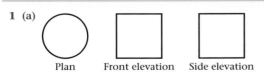

Plan   Front elevation   Side elevation

(b)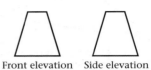

Plan   Front elevation   Side elevation

(c)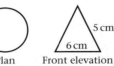

Plan   Front elevation   Side elevation

2 (a)

Plan   Front elevation   Side elevation

(b)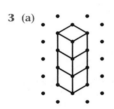

Plan   Front elevation   Side elevation

3 (a) 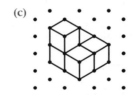 (b)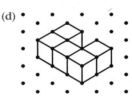

(c) 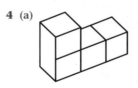 (d)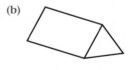

4 (a) (b)

(c)

Exercise 12H

1 (a) 40°   (b) 140°
   (c) Sum of interior angles = 1260°
2 24 sides
3 10

4 (a) $a = 91°$
(b) $b = 60°$, $c = 120°$
5 (a) $150°$ (b) $135°$
(c) $147°$ (d) $90°$
6

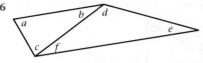

$a + b + c = 180°$ (angle sum of triangle)
$d + e + f = 180°$ (angle sum of triangle)
So $a + b + c + d + e + f = 360°$

Exercise 12I

1 $YZ = 4.5\,cm$, $PR = 6\,cm$
2 $AC = 2.8\,cm$, $EF = 6.3\,cm$
3 (a) $2.4\,cm$ (b) $6\,cm$ (c) $3.6\,cm$
4 (a) (ii) and (iii)
(b) (i) and (ii)
(c) (ii) and (iii)
5 (a) The bases of the triangles are parallel so corresponding angles are equal. The third angle is common to both triangles, so all corresponding angles are equal.
(b) $x = 1.8\,cm$, $y = 3.6\,cm$
6 (a) $BE = 4\,cm$
(b) $DE = 12\,cm$
7 (a) $DE = 13.5\,cm$
(b) $CE = 2.5\,cm$
8 (a) $AB = 24\,cm$
(b) $AE = 40.5\,cm$
9 (a) All squares are similar. Corresponding angles are equal (all equal 90°). Corresponding sides in the same ratio.
(b) Any two rectangles are not necessarily similar because corresponding sides are not always in the same ratio.
(c) Any two circles are always similar because the ratio of circumference to radius is always the same.

Exercise 12J

1 (a) **A and B, SSS** (b) **A and C, SAS**
(c) **A and C, ASA** (d) **A and C, RHS**
2 (a) Yes, SAS (b) No
(c) No (d) Yes, ASA
(e) Yes, SAS
3 For example
(a) (b) 15° (all three sides are smaller)

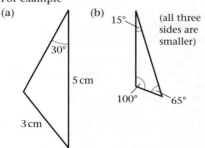

Exercise 12K

Note that there may be more than one way to prove congruence.

1 Opposite sides of a rectangle are equal, so $AD = BC$
Clearly, $CD = CD$
And diagonals of a rectangle are equal, so $AC = BD$
So triangles ADC and BCD are congruent (SSS)
2 Opposite sides of a parallelogram are equal ∴ $PQ = RS$
Z-angles are equal $\left(\text{i.e.} \right)$ so $\angle QPX = \angle SRX$
and $\angle PQX = \angle RSX$.
Therefore SXR and QXP are congruent (ASA)
3 E is the mid-point of AC, so $AE = EC$
D is the mid-point of AB, so $AD = DB = FC$
Z-angles are equal so $\angle DAE = \angle FCE$
So, DAE and FCE are congruent (SAS)
4 $ABCDE$ is a regular pentagon so $AB = BC$, $AE = DE$ and $\angle BAE = \angle BCD$
So, EAB and BCD are congruent (SAS)
5 $\angle ABC = \angle ACB$ (since $AB = BC$), so $\angle ABX = \angle ACY$
$\angle AXY = \angle AYX$ (since $AX = AY$),
so $\angle AXB = 180° - \angle AXY = 180° - \angle AYX = \angle AYC$
So $\angle BAX = 180° - \angle AXB - \angle ABX = 180° - \angle AYC - \angle ACY = \angle CAY$ (angles in a triangle add up to $180°$)
Also $AB = AC$ and $AX = AY$
So, BXA is congruent to CYA (SAS)
6 $WXYZ$ is a kite, so $WX = WZ$ and $XY = ZY$
Also, $WY = WY$
∴ WZY and WXY are congruent (SSS)
Hence $\angle X = \angle Y$
7 $\angle ABX = \angle ABC + \angle CBX = 90° + 60° = 150°$ (since $ABCD$ is a square and BXY is an equilateral triangle)
$\angle ABX = \angle XBY + \angle ABY = 360°$ (angles at a point add up to $360°$)
So $\angle ABY = 360° - 150° - 60° = 150°$
(since $\angle ABX = 150°$ and BXY is an equilateral triangle)
$BX = BY$ (since BXY is an equilateral triangle)
So ABY and ABX are congruent (SAS)
8

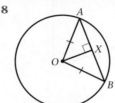

Call the centre of the circle O, and the end points of the chord A and B
Call the mid-point of the chord X.
$OA = OB$ (both radii)
$OX = OX$ (same)
$AX = XB$ (as X is mid-point of AB).
So triangles OAX and OXB are congruent (SSS)
Therefore $\angle AXO = \angle OXB$
Since AB is a straight line,
$\angle AXO = \angle OXB = 180° \div 2 = 90°$
Therefore OX is perpendicular to the chord

Mixed exercise 12

1 (a), (b) Half size

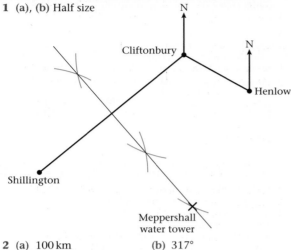

2 (a) 100 km   (b) 317°

3

4

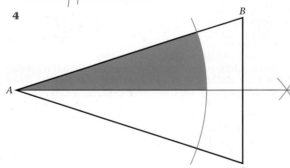

5 (a) Half size:

(b) Half size:

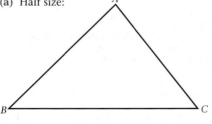
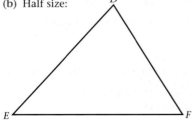

6 (a) $x = 120°$ (b) $y = 60°$
(c) (d) construction

7 (a) 4 cm should be 6 cm
(b) $x = 8$ cm $y = 8$ cm
(c)

8 (a)

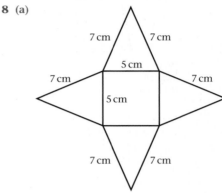

(b)

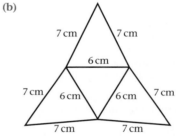

9

Plan   Front elevation   Side elevation

10

Plan   Front elevation   Side elevation

11 (a) 22.5°   (b) 157.5°

12 $x = 110°$

13 (a) 6 cm   (b) 15 cm

14 (a) $AE = EC$ and $EF = EB$
$\angle AEF = \angle BEC$ (vertically opposite angles)
So $\triangle AEF$ and $\triangle BEC$ are congruent, SAS.
(b) $\triangle BDC$
(c) $\angle FAE = \angle BCE$ and $\angle GAD = \angle CBD$
(d) $\angle BAC + \angle CBD + \angle BCE = 180°$ (angle sum of triangle)
So $\angle BAC + \angle GAD + \angle FAE = 180°$
Therefore GAF is a straight line.

15 (a) $CF = CD = BC = CE$ (since $ABCD$ is a square, and BEC and DCF are equilateral triangles)
$\angle DCE = \angle DCB + \angle ECB = \angle DCB + 60°$
$= \angle DCB + \angle DCF = \angle BCF$ (since BEC and DCF are equilateral triangles)
So ECD and BCF are congruent (SAS)
(b) $BF = ED$ (since ECD and BCF are congruent)
$EG = BF$ (opposite sides of parallelogram)
So $ED = EG$

16

17 (a) $PR = 39$ cm   (b) $BC = 30$ cm

Exercise 13A

1 (a) $a = 19.2$ cm (3 s.f.)   (b) $b = 11.7$ cm (3 s.f.)
   (c) $c = 7.40$ cm (3 s.f.)   (d) $d = 16.8$ cm (3 s.f.)
   (e) $e = 3.14$ cm (3 s.f.)   (f) $f = 8.49$ cm (3 s.f.)
2 (a) $AB = 5$ (b) $AB = 15$
   (c) $AB = 8.06$ (3 s.f.)   (d) $AB = 5$
   (e) $AB = 3.61$ (3 s.f.)   (f) $AB = 8.94$ (3 s.f.)
3 (a) $(2, 3)$ and $(-1, -2)$
   (b) $AB = 4.5$ (1 d.p.)
     $BC = 10$
4 PQ: midpoint $(4, 7)$, length 12.8 (1 d.p.)
   QR: midpoint $(6, 9)$, length 7.2 (1 d.p.)
5 AB: midpoint $(-4, 4)$, length 4.5 (1 d.p.)
   AC: midpoint $(2, 0)$, length 10.8 (1 d.p.)
   BC: midpoint $(1, 2)$, length 14.4 (1 d.p.)
6 (a) $a = 8$ cm   (b) $b = 12.0$ cm (3 s.f.)
   (c) $c = 6.29$ cm (3 s.f.)   (d) $d = 4.86$ cm (3 s.f.)
7 30.5 cm (3 s.f.)
8 10.9 cm (3 s.f.)
9 (a) $x = 12.8$ cm (3 s.f.)
     $y = 18.0$ cm (3 s.f.)
   (b) $x = 24$ cm, $y = 39.7$ cm (3 s.f.)
   (c) $x = 13.7$ cm (3 s.f.)
     $y = 24.3$ cm (3 s.f.)
   (d) $x = 12$ cm, $y = 23.3$ cm (3 s.f.)

Exercise 13B

1 17.03 cm (2 d.p.)
2 $\sqrt{p^2 + q^2 + r^2}$ cm
3 (a) 22.36 cm (2 d.p.)   (b) 22.91 cm (2 d.p.)
4 (a) $AC = 8.49$ cm (2 d.p.)
   (b) $AV = 15.59$ cm (2 d.p.)
5 (a) $EB = 21.54$ cm (2 d.p.)
   (b) $EC = 33$ cm

Exercise 13C

1 (a) 5.14 (3 s.f.)   (b) 0.141 (3 s.f.)
   (c) 1.25 (3 s.f.)   (d) 0.557 (3 s.f.)
2 (a) $60.945°$ (3 d.p.)   (b) $29.683°$ (3 d.p.)
   (c) $77.444°$ (3 d.p.)   (d) $68.962°$ (3 d.p.)
   (e) $80.823°$ (3 d.p.)   (f) $36.870°$ (3 d.p.)
3 (a) $a = 33.7°$ (3 s.f.)   (b) $b = 72.6°$ (3 s.f.)
   (c) $c = 54.2°$ (3 s.f.)   (d) $d = 50.1°$ (3 s.f.)
   (e) $e = 67.4°$ (3 s.f.)   (f) $f = 59.4°$ (3 s.f.)
4 (a) $a = 10.62°$ (2 d.p.)
   (b) Bearing on Hitchin from Bedford = $169.38°$ (2 d.p.)
5 (a) $a = 9.60$ cm (3 s.f.)   (b) $b = 10.1$ cm (3 s.f.)
   (c) $c = 7.85$ cm (3 s.f.)   (d) $d = 21.6$ cm (3 s.f.)
   (e) $e = 13.0$ cm (3 s.f.)   (f) $f = 5.04$ cm (3 s.f.)
6 Height ladder reaches up wall = 5.23 m (3 s.f.)
7 Length = 21.4 cm (3 s.f.)

Exercise 13D

1 (a) $a = 48.6°$ (3 s.f.)   (b) $b = 41.8°$ (3 s.f.)
   (c) $c = 48.7°$ (3 s.f.)   (d) $d = 37.4°$ (3 s.f.)

2 (a) $a = 4.23$ cm (3 s.f.)   (b) $b = 5.14$ cm (3 s.f.)
   (c) $c = 25.6$ cm (3 s.f.)   (d) $d = 18.8$ cm (3 s.f.)
   (e) $e = 24.5$ cm (3 s.f.)   (f) $f = 20.6$ cm (3 s.f.)
3 (a) 6.21 cm (3 s.f.)   (b) 24.9 cm (3 s.f.)

Exercise 13E

1 (a) $a = 4.12$ cm (3 s.f.)   (b) $b = 9.12$ cm (3 s.f.)
   (c) $c = 9.53$ cm (3 s.f.)   (d) $d = 3.60$ cm (3 s.f.)
   (e) $c = 24.2$ cm (3 s.f.)
2 (a) $a = 65.4°$ (3 s.f.)   (b) $b = 54.3°$ (3 s.f.)
   (c) $c = 41.8°$ (3 s.f.)   (d) $d = 57.5°$ (3 s.f.)
   (e) $c = 65.3°$ (3 s.f.)
3 Length of rope = 20.6 cm (3 s.f.)

Exercise 13F

1 Height of window above ground = 8.40 m (3 s.f.)
2 Height of tower = 46.9 m (3 s.f.)
3 (a) 22.1 km east (3 s.f.)
   (b) 11.7 km north (3 s.f.)
4 (a) $DC = 14.0$ cm   (b) $AC = 20.7$ cm
   (d) $AB = 14.79$ CM   (d) $\angle BDC = 23°$
   (e) $\angle ADB = 33°$ (Lengths to 3 s.f., angles exact)
5 $34.45°$ (2 d.p.)

Exercise 13G

1 $4.6°$ (1 d.p.)   **2** $71.7°$ (1 d.p.)   **3** $7.2°$ (1 d.p.)

Exercise 13H

All answers to 3 s.f.
1 4.28 cm^2 **2** 12.9 cm^2 **3** 15.9 cm^2
4 10.2 m^2 **5** 18.0 m^2 **6** 156 m^2
7 29.4 cm^2 **8** 75.0 cm^2 **9** $A = 30.6°$ or $149°$

Exercise 13I

1 $a = 26.39$ (2 d.p.)   **2** $b = 20.63$ (2 d.p.)
3 $c = 13.67$ (2 d.p.)   **4** $d = 14.45$ (2 d.p.)
5 $e = 22.89$ (2 d.p.)   **6** $A = 15.8°$ (1 d.p.)
7 $B = 52.6°$ (1 d.p.)
8 $C = 47.8°$ or $132.2°$ (1 d.p.)

Exercise 13J

Lengths to 2 d.p., Angles to 1 d.p.
1 $BC = 20.22$, angle $B = 40.0°$, angle $C = 20.0°$
2 $DE = 2.80$, angle $D = 123.0°$, angle $E = 34.0°$
3 $PR = 13.06$, angle $P = 98.6°$, angle $R = 47.4°$
4 $JL = 13.18$, angle $J = 38.6°$, angle $L = 24.4°$
5 $ST = 11.69$, angle $S = 21.4°$, angle $T = 15.6°$
6 $YZ = 2.57$, angle $Y = 137.9°$, angle $Z = 30.8°$
7 angle $A = 89.0°$, angle $B = 61.0°$, angle $C = 30.0°$ (1 d.p.)
8 angle $D = 56.3°$, angle $E = 93.8°$, angle $F = 29.9°$ (1 d.p.)
9 angle $J = 125.1°$, angle $K = 30.8°$, angle $L = 24.1°$ (1 d.p.)
10 angle $P = 25.9°$, angle $Q = 149.6°$, angle $R = 123.8°$ (1 d.p.)
11 (a) 11.7 cm
   (b) angle $ABC = 42.5°$
12 Distance from starting point = 462 km (3 s.f.)
   Bearing of $064.9°$ (3 s.f.)
13 (a) Averge speed = 15.4 km/h (3 s.f.)
   (b) $LM = 20.8$ km (3 s.f.)

Exercise 13K

1
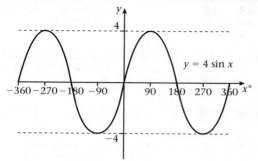

2
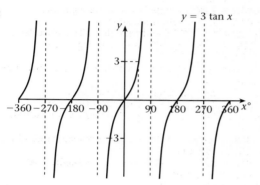

3
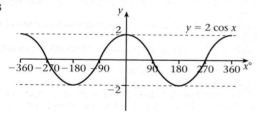

4
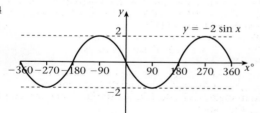

5
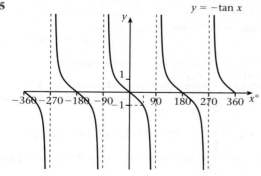

6
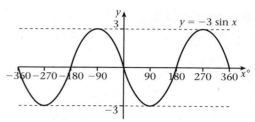

7
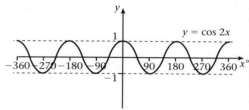

8
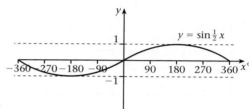

9
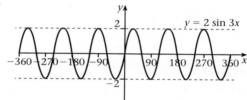

10
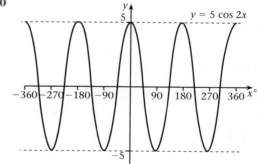

Exercise 13L

1 $x = 14.5°, 165.5°$ (1 d.p)
2 $x = 56.3°, 236.3°$ (1 d.p)
3 $x = 30°, 150°, 210°, 330°$
4 $x = 33.2°, 146.8°$ (1 d.p.)
5 $x = 26.2°, 86.2°, 146.2°, 206.2°, 266.2°, 326.2°, 386.2°,$
446.2°, 506.2°, 566.2°, 626.2°, 686.2° (1 d.p.)
6 $x = -160.5°, -19.5°$ (1 d.p.)
7 $x = -84.2°, -5.8°, 95.8°, 174.2°$ (1 d.p.)
8 $x = -118.2°, -28.2°, 61.8°, 151.8°$ (1 d.p.)

Mixed exercise 13

1 (a) 7.21 (2 d.p.)   (b) 7.07 (2 d.p.)
2 41.6° (1 d.p.)
3 11.1 cm (3 s.f.)
4 (a) 23.9 cm² (3 s.f.)   (b) 78.4° (1 d.p.)
5 (a) $AC = 9.86$ cm (3 s.f.)
  (b) Area of $ABC = 13.3$ cm² (3 s.f.)
  (c) Area of $ABCD = 40.0$ cm² (3 s.f.)
6 (a) Height $= \sqrt{6}$ (b) Area $= 6\sqrt{2}$
7 (a) 12.7 cm (1 d.p.)
  (b) 13.6 cm (1 d.p.)
  (c) 64.9° (1 d.p.)
  (d) 50.2° (1 d.p.)
  (e) 64.9° (1 d.p.)
8 69.4 m (3 s.f.)
9 243 m (3 s.f.)
10 17.3 cm (1 d.p.)
11 74°
12 64°
13 (a) 15 feet   (b) 35 feet   (c) 6 hours
14 (a)

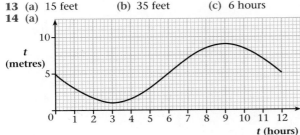

  (b) 3, 15
15 (a) $A = (90°, 0)$, $B = (0°, 1)$
  (b)

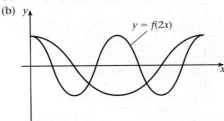

16 (a) 15.1 cm (1 d.p.)   (b) 25.1 (1 d.p.)
  (c) 11.11° (2 d.p.)
17 (a) 11.7 cm (1 d.p.)   (b) 68.7° (1 d.p.)
  (c) 32.2 cm (1 d.p.)

Exercise 14A

1 $a = 57°, b = 57°$ **2** $c = 44°, d = 88°$
3 $e = 65°$ **4** $f = 22°$
5 $g = 25°$ **6** $h = 37°, i = 37°$
7 $j = 66°$ **8** $k = 56°, m = 56°$

Exercise 14B

1 $a = 108°, b = 85°$ **2** $\angle B = 76°$
3 $\angle XTY = 117°$ **4** $\angle TYS = 112.5°$
5 $\angle ABC = 124°$
6 $\angle ADC = 75°, \angle ACD = 63°$
7 $\angle ABC = 56°, \angle BAC = 34°$
8 (a) $\angle OCE = 90°$ (tangent at right angles to radius)
    $\angle EOC = 180° - 90° - 36° = 54°$ (angles in a triangle)
    $\angle ABC = \frac{1}{2} \times 54° = 27°$ (angle at centre = 2 × angle
                  at circumference)
  (b) $\angle ADC = 180° - 27° = 153°$ (opposite angles in a
                  cyclic quadrilateral)

Exercise 14C

1 $\angle TBA = 42°$ **2** $\angle ABT = 56°, \angle BTC = 46°$
3 $\angle ABT = 73°$ **4** $\angle BTA = 60°$
5 $\angle CBT = 37°$
6 (a) 40°   (b) 12°
  (c) $\angle EAD = \angle BAC + 38° = 78°$. If a circle could be
      drawn as described then $\angle EAD$ would have to be
      an angle in a semicircle i.e. 90°.

Exercise 14D

1 $\angle AXB = \angle CXD$ (opposite angles).
  $\angle ABX = \angle CDX$ and $\angle BAX = \angle DCX$ (angles in the
  same segment). So, BXA and CXD have the same
  angles so are similar.
2 $\angle BAX = \angle DCX$ (angle in the same segment)
  $\angle BAX = \angle CDX$ (alternate angles)
  So, $\angle DCX = \angle CDX$ and triangle CXD is isosceles.
3 $\angle TPB = \angle TBA = \angle ATP$ (alternate segments)
  $\angle TPA = \angle TPB$
  So, triangles PAT and PTB are similar (since two angles
  are the same)
4 $\angle APT = \angle ATP$ (triangle PAT is isosceles)
  $\angle ATP = \angle AXT$ (alternate segment theorem)
  So, $\angle APT = \angle AXT$ and so triangle PTX is isosceles.
  So, $PT = TX$.
5 $\angle AQR = \angle PQR = 180° - \angle PSR$ (opposite angles in a
  cyclic quadrilateral)
  $\angle ASP = 180° - \angle PSR$ (angles on a straight line)
  So $\angle AQR = \angle ASP$
  Also, $\angle RAQ = \angle SAP$
  So, triangles APS and AQR are similar (since two angles
  are the same)
6 $\angle APR = \angle ABP$ (alternate segment theorem for smaller
  circle)
  $\angle XPR = \angle XYP$ (alternate segment theorem for larger
  circle)
  So, $\angle XYP = \angle XPR = \angle APR = \angle ABP$
  But PY is a straight line, so AB and XY are parallel.
7 $\angle OSQ = 90°$ (angle between a tangent and a radius)
  So $\angle QOS = 90° - \angle OQS$ (angles in a triangle add up to
  180°)
  $\angle QTR = 90°$ (angle between a tangent and a radius)
  So $\angle TRQ = 90° - \angle TQR = 90° - \angle OQS$ (angles in a
  triangle add up to 180°)
  We now have $\angle TRQ = 90° - \angle OQS = \angle QOS$
  But $\angle XYT = \angle QOS$ (alternate angles)
  So $\angle XYT = \angle TRQ$
  We also have $\angle QTR = 90° = \angle YXT$ (angle between a
  tangent and a radius, and angle in a semi circle)
  So triangles TXY and TRQ are similar (since two angles
  are the same)

Mixed exercise 14

1 $\angle ABC = 90°$ (angle in a semicircle)
    $x = 180° - 90° - 35°$ (angles in a triangle)
      $= 55°$
    $y = 35°$ (angles in the same segment)
2 $OD = OB$ (radii)
    $\angle ODB = 20°$ (base angles of isosceles triangle)
      $x = 90° - 20°$ (angle between tangent and radius
              is 90°)
      $= 70°$
    $\angle ADB = 180° - 70° - 35°$ (angles on straight line)
      $= 75°$
    $y = 2 \times \angle ADB$ (angles at centre and circumference)
      $= 150°$

3 $PA = PC$ (tangents from a point)
So $\angle PAC = \angle PCA$
So $\angle PAC = \frac{1}{2}(180° - 56°) = 62°$
$x = 90° - \angle PAC = 90° - 62°$ (angle between a tangent
and a radius)
So $x = 28°$
We now also have $y = 28°$ (alternate segments)

4 $\angle OAB = 180° - 160° = 20°$
$OA = OB$ (radii), so $\angle ABO = \angle OAB = 20°$
$x + \angle ABO = 90°$ (angle between a tangent and radius)
So $x = 70°$
$\angle AOB = 180° - \angle OAB - \angle OBA = 140°$
So $\angle BOC = 180° - 140° = 40°$
$\angle OBC = 90°$ (angle betwen a tangent and radius)
So $\angle BCO = 90° - \angle BOC = 50°$
So $y = 180° - \angle BCO = 130°$

5 $OB = OC$ (radii)
So $\angle OCB = \angle OBC = 56°$ (base angles of isosceles triangle)
$\angle OBA = 124°$ (angles on a straight line)
$\angle BOA = \angle BAO$ ($OB = BA$)
$x = \frac{1}{2}(180° - 124°) = 28°$
$\angle TOA = 360° - 200° - 68° - 28° = 64°$
$\angle OTA = 90°$ (tangent and radius perpendicular)
$y = 180° - 90° - 64°$
$= 26°$

6 $\angle QPS = 180° - 45° = 135°$
$x = 180° - 135°$ (opposite angles in a cyclic
quadrilateral)
$= 45°$

7 $\angle CFD = 50°$ (angles in the same segment)
$x = 180° - 50° - 30° - 25°$ (angle sum of triangle)
$= 75°$

8 $\angle JNL = 180° - 36° - 64°$ (angles on straight line)
$= 80°$
$x = 180° - 80°$ (opposite angles in a cyclic
quadrilateral)
$x = 100°$

9 $\angle ADE = 32°$ (angles in the same segment)
$\angle DPE = 180° - 80° = 100°$ (angles on a straight line)
$\angle BED = 180° - x$ (opposite angles in a cyclic
quadrilateral)
So $180° - x + 100° + 32° = 180°$ (angle sum of
triangle DEP)
$x = 132°$

10 $\angle GFJ = 180° - \angle GHJ = 86°$ (opposite angles in a cyclic
quadrilateral)
So $\angle JFH = 86° - 30° = 56°$
So $\angle HJL = \angle JFH = 56°$ (alternate segments)
$HL = JL$ (tangents meeting at a point)
So $\angle JHL = \angle HJL = 56°$
$x = 180° - \angle JHL - \angle HJL = 68°$

11 $\angle PSR = 180° - 111°$ (opposite angles in a cyclic
quadrilateral)
$= 69°$
$x = 180° - 29° - 69°$ (angle sum of triangle)
$= 82°$

12 $\angle BAD = 90°$ (angle in a semicircle)
$\angle BAC = 90° - 33° = 57°$
$\angle BDC = \angle BAC$ (angles in the same segment)
So $x = 57°$

13 $\angle BAE = \angle FEB$ (alternate segment theorem)
$= 77°$
$\angle BOE = 2 \times 77° = 154°$ (angle at centre twice angle at
circumference)
$OB = OE$ (radii)
$\angle OBE = \angle OEB$ (base angles of isosceles triangle)
$= \frac{1}{2}(180° - 154°) = 13°$
$\angle BEA = \angle BAE$ (base angles of isosceles triangle)
$= 77°$
$x = 77° - 13° = 64°$

14

$a = 40°$ angle subtended at circumference half the
angle subtended at the centre
$b = 180° - 65° - 80° = 35°$
$80° + b + x + c + 2 \times 90° = 360°$ (angles in a
quadrilateral)
So $x + c = 65°$
$c = 180° - 90° - a = 90° - 40° = 50°$ (angles in a
triangle)
$x = 65° - c$
So $x = 15°$

15 $\angle ADC = 180° - 100°$ (angles on straight line)
$= 80°$
$\angle DBC = \angle CAD$ (angles in the same segment)
$= x$
$\angle ABC + \angle ADC = 180°$ (opposite angles in a cyclic
quadrilateral)
So $x + 32° + 80° = 180°$
$x = 68°$

16 $\angle BEC = \angle BAC$ (angles in the same segment)
$= 52°$
$\angle CED = \frac{1}{2}x$ (angle at centre twice angle at
circumference)
$\angle BEC + \angle CED = 180°$ (angles on straight line)
$\frac{1}{2}x = 180° - 52°$
$x = 256°$

Exercise 15A

1 (i) (a) Area $= 256\pi$ cm^2, circumference $= 32\pi$ cm
   (b) Area $= 144\pi$ mm^2, circumference $= 24\pi$ mm
   (c) Area $= 6.86\pi$ m^2, circumference $= 5.24\pi$ m
   (d) Area $= 792.99\pi$ m^2, circumference $= 56.32\pi$ m
(ii) (a) Area $= 804.25$ cm^2 (2 d.p.)
   circumference $= 100.53$ cm (2 d.p.)
   (b) Area $= 452.39$ mm^2 (2 d.p.)
   circumference $= 75.40$ mm (2 d.p.)
   (c) Area $= 21.57$ m^2 (2 d.p.)
   circumference $= 16.46$ m (2 d.p.)
   (d) Area $= 2491.24$ m^2 (2 d.p.)
   circumference $= 176.93$ m (2 d.p.)

2 (a) 2199.1 mm (1 d.p.)
   (b) 109.96 m (2 d.p.)

3 Area $= 181.46$ cm^2 (2 d.p.)

4 Area $= 907.9$ m^2 (1 d.p.),
   circumference $= 106.8$ m (1 d.p.)

5 Diameter $= 26.42$ m (2 d.p.)

6 Diameter $= 1.73$ cm (2 d.p.)

7 (i) (a) Area = $8\pi\,cm^2$, perimeter = $(8 + 4\pi)\,cm$

(b) Area = $28.125\pi\,cm^2$,
perimeter = $(15 + 7.5\pi)\,cm$

(c) Area = $6.48\pi\,cm^2$,
perimeter = $(7.2 + 3.6\pi)\,cm$

(d) Area = $3.7538\pi\,m^2$,
perimeter = $(5.48 + 2.74\pi)\,m$

(ii) (a) Area = $25.13\,cm^2$ (2 d.p.),
perimeter = $20.57\,cm$ (2 d.p.),

(b) Area = $88.36\,cm^2$ (2 d.p.)
perimeter = $38.56\,cm$ (2 d.p.),

(c) Area = $20.36\,cm^2$ (2 d.p.)
perimeter = $18.51\,cm$ (2 d.p.),

(d) Area = $11.79\,m^2$ (2 d.p.),
perimeter = $14.09\,m$ (2 d.p.)

8 Area = $9.82\,m^2$ (2 d.p.), perimeter = $12.85\,m$ (2 d.p.)

9 $3.00\,cm^2$ (2 d.p.)

10 Area = $1.33\,m^2$ (2 d.p.), perimeter = $4.64\,m$ (2 d.p.)

11 (a) Area = $8827.43\,m^2$ (2 d.p.),
perimeter = $388.50\,m$ (2 d.p.)

(b) Area = $388.36\,cm^2$ (2 d.p.),
perimeter = $78.56\,cm$ (2 d.p.)

12 (a) $135.45\,cm^2$ (2 d.p.)

(b) $81.46\,cm^2$ (2 d.p.)

(c) $85.84\,cm^2$ (2 d.p.)

Exercise 15B

1 $520\,m^2$ **2** $344\,m^2$ **3** $2969.1\,m^2$ (1 d.p.)

4 Surface area = $150\,cm^2$, volume = $90\,cm^3$

5 $BE = 5\,cm$, surface area = $320\,cm^2$

6 (a) Volume = $500\,cm^3$,
surface area = $400\,cm^2$

(b) Volume = $4.725\,m^3$,
surface area = $21.3\,m^2$ (1 d.p.)

7 Surface area = $785.9\,m^2$ (4 s.f.),
volume = $1319\,m^3$ (4 s.f.)

Exercise 15C

1 (a) $300\pi\,cm^3$ (b) $512\pi\,cm^3$

(c) $180\pi\,cm^3$ (d) $3200\pi\,cm^3$

(e) $63.487\,cm^3$

2 (a) radius $1.55\,cm$ (3 s.f.)   (b) radius $2.06\,cm$ (3 s.f.)

(c) radius $2.60\,cm$ (3 s.f.)   (d) radius $1.46\,cm$ (3 s.f.)

(e) $1.91\,cm$ (3 s.f.)

3 (a) Surface area = $478\,cm^2$, volume = $754\,cm^3$

(b) Surface area = $1280\,cm^2$, volume = $3170\,cm^3$

(c) Surface area = $6440\,cm^2$, volume = $15\,700\,cm^3$

(d) Surface area = $99.0\,cm^2$, volume = $63.6\,cm^3$

(e) Surface area = $4750\,cm^2$, volume = $5890\,cm^3$

(f) Surface area = $567\,000\,cm^2$, volume = $226\,000\,cm^3$

4 $2806.86\,m^3$ (2 d.p.)

5 $22.0\,m^2$ (3 s.f.)

6 Volume = $8580\,cm^3$ (3 s.f.),
surface area = $5480\,cm^2$ (3 s.f.)

Exercise 15D

1 (a) $50\,000$ (b) $280\,000$

(c) $12\,000$ (d) $1\,050\,000$

(e) 2.6 (f) 0.34

(g) 800 (h) 2200

(i) 24 (j) 362

2 (a) $2\,300\,000$ (b) $40\,000$

(c) $304\,000$ (d) 7

(e) 0.53 (f) 0.0265

(g) 4000 (h) $13\,050$

(i) 8.4 (j) 0.43

3 (a) (i) $6.3\,m^2$ (ii) $63\,000\,cm^2$

(b) (i) $0.882\,m^3$ (ii) $882\,000\,cm^3$

Exercise 15E

1 (a) Arc = $\frac{4}{5}\pi\,cm$, perimeter = $12 + \frac{4}{5}\pi\,cm$,
area = $\frac{12}{5}\pi\,cm^2$

(b) Arc = $4\pi\,cm$, perimeter = $36 + 4\pi\,cm$, area = $36\pi\,cm^2$

(c) Arc = $\frac{110}{3}\pi\,cm$, perimeter = $120 + \frac{110}{3}\pi\,cm$,
area = $1100\pi\,cm^2$

(d) Arc = $7\pi\,cm$, perimeter = $9 + 7\pi\,cm$, area = $\frac{63}{4}\pi\,cm^2$

2 (a) Arc = $6.0\,cm$, perimeter = $36.0\,cm$, area = $45.2\,cm^2$

(b) Arc = $6.3\,cm$, perimeter = $18.9\,cm$, area = $19.7\,cm^2$

(c) Arc = $11.6\,cm$, perimeter = $23.4\,cm$, area = $34.3\,cm^2$

(d) Arc = $32.0\,cm$, perimeter = $48.6\,cm$, area = $132.9\,cm^2$

3 (a) $\theta = 43.0°$ (3 s.f.)   (b) $a = 24.6°$ (3 s.f.)

(c) $b = 115°$ (3 s.f.)   (d) $c = 306°$ (3 s.f.)

Exercise 15F

1 (a) (i) $0.979\,cm^2$ (ii) $3.125\pi - 8.84\,cm^2$

(b) (i) $28.5\,cm^2$ (ii) $25\pi - 50\,cm^2$

(c) (i) $138\,cm^2$ (ii) $75\pi - 97.4\,cm^2$

(d) (i) $2.26\,m^2$ (ii) $\frac{75}{18}\pi - 10.8\,m^2$

Exercise 15G

1 $804.2\,cm^2$ (1 d.p.)   **2** $204.2\,cm^2$ (1 d.p.)

3 $706.9\,cm^2$ (1 d.p.)   **4** $138.2\,cm^2$ (1 d.p.)

5 $339.3\,cm^2$ (1 d.p.)   **6** $339.3\,mm^2$ (1 d.p.)

7 $63.3\,cm^2$ (1 d.p.)

Exercise 15H

1 $47.1\,cm^3$ (3 s.f.)

2 $11.2\,cm^3$ (3 s.f.)

3 $320\,cm^3$

4 $24\,429.0\,cm^3$ (1 d.p.)

5 $45\,000\,cm^3$

6 $904.8\,cm^3$ (1 d.p.)

7 (a) $111.3\,m^3$ (1 d.p.)

(b) 7.0 litres (1 d.p. but rounded up)

Exercise 15I

1 $15.87\,cm$ (2 d.p.)

2 (a) $1105.92\,cm^3$ (b) $144\,cm^2$

3

Measurement	Aeroplane	Model of aeroplane
Area of roundel	$3\,m^2$	$12\,cm^2$
Number of wheels	4	**4**
Width	**3.25 m**	$6.5\,cm$
Volume of cabin	**200** m^3	$1600\,cm^3$

4 (a) $4:25$ (b) $8:125$

5 $216\,000:1$

Exercise 15J

1 (a) (i) $2400\,cm^3$ (3 s.f.)   (ii) $\frac{2290}{3}\pi\,cm^2$

(b) $796\,cm^3$

(c) $162\,cm^3$ (3 s.f.)

(d) $1700\,cm^3$ (3 s.f.)

2 $654.50\,cm^3$ (2 d.p.)

3 $458\frac{1}{3}\,m^3$

4 $1520.00\,cm^3$ (2 d.p.)

Exercise 15K

1 (a) Volume; number × (length)^2 × length gives volume
(b) Area; number × length × length gives area
(c) Volume; (length)^3 gives volume
(d) Length; length + length gives length
(e) Area; number × length × length gives area
(f) Volume; number × number × (length)^2 × length gives volume
(g) Volume; number × length × length × length gives volume
(h) Area; number × number × length × length gives area
(i) Area; length × (length + length) gives area
(j) Length; length × length gives area, area + area gives area, area ÷ length gives length
(k) Volume; length × length × (length + length) gives volume
(l) Area; length × length × (length + length) gives volume, volume ÷ length gives area

2 a^2 represents area, b^2 represents area, but c represents length and area + area + length does not give an area

3

Expression	$a + b + 2c$	πr^2	$2l + w^2$	xyz	$\sqrt{3a}$	$mnpq$	$6s^2$
Length	✓				✓		
Area		✓					✓
Volume				✓			
None of these			✓			✓	

4 (a) Volume; $\frac{4}{3}$ and π are numbers so are dimensionless, r is a length so r^3 has dimension 3. So $\frac{4}{3}\pi r^3$ has dimension 3.
(b) Volume; π is a number so is dimensionless, r is a length so r^2 has dimension 2. h is a length so h has dimension 1. So $\pi r^2 h$ has dimension 3.
(c) Length; π is a number so is dimensionless, d is a length so d has dimension 1. So πd has dimension 1.
(d) Area; $\frac{1}{2}$ is a number so is dimensionless, a and b are lengths so $a + b$ has dimension 1. h is a length so h has dimension 1. So $\frac{1}{2}(a + b)h$ has dimension 2.
(e) Length; 2 is a number so is dimensionless, l and w are lengths so l has dimension 1 and w has dimension 1. So $2l$ has dimension 1, $2w$ has dimension 1 and $2l + 2w$ has dimension 1.
(f) Area; π is a number so is dimensionless, r is a length so r has dimension 1. l is a length so l has dimension 1. So $\pi r l$ has dimension 2.
(g) Area; π is dimensionless, while r, h, d and l each have dimension 1. So the top of the fraction has dimension 3; divided by the bottom (dimension 1) this gives an expression with dimension 2.
(h) Length; π and 2 are dimensionless, while r is a length so $\pi r^2 + 2r^2$ has dimension 2; divided by r (dimension 1) this gives an expression with dimension 1.

5 (a) Area; λ is dimensionless. x and y both have dimension 1. So λxy has dimension 2.
(b) Volume; λ is dimensionless. x, y and z all have dimension 1. So λxyz has dimension 3.
(c) Area; λ is dimensionless. y^2 has dimension 2. So λy^2 has dimension 2.
(d) Area; λ^2 is dimensionless. x^2 has dimension 2. So $\lambda^2 x^2$ has dimension 2.
(e) Length; λ is dimensionless. x, y and z all have dimension 1, so $x + y + z$ has dimension 1. So $\lambda(x + y + z)$ has dimension 1.

Mixed exercise 15

1 πr^2 represents area, $\pi r^2 h$ represents volume and area + volume does not give a volume.
2 360 000 cm^3
3 (a) 754 cm^3 (3 s.f.)
(b) 478 cm^2
4 6600 square inches (3 s.f.)
5 Volume = 2025 cm^3 (3 s.f.)
Area = 1060 cm^2 (3 s.f.)
6 (a) 8910 cm^2 (3 s.f.)
(b) 20 300 cm^2 (3 s.f.)
7 (a) 602 m^2 (3 s.f.)
(b) 869 m^3 (3 s.f.)
8 6.20 cm (3 s.f.)
9 2 420 000 (3 s.f. but rounded down)
10 Volume = 2680 cm^3 (3 s.f.)
surface area = 1250 cm^2 (3 s.f.)
11

Thickness	Length	Width	Volume
12 mm	1.8 m	5 cm	**1080 cm^3**
9 mm	2.4 m	8 cm	**1728 cm^3**
15 mm	3.0 m	**20 cm**	9000 cm^3
5 cm	**8.0 m**	5 cm	0.02 m^3

12 (a) 8.38 cm (3 s.f.)
(b) 8.13 cm (3 s.f.)
(c) 4.73 cm^2 (3 s.f.)
13 Volume; λ is dimensionless and a and h each have dimension 1. h^2 has dimension 2 so λah^2 has dimension 3.
14 (a) 9 : 49
(b) 27 : 343
15 2666π cm^3
16 (a) 21.8 cm (3 s.f.)
(b) 66.4 cm^2 (3 s.f.)

Exercise 16A

1 (a) $\begin{pmatrix} -3 \\ 1 \end{pmatrix}$ (b) $\begin{pmatrix} 3 \\ -1 \end{pmatrix}$

(c) $\begin{pmatrix} -4 \\ -8 \end{pmatrix}$ (d) $\begin{pmatrix} -1 \\ -9 \end{pmatrix}$

2 (a) (i) $\begin{pmatrix} -2 \\ 2 \end{pmatrix}$ (ii) $\begin{pmatrix} 2 \\ -2 \end{pmatrix}$

(b) (2, 8)

3 (a) $\begin{pmatrix} 7 \\ 2 \end{pmatrix}$

(b)

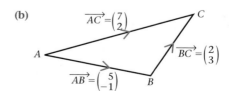

4 (a) $\begin{pmatrix} 5 \\ -3 \end{pmatrix}$ (b) $\begin{pmatrix} 1 \\ 7 \end{pmatrix}$ (c) $\begin{pmatrix} 9 \\ 6 \end{pmatrix}$

   (d) $\begin{pmatrix} 4 \\ -10 \end{pmatrix}$ (e) $\begin{pmatrix} 5 \\ 16 \end{pmatrix}$

5 (a) $\begin{pmatrix} -3 \\ 5 \end{pmatrix}$ (b) $\begin{pmatrix} 3 \\ -5 \end{pmatrix}$ (c) $x = \begin{pmatrix} 1 \\ -\frac{1}{2} \end{pmatrix}$

6 (a)

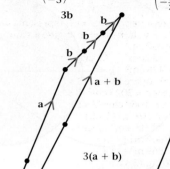

(b)

Exercise 16B

1   $x = \begin{pmatrix} 4 \\ 3 \end{pmatrix}$

2   $y = \begin{pmatrix} -\frac{1}{3} \\ -\frac{4}{3} \end{pmatrix}$

3   $z = \begin{pmatrix} -11 \\ 7 \end{pmatrix}$

4 (a) $5a - 3b$ is parallel to x-axis, for example
   (b) $3a - 2b$ is parallel to y-axis, for example

5   $p = -2$

6   $p = 2\frac{1}{5}$, $q = 1\frac{1}{5}$

7   $\frac{9}{7}a + \frac{4}{7}b = \begin{pmatrix} 2 \\ 5 \end{pmatrix}$

Exercise 16C

1   Let M be the midpoint of AB. $\overrightarrow{OM} = \begin{pmatrix} 5 \\ 5 \end{pmatrix}$

2   $\overrightarrow{OC} = c = \frac{4}{5}a + \frac{1}{5}b$

3   Coordinates of C are $(5, -1)$

4 (a) (i) $(2\frac{1}{2}, 3\frac{1}{2})$ (ii) $(1, \frac{1}{2})$
     (iii) $(\frac{1}{2}, 2)$
   (b) Coordinates of G are $(1, 8)$

5   $\overrightarrow{OD} = \begin{pmatrix} -5 \\ -1 \end{pmatrix}$

   Let M be the midpoint of BD, $\overrightarrow{OM} = \begin{pmatrix} -4\frac{1}{2} \\ 3\frac{1}{2} \end{pmatrix}$

Mixed exercise 16

1 (a) $\begin{pmatrix} -3 \\ 1 \end{pmatrix}$ (b) $\begin{pmatrix} 4 \\ -10 \end{pmatrix}$ (c) $\begin{pmatrix} -4 \\ 10 \end{pmatrix}$ (d) $\begin{pmatrix} 7 \\ -11 \end{pmatrix}$

2 (a) $\begin{pmatrix} 3 \\ 6 \end{pmatrix}$ (b) $\begin{pmatrix} -7 \\ 0 \end{pmatrix}$ (c) $\begin{pmatrix} -6 \\ 9 \end{pmatrix}$ (d) $\begin{pmatrix} 16 \\ -3 \end{pmatrix}$

3 (a) $\begin{pmatrix} 1 \\ -3 \end{pmatrix}$ (b) $\begin{pmatrix} 13 \\ 11 \end{pmatrix}$ (c) $x = \begin{pmatrix} \frac{1}{2} \\ 1 \end{pmatrix}$

4   $x = \begin{pmatrix} -4 \\ 5 \end{pmatrix}$

5   $a - b$ is parallel to the y-axis, for example

6   $p = 2$, $q = 3$

7 (a) $a + c$ (b) $c - a$

8   $\overrightarrow{OC} = c = \frac{2}{3}a + \frac{1}{3}b$

9   M and N are the midpoints of OA and OB,
   so $\overrightarrow{OM} = \frac{1}{2}\overrightarrow{OA}$ and $\overrightarrow{ON} = \frac{1}{2}\overrightarrow{OB}$
   $\therefore \overrightarrow{MN} = \overrightarrow{ON} - \overrightarrow{OM} = \frac{1}{2}\overrightarrow{OA} - \frac{1}{2}\overrightarrow{OB}$
   $= \frac{1}{2}(\overrightarrow{OA} - \overrightarrow{OB}) = \frac{1}{2}\overrightarrow{AB}$ or $\overrightarrow{AB} = 2\overrightarrow{MN}$
   This shows AB is parallel to MN, and twice the length.

10 (a) $\overrightarrow{AM} = b + \frac{1}{2}c$, $\overrightarrow{DC} = \frac{2}{3}b + \frac{1}{3}c$
    (b) $\overrightarrow{AM} = \frac{3}{2}\overrightarrow{DC}$ so $AM:DC = 3:2$ and clearly AM and
       DC are parallel

11 (a) $\begin{pmatrix} 4 \\ 3 \end{pmatrix}$

    (b) $\begin{pmatrix} -4 \\ 1 \end{pmatrix}$

12 (a) $p + q$ (b) $q - p$

13   $\frac{1}{2}(p + q)$

Examination practice paper

Section A (calculator)

1. Mark £3200, Anne £2400, Barbara £1600
2. (a) £940   (b) 12.5%   (c) £600
3. 154 cm^2 (3 s.f.)
4. 3.53
5. (a) $3.5 < n < 7$ (b) $-2, -1, 0, 1$
6. £2756.84
7. 352 cm^2 (3 s.f.)
8. 4.47 cm (3 s.f.)
9. 12 cm
10. (a) (i) upper bound 200.5 g, lower bound 199.5 g
      (ii) upper bound 114 glasses, lower bound 105 glasses
    (b) 1.91 g (3 s.f.)
11. (a) 47.34° (2 d.p.)   (b) 35.14° (2 d.p.)
12. $t = \frac{1}{5}(7 - 2y)$
13. (a) $y = 11.2$ (b) $u = \pm 3\frac{1}{3}$
14. $x = 2.35$ or $x = 7.65$ (2 d.p.)
15. $p = 2.5$, $q = 4$

Section B (non-calculator)

1. (a) $\frac{11}{40}$ (b) $6\frac{2}{3}$
2. (a) On Monday cost is $P \times 80\%$
      On Tuesday cost is $P \times 80\% \times 80\% = P \times 64\%$
    (b) 25%
3. 150 g butter, 120 g sugar, 3 eggs, 135 g flour, 45 ml milk
4.

Plan   Front elevation

5. (a), (c)

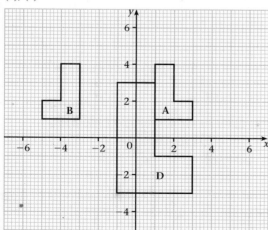

(b) Rotation 90° clockwise, centre (0, 0)

6.

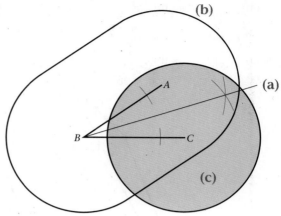

7. $c(a + b)$, $2(a^2 + b^2)$
8. (a) $3x + 120 = 360°$ (b) 100°
9. $50x + 10y$
10. (a) $x = 14$ (b) $x = -3$
11. $x = \frac{3}{4}$, $y = -\frac{1}{2}$
12. 1600 g or 1.6 kg
13. $\frac{3}{4}\mathbf{a} + \frac{1}{2}\mathbf{b}$
14. $4 + 2\sqrt{3}$
15. $y = 3x + 2$
16. Surface area of cylinder $= 2\pi x^2 + 4\pi x^2 = 6\pi x^2$
    Surface area of sphere $= 4\pi r^2$
    So $3x^2 = 2r^2$
          $r^2 = \frac{3}{2}x^2$
           $r = \sqrt{\frac{3}{2}}x$